Christian Mission in the Third Millennium

UNITED METHODIST CHURCH

HISTORY OF MISSION SERIES

Christian Mission in the Third Millennium

CHARLES E. COLE, EDITOR

GENERAL BOARD OF GLOBAL MINISTRIES
The United Methodist Church
New York, New York

Published by GBGM BOOKS
Copyright © 2004
The General Board of Global Ministries
The United Methodist Church
475 Riverside Drive
New York, New York 10115

All rights reserved.
Permissions listed on page 315
Printed in the United States of America

LIBRARY OF CONGRESS
Control Number 2003107311

ISBN 1-890569-65-8 CLOTH
ISBN 1-890569-78-X PAPER

COVER PHOTOS *(left to right from top left):* Ben Hill UMC at Mutare; PFC Jessica Lynch; Border Patrol; Shawl dancer; Chicano Park; Theology student, Nigeria; Iowa peace protestor.

[Contents]

List of Illustrations, vii
Foreword, ix

1. The Future of Christian Mission in Ghana
   Mercy Amba Oduyoye, 1

2. Asian Mission to Asians
   Scott W. Sunquist, 21

3. The Challenge of Christian Mission in Islamic Southeast Asia
   Robert Hunt, 45

4. Women in Mission: A Philippine Experience
   Elizabeth S. Tapia, 65

5. The Future of Methodist Mission in Europe
   James A. Dwyer, 77

6. The Methodist Educational Mission in Latin America: History, Meaning, Perspective
   Norman Rubén Amestoy and Néstor O. Míguez, 121

7. Christian Mission in a Religiously Pluralistic Society
   Sudarshana Devadhar, 153

8. The Future of Native American Ministry
   Marvin B. Abrams, 169

9. The Future of African Americans and Mission
   Anthony J. Shipley, 183

10. "Looking Forward Inwardly": The Future of the Korean Mission in the United States
    Stephen S. Kim, 203

11. A Latino Perspective
    José M. Fernández, 219

Contents

12. Women, Mission, and the Future
Peggy Halsey, 251

13. Youth and the Future of Mission
John O. Gooch, 273

Notes, 295
Contributors, 313
Permissions, 315
Index, 317

[Illustrations]

[Charts and Tables in text]

UM Latinos and U.S. Latinos, 227

California Methodist and UM Latinos, 228

Latinos in Mainstream America, 245

Population Trends in the U.S. in Jurisdictions of The United Methodist Church, 246

Latino Membership in The United Methodist Church (U.S.) 1998, 247

U.S. Border Patrol Apprehensions of Undocumented Aliens, Fiscal Year 1999, 249

[Photographs]

Prenatal injection, Accra, Ghana, 7

Theology student, Nigeria, 17

Miao boys from South China, 29

Phnom Penh school, 33

Women preparing for Muslim wedding, Malaysia, 51

Jakarta scholar and students, 55

Filipina evacuee, 69

Muslims and Christians, Philippines, 73

Prague church, 99

Smolensk students, 107

Thomas B. Wood, 126

John F. Thomson, 138

Frederico Pagura, 146

Buddhist temple and Praise Tabernacle, 154

LA Muslims praying, 157
Shawl dancer, 170
Cities of Gold casino, 179
Windsor Village UMC, 186
Ben Hill UMC at Mutare, 191
Honolulu sculpture, 206
Mongolia, 213
Border Patrol, 224
Chicano Park, 231
Jet remains, Puerto Rico, 240
Young UMWs, 261
Soldier Lynch, 279
Iowa peace protestor, 291

[Foreword]

*M*ORE THAN FIFTY years have passed since a history of mission series was begun by The Methodist Church Board of Missions. Wade Crawford Barclay wrote *Early American Methodism, 1769–1844* as the first of what would become a four-volume series.

In that first volume, Barclay explained that the series was "designed to present a comprehensive, detailed, and accurate history of American Methodism in its character as a Christian missionary movement." He laid out the publishing program as including the content of volume one, early American Methodism, and then the mission histories of the three divisions of mainstream Methodism prior to 1939: the Methodist Episcopal Church (MEC), the so-called northern church; the Methodist Episcopal Church, South (MECS), the so-called southern church; and the Methodist Protestant Church (MPC).

By the time of the third volume, however, Barclay was apologetic: "The writing of this volume has required more time than was anticipated." The second volume had brought the history only up to 1844, and that only of the MEC. The third volume advanced the MEC history to 1895. A fourth volume, written by J. Tremayne Copplestone after Barclay's death, completed the MEC mission work, ending in 1939. With the publication of this volume in 1973, however, the project stopped. The four volumes had taken a quarter century and the Board of Missions had by then evolved into the Board of Global Ministries of a new denomination, The United Methodist Church. The Board decided the histories did not articulate an adequate vison of mission.

By the end of the twentieth century it seemed apparent to many that a continuation of the history of mission was needed. There were several reasons. The Women's Division almost alone in The UMC had continued to educate an important constituency about mission, supporting the National Council of Churches of Christ in its publication of annual mission resources and publishing many resources of its own. When the NCCC found it could no longer continue publishing these books, the Women's Division led the General Board of Global Ministries to continue their publication. The Women's Division more than most was conscientious in publishing works about mission. Yet many in the rest of the denomination remained untouched by any serious study of mission, present or past.

A second large reason consisted of the bridges that had flowed under the water since the conclusion of the Barclay/Copplestone series. The history of mission of The Methodist Church, in existence from 1939 to 1968, had never been written. The history of mission of the Evangelical United Brethren, in existence from 1946 to 1968, had never been written. Since these two merged to become The United Methodist Church, critical changes had occurred in the comprehension, strategy, and practice of mission in the newly united denomination. The very nature of the denominations had altered greatly in relation to the rest of the culture and in relation to the ecumenical movement. A need existed to write all these histories taking these changes into account. Furthermore, the MECS and MPC histories need to be written and published.

A third reason lay in the religious and cultural changes that affected the way history is conceived and written. At the time Barclay began his series, women were almost totally absent from the official leadership of the mainline churches. African Americans, Hispanics, Asian Americans, and native Americans were not well represented in that leadership. Bishops, officers of the major program boards like the Board of Missions of The Methodist Church, and other denominational officials consisted almost entirely of white men.

The need, then, was to develop a history of mission that did justice to the role of women, ethnic minorities in the United States, and also indigenous leaders in various countries. For most of the histories of mission previously published had ignored the leadership and contributions of indigenous leaders as well.

Finally, the field of history itself had changed. Chronicles of official events and even large-scale interpretations, or "metahistories," had given way to more detailed studies of local and culturally specific developments. "Thick description" was preferred to chronicles of facts and dates. Traditional histories are still being written, those that take a large field and attempt to provide an overriding image or concept for interpretation and those that relate personal histories. These efforts, while entertaining and even popular, eventually fail because of their biases, the inevitable inability of a single historian to know that large field, or simply because they ignore the human race in its diversity.

This series might seem to be attempting such large-scale interpretations. Writers were advised to provide an interpretive framework while avoiding the attempt to create "repositories of facts," to "provide readable narratives" that would be placed "within the context of culture/religion interaction." We were keenly aware of the dangers of attempting histories "from the center," as it were, rather than "from the periphery," that is, from the perspective of previously neglected people. We hoped, however, that by breaking the histories into periods of fairly brief epochs and by seeking diligently to give voice to the voiceless inasmuch as the historical record allowed, we could fill the vacuum left in mission history since the conclusion of the Barclay/Copplestone series.

We hoped even more that we could produce histories that might be actually read by United Methodists and others committed to mission. This may seem an even more dubious undertaking, since the advent of electronic media has threatened to abolish reading entirely. Yet the publication of books and magazines on the electronic media itself gives us some hope that reading may extend into the next generation.

The General Board of Global Ministries, through grants provided by the office of the general secretary, initiated the "United Methodist History of Mission" in 1999. It was conceived as a way to accomplish four goals:

1. To complete the outlines of the history of mission of The Methodist Church and its predecessors as given in *The History of Methodist Missions* by Wade Crawford Barclay and J. Tremayne Copplestone.
2. To provide readable narratives or thematic treatments that can be used by both scholars and the general church membership.
3. To do justice to the contributions of women, ethnic minorities, and indigenous leaders to the history of mission.
4. To provide the basis for a video and other resources to be used in orienting GBGM staff and missionaries in our history.

This volume is one of a series that will consist of the following:

- the history of mission of the Methodist Protestant Church, 1830–1939
- the history of mission of the Methodist Episcopal Church, South, 1845–1939
- the history of mission of The Methodist Church, 1939–1968

- the history of mission of the Evangelical United Brethren Church, 1946–1968
- the history of mission of The United Methodist Church, 1968–2000
- reflections on Christian mission in the early decades of the third millennium of Christian history
- first-person accounts of presidents and directors of the United Methodist General Board of Global Ministries in undertaking significant mission initiatives from 1980 to 2002.

These histories are dedicated to past and present generations of Methodists, EUBs, and United Methodists who helped to fulfill the commitment "to reform the Continent and to spread scriptural Holiness over these lands." They are also offered in the hope that future generations will find in them not only information and interpretation of Christian mission but inspiration to continue that mission in the future. Although a reading of these histories will reveal failures as well as successes, contemporary Christians cannot but be grateful for the accomplishments of our foreparents in the faith. "We feebly struggle, they in glory shine."

Charles E. Cole, EDITOR

Christian Mission in the Third Millennium

CHAPTER 1

The Future of Christian Mission in Ghana

Mercy Amba Oduyoye

THE MANIFESTATION OF Methodism in Africa is as varied as you would find anywhere that Euro-American Christianity has had an impact. It seems to me, however, that Africa's colonial history made British Methodism more widespread, especially in areas that used to be under the British sphere of influence.

The twentieth-century unions of the various families of Methodism left Africa with a few primitive Methodists, Methodists of the Duchess of Huntington, and United Methodists, mainly of the provenance of the United States. We also have some African Methodist Episcopal churches and African Methodist Episcopal Zion churches. At the inception, Sierra Leone alone featured several, separated on the lines of American republican and British loyalist types.[1] Given this variety and the breadth and length of Africa, I believe it is more realistic to speak not even of West Africa but more specifically of Ghana. Nevertheless, a general picture of this area is not out of place here.

In West Africa there are several churches of the Methodist communities to be found in Gambia (founded 1820), Sierra Leone (1811), Liberia, Cote d'Ivoire, Ghana, Togo, Benin, and Nigeria. Of these, my firsthand experiences are with Ghana (a part of which was called the Gold Coast, 1835) and Nigeria (1841). Ecumenical encounters in the All Africa Conference of Churches (AACC), the World Council of Churches (WCC), and the Circle of Concerned African Women Theologians have given me some indications as to the ethos of the other churches. Working together as Methodists in West Africa has been a struggle, but these churches do share one another's significant occasions.[2]

With regard to Ghana and Nigeria I have had closer contact. I grew up in the former and made a study of the latter during the critical period of the mid-1970s to the mid-1980s. My reflection would be informed by both but limited to the churches that spring out of the Wesleyan Methodist Missionary Society (WMMS). Specifically then, I have in mind Methodist Church Ghana and Methodist Church Nigeria (MCN). Both of them were at one point a single district that included present Togo and the Republic of Benin. They have roots in the invitation issued by Ghanaians that brought Joseph Rhodes Dunwell to Cape Coast in 1835 and another by Nigerians that took Thomas Birch Freeman and William de Graft (Ghanaian) to Badagri, Nigeria, in 1842. These are churches that reached their centenary years in the middle of the twentieth century of the existence of the Christian religion.

What challenges did they meet in that period and what is ahead of these churches in the next century? We may be able to summarize the past but for the future all we can do is spell out in a "wish list" what we see the present calling for and what we would like to see happen.

The Planting

The twentieth century became a traumatic and eventful period for the whole of the continent following the nineteenth-century decision of Europeans to share the continent among themselves, ignoring the fact that there were peoples, nations, civilizations, cultures, and religions in existence. The story of this unbelievable arrogance has been told and retold, and, though it bears retelling, I'll save myself the pain of doing so. Pertinent to review though, is what the propagators of Christianity saw as their duty to Christ to do in Africa. Of course, there were earlier Christian missions that coincided with the trade in human beings and in gold dust and nuggets.

The Methodist story in West Africa begins, however, with the return of Africans enslaved in America, Europe, and the Caribbean and from boats bound for those regions. The earliest would be Wesleyans and Methodists in Sierra Leone, Liberia, and the Sene-Gambia at the turn of the eighteenth century and the beginning of the nineteenth century. Andrew Walls notes that "the modern Church of tropical Africa did not begin by missionary agency at all; it arrived, a ready-made African Church."[3] Referring to the story of the Lady Huntington congregation in Sierra Leone, he said there were Methodist congregations that had never known a Methodism that was inside the Church of England. When sometime afterwards, the conference came to send out a superintendent from Britain to Nova Scotia, he was a disastrous failure. For the Nova Scotians, for example, British patterns were completely alien. The current challenges of British Methodists "going episcopal" gives us some indications of what Sierra Leone at the close of the eighteenth century must have gone through.

The story I tell here, however, limited as it is to Ghana and Nigeria, begins only in 1835. But up until the middle of the twentieth century the ethos of Euro-American Christian mission in Africa did not see much change. It was conceived as an aggressive work to save the souls of Africans and adhered to the patterns of the church as known in "the sending" churches. The African collaborators in the mission, including those who invited the missionaries, were of the same conviction that Africans needed to be saved from paganism; that is, from their own indigenous religions and cultures.

The work consisted of westernizing Africans. There were situations in which it was impossible to distinguish the agents of the colonial government and those of the gospel. It seemed that to assure conversion the singular way was to alienate them from their traditional religions and culture. The result was the planting of Western Christianity in most parts of Africa. The Methodist story is part of this larger picture. The hymnbooks and the Order of Service, as well as of business both in Ghana and Nigeria, were from Britain and were translated also into local languages. In Ghana the 1933 hymnbook and Order of Service of the British Conference are still in use. The order of church business in synods and conferences follow the "Methodist usage" of Great Britain. Very little has changed. The most dramatic change that happened to Methodism in Nigeria was the change in the ordering of the clergy, and in Ghana just in 2000, episcopal nomenclature has been adopted.

Making the Gospel Concrete

The context of the planting was competition with Islam and African religion. It was also a period of harsh economic realities following the abolition of slavery and the beginning of cash-crop agriculture for export. Living conditions were difficult for Europeans, especially those who needed a European style of life in West Africa. Communication was a challenge for all. The hard work of planting Western education was in part stimulated by the need to communicate. Communicating the gospel as in proclamation resulted in the need for linguistic studies. Making the gospel a positive force in people's daily lives was equally daunting, since that came into competition with traditional religion, which governed the ethics and morality of the African people.

Ignatius of Antioch said Jesus Christ is the good news whom we must receive, live, and proclaim. To evangelize is to present this good news and to make it visible. To make it visible is to make it affect the lives of the audience in concrete terms. Contemporary efforts in mission are geared to this unveiling or making efficacious the presence of Jesus Christ in Africa. This has remained the task of mission till today.

The Methodists in both Ghana and Nigeria have kept up with educational and health ministries and to some extent intentional extension of evangelization to the "un-evangelized" areas. It is true that some of the challenges of 1835 remain today and may be with us in 2035 because they have their roots in endemic economic disadvantage and a view of mission that concentrates on church membership. Above all, cultural change is slow, and a people's primal religion cannot be made to disappear overnight. The challenges of incarnating the gospel remain with us.

Things and ideas and symbols that are African remain excluded from the purviews of those shaping the ethos of the church in Africa. One area of accommodation of African culture and spirituality in the Methodist Church in Ghana is in the services of worship. But this is limited to the addition of Ghanaian lyrics and dance as praise. The same goes for Nigeria. The predominant language of prayers reflects the antipathy towards traditional religion, the concern for prosperity, and imprecations on Satan and demons. Exorcism in the form of deliverance from demons and curses that derive from one's ancestors has spread from the new charismatic movement to the Western churches, including the Methodist. Prayer camps and special praying grounds that used to be the preserve of African Instituted Churches are becoming a regular feature of Christianity in Ghana and attracting Christians from all communities.

African Collaborators

Preparing persons for mission, ministerial formation, and the making of a theologically enlightened laity remain for me the continuing challenge as far as the church's own ethos is concerned. The sociopolitical, economic, and cultural context shall continue to shape the church's participation in mission. Taking account of this context requires that the theological sophistication be enhanced among both laity and clergy. In the congregation I attend, a teaching period has been created to expound the tenet of the "Apostle's Creed." This is a necessary move to inform "Bible reading" and what is derived from the "Bible preaching."

If there is one field in which the church as a whole has succeeded it is in formal education. From the days of Methodism in Sierra Leone, education had "distinguished" as well as "propped up" the work of the Methodist missions. As Walls comments on education, it was "one of its [Methodism's] distinctive institutions, initiated by agents of the Methodist Conference, supported by funds from England" as well as from local contribution and later that of the colonial administration.[4] The Methodists in particular did pioneer secondary education of a quality that became a model for others.

Mfantsipim Secondary School on its rough road to fame exhibited the cardinal challenges of the mission enterprise; the key ones being financial resources and the acquisition of land. As in Sierra Leone funding the mission and especially its educational work was always a source of tension. Finance was one of the reasons for Thomas Birch Freeman's withdrawal from the WMMS in West Africa.[5] Together with Wesley Girls High School, the success of this aspect of mission is unquestionable. One could say the same for teacher training as attested by Wesley College (in Kumasi, Ghana, and Ibadan, Nigeria).[6]

Health delivery services were less developed. In both countries the Methodists could provide only a few hospitals, but the idea of a sound mind in a sound body was ever present and remains top priority in the challenges of following the footsteps of Jesus of Nazareth. It was concern for the health of the missionaries that brought the architectural principle of "Boy's Quarters" into the language of West Africans.

Existing Foundations for Mission

The traditional interpretation of Matthew 28 that fueled Euro-American missions in other continent continues to hold sway. The "other" is the pagan "over there" who must be rescued from sure perdition. The farther away from your own immediate environment, the better. It is the foundation on which Methodism, too, was built, although circumstances dictated that the task must begin at home, urging John Wesley to ride many hundreds of miles on horseback. He is said to have uttered the famous dictum "the world is my parish."

In both Ghana and Nigeria, Africans were collaborators and active participants in the conversion of other Africans to Christianity. On this foundation is being built the outreach missions to parts of Ghana where the church is weak or nonexistent or is very marginal to the life of the community. Mainly, this means northern Ghana and the rural areas that continue to be off the limits of modern developments. But also there are people who have made a deliberate choice not to abandon the traditional religion of their ancestors. Primary evangelization challenges this choice, sometimes causing violent confrontations even in metropolitan communities like Accra.

Building on Western missions' foundation has become precarious, since the institutional models left by the previous effort have become economically beyond the means of the present church. The educational need of Ghana as elsewhere in Africa continues to expand against the dwindling financial resources necessary for infrastructure and training and maintenance of personnel. The church acknowledges this need to participate in formal education as well as in general public education. Continuing health ministry is even more challenging. In the formal Western medical stream, the church is almost absent. Neither has it begun to join in the enhancing of health care delivery through the traditional herbal medicine. The normal challenges of health care in the tropics have been augmented by the HIV/AIDS pandemic. Today if we received a letter crying for medical health it would have to say people are flocking to the Deliverance Ministries, plagued as they are by demons of poverty and ill-health. (In Deliverance Ministries, Christians deliver people from Satan and evil spirits in a form of exorcism.)

In recent times under the impetus of the Roman Catholic Church, issues of inculturation of Christianity in Africa have been heightened. Throughout the previous period it was a minority of Western missionaries in Africa who would have anything to do with things African beyond the language study necessary for the translation of the Bible. It is, however, the vernacular Bibles that have delivered Christianity into the hands of Africans. The initiators of African Instituted Churches worked with these vernacular Bibles augmented by direct revelation through dreams

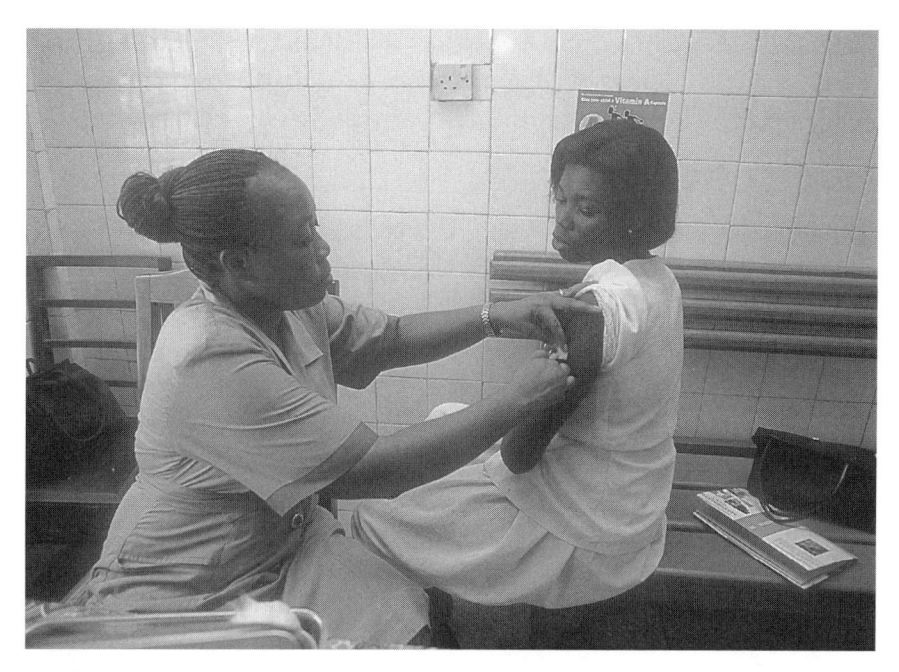

A woman receives a prenatal injection in a private clinic in Accra. The Methodist Church in Ghana affirms Western medical practices but struggles with integrating such scientific methods with indigenous approaches like "Deliverance Ministries," which emphasize demons. *(Richard Lord photo)*

and visions. They appreciated biblical spirituality, especially those practices that are similar to traditional African spirituality, like not wearing sandals to go before the deity and praising God with drums and clapping of hands. The charismatic churches today have gone "Western" again. However, replacing the pipe organ with a jazz ensemble has democratized the music-making in church and made it more participatory. The words that are sung reveal the challenge to theological articulation of the faith once given, so that it responds in a salvific way to the needs of the people.

Not long ago Bishop Kwasi Sarpong of the Roman Catholic Church in Ghana sparked a lot of controversy by his advocacy for Africanizing Christianity. African Christianity caught the attention of Western Christians in the 1960s with its numerical strength and the prospect of its being the definitive ethos of world Christianity as we enter the third millennium of the Christian era. Statements such as this one by Sarpong could be heard and read at all mission conferences: "At a time when the church is losing ground in Europe and America as well as making little enough impression on the millions of teeming masses in Asia, in Africa, the increase in numbers of Christians over the past few years has been phenomenal."[7]

The bishop was, however, critical: "All this seems to me to be superficial." It is a fact that on Sundays our churches are packed, open-air crusades bring in thousands more, and church buildings are becoming more and more expansive. Christianity is having a heyday in Ghana, indeed in Africa. But the superficiality of it all is demonstrated by the upsurge of Deliverance Ministries, the condoning of evil practices, the absence of prophetic mission, and the lack of influence on politics and public morality. There is a lack of depth in Christian life, since it is not integrated into life in Africa, and globalization has only served to establish its colonial ethos and mentality. Without respect for humanness as exhibited in Africanness, this colonial mentality has been difficult to shed, and Africans remain and seem to enjoy and approve of being mimics.

The anger against the bishop, I suggest, came out of touching a sore nerve. Sarpong insists that "inculturation has to do with transforming people."[8] The challenge of mission today is that of transformation of life in Africa. Hence Teresa Okure writes, "Theologically speaking, inculturation belongs to the very core of the history of the fulfillment of the Church's universal mission of evangelization."[9] It arises from living our faith and so must be contextual if we are not to demonize our past and consign all things African to the power of Satan and his demons.

Methodist missionaries have gone down as having crafted a constitution for the church, which prohibited the use of drums in the churches and declared the enstoolment of chiefs as idolatrous. It is the lack of sensitivity to the task of contexualization that led the missions of the previous centuries to concentrate on "snatching the Westernized African from the grip of the devil and has resurged in the concentration on deliverance from the power of Satan."[10]

The challenge of mission today arises out of the doctrine of incarnation as it has always done. Teresa Okure reminds us that this challenge is foundational to Christianity. At its inception the Christian religion was perceived as "a set of external and imported practices to be performed rather than as a way of life, to be lived."[11] This misconception resurfaced in the early period of evangelizing Africa. Is salvation in Christ or in the laws set by Western missionaries? Should inculturation not be understood as incarnation, "the union of two realities?" asks Okure. She refers here to the context and realities of Africa (Ghana/Nigeria) and the Western context (the Euro-American) to which Africans seem happy to succumb.

The problem is that this type of Christianity treads a path of inculturation that does not derive from a living faith (John 4:39-42, Acts 4:12). Methodism in British clothes still reigns in Ghana, together with megachurch charisma that even speaks American-English and mimics the speaking and singing styles of African Americans. The failure "to grasp and understand" both the particular culture of the missionaries (and of the host country) involved and the gospel of Jesus Christ has produced a Christian people that do the dance of the priests of the Baalim of old (1 Kings 18:20-21). "We are faced with a call to commitment to a personal God through Jesus Christ," says Okure. How we respond to this call is the challenge of the coming decades.

Contextualization of the Gospel

Following this train of thought I would then ask how does the Methodist Church participate in the contextualization of the gospel? Mission today should become more sensitive to the quality of its reception by the target audience. In addition to snatching people from their private hells, the focus on witnessing to Jesus who is the gospel should be augmented. We need to discover how to do this in all aspects of life. Confessing or witnessing to Jesus requires bringing Jesus to live with us. This calls for the sanctification of our very environment, straightening the crooked, lifting up the valleys, and bringing low the hills. It means radical change that will enable Africans to see themselves as worthy temples for the Spirit of God. This will enable people to see themselves as African Christians and to curb the propensities for mimicking which result in superficiality.

There is another side to contextualization of Christianity, which could perhaps became the focus of the next few decades. It is that of self-emptying. As persons in mission among people in our own countries in Africa we need to rid ourselves of the self-degradation and abasement we have accrued as a result of being colonial and having entered into a slave economy. The negative self-image of the colonized has also turned us into consumers who have no creativity to contribute to the economic developments beyond producing primary materials and opening our countries to the ravages of tourism. We have to rid ourselves of the self-hatred that make us value others and their cultures more than ours and ourselves. The attachment to things American can mount to nauseating proportions and thus have a debilitating effect on all, especially on young people in Africa.

Where will the Methodist Church stand in relation to this challenge? It is my view that more in-depth study of what it means to be human, based on the Bible, will stimulate a re-evaluation of Africanness. In the attempt to Christianize life in Africa, some African Christians have adopted a very negative and judgmental attitude towards our history and culture. Christians have invented something called "the ancestral curse," by which they explain every adversity. No sociopolitical or economic analysis is demanded. All that it takes to put things right is to annul the ancestral curse, to deliver people from the resultant absence of prosperity. Wholeness of life has come to mean separating oneself from one's heritage. I find this an unsatisfactory approach and evidence of the unwillingness to face certain realities. Methodists may join in the Deliverance Ministries, but it is also imperative that we promote in-depth study of African culture and heritage so that we condemn or promote not out of ignorance but from what we have come to discover the intent of what culture demands.

Studies and research will provide the basis for the contextualization of liturgies. From my observation of Methodism in Nigeria it is possible to make baptism more meaningful by introducing the symbols of traditional naming ceremonies that point the infant to cultural wisdom. Since the infant understands none of this, it is in fact the occasion to remind all participants in the ceremony about the joys and sorrows of life as well as the individual's and the community's responsibilities and entitlements. These are ceremonies at which the values of the community are rehearsed in order to reinforce them. Christian baptismal rite could therefore be enhanced. The renewal in eucharistic liturgy that swept Africa in the 1960s seems to have bypassed the Methodists. We have remained tied not only to the language and to the symbolic gestures of nineteenth-century Methodism but also the 1662 Book of Common Prayer of the Anglican Church. (Incidentally, in Britain both the Anglicans and the Methodists have crafted alternative liturgies.)

Since the Methodist churches have come together in the World Methodist Council, and many also meet at the Oxford Institute of Wesleyan Studies, we could make the challenge of gospel and culture in Africa one of the focal points in the next couple of decades. Africa too does have a responsibility to contribute to the ethos of world Methodism.

Globalization and Communication

Christianity can claim to be the first religious impulse that was universal in its vision and practice. It freed itself from Judaism and headed for the world out there at a very early stage. The challenge here was one of communication. Aramaic was its "mother tongue," but it had to read Hebrew and Greek Scriptures, document the faith in Koiné Greek, and later make itself understood also in Latin. Very early its Scriptures were to be found in Syriac and other languages of West Asia and the Holy Land. It vied with the religions of the Roman world and came up supreme. Since then, it has claimed universality by being "translatable." Throughout its development it has encountered several obstacles. The development in Africa is no different.

Reviewing this history one could count several obstacles to the Christianization of Africa. Prominent among the causes of the rejection of Christianity by Africa are

- the slave trade
- the strength of traditional political systems and attitudes
- the presence of Islam
- the challenge of communication across the language barriers
- the demeanor of persons in missions.

Related to all this is the association of Westernization and Europeans with the Christian religion. It took a long time to demonstrate that Christianity was not the "white man's religion." Unsuccessful attempts at evangelization may be due to any or combinations of the above.

The earliest "missionaries" to Ghana were not missionaries at all but chaplains to European trading establishments who on occasion showed some paltry interest in the conversion of the Africans around the forts and castles of the Europeans as these traders joined "the Evil and Wicked Traffic of the slavery and commerce of the human species." Later the Wesleyan mission was to admit that Britain owes a vast debt of reparations for the wrong and miseries of the accursed "slave trade."[12] These reparations are yet to be made. Christianity failed to interest not only the Africans but the mestizos and their European fathers who inhabited the strongholds. Several of the "governors" of the castles were either disinterested or hostile to Christianity. The new religion did not seem able to help people cope with the impact of the new politico-economic situation that had come upon them. So the Africans could not see any reason to change their religion. Trade, not religion, was the face of the new era that had dawned, and Christianity was tolerated as a means to create relations with the traders from overseas.

The trade moreover proved to be one in which both Europeans said to be Christians and Africans said to be heathens exhibited humanity's greed and inhumanity. The chaplains had a hard time trying to dissociate their mission from that of the traders and later even from that of the colonizers. "In the pre-abolition period, the circumstances were such that trade became the main activity around which all others including the missionary enterprise revolved."[13] That the terminology associated with mission was "enterprise" is in itself quite significant.

Much-observed is that where the traditional political authority was centralized in monarchies, missionaries had a hard time overcoming the religio-culture that supports the political system. The internal political upheavals of the previous period made it quite impossible to travel safely, let alone preach the gospel beyond the range of the castles and forts. S. K. Odamtten observes that subjecting Basel missionaries to the authority of Danish merchants and governor thwarted the ideas of the missionaries until they freed themselves by moving to Akropong in the Akuapem hills some 60 km from the Danish castle at Christiansborg. In the Akuapem area, Odamtten concludes that "the people were prepared to receive the missionaries not because they were convinced of the superiority of the Christian doctrine but because of the political, economic and social processes it brought in its train." To this day Akuapem attracts tourists who wish to experience African traditional worship of local deities, especially Akonodi. Yet the hills also feature some of the oldest Presbyterian and later Methodist work. Receiving the message was one thing, living by it was another.[14]

Evangelization, as noted, has to do with social change, and the people had very strong religious bases for what they did, so the challenge was very deep and very complex. Carriages and cars may arrive to boost the prestige of traditional royalty, but for really significant occasions royalty continue to be carried in palanquins. Being in mission in Ghana today requires that one recognizes the significant events in people's lives and helps them cope or celebrate in a manner befitting Methodists, indeed Christians. In mission we attempt to present "the story of the church."

The presence of Islam was and continues to be a factor in the environment in which we wish to proclaim the gospel. Initially, it was British administration that prevented missionaries from going to northern Ghana and northern Nigeria. The reason was the assumption that they were Islamized areas. The British policy of administration through traditional rulers demanded that they screened off people who were not Muslims too. Thus it is only with political independence that the north has been formally open to evangelization. Prior to independence the churches in the north were regarded as "chaplaincies" for immigrants from the south.

Religion and Politics in Ghana

The colonial administration used Islam as an excuse to keep missionaries out of the north, which also meant isolating them from Westernization and Western education that was championed by the mission. Today Muslim persons and voices are loud and clear in Ghana's media and public affairs and louder in Nigeria. The situation described by J. S. Pobee has changed, and many Muslims—Gas, Fantes, Asantes—are to be counted in Ghana. Islam is no longer a religion of immigrants, not even in southern Ghana.[15] One of the reasons for sponsoring Portuguese exploration of Africa was "to ascertain the extent of the Muslim power which had been a serious threat to Christendom in Europe itself. Prince Henry (1395–1460) sponsored the effort to evangelize the peoples of Africa so as to undermine any Muslim influence in Africa South of the Sahara."[16]

Today we continue to have the challenge of Islam in various forms— *sharia* (law), Muslim festivals, and occasional confrontation and destruction of property. All are indications that without proper dialogue to inculcate mutual respect and coexistence, we are headed for religious tension that Africa does not need. A critical area calling for attention is study and counseling in interfaith marriages. Being in Christian mission in West Africa today calls for the promotion of the task undertaken by the Project on Christian Muslim Relations in Africa, based in Nairobi and covering all of sub-Saharan Africa. In Ghana, churches working in the north are conscious of these challenges, but the mindset remains conversion rather than discipleship. Persons in mission need to enable a reorientation of the Christian endeavor so that we might make disciples rather than swell the church roll, especially where other faiths predominate.

Another obstacle to early mission was the attitudes of Europeans towards Africans and their own European style of life. The Basel mission succeeded when it brought Africans from the Caribbean. The Methodists always paired their European personnel with African collaborators. Where Europeans were caring, Africans admired their religion. This is one area where the not-distinguishing of missionaries from other Europeans became an obstacle to the acceptance of Christianity. Racism remains to be uprooted, and though none would judge Christianity by the behavior of Europeans, most would say being Christian makes no difference when they see no unique contribution. All have sinned, and all continue to sin. And *all* includes professed Christians.

Translation was indeed a challenge. European persons in mission and even some Africans needed interpreters for communication in the early period. The Bible, the hymns, the order of service, the sermons were all in English. Training a cadre of Africans in English language was the chosen path of the Methodists on the West Coast. Although in preparing persons for mission "the one over-riding demand of the WMMS on its missionaries was a knowledge of the language of the people they served . . . for effective preaching of the gospel, the hearer's mother tongue is best." The society recognized that "in order to hunt down evil, it is necessary to be acquainted with the habits of the people." You cannot get into a people's way of life, their culture, without adequate knowledge of their vehicle of communication.[17] The Presbyterians trained their missionaries to speak the African languages. There was a significant difference here at the beginning, but now the language issue is more complex. In eastern Nigeria, for instance, the problem was that of a minister whose only language was Efik, while more people were moving into the area who had other African languages but not Efik.

Multilingual Africa is an expensive challenge when we need to do ecumenical conferences across the continent and across educational levels.[18] How do people understand and interpret the Bible, never mind what language, is the most crucial issue. Globalization of Christianity has meant, for the African, taking on Christianity that has absorbed European culture and making it our own. The question is: What is Africa's contribution to this global religion? If, as Stephen Neil says, "the essential uniqueness and power of Christianity is the way of Salvation for the whole world," and this is what impels our mission, then we should ensure that the whole world is present in Christianity.[19]

An objective of mission which was a signal failure was the early Latin/Roman Catholic effort to claim the whole of Africa south of Cape Bojador (in former Spanish Sahara, now known as Cap Boujdour in Western

Sahara) for Christ. The story is ably summarized by J. S. Pobee in his *AD 2000 and After: The Future of God's Mission in Africa*. In 1494, by the *Padroado*, the then-Pope Alexander VI made the king of Portugal "responsible for founding and supporting missionaries and endowing bishoprics in Africa and Brazil."[20] In West Africa this policy did not work, and where it worked, as in Congo, Angola, and Mozambique, the politicization of mission had unsavory results. By the *Padroado*, pope, king, and merchant were to join hands in claiming Africa for Christ. In the event the mercantile interests proved the strongest. By 1884 the church had become "an accomplice" of colonialism with mixed results, and African objections to colonial administrative style were frowned upon by missionaries. This and the racism of apartheid resulted in the deeper failure of Christianity in Africa. The universal religion wore a Western face that was not all pleasant and caused many to label it a foreigner even while acknowledging its benefits.[21]

Dealing with success or failure of attempts at mission requires that we state explicitly what we consider as success. In 1928 this was a subject among those participating in the work of the WMMS in Nigeria. London was of the opinion that gains were to be consolidated and that attention was to be concentrated on the training in Christian living rather than the urge for geographic expansion that those in Lagos were clamoring for. One case in point was Badagri, the landing place and first post of Methodism in Nigeria. Badagri was a neglected place, described as "under the spell of traditional religion." A contemporary letter stated, "As in Freeman's days, paganism is so strong that progress for Christianity is hardly won." But the pro-Badagri lobby always responded with "an area sacred to Methodism as the scene of Freeman's early work in Nigeria might not be abandoned wholly to heathenism." One reason often given was the inadequacy of local resources. But it was more than that. Badagri's location was the problem: "Lagos has taken over its economic role and missionaries had emigrated with their compatriots. Further, it did not stand a chance of growing in importance as the traditional religion proved dominant in people's minds."[22] Here coming together in one pot were all the obstacles to mission in West Africa. Other parts of Africa would add overt white racism.

We cannot review Christian missions in Africa and neglect the ecumenical aspect of mission. After all the oneness of the church is a condition for authenticating our preaching of the Christ. I therefore insert here, even if it is only a short note, a comment on the challenge of the *oikoumene*. Interchurch relations, the ecumenical movement among Christians, has been an area of strong witness by Methodists the world over. Persons in mission must promote the visible unity of the church, since it is an important aspect of witness to the mission of Jesus, our only Christ. Dialogue within the family of Jesus must continue as must dialogue within the family of Methodists. It is so easy to disagree and part company. Staying together to work together demands our prayer and openness to the Holy Spirit. It is thus that we shall show ourselves to be Methodists.

Mixed Blessings

As Leslie E. Shyllon points out, conversion to Christianity was not without an element of self-interest where the African was concerned. Christianity facilitated the creation of the Krio "ethnic" group in Sierra Leone. But the tragedy of the Krio was an "imperfect imitation of European manners and customs" by a people who "had lost their homeland, their society, their cohesion."[23] But with Christianity as a common and newly adopted heritage they were able "to blend cultural aspects" of the African backgrounds to become a new people. The Krio even produced a Methodist Reverend W. H. Durington, who from 1880–1884 was a missionary to Kenya. Even the architecture in West Africa has been influenced by mission houses, manses, and churches. The schools they built became models and some still stand. Methodists fostered indigenous ministry, howbeit as auxiliaries, for a long time. The resultant inadequacy of theological foundations for both laity and clergy is thoughtfully dissected by K. A. Dickson in his *Uncompleted Mission*. There was an ambivalence in mission policy as to how to involve Africans, especially in leadership positions.

One could detect some of these swings in the development of racism that accompanied the attempt to justify colonialism and the expropriation of Africa's resources. It is interesting to note that as the nineteenth century was closing (1884), Africa was made to begin laboring under the yoke of European cultural superiority complex. Parallel this with the 1980s, the closing decades of the twentieth century and Africa's position as a heavily indebted continent fit only for milking and discarding. Will the twenty-first century end this unjust process of marginalization? Will the Methodists, indeed Christian churches, play a role worthy of the name they bear in the process?

Future in Ghana [17]

Namasta Baraya, a visually impaired person, was a student at the Theological College of Northern Nigeria at Bukuru in 1976. He represents the eagerness with which Nigerians have sought education through church-related schools, colleges, and seminaries. But today the challenge is to relate education to the economics and social environment of Africa.
(Photo by John Goodwin)

The combination "learning and piety" which the Methodists represent has served well the educational ethos of Ghana and several African countries.[24] Today the challenge is to adapt education to the economics and social environment of African nations. Will the Methodists be found here? A related challenge here is that of communication in general. Pobee notes, "Methodists produced some of the earliest newspapers which were committed to the defense of the oppressed Africans."[25] Among these papers was *The Christian Messenger and Examiner* (1839). Through this public education and advocacy Europeans joined Africans to propagate the ideas that promoted the liberation of the individual and contributed positively to social services. Africans like Akrofi joined Europeans like Christaller to produce the grammar of African languages, wrote them, and documented

African thoughts to be shared as part of our global heritage. Thus in the midst of much that was traumatic, Africans were gaining self-confidence and self-consciousness as people who are contributors to the "spiritual achievements of mankind."[26] They were imbibing the ideas and ideals of human rights as presented through the gospel. Will Methodism, indeed Christianity, be found in the efforts to reconstruct a positive and empowering self-understanding for the African?

Christianity has been assessed as agent both of oppression and liberation. In the century that has opened for us we preen ourselves with increase in numerical strength but are the nations Christianized in their policies and dealings with the populace? Pobee highlights the role of the church as the conscience of the nation. That indeed is a heavy responsibility. How do Methodists enable this? Religion is becoming more and more visible in daily life, what with all the slogans on vehicles and names of stores and enterprises. But is Christianity an integral part of the people's daily lives? How is Christ made evident in the lives of the people called the Methodists?

The Appeal of Methodism

In Ghana I have observed car stickers that say, "I am a Methodist/I love my Church." I have not asked why but from casual conversation and prayers I can identify a couple of reasons. Sure is the fact that people love to sing Methodist hymns, and in Ghana they have indigenized the rhythm of several of the hymns in the 1933 Methodist hymnbook. The lay participation in liturgy, administration, and governance of the church give people a sense of ownership and belonging. Ghana Methodists keep the ancient society classes, Bible classes, and Sunday school for literacy education. They were pioneers in the use of Ghanaian lyric style in telling the Christian story and still hold first place in lusty singing and extempore praying.

People like to be known and recognized, and so each belongs to a small group and that ensures this group care. The churches' openness to these groups is another attraction. People belong to one or two of them: choir, singing band, Christ's little band, the women's fellowship, the men's fellowship, and the youth fellowship. The Sunday service and school for children is always a lively program in the church. The rituals of baptism, confirmation, communion, and special thanks offering all create an atmosphere of a joyful and supportive community that empowers Christian living.

We also have stickers that say, "I am Methodist and proud of my church." Maybe we need a survey to collect the reasons for such pride. Meanwhile, we go by the old adage, "We witness, we worship, and we work," and by these we continue in God's mission.

CHAPTER 2

Asian Mission to Asians
Scott W. Sunquist

THE BOXER REBELLION of 1900 provides an instructive illustration for the future of Asian missions in Asia. The social and economic context was, of course, quite different from today, but many of the issues involved in this antiforeign rebellion should not be forgotten as we enter a new century of mission in Asia. What is often interpreted as a violent response to centuries of foreign domination, headlined by the oppressive opium trade, is much more complex. The Boxer Rebellion also represents the Christian struggle for identity and meaning in Asia, for Chinese Christians suffered in the rebellion as foreign agents. Asian Christians involved in missionary work in Asia today are still a pilgrim and minority community seeking to present the Kingdom of God in a foreign land.

The results of the Boxer Rebellion are fairly well known: Five Roman Catholic bishops were killed along with another thirty-one European priests, nine European sisters, and two Marists. Approximately 30,000 Chinese Catholics were killed as well as 135 Protestant missionaries, 52 missionary children, and more than 1,900 Chinese Protestants. By August 1900 the "foreign relief army" had crushed the rebellion, enforcing peace but with little concern for justice. It would not be a lasting peace. Less well known are some of the issues surrounding the rebellion; issues which still have some relevance for Asian mission involvement today.

The Boxers ("Religious Harmony Fists") were both a religious and a patriotic sect. They were motivated by concerns for Chinese independence, economic justice, and the removal of "foreign devils." The economy was dominated by foreigners, and Chinese were often losing jobs, or, if employment was to be found, it was often employment working for westerners. The Boxers were also driven by religious concerns, and these concerns were not easily separated from the social. They were concerned about how the new Western-built railroads were destroying the *feng shui* of the countryside. The Boxers engaged in occult or magical rites which would protect them from bullets and swords and disable the foreign devils. In the midst of the social transformations (both religious and cultural) of their land, the Boxers took up arms to defend China and the Qing Dynasty. The dowager herself was supportive, as were many of the Chinese secret societies (religious societies of gangs). The rallying cries of the Boxers made clear the purpose of their attacks: "Protect the country, destroy the foreigner"; "Establish the country, destroy the foreigner." Three groups of people in China were the targets. The "Primary Hairy Men" were the Christian missionaries (religious imperialism was the first concern). "Secondary Hairy Men," or Chinese Christians, were the next concern, and finally there were "Tertiary Hairy Men," or those who used foreign goods. The majority of those killed were not people using foreign goods (Tertiary Hairy Men) and were not even foreigners (Primary Hairy Men). The greatest threat to Chinese order was perceived to be the Chinese Christians, and so they suffered the greatest losses. A century later this anxiety over social and religious order, often expressed as Confucian conservatism, is still a primary concern even as mission work now originates in Asia. Today, most of the crosscultural mission work in Asia is from Asia. It is helpful to review some of this history as Asian Christians in mission prepare for their witness in the third millennium.

Asian Witness to Asians before Independence

Prior to the independence movements which followed the Second World War, Christian missions in Asia were both aided and hindered by three important factors. First, in almost every region of Asia, mission work took place in the context of foreign domination. Western powers determined the rules of the game.[1] If the British found missionary work harmful to the East India Company's economic progress, missionary work was outlawed. On the other hand, if missionary schools were found to be helpful in training a local civil service sector, then missionaries would actually receive financial support for their educational work. As we saw in the Boxer Rebellion, missionaries were easily confused with political domination, and yet the foreign powers could also be called in to enforce social order, making missionary work possible.

Second, missionary work was guided by, or often followed in the wake of, foreign trade. Trade would open the doors for work, not only in providing the infrastructure but also in providing the most basic of needs: transportation to the mission field. Even those missionaries who wanted to separate themselves from the trade and who tried to keep their distance from trading companies found that local people did not make such a distinction. The opium chests came off the same boat as the missionaries. One person was selling a drug, the next person was selling Scriptures, and so local residents saw one mission from the West.

Third, before independence, missionary work was clouded by the power of Western currency. Missionaries could afford to build massive mission stations, churches, hospitals, and schools. They could often afford to hire local people to work on the mission stations, and they could even pay local preachers. What this meant is that the influence of the missionary endeavor was often more closely related to the power of the British pound than to the goodness of the gospel. Who could tell the difference? Who is to say if people were becoming "rice Christians," genuine believers, or just new Asian entrepreneurs? All three of these—the foreign political power, trade, and financial strength—made Western missionary work in Asia possible, but the confusion of purposes, goals, and methods made genuine discipleship a clouded concern.

And yet, in the midst of this Western domination of the missionary task in Asia, there were Asian Christians who were pioneers in developing what might be called missionary ministries. These were ministries that were not limited to the Asians' own language, culture, or nation. In many cases these Asian missionary pioneers developed their crosscultural ministry vis-à-vis the representatives of Western missionary and colonial powers. As pioneers they were often misunderstood because of their antiestablishment (often antimissionary) rhetoric, but in retrospect we can see that they were pointing to the future of indigenous Asian missionary work.

A number of individuals of pre-independence Asia could be cited as models of Asian missionary work for today. Sadhu Sundar Singh is a good model to begin with because numerous themes of these early Asian missionaries are represented in his life. Sundar Singh was born in 1889 into a Punjabi family, his mother being a devout Hindu and his father a Sikh. His mother left the greatest early impression on him as she prayed that he would one day become a religious holy man, a *sadhu*. Although Sundar

Singh studied the Bhagavad-Gita with his mother, and although he was violently opposed to Christianity—even to the point of burning copies of the New Testament—his search for God eventually brought him face to face with Jesus Christ. In December 1904, at the age of fifteen, he prayed a prayer of deep longing and frustration in his search to know God. As he recounts the story, he prayed, "O God, if there be a God, reveal yourself to me tonight."[2] After his prayer he found himself in a room bathed in light, and the resurrected Christ appeared before him, and he heard a voice which said in Hindustani, "How long will you persecute me? I died for you; I gave my life for you." As is often the case, Sundar Singh's call to salvation was a call to ministry and a call to suffer. He immediately dedicated his life to serving Jesus Christ, but he did so, in answer to his mother's prayer, as a *sadhu*. For the remaining twenty-four years of his life Sadhu Sundar Singh would be an itinerant missionary, traveling throughout the Punjab, Jammu, Kashmir, Tibet, India, Nepal, Baluchistan, and Afghanistan. He spoke to groups in the United States, Europe, and Australia, but most of his time was spent walking throughout the mountains of central and south Asia. For a brief time he began theological studies in Lahore, but he would not be confined by denominations, seminaries, or (especially) Western missions.

A few themes which became central in Sundar Singh's itinerant ministry are worth noting. First, from the very beginning he recognized that his call was in part, a call to suffer. On a number of occasions he narrowly escaped death. He was imprisoned and was often very ill. One could argue that much of this he brought on himself, but that is missing the point. For Sundar Singh the call to be a servant of Jesus Christ was a call to the margins of "acceptable" missionary methods and regions. Second, his call was to an Indian Christ who called him in an Indian tongue. He carried around with him only a blanket and an Urdu New Testament. His ideal was to imitate Christ in very literal ways. He wandered around preaching, teaching, and healing. He would spend long periods in prayer, and he was directed by these sessions of prayer and the visions which often accompanied them. Third, Sundar Singh's ministry often came in conflict with the local missionaries from the West. His brief stay at St. John's in Lahore made it clear that he neither wanted to join a denomination, nor would he easily fit the expectations of missionary personnel. He not only rejected the Christian divisions which he observed, but he also rejected much of the Western scholarship, describing some of these theologians as "Christians without Christ."³ Finally, the *sadhu* was a missionary of one book. Typical of his upbringing by his mother, he was committed to the study and memorization of passages of the holy book, only now the holy book was the New Testament, rather than the Bhagavad-Gita.

Four years before his apparent death Sadhu Sundar Singh made out a will.⁴ His writings were becoming quite profitable, and he wanted this money used for purposes which he would outline. Three executors were named: a Presbyterian missionary, an Indian from the Christian Missionary Society, and the general secretary of the National Missionary Society (an indigenous Indian mission). Six purposes were given: training of evangelists for the hill states of the Himalayas, Scripture prizes for boys competing in proficiency of the New Testament, prizes for missionaries (Indian) for proficiency of the whole Bible, scholarships for boys to study, scholarships for evangelists to study theology, and scholarships for others to study in preparing to teach the New Testament. Here we see Sundar Singh's basic missionary concern to train indigenous young missionaries through knowledge of the Bible.

Many of the themes mentioned above could be traced in the ministries of other Asian missionaries such as Pandita Ramabai Sarasvati and Krishna Mohan Banerjea, Bishop V. S. Azariah⁵ in India, or John Sung in China and throughout Southeast Asia.⁶ As these Asian missionary pioneers began to develop patterns of crosscultural ministry, they did so in ways which became more Asian and less Western, with less dependence upon Western structures and finances, even before those Western structures were shattered. Biblical training was central to their work, they developed their own Asian forms of mission, and there were tensions with the Western missionaries and their theology. Their missionary work was generally done within their own political borders but often in different languages or with people of different religious backgrounds than their own. These early pioneers provide models for contemporary Asian missionaries, who may resemble Christian *sadhus* more than modern missionaries.

Complexity of Asian Mission Today

Asian missionary involvement today is so complex that even keeping track of the numbers is nearly impossible. Some local congregations are developing their own mission agencies, other churches cooperate, and in some areas, individuals launch out on their own or send out people on their own. Thus, the first problem that confronts us in our study of Asians in mission today is fairly basic: How many Asian missionaries are there? Where are they and what are they doing? How are they supported? How can we find out this information?

Asians in mission in Asia today are more numerous than the number of westerners who have ever worked at one time in Asia. This should give us a pause to reflect. It would be very difficult to give exact numbers of Asian missionaries working in Asia, but a quick look at one country, India, will reveal how complex the missionary involvement is and how hard the numbers are to validate. According to Brierley and Wraight's *Atlas of World Christianity*, there are 171 Protestant and 5,561 Roman Catholic missionaries serving from India in other countries.[7] This does not mean they are all serving in Asian countries, but it gives an idea that there are a good number of missionaries serving from India.

Another statistic gives a different picture and a different perspective. The India Missions Association (IMA) is a Protestant association of indigenous Indian missions which cooperate in their missionary work in and for India. Some of these societies only work in certain states, many work all over India. What defines their people as missionaries is that they are "full-time teams who serve across geographic or linguistic or ethnic or socioeconomic distance."[8] In the 1995 directory it was mentioned that IMA represented eighty-one missions with more than 10,000 missionaries. Another twenty-five missions had applied for membership, which means there are a number of other Indian mission societies not included in the IMA. It would be difficult to know how many other missions there are in India which are not members of IMA and how many missionaries they have sent out. For example, the Church of North India, the Church of South India, the Lutheran Church, and the Methodist Church are not members of the IMA. To confuse matters a little more, Patrick Johnstone's *Operation World* estimated in 1993 that there were fewer than 12,000 Indian missionaries serving both outside and within India.[9] In light of the statistics from the IMA alone (which can be verified by contacting each of the missions listed) it seems that Johnstone's estimates are very conservative. If we were to add up what seems to be fairly reliable statistics for all Protestant and Roman Catholic Indian missionaries working in Asia the total would easily be more than 17,000 full-time missionaries. And this is just India. By comparison, in all of Asia there are only about 24,000 Western missionaries working today. In fact there are only about 50,000

Western missionaries working in the whole world today.[10] What does this mean for our purposes?

First, the difficulty we have getting reliable statistics reveals to us something of the nature of the modern mission movement in Asia: the movement today is more of a movement of the Spirit, rather than an institutionally directed program. The multifaceted, spiritual nature of Asian missions is explained in part from the history of missionary work in Asia. Some Asians are working with Western agencies, others with agencies patterned after Western societies, and some are doing something completely new. When Asian churches, moved by the Spirit of God, begin to reach out in mission involvement, they move ahead with whatever institutions or structures are available. Because of the long history of mission involvement in Asia, there are many different structures available.

Another example may help to illustrate. We know from the Singapore Centre on Evangelism and Mission (SCEM) that there are more than two hundred full-time missionaries from Singapore working overseas, but these are only those not working with overseas Chinese. And these two hundred are only the Protestants who can be discovered through surveys: asking local churches and mission agencies. The numbers are very conservative. When I read this statistic in 1992, I was pastor of a Presbyterian Church in Singapore with seven overseas missionaries sent out by this one local congregation.[11] These missionaries were working with Western agencies (WEC International, Child Evangelism Crusade) and Asian groups as well as newer independent structures. In addition we had a medical doctor who, from his own means, supported a Christian medical clinic (two or three doctors and their families) in peninsular Malaysia working with tribal peoples. We were not contacted by the SCEM, so I would have to conclude that there are at least 207 missionaries from Singapore.[12] It is all very complex: a Presbyterian Church in Singapore with seven missionaries and a Presbyterian doctor with his own little mission.[13]

Second, the organization and coordination of Asian missions which began with the two earliest Indian indigenous mission societies (established in 1903 and 1905) no longer holds. The local, regional, national, and international Asian initiatives are numerous and constantly changing. Asian missionary activity is spreading like a blowing wind across the continent, and like the wind, it is blowing both chaff and seed.

This "pneumatic" (as opposed to programmatic) nature of the modern Asian mission movement means that it is less coordinated and more varied and thus makes it more difficult to make generalizations that adequately summarize what is happening. With this caution, let me go ahead and make some generalizations, not from statistics, but from stories. We must realize that this may not be the best way to do church history. A single story, for example, can never be the whole picture, but stories have a certain power that often becomes "the whole" in the memory of the listener. A person who hears a story which is meant to illustrate a lesson may remember with vivid accuracy the story but forget the lesson. Let this warning be given as a way of providing boundaries to these stories: Each of these stories actually happened, and all reflect types of missionary work taking place in Asia today. They illustrate something of the problem with statistics and the complexity of the movement. For each story there are hundreds of other unrecorded mission movements with similar purpose and passion. Few of these stories will be written because they come more from the grassroots of Christian faith rather than from the institutional church. But this is where most of the mission work is being done in Asia today. Taken in this light, it can be assumed, as often happens, these Spirit-induced (one might say prophetic) movements often become part of the institutional church through the years. The accumulation of smaller movements and the linking of these together become established over time. The process of "rationalization" is a normal sociological process that helps to maintain a movement and ensures that its message and concerns are passed on to those who come later. After telling these stories some very tentative generalizations will be made regarding the missionary work of Asians today and what seems to be on the horizon for the twenty-first century.[14]

Story 1: Anna and Mission Back to China

Anna was one of the best seminary students I had at Trinity Theological College (TTC) in Singapore. Her theological ability, humility, and faithful service was recognized by the faculty. Although both Chinese- and English-educated in East Malaysia, Anna was studying in the English language department at TTC. Going into her last semester she set up an appointment to ask me about an assignment and during the appointment I asked, as I did with most students, what her plans were upon graduation. She informed me that it was not definite yet, but she would probably be a missionary to China. I asked her to explain, since it is illegal to go to

Miao boys in South China sing songs of praise to Amity International visitors. Many Chinese Christians in southeastern Asia are looking for ways to go to China and witness to their Christian faith. *(Scott Sunquist photo)*

China as a missionary, and she very humbly mentioned that her father was from a small village in south China which still had no church. Since he was getting older he wanted to send his daughter to his home village to evangelize his friends and relatives and then to plant a church so, when the time comes, he can have a proper Christian burial in his home village in China. Anna spent one of her holidays making the trek to the village, buying a small shop house, and handing out Chinese New Testaments. She started a small Bible study and then returned to finish seminary training. To my knowledge she did as her father planned for her to do. Anna's loyalty to her father and to the gospel, along with the concern of the Nanyang (southern diaspora) to evangelize China are all very typical. This is a common theme among, not only the Chinese, but also Vietnamese and Cambodian Christians who are looking for ways to return or to evangelize their home villages. There are many stories needing to be recorded of Cambodians returning to their home country after being evangelized in refugee camps or in their new Western countries. Many Chinese who "escaped" after 1948 are looking for ways they can be involved creatively in mission in China today.

Story 2: Kachin's "300 for three years" Evangelistic Mission[15]

This special mission event in Myanmar was the response to the Kachin Baptist centennial celebration. After much prayer it was decided by many of the Kachin Christian leaders that their response to what God had done among their people should be to dedicate themselves to greater mission. The leader who was appointed in 1977 was a Reverend Ka Maw, a retired army general who was, at the time, a part-time student at the Burma Institute of Theology (BIT, now called the Myanmar Institute of Theology). The quiet but dedicated retired general took his responsibility very seriously, spending ninety-eight hours in prayer and fasting for clear direction from God. With a small band of helpers he next went throughout the Kachin Hills looking for three hundred missionary volunteers who would each dedicate three years of their lives to help evangelize the Kachin area even up to China. Close to seven hundred volunteered, and so a selection process was necessary to bring the number down to three hundred. In imitation of our Lord, these three hundred spent forty days and nights in training and prayer. The training was a holistic curriculum involving basic health care, physical exercise, devotions, sermons, lessons on Christian drama, songs, basic Christian beliefs, and early morning prayers on a hill (named Mount Zion) about one mile from the camp. After forty days of training the three hundred were commissioned and sent out to seven different mission areas throughout northern Myanmar under the theme: "Jesus Saves, Jesus Liberates and Jesus Unites."

It is helpful to note some of the guidelines that were to be used by the three hundred. They were to work with local church leaders, and leaders from the "command post" (the leader of the mission was a former general) would make occasional visits to the various mission fields. In the larger towns they would engage in open-air meetings, witness in the market places, visit hospitals to pray for the sick, and visit those in prisons. In the more rural areas where superstitions and spirits prevailed the missionaries would perform miracles and pray for demons to be cast out of the sick.

The missionaries more than ever before were encouraged to engage in crosscultural missionary work. Among the most "successful" mission work of the three hundred was the work among the Shan in and around Waingmaw (on the far side from Myitkyina on the Irrawaddy River) as well as among the Palaungs and Wa tribesmen. Many Kachin and related peoples live beyond the borders of Myanmar in China, and so the missionary work reached out to Kachin peoples in the People's Republic of China as well. By the time the three-year period was over, twenty-four Chinese villages had been reached by Burmese Baptist missionaries.

It is difficult to measure all of the results of this unique mission, but records were kept of those healed ("nine blind, 12 deaf and dumb and 15 lame were healed"), those who had demons cast out, those who were baptized (8,366), those who pledged to give up drugs or alcohol (23,414), and the total number of villages reached (8,576). When this report was written up, Rev. Ka Maw and the Kachin leadership were planning a similar campaign to Tibet and China. Other missionaries had gone off to Bible schools to prepare for full-time ministry and some had rededicated themselves for another three years of voluntary mission work.

Story 3: Jonathan's Personal Mission to Indonesian Youth

Jonathan was a student at TTC in Singapore in the early 1990s. While teaching my first class on evangelism in Asia, a class where I was more student than teacher, I asked the forty-two students how many had helped to lead at least one person to Christ in the past year. Everyone stood up. I then asked how many had at least helped in leading five or more people to Christ in the past year. A few people sat down. By the time I got to fifty, Jonathan was still standing up. When asked exactly how many people he had helped lead to Christ in the past year, he paused and then quietly said that he had probably helped to lead between fifteen hundred and two thousand people to Christ. During the class coffee break I got the full story.

Jonathan had been a triad society member (Chinese gang), and after beating someone up with a pipe and leaving him in a gutter, he went home under a great cloud of guilt and then accidentally picked up a New Testament and began reading the Gospel of John. Jonathan thought that he would be killed as soon as the rival gang found the body of the young man he had beaten up. At the age of fourteen Jonathan was ready to die. Instead he was saved. This was the first time he had read about Jesus, and he was so overwhelmed by the love that Jesus showed his persecutors ("Father, forgive them, for they know not what they do") that he asked a local pastor exactly who this Jesus was. The pastor quietly said, "Well, this is God. Jesus is God who came to earth to show us his love." Immediately Jonathan gave his life to Jesus and began telling other young people about the love of God in Christ so they would not turn to gangs. Jonathan began his own little mission to islands around Singapore and Batam, Indonesia, to reach young people. He would preach, call for commitments, and provide educational material to be used after he left. Jonathan trained other people to help in the follow-up, and then he asked me about developing material that would be contextually appropriate. I pointed him to people who already produced material for use in Chinese and Indonesian cultures.

Story 4: Singapore Methodist Missions

The Singapore Methodist Church is a slightly different type of story, for it is actually a network of stories which illustrate some of the complexities of Asian mission work today. The Methodist Church of Singapore has three annual conferences organized according to language: the Tamil, Chinese, and English language annual conferences. Until 1991 all missionary activity of Singaporean Methodists was initiated by individuals or local churches and then partnerships or links with overseas regions was done either individually or through international missions (Overseas Missionary Fellowship, Youth with a Mission, Summer Institute of Linguistics, etc.). Since the 1970s there has been a great deal of interest in overseas missionary work (especially in Asia) among Singaporean Methodists. This zeal for missionary involvement often runs ahead of careful theological thinking and planning, and yet the concern to be witnesses is steady and tends to be self-correcting. More on this later.

In July 1990 I began a new semester teaching Asian church history to first-year students. One student did not show up for the first class, which was highly unusual. Cheng Huat came to the second class and profusely apologized, saying that he had been in Vietnam for two weeks setting up a new factory for his business. It turns out that the factory would employ a hundred or so Vietnamese to assemble electronic instruments. I asked him if this was going to be a recurring problem, and he assured me that it would only be this one time; he had decided to stay on longer because he

This bilingual school in Phnom Penh, Cambodia, is run by the Singapore Methodist Church, which has its own mission society. *(Richard Lord photo)*

was setting up the factory Bible study program: Ah, yes, the all-important factory Bible study program. I asked him to explain. Cheng Huat had decided that even though it was not necessary to set up a factory in Vietnam, he thought it would be a good Christian thing to do, because it would give him an opportunity to help the Vietnamese by providing jobs and teaching people about Jesus. And so six mornings a week, one hundred or so factory workers show up at 7 A.M. to begin work at 8. The Bible study is part of their job, and so they get paid for that first hour, from 7 to 8. At the end of the Bible study there is the opportunity to share personal needs to be prayed over, and there is also a brief time to talk about personal concerns (clothing, education for children, medicine, etc.). Cheng Huat then learns about how his "factory mission" can begin to meet other needs as he learns how to pray for his employees. I don't know how long the factory mission continued, or if it continues today, but I mention it as a type of mission model which is not all that rare in East Asian countries where the economy is very healthy and there is the opportunity to link missionary vocation with business occupation. This model of mission raises a number of questions, especially in light of the often oppressive relationship of capitalism and mission in the last century; these issues we will pick up in a later section.

Another type of missionary work Singapore Methodists engage in is local church involvement with local churches in a poorer country. A few Methodist churches have helped pay for the education of Methodist theological professors from Myanmar or Thailand as they study in Singapore. When these pastors return to Myanmar (or Thailand) the local Singaporean churches make visits and begin to find ways to support missionary work in that country. Once again the power of the Singapore dollar makes the relationship an unequal economic partnership, but the variety of missionary activities prevents us from being too quick in our judgment on these mission trips.

In 1991 the Methodist Church in Singapore formed its own missionary society: the Methodist Missions Society (MMS). As a brochure makes clear concerning the society: "She [MMS] represents the commitment of the Methodist Church in Singapore to the task of world missions. She works with Methodist churches to strengthen the involvement of the congregation to the cause of world missions. MMS commissions Methodist missionaries and assigns them for service and support in overseas missions fields." Thus, this new venture is denominational but is not the sole missionary agent for Methodists. Very few denominations in Asia have their own sending agencies, as a denomination. What is interesting about this mission society is that it exists for the Methodist Church in Singapore but solicits support much as an interdenominational mission would, and it has a focus on four countries in the region: Thailand, Vietnam, Cambodia, and China.[16] Three of these countries are considered "closed" to missionary activity and yet they are the first countries in the "start-up phase of the mission work." At present the MMS is supporting work in Cambodia, Nepal, China, Thailand, and Vietnam. It has twelve full-time missionaries working and a number of doctors who do short-term medical work with children in Vietnam.

These missionary stories illustrate something of the variety of Asian missionary work today, but they cannot do justice to the complexity of the missionary structures and activities. New mission initiatives in Asia are impossible to track. Once we begin to understand something of the Presbyterian missionary work from Korea, we find out that a completely different pattern is developing in Nepal and Cambodia among Methodists and Anglicans. To get a more accurate picture we would have to travel to Nagaland and talk with church leaders about all of the initiatives in Nepal, Sikkim, Bhutan, Tibet, and China. We would have to travel to Hong Kong and talk to church leaders who have exhibited special concern for China during the past decades. We would also have to talk to Bataks from Sumatra who have been planting churches throughout Indonesia. Then there are the Filipinos working among various islands and among ethnic Malay in East Malaysia. And I haven't even mentioned Korean initiatives. What these stories have done is opened our minds to the fact that Asian missionary activity to Asians is vital, growing, varied, and imperfect.

Issues for Asian Missions in the Near Future

Rather than drawing conclusions or generalizations about Asian missionary work in these many contexts, a task which is outdated as soon as it is recorded, it is more useful to note some of the issues which will be facing these Asian missionaries in the coming years. These issues are not given as an agenda, or as a critique, but as a description that should be helpful for Asians preparing for mission in the coming years. I offer these in descending order of what seem to be the most crucial or critical for the future of missionary work in Asia.

1. *Persecutions, Restrictions, and Martyrdoms*

This is clearly the most critical issue for Asian missionary involvement in the coming decades. In recent years the places of persecution against Christians and Christian missionary activity have largely been in Muslim lands (and transitional territories) such as Sudan, Nigeria, and Egypt, but also in Asia (India, Indonesia, Myanmar, China, Laos, Pakistan, etc.). Indeed, in most countries of Asia there is the present reality of restriction and the future possibility of religious persecution, generally of a popular, nonpolitical nature, at any time. Many factors contribute to the thin-ice situation on which missionary activity is carried out in Asia. One of the contributing factors is the great economic contrasts that exist in Asia. We have seen in Indonesia how anger at the economic disparity spills over into violence against Chinese and against Christians; two groups who are faring better in the modern world. But this is not the whole story. Governments also may encourage popular religious persecution, and then the military intervenes and appears to be the savior of the nation. Until there are greater internal checks and balances on governments in Asia, religious persecution will always be a daily concern.

A third contributing factor to the persecution of Christians in Asia is ideology. Totalitarian systems of government have no room for communities which honor a higher authority. One of the reasons that the twentieth century has had the highest rate of martyrdom is the rise of totalitarian governments with new technologies. David Barrett estimates that there were about 35,600 Christian martyrs per year at the turn of the century (1900), but after the rise of Communist states the rate shot up to 230,000 martyrs per year.[17] Barrett estimates that the rate has gone down since the fall of Communism and the greater openness of the People's Republic of China, but this assumption should be questioned. As we witnessed in the Boxer Rebellion in the early 1900s, the mix of social injustice, social and religious change, and government encouragement can easily unleash violence against minority communities. Many countries in Asia have these elements in their mix, and the globalized economy of Asia acts as a catalyst to violence as the gap between the poor and rich widens. It would be quite surprising if the rate of martyrdom would decrease in light of the present social and political situation in Asia.

Here we have spoken mostly about popular violence (unofficially supported by governments) against Christians and the Christian missionary enterprise, but the prospect of official, government-sanctioned persecution is equally likely. Many of the governments in Asia are fragile coalition governments with constant internal struggles for control. India, for example, has surprised the rest of the world with the sudden rise of the Bharatiya Janata Party (BJP). Although not the ruling party at the moment, this party still is a key player in the government, with special concerns for a strong Indian nationalism rooted in the Hindu tradition. One of the key ideological words is *Hindutva*, which the BJP defines as "cultural nationalism," but in fact its meaning must be understood in the context of Muslim intolerance and the imposition of Western Semitic religions of monotheism.[18] It is easy to find both the language of Hindu resurgence in the BJP's rhetoric and, after the 1999 elections, a more tolerant, softer BJP rhetoric. The fact is that the resurgence of Hinduism is not just a religious renewal; it means continued oppression for minorities and scheduled castes. The caste structure is integral to Hinduism, and there has been much written in the major papers of India about the relationship between the BJP's Hindu rhetoric and the popular revolts against Dalits, Christians, and other minorities. Similar issues could be discussed for Pakistan, where the role of Islam in the government is a constant political issue which seldom promotes greater security for Christians, other minorities, and women. The political climate in many countries of Asia is such that at any time either popular or political persecution against Christians may break out, and those involved in missionary activities would be the first to suffer. It may be that the present complexity of structures and programs in Asian missions is a blessing in light of imminent persecution.

2. Asian Military and Mission

Closely related to the first concern for Asian missions is the role of the military in Asian countries. In many countries in Asia the military is more of an internal policing force than a type of protection from invasion. Myanmar, for example has the fourth-largest military in Asia, and yet there are no countries threatening Myanmar's borders. Military takeovers and restrictions of travel, meeting, or publication are often enforced via a strong and well-funded military. What role will the military play in the future of Indonesia, Vietnam, Cambodia, Thailand, China, Laos, and Myanmar, and can we envision that the military would ever step in to defend Christian communities? Probably not, since on the missionary frontiers of the church social change is a characteristic trait, and the military is threatened by change. When the military is in power, or has power by virtue of its political muscle in parliament, change can only mean a loss of power and control.

As we know from North Korea, the church can be nearly if not completely silenced by military resolve, supported by a totalitarian ideology, and directed by a dictator. This is a lethal mix for social injustice and minority suppression. The extreme paranoia mixed with the absolute power of Mao in China also created an oppressive climate for all minorities, but for both North Korea and China it was the military which made it all possible. Military spending indicates that military oppression will not be as likely in Vietnam or North Korea where military spending has nearly collapsed in the past ten years, but in China military spending continues to increase, as it does in India, Pakistan, Indonesia, and many countries friendly to the United States.[19]

3. Western Involvement

The third important factor in the future of Asian missionary work is the role that Western churches, theology, and money will play in this great missionary enterprise. It bears repeating that the Asian missionary enterprise today is stronger in terms of missionary force than Western missions ever were in Asia, and so it is clear that Asian mission societies do not "need" Western support. They are doing quite well without it. And yet one of the great advances in global mission that began to be noticed in the 1960s is the concept of "mission to six continents" (and from six continents). Mission is not a one-way road but a web of communications expressing, to all of creation, the redemption offered in Jesus Christ. It would be a step backwards in mission development for any region to withdraw from missionary activity. The type of involvement must change, but the ecumenical nature of Christianity necessitates missionary expression in all contexts, in each place.

This being said, the present situation must be recognized as holding great promise and great problems for the future. On the one hand there is great promise for partnership activity with Asian mission societies. And yet partnerships often devolve into one of Western financial support for Indian or Nepalese initiatives. This relationship repeats in a new key the same old tune of Western domination or imperialism. Happily, most ecumenical as well as independent agencies are aware of the weakness of this type of relationship. The possibilities for other types of partnerships — such as Western medical teams working with Asian church planters and intercultural mission teams — are endless and are being explored with great benefit thanks to the growth in communication networks.

On the other hand, the power of the dollar and the Euro can often overwhelm theological conviction. Writing a quick check, or transferring a quick sum of money can make so much happen, so quickly. This quick fix, as we all know, generally creates more problems than solutions, but it goes on repeatedly, and churches East and West must be constantly vigilant. It is not only the seduction of Western money that creates unequal partnerships; it is also the power of Western Christian culture. For example: most Asian churches are churches of only one Holy Book, a situation which, in large part, economics has determined — books and translation are expensive. And yet when churches become wealthier and their members are able to travel more to the West, Western literature, music, liturgy, and theology begin to creep in. On one level this is a natural outcome of ecumenical relationships. It is to be expected that the sharing of ideas, East and West, will bring about the adoption of some of these ideas. What too often happens, though, is that "Scripture songs" from Sydney or "contemporary worship" from Wheaton become part of the missionary message as Singaporeans work in Cambodia or as Malaysians work in Thailand. Dominant cultures tend to overwhelm contextualization once a certain level of prosperity sets in.

Korean missions present a particular paradox here. The earliest Presbyterian (1884) and Methodist (1885) missionaries to Korea invited the Presbyterian missionary from Cheefoo, China, John L. Nevius, to address the combined group of missionaries to Korea at a training conference in 1890. Nevius presented his principles that had been published in his *Planting and Development of Missionary Churches*.[20] The main principles involved:

1. Local churches supporting their own work and their own workers,
2. equipping new Christians to be witnesses in their present vocation, and
3. systematic Bible study and enforced discipline according to Scripture, for all.[21]

By the time of the first Presbytery meeting in Korea in 1907, the majority of the presbyters were Koreans, and a Korean mission society was established with twelve members. Thus, in the early stages, the principles of handing over leadership and building up local leadership were well understood. Today, however, there are many examples of Korean missionary work which are not marked by the respect for local peoples and cultures and the cooperative spirit the Western missionaries strove for. And yet the strong emphasis upon the Bible and biblical discipline is still a hallmark of Korean spirituality in mission. Korea has become a dominant culture, both in terms of the economy and strong church development, and so the issues of contextualization tend to slide into the background. Christian cultural imperialism is not always Western.

Our concern here for Asian missions is that the missionary work done by the wealthier Asian nations (Taiwan, Singapore, and Korea) may be less relevant to the Asian context because of the subtle Westernization that has taken place in these churches. This is not a problem that is solved once and for all, but, as with all theology, there must be constant scriptural vigilance in light of the present, ever-changing context.

4. Mission Trips

Missionary activity in Asia can be discussed in two broad categories: those long-term workers who have moved to new regions, and those churches which send teams of people on "mission trips" for one or two weeks of work, prayer, or education. Of the former, little needs to be said. Of the latter, many questions need to be raised. There are at least three types of mission trips. First there are those mission trips where a group from a church (or a few local churches) travel to a second country and help in evangelistic work, building a school or providing education for pastors, lay people, or children. Some of these trips are arranged by local churches in the receiving country and therefore some degree of control is retained by the local churches. Other trips are arranged with little concern or communication with the local churches. In these cases, the one- to two-week "blitz" does little to establish worshiping communities. The zeal of missionary churches, in these cases, runs ahead of their theology.

A second type of mission trip is the ongoing relationship with a local community in a neighboring country where periodic trips are planned to help in medical, educational, or social welfare. It may not be possible to move to the mission area, but that does not prevent an ongoing, albeit sporadic, Christian witness.

A third type of mission trip, one which is common among Western societies also, is more of an educational mission trip. Local churches become aware of the problems, struggles, and needs of struggling Christian communities as their members talk to local church leaders, stay in local villages, and witness the vitality in the local worship. In all cases where mission trips are a part of the missionary activity there is the need for close monitoring lest the mission trips become mission vacations, with little personal sacrifice and only superficial awareness of the local context.

5. Theology of Mission

A final concern for the future of Asian missions is the need to stay close to the model of Jesus in ministry involvement. The penetration of Western theological dichotomies in Asian theology is troubling and very often leads to missionary work that involves verbal witness and church planting to the exclusion of ministries of mercy, healing, and justice. This is a very difficult issue to measure, but it seems that the overwhelming human needs in Asia have made it natural (if we can use that loaded term) to minister to the whole person in the name of Jesus Christ. Where we see "evangelistic raids" and a narrow missionary understanding (evangelistic preaching), it is generally among those most influenced by Western missions and theologies. In most contexts when missions develop locally in Asia there is no question of whether or not to respond to the social needs. Pentecostal and evangelical seminaries and training centers in India, for example, teach basic health care and literacy along with Bible and mission strategy. We should remember that the "300 for three years" evangelistic program in Myanmar ministered to people with drug problems, illnesses, and ignorance. Many returned to develop the local ministries where they had first worked. The Asian contexts of poverty, illness, and suffering speak to the Asian missionary, and the Asian missionary, equipped with the Word of God, brings the hope of the gospel.

One theological concern for westerners, as they observe the development of Asian missiology, is that there seems to be little place for political engagement in Asian missiology. Whereas Latin American mission involvement includes struggles for justice and structural changes in society, this seems to be totally lacking in Asian missiology, except for the Philippines. This is the rub: the Philippines is the only Asian nation where Christians are in the majority. Excluding the Philippines, Asians have been involved in missionary activity in Asia for nearly two thousand years as minority communities, in most cases where other religions were the national religion. Christians have struggled for centuries in Persia where the empire (and later country) was Zoroastrian and then Muslim, in India where the religion was Hindu or Muslim, or in Thailand, Sri Lanka, and Burma where the national religion is Buddhism. Both the dominance of a non-Christian religion and the lack of history of democratic republics have meant that Christian mission is a sensitive and often dangerous enterprise. Protest and opposition to oppressive regimes are quick paths to persecution or annihilation. Struggles for justice have to be much more subtle, nuanced, and carefully carried out. The Asian way to justice is not the Western, democratic way. Westerners may criticize the lack of documented Christian struggles for justice in Asia, but that does not mean that there is no concern or no action. The Christian Conference of Asia (CCA) has consistently spoken out against injustices and in 1987 paid the price: its offices were closed in Singapore, and its members had to leave the country because they were perceived to be a threat to national stability.

A contemporary example may help. The treatment of refugees or migrants to Hong Kong from the mainland after 1997 is an important justice issue. At present the church in Hong Kong is able to continue in worship, training, and mission work as it has before. What would happen, however, if church leaders in Hong Kong began to protest the unjust treatment of immigrants to Hong Kong? Even the most enlightened and concerned church leaders would tell you that it would be foolish to confront the government on this or similar issues. Political involvement in China, as in most Asian nations, must come through church example (establishing ministries of mercy) and then the quiet persistent discussions with those who will hear the concern. Having said this, it is clear that Asians do not make these decisions in isolation. The ecumenical nature of the church demands that dialogue between Asians in mission and Western partners must include the ever-changing political contexts in which mission is carried out.

Signs of Hope and Glory

These five issues (persecution, military, the West, mission trips, and theology) are actually the context for Asians in mission for years to come. These issues will not be "solved," because they are, more accurately, the Asian reality. Part of the Asian reality also includes present signs of hope and glory that point to a promising future for Asian missions. Any theological discussion of mission must include or even end with hope.

One example of the hope for the future of Asian mission involvement is the cooperation of regional seminaries for the training of leaders in the various countries and regions. Trinity Theological College (TTC) in Singapore, an ecumenical seminary of the Methodist, Presbyterian, Anglican, and Lutheran churches of Singapore and Malaysia, is one such example. TTC has two different language tracks, English and Mandarin Chinese, which make it possible for people from different ethnic and national backgrounds to attend. In many countries of Asia, English is either the language of education or is a popular language used in research and writing. Chinese is used by many churches in Malaysia, Vietnam, Indonesia, and Thailand as well as in Taiwan and China. TTC has understood for decades that it has a responsibility for training church leaders, missionaries, and lecturers for Bible colleges and seminaries in Asia. Students from throughout Asia are usually in attendance: from the Philippines, China, Indonesia, Vietnam, Thailand, India, Pakistan, Sri Lanka, Myanmar, Malaysia, and, more recently, from Cambodia and Nepal. The administration has a special relationship with the Myanmar Council of Churches to help provide education for theological faculty in Myanmar. TTC is expanding its graduate program and developing a mission study center specifically for missional involvement in Asia. Most all of the funding for TTC comes from Asian churches and individual Christians. This is a sign of hope for the future of Asian mission.

Another sign of hope comes from the thousands of individual stories of individual Christians involved in pioneering Christian work, not only in Asia, but throughout the world. One example will suffice. Amy is an ethnic Chinese woman from a Presbyterian church in Singapore. From the time she became a Christian she had a concern for pioneering mission work. Upon graduation from college she worked briefly and then went to France to study French for a year before going to Senegal in West Africa. With one other Chinese woman she moved into a small village in the interior to establish a Christian presence in a Muslim village. Local people helped the women build a small house. After two years Amy's friend could not carry on. The loneliness and lack of responsiveness were too much for her. Amy returned to her home church to discuss what she should do. Sensing that her call to mission had not changed, she returned and prayed for a companion. When Amy returned to Singapore again after four years in Senegal, I remember her telling a story of how the local people were beginning to accept her. She showed some of the women in the village pictures of her apartment and car in Singapore. The women were amazed. They had never seen such wealth, nor had they ever seen such a modern city. "Why," they asked, "did you ever leave such a beautiful and wealthy place?" Why, indeed?

Here is the image which remains with us. Amy, a young Chinese woman, grinding her grain by hand, baking her flat bread, and then sitting down in the evening with some Senegalese women to study the words of Jesus.

CHAPTER 3

The Challenge of Christian Mission in Islamic Southeast Asia
Robert Hunt

WHEN I FIRST arrived in Malaysia in 1985 my plane landed in the late afternoon of a day in Ramadan, the Muslim fasting month. I went to get the packages I had sent by air freight only to discover that the entire freight section of the airport was quiet. It was only a few minutes before sundown, and the workers, all of whom had gone without food or water for twelve hours, were preparing to break their fast. None appeared interested in the tedious process of helping a foreigner get his boxes from the warehouse and navigate the complex way through customs. But one did. An elderly gentleman whose white cap indicated that he had made the holy pilgrimage to Mecca got off his stool behind the counter and left his dinner behind. For more than an hour he helped me; filling out forms, finding my boxes, and literally leading me by the hand through customs, until I and my boxes were safely in a car bound for my new home. Only then did he go to his long-delayed meal.

When Christians embark on ministry to others in the name of Christ we discover quickly that the nations to whom we are commanded to go are populated with neighbors who love us, and whom we are to love as our very selves (see Luke 10:25-37). In our obedience to the command, "Go therefore and make disciples of all nations, baptizing them in the name of the Father and of the Son and of the Holy Spirit," we discover not only the nations, but ourselves. The "other" whom we construe as an object of our charity, evangelism, or instruction turns out to be inextricably bound up with us as we seek to be faithful to Christ; to the point that the other can become the subject and we the object of God's mission of grace. The challenge of mission in the twenty-first century among Southeast Asian

Muslims is to find ways of living together as neighbors toward the Kingdom of God. This demands that we both love, and learn to be loved, in ways that transform our lives together.

Islam in Southeast Asia

The Pre-Islamic Culture of Nusantera

The islands of the Indonesian archipelago, and the Malay peninsula to which they have always been related culturally and economically, have seen a succession of religious influences. More than one thousand years ago trade between the small coastal kingdoms of the archipelago and India brought Hinduism and then Buddhism to the region, the latter waning as India finally became dominantly Hindu. Within the islands religious influences also traveled with trade. The coastal kingdoms taught their inland neighbors new religious practices and paths of spiritual power while remaining bound to them by indigenous beliefs about the divine status of royalty and the sacred forces at work in the natural world which they shared. These kingdoms were also linked with one another by trade, culture, and family ties. Most importantly, the island of Java traded rice in exchange for valuable spices grown much farther east. Thus religious ideas which came first to coastal Sumatra, Java, and the northern Malay peninsula soon moved south and east into the more distant islands. Through trade there developed a broad cultural area called Nusantera, which had a common trade language (Malay), recognized customs of trade and statecraft, and a complex and varied religious life combining Hindu, Buddhist, and animist influences.

Early Islam in Southeast Asia

Sometime in the twelfth century, or perhaps earlier, Muslim influence arrived with Arab traders who bypassed India in search of spices. As Islam moved into the subcontinent it was followed by Indian traders who had converted to Islam. Arab, Persian, and Indian Islam would all be influential in different periods, shaping the concept of Islam in Nusantera and particularly its port cities. Islam had several attractions for the people of the coastal trading towns. The early Arab traders brought both a script, which could be used to render local languages in writing, and a holy book whose numinous power was accepted and respected. Moreover Islam brought both "international" rules of trade and commerce, and a God whose protection and power extended across oceans; something different from the protection of local spirits upon which traders usually relied. When the major Indian trading partners became Muslim there were more direct trade advantages to conversion. And local rulers found that by adding Islamic titles to their existing Hindu and indigenous titles they could increase their prestige and spiritual power.

Conversions outside the port cities occurred more slowly. Yet Sufi missionaries, representing Islamic mysticism, were willing to travel inland beyond the trade centers and played a strong role in making Islam comprehensible and attractive within the framework of indigenous mysticism and its quest for spiritual power. By the time the Portuguese arrived in Southeast Asia in the early sixteenth century, most of the coastal kingdoms were Muslim, while Islam was beginning to spread into the more accessible areas of the interior.

A final factor in the spread of Islam was the arrival of the Europeans. The Portuguese, and then Dutch, sought to monopolize trade in Southeast Asia. It appears that this European presence spurred the Malay kingdoms to cement ties with each other and their traditional Muslim trading partners through Islam. Moreover, the economic pressures which increasingly opened the interior to direct outside influence allowed for the spread of Islam as well as Western influence. And the military interventions of the Portuguese, Dutch, and finally British tended to unite the indigenous population against them through a deeper embrace of Islam. By the end of the nineteenth century, Malay-speaking Southeast Asia was Muslim and conscious of being part of an alternative civilization to that of the West.

Christianity in Southeast Asia

The First Period

In addition to spurring the growth of Islam as a hedge against the colonial monopolizing of trade, the arrival of Portuguese ships and traders in the Straits of Malacca, and later throughout the archipelago, determined one part of the pattern of Christian-Muslim relations and created the first Christian communities. Because the Portuguese came into Southeast Asia still fighting a holy crusade against Islam in the Levant and Turkey, relations between Christianity and Islam were assumed to be, and were realized, in terms of conflict and conquest—fixing for centuries Muslim attitudes toward Christianity and Europeans in general. However, in areas where Islam was weak or nonexistent, or where nominally Muslim rulers or populations had been in conflict with more powerful Muslim neighbors, converts to Christianity were won. In the eastern islands of Ambon and East Timor the work of mission was carried out primarily by humble friars with little or no political and military support from the distant Portuguese power base in Malacca. What is known of their methods suggests that like the Sufi missionaries of Islam they were willing to live with the people and to make Christianity comprehensible by relating it to both indigenous mysticism and animism. The populations in these areas were largely Christianized by the time the Dutch arrived between 1599 and 1605.

The arrival of the Dutch East India company, which quickly forced the Portuguese out of the islands, brought with it new attitudes toward Islam and approaches to Christian missions. The Protestant Dutch had no immediate cause for conflict with Islam per se, and as representatives of a trading company gave commercial efforts to establish trade relations with local rulers first priority. However, it was Dutch policy to use superior sea power to establish an absolute monopoly on trade in spices from the islands. This policy was economically ruinous to the many small kingdoms which derived their income from hosting traders coming from as far east as China and as far west as the Arabian peninsula. And when the Dutch government decided actually to control and colonize the archipelago in order to maintain this monopoly and exploit it agriculturally, conflict with Islam, and Muslims, was inevitable.

Dutch mission work in this period went through several phases. At first it was carried out in idiosyncratic fashion by Christian traders and chaplains because Dutch policy did not support a systematic church-led missionary effort. The first Christian congregations were thus established in port cities, and often consisted of resident Chinese and other nonindigenous groups. The forced conversion to Protestantism of the Roman Catholic population of Ambon re-established that island as Christian, while East Timor remained Catholic. In the eighteenth century more systematic efforts were carried out as the Dutch gained access to the interior populations, particularly in Sumatra and Java. The Bible was translated into Malay and several other important indigenous languages as well. As had been the case with the Portuguese, willing converts were found among peoples as yet uninfluenced by Islam or living in conflict with Muslim rulers. Christianity continued to be an alternative religion to Islam, linked to Europeans who were in trade or political conflict with Muslims.

The Nineteenth Century

The seventeenth and eighteenth centuries, in addition to establishing a complex rivalry between Christianity and Islam in island Southeast Asia, laid the groundwork for Christian missionary understandings of Islam. Efforts to translate the Bible had brought to the fore the need to find religious terminology which communicated biblical concepts to Muslims. It also became obvious that a Bible which used special Islamic terms might not be appropriate to other indigenous speakers of the vernacular. In the nineteenth century these insights were deepened by philological studies of Malay texts and the rapidly developing knowledge of the Arabic and Persian roots of many Muslim religious terms.

With the development of systematic studies of Islam in European universities, the variety within Southeast Asian Islam had also become apparent. Missionaries had early recognized that non-Muslim communities were easier to convert to Christianity than communities with an established Muslim identity. In the nineteenth century an increasing body of literature on Islam appeared in Europe, as well as more and more detailed reports on local religious practices from Dutch and British civil servants. Based on these as well as personal experience, missionaries in the latter part of the nineteenth century would also come to recognize the distinctive ways in which Southeast Asian Islam varied from that in the Middle East and India, and the peculiar variations which arose within Southeast Asia. Yet it proved difficult for missionaries to apply many of these insights to the practice of evangelism.

The problem was largely theological. It mattered little how much information on the variety of Islam was gathered if it all had to be placed in an evangelistic framework which saw the essential human, and thus Muslim, problem as sin beyond the reach of human atonement, and the only answer as an acceptance of the whole range of beliefs and practices characteristic of orthodox Christianity. Generally disregarding the self-understandings and very real fears and desires of Muslims, missionaries concentrated on an apologetic approach to the gospel. It was designed to undermine Muslim beliefs, establish the truth of original sin and total depravity, and finally the truth that Jesus Christ had atoned for human sin through his death on the cross. The tenor of this literature was usually polemical.

While often well informed about specific Islamic teachings, these attacks were heavily influenced by a missionary sense of European moral superiority, superior rationality, and cultural vigor. Missionaries frequently attacked the moral character of Mohammad and other Muslim leaders, derided Islamic beliefs as superstitious, and attacked what was seen as fatalism. As one might expect, Muslim reactions ranged from incomprehension to outrage.

The ferocity of missionary attacks upon Islam arose in part because Christian missionaries came to see Islam as not merely another religion but a powerful rival in their quest for universal religious hegemony. Despite Christian representations of Islam as a moribund religion which had failed to evolve, and attacks on Muslim character and rationality, Islam was, particularly in Southeast Asia, a vital and growing missionary faith from the sixteenth century onward. In the late nineteenth and early twentieth centuries, Islam was penetrating many of the non-Muslim groups in the interior of the Malay peninsula, Sumatra, Borneo, Sulawesi (Celebes), and New Guinea at the same time Christian missionaries were establishing their work among the peoples of these territories. And vigorous Islamic reform groups in both Malaya and Indonesia were renewing the faith of nominal Muslims whom Christians hoped to win over for Christianity. Thus an attitude of fear sometimes shaped the Christian approach toward Christian-Muslim encounter.

Central Questions: Religion and Culture

In the history of Christian-Muslim encounter in Southeast Asia there was a fundamental shift when, in the 1890s and early twentieth century, Christians began to grapple with the question of whether Islam prepared Muslims to hear the gospel. Along with missionaries in many cultural and religious contexts they began to move close enough to Islam as the living religion of Muslims that they could no longer regard it simply as the target of polemical attacks. Empirical evidence suggested that Islam certainly did *not* prepare Muslims to respond to Christian missionaries. Yet as missionaries became more familiar with both Islam and its effect on individual Muslims they began to see ways in which its basic teaching and worldview had similarities with Christian worldviews and spirituality which might indeed make it possible for Muslims to begin to understand the gospel. However, this could happen only when the gospel itself was presented from a different angle than simply the reality of sin and the necessity of a

Islam in Asia represents a rich blend of culture and religion. Here Muslim women are preparing for a wedding in a village near Kuala Selangor, Malaysia. *(Robert Hunt photo)*

divine atonement. In other words the "problem" of Islam began to force Christian missionaries to reflect on the nature of their gospel and their mission on its behalf. At the same time the devastation of the First World War undermined Western claims of superiority. Missionaries could not take it for granted that Westernization was an appropriate partner in Christian missions. Finding a way forward in Christian mission would also involve understanding the relation of Islamic *cultures* to the gospel.

This process of reflection had begun with various regional conferences of missionaries in the nineteenth century and began to bear real fruit with the World Missionary Conference of 1910 in Edinburgh and the conference of the International Missionary Council in Jerusalem (1928) and Tambaram, near Madras, India (1938). Out of these emerged a host of questions which ultimately put theological reflection on the nature of religion and faith on equal par with questions about mission strategy and evangelistic method.

The question of whether Islam prepared people to hear the gospel led to the larger question of the value of non-Christian cultures in general — not only as environments in which the gospel might be preached, but as part of God's plan for the world. Missionaries began to wonder whether Christ could transform culture without destroying it, and whether the link between culture and religion could, or should, be broken so that one could be preserved without the other. Could the cultures of the Islamic world exist without, or beyond, Islam? Could Christianity exist apart from its Western cultural context? There were, and are, not obvious answers to such questions. Yet the kind of shift taking place in the early twentieth century was well illustrated by Methodist missionaries in Malaysia. Robert Blasdell, a Methodist missionary, made a survey and analysis of Islamic literature available in Singapore in the 1920s. He concluded that since most Islamic literature dealt with legal matters (*fiqh*) it was of little religious value. For a Christian who saw the law as either prior to or opposed to salvation such an observation is not surprising, but it would have amazed a Muslim, for whom faithful obedience to God's law was central to faith. By the 1930s and 1940s the same missionary who made this survey was actively studying and reprinting Islamic literature as a basis for discussing with Muslims common attitudes towards worship, faith, and morals.

Such questions became more urgent as Christian missionaries realized that they lived in an increasingly secularized world, and that they also shared with Muslims a religious outlook which should have made them allies against secularism and antireligious forces such as Communism. Muslim-Christian encounter could thus be seen as a gathering of fellow religionists to oppose secularism. This view was strongly advanced by Duncan Black McDonald in the 1920s and 1930s and influenced a generation of missionaries to Southeast Asia who studied under him. The conflict with secularization also emerged as part of a larger conflict between the goals of Christian mission and those of colonial government. By the 1930s we find in Malaysia both local Christians and missionaries wondering whether the use of the mission schools for a government-sponsored secular education was really beneficial for the students, particularly Muslims, who, it was asserted, were encouraged to shed their old religion but given none in return. By the time the Second World War ended, missionaries were beginning to see the problem of how religion related to culture was not simply a problem for missionaries, but a problem which all religious people shared in a secularizing cultural context.

Central Questions: Mission and the New Nations

The post-World War II struggle for independence in both Malaysia and Indonesia created conflicts within the Christian community over where its interests lay. In Indonesia the Christian community contributed a number of prominent leaders in the struggle for independence, and this brought Christian insights into play in defining national values and identity. In Malaysia, Christians were more wary of independence but ultimately provided leadership to the political movements which shaped the new nation. Yet the relation in newly independent nations between Christian minorities and the Muslim majority was problematic. In Malaysia and Indonesia these communities had often been competitors for political and economic power. In Malaysia Christianity was associated exclusively with the Chinese and Indian ethnic minorities, so that religious issues were (and are) inextricably bound up in ethnic rivalries and political power-sharing arrangements. In Indonesia, Christians, although a tiny minority of the population overall, formed (and form) local majorities on many resource rich islands. Christian missionaries, both Western and local, who had struggled to find some kind of solidarity and common ground with Muslims for the sake of sharing the gospel and struggling for independence now find their loyalties divided.

The problems faced by Christians in these new nations were addressed in part by the discourse of democracy, which spoke of majorities and minorities, and cast all religious (as well as ethnic and linguistic) encounters into political terms. Central to these political terms was the concept of "human rights" of minority communities. Many, including many Christians, have hoped that this concept would, in the world's cornucopia of cultures, political systems, and social structures, provide some universal basis for maintaining justice and order in the face of political chaos or totalitarian states. Yet appeals to human rights have also been problematic for Christians in both Malaysia and Indonesia. When directed toward protecting Christian institutions or established social privileges they can appear to be placing communal interests before those of the nation. Moreover they can seem to represent a Christian appeal to political power structures beyond the nation rather than a Christian willingness to work positively within the national political life. For this reason many Christians in both countries prefer to avoid seeing themselves as "minorities" and understand that mission to Muslims means seeking to be seen as partners in nation-building.

Yet the division between Christians and Muslims is deeper than simply long-standing political and economic conflicts. For Southeast Asian Christians, modernity and Christianity arrived and developed together, even if they were not always comfortable bedfellows. Christians were familiar with the overwhelming power of the nation-state to intervene in private and community life, the development of education toward technical competence rather than humanity or piety, and the dominance of economic development in shaping national life. And Christians had, to some extent, found ways of living with these realities. The effort to define a universally recognizable list of "human rights" was one way of protecting matters of religious faith from the overwhelming power of the state. Political ideologies which insisted on a complete separation of the state from the power of any one religion were another. Finally, defining Christianity as not only a personal but largely a private religious faith shared primarily within a voluntary association called a "denomination" was a third.

These approaches have not commended themselves to Muslims. For them each aspect of modernity struck at the roots of their culture and faith. Islamic law protected individuals, not by pitting human rights against those of the state, but by clearly defining the role of individuals, families, communities, and national governments under God's law. Islamic education had been centered on teaching children the ways of both obedience to God and personal piety and spirituality. Success at God's judgment and the attainment of paradise were the idealized values of Islamic society, rather than wealth. While political power was held in the distant capitals of colonial empires, Muslims were excluded from the process of realizing their values in political structures. With the rise of independent Muslim nations in the mid-twentieth century, this has changed dramatically. For many Muslims the central struggle of the early twenty-first century is how to realize their religious faith through the seeking and wielding of political power. And Christians in mission must ponder whether this struggle on the part of Muslims should be supported as a legitimate impulse of religious faith or should be opposed as overthrowing now-accepted ideas about human rights and the power of the state.

This task is made more urgent because of the late-twentieth century influx of new Christian missions and sects in the wake of "globalization." In many ways the complex forces which make up globalization—although not directly controlled by any one nation—represent a movement which, much like colonialism, has brought Christian mission and missionaries in its wake. In Malaysia, for example, an influx of new Christian groups has resulted in a multiplication of denominations and independent churches. These groups seek to win converts, find places to hold meetings and wor-

Muslims in Southeast Asia take different attitudes toward their adoption of Western ways. Here a Fulbright scholar in Jakarta talks with two Muslim students, the young man choosing to dress in Western garb and the young woman in traditional Muslim dress. (Richard Lord photo)

ship, and seek some type of legal status for their organizations. These activities upset, and even overturn, the social and political accommodations reached between older Christian churches and the Muslim majority. And they only heighten the threat felt by Muslim communities already concerned about their cultural identity and integrity.

Globalization in this form also sharply focuses the question of the purpose of the church. Does mission consist of gaining adherents until other religions are essentially elbowed out of a community and Christian standards come to dominate? Does the church exist to maintain the purity of Christian belief and practice against a hostile world; thus building defenses against the establishment of any non-Christian influences? Both of these understandings are found among Christian minorities in Southeast Asia and elsewhere. Mission in the twenty-first century will need to move away from this dichotomy and develop an understanding of the gospel and the church which allows for Christ to be present in the witness of the church to the gospel.

The Twenty-first Century: No Easy Answers

Three Phases to Christian Mission in Southeast Asia

In the history of Christian mission to Southeast Asian Muslims sketched above there are three discernible phases. In the first, "mission" was seen primarily as extending the reach and breadth of the church in its full Western garb in Muslim lands. The church moved physically, but Muslims were required to move culturally, socially, and spiritually if they wished to join this movement. The second phase, which really only began in this century, sought to narrow the cultural and social distance between Christian witness and Muslim life so that the gospel addressed directly the experience of individual Muslims. That this approach had little or no success points to the ongoing reality that Islam is a faith held not so much by individuals as by the family and community within the larger *ummah*.[1] It also suggests that most Muslims find their religion adequate both to understand themselves and meet their spiritual needs. Efforts to extend this approach to address the concerns of Muslim communities, whether through joining in the nationalist struggle or through community development and services in Malaysia, has generated goodwill but did not spur any substantial interest in Christianity as a religion. Positive community involvement seemed to suggest to Muslims simply that Christians could be good neighbors, and not that they had some superior spiritual insight or object of worship. A third phase, very much part of the postwar era, has been to seek to dress Christianity in Muslim garb; thus in theory allowing the continuation of indigenous culture but with its religious life directed toward Jesus Christ. At least in Southeast Asia, however, this has been more of an academic exercise by those from long-time Christian traditions than a creation of an indigenous Christianity from within the culture of Muslims. Southeast Asian Muslims look at such approaches with utmost suspicion, often fearing that they are simply a way of tricking weaker or less knowledgeable brothers and sisters into apostasy.

For some Christians this history of failure to find any certain means of sharing the gospel with Muslims is ultimately a call to more perseverance. They continue to concentrate on winning converts, using whatever means are necessary and effective out of the repertoire of strategies already developed while constantly looking for new ways, or opportunities, to share the gospel. Recently, for example, some have sought to use the sense of cultural displacement felt by students or recent immigrants to the West as a moment of psychological and community weakness in which the message of Christ might penetrate Muslim defenses. Whatever the merits of this approach it has the disadvantage of making Muslim parents and families suspicious of the motives of any Christian who seeks to work positively with Muslims.

Other Christians see their history as a pointer to a future in which evangelism should be abandoned so that the church can concentrate on neighborly cooperation that builds up both Christian and Muslim communities and communicates at least the ideals of Christianity. The focus is on finding and working on a common nonreligious agenda and through this the creation of mutual trust and appreciation. Given the long history of animosity and mistrust this is seen by many as a sufficiently forward step for Christian mission in the twenty-first century. Yet I would argue that taken by itself this approach is a betrayal of the fundamental impulse of Christian mission, which centers not on demonstrating that Christians are good people, or even on being good neighbors, but in the realization in human life of the Lordship of Christ and the presence of God's Kingdom.

Given our history of missionary endeavor it appears that this realization will not happen through our efforts, however clever, to force, insinuate, or inject the gospel into Muslim lives and cultures. Instead I believe it will happen when Jesus can be seen and heard *within* the Muslim consciousness and community of faith rather than from outside. Or as Harold Voglar so aptly puts it, "when Jesus is a crisis within Islam instead of against Islam."[2] And to draw the distinction further, when it is Jesus rather than Christianity who stands at the center of mission.

Rethinking our mission in terms of who Jesus is within Islam will require: first, a fresh look at our normative models of mission; second, a reevaluation of what it means to respond in faith to Jesus; third, an examination of the context in which faith arises; and finally, development of a spirituality which allows the church and individual disciples to live out a missionary vocation which may lack all the ordinary forms of emotional support and psychological comfort expected of modern Christians.

Normative Models of Mission

The New Testament accounts of how Jesus calls his disciples into mission have provided the impetus which shapes much of Protestant Christian mission in the last several centuries. Going out to the nations is just what Western Christians in a colonial era, and now virtually all Christians in an era of globalization, are doing anyway. Making disciples and baptizing them could be seen as simply the completion of the process. And in the nineteenth and twentieth centuries the declaration of good news to the poor, the imprisoned, the enslaved, the sick has been equally a part of these movements: the decent thing to do when a Christian arrives rich in resources (political and economic) among people who lack the same. Of course the two driving texts of this missionary endeavor, Matthew 28 and Luke 4, can push us to much more nuanced understandings of our mission, as can Luke 10:1-12, another oft-cited text.

What is problematic in using these texts is that we as Christians no longer stand in the same relationship to the world around us as did the first disciples, and indeed the first Christian communities. Today we understand ourselves, and are understood, as followers of a religion in the midst of many religions, as church members in mission to members of other religious organizations. Our Christianity is thus vested with a political significance and power which is proportional to the number of its followers and its wealth. That power clings to us and hangs over us like a shadow whenever we "go out" in mission so long as we remain part of the church, and the church remains a power among powers in the world. And so long as our mission, in the least way, suggests the transfer of members from one religion to another it becomes part of the struggle for power between competing religions.

This may not appear to be a problem for appropriating the biblical texts on mission, since both first disciples of Jesus and the generation which followed were caught up in conflicts with powers both temporal and spiritual. Yet these conflicts were fundamentally different from those we face today. The "power" which filled Jesus, the disciples, and for that matter Paul, was the power to accept complete humility and indeed humiliation in the face of all the "powers" of the world. The presence of such humility evoked an *internal* crisis within these power structures. When we see the conflict of the religious authorities with Jesus, or the first disciples, we are seeing a projection of this internal crisis onto those whose powerlessness evoked it. When gospel writers recount the attacks upon Jesus at the Passover we know that the real struggle is within the religious establishment, the government, and the hearts of the religious leaders and Pilate. Similarly the accounts of conflict in the Book of Acts do not show disciples of Christ struggling with the powers of the world, but rather the way in which the complete submission, humility, and humiliation of the apostles of Christ evoke a crisis within these powers. That the powers lash out against these followers of Jesus is an indicator of the depth and nature of their internal crisis, not that mission should be equated with struggles between the power of the church and the power of the world.

Thus the texts of the New Testament which call the disciples of Christ to mission are relevant when the disciples who hear that call are, like

Jesus himself, both humble and willing to be humiliated. If we are to re-appropriate the scriptural accounts of mission for our own time we will have to shed our power, our "Christianity," and go to witness to Jesus clothed only in the power of the Holy Spirit and our conviction that we cannot go where he has not gone before.

A Biblical View of Conversion

Just as the New Testament accounts of the call to mission must be understood in their context, so also we must understand what the New Testament understands as the human context in which people respond to the gospel and come to faith in Christ. When we read that the witness of the disciples is met with faith it is not because they "overpowered" the other faiths. Rather the New Testament suggests that those who respond to the gospel with faith have been first called to faith by God. They are of the elect. They have been chosen. The preaching of the gospel is not the cause of faith but the occasion of it. The power to convert is a power owned solely by the Spirit.

This understanding enables us to grasp better what the presence of Jesus in the spoken word, and in deeds of love and service, means. For those being led toward repentance by the Spirit, the gospel of Christ both focuses and refracts their vision toward the Kingdom of God. Jesus directs their path, heretofore moving haphazardly toward the Divine, into the straight way to God. We need not undertake mission with the intention of pushing, controlling, or manipulating people toward repentance and a change of direction in their lives. God is drawing all people to God's self. Yet neither can we simply wait patiently in the hope that all those wandering, often aimlessly, toward God's summons will finally make it in the end. Rather our task is introduce Jesus to them so that they can find in him, and choose in him, to set their lives on the straight way.

A Theology of the Nations

Third, we must reconsider the social context in which faith in Christ arises. The answer given in the New Testament is that it arises first among the Jews, and then in "the nations." We commonly think of the gentile context in which the disciples preached as a particular cultural space to which the preaching of the gospel had to be adapted. And this is true. But the gentile context was also a religious space, and those who heard the gospel and responded with faith were all followers of other religions first.

In some cases this religious context was hostile to Jesus, and his presence in proclamation created a personal crisis in which those called to faith were forced to decide between him and the gods they had been worshiping. In other cases, however, the presence of Jesus in proclamation was not the negation of religion but its fulfillment. This is most obvious in its relation to Judaism, but it was also the case in those Greek religions which acknowledged an unseen and transcendent God (see Acts 17). In either case the understanding of mission presented in the New Testament, and particularly the Book of Acts, is not as an attack upon the religious context, but a proclamation within it. (See Acts 19:37, where it is made clear that Paul never blasphemed or attacked the Greek goddess Artemis.)

At the same time, neither Paul and his companions, nor the other apostles, pretended that they were something they were not in order to speak from within the religious cultures of their day. Theirs was not a strategy of subversion but of sympathy with the human situation they encountered among the Jews and among the nations. They made themselves part of the ongoing dialogue which exists in every religious tradition which seeks a deeper understanding of its goal in relation to its context. In Southeast Asia, entering into the existing dialogue within Islam, and the Muslim community, means in part engaging in the particularly theological dialogue which seeks to express in each generation the meaning of the call, "There is no God but God, and Mohammad is God's prophet." It also means understanding the search for a contemporary spirituality which has moved Muslims both to the renewal of mysticism and a deepening of commitment to an "Islamic lifestyle" in all its dimensions. Finally, and perhaps most importantly, it means somehow entering into the deep desire of Muslims to bring their national social, economic, and political lives into conformity with God's law.

If we are to be the instruments through which Jesus speaks, then we must be among Muslims, not as religious saboteurs, but as genuine fellow seekers after *islam*: submission to God. Where this is most problematic is in the desire of Muslims fully to submit their lives to God through the implementation of *sharia*, or Islamic law, in Muslim society. Historically Christians have found their interests best served when states did not support or regulate religious activities and when their freedom was ensured by the constitutional guarantee of their human rights. The *sharia*, which establishes state support for religious activities and implements not human rights, but a divine order, seems in theory to diminish the power and freedom of non-Muslim communities, and thus moves against their interests.

Our response to this must be to face squarely some questions about our assumptions concerning mission. First, as Christians we must ask whether the mission of God in Christ really hinges on protecting the interests of Christians, or whether instead the power and freedom of the Christian community to give up its claims to power can actually be an indicator of the imminence of God's Kingdom. Second, we must consider whether efforts to implement the *sharia* will necessarily diminish the interests of non-Muslim communities. The exact role and nature of the *sharia* itself is the object of intense debate among Muslims, as is the nature and role of religion in secular democracy among Christians in the West. It seems to me that our faith demands that we pursue with Muslims ways in which the human community should live under God's reign, rather than asserting that humanity is best served by governments which deny the claims of God on human life. In recent years in Malaysia, Muslims themselves have promoted "civilizational dialogue," which brings together people of different religions to discuss precisely what it means to cooperate in implementing *sharia*, not as a static set of laws, but in its more basic meaning as the way of a society towards submission to God's will. In Indonesia the long-standing dialogue between Christians and Muslims over the meaning of the national ideology, Pancasila, is likewise a means by which Christians and Muslims have shared in a common concern that the social context support *islam*, if not a formal implementation of Islamic law.[3] When we can work alongside Muslims as they seek to make real in society their commitment to God's reign then perhaps the Jesus whose ministry was to fulfill, and not subvert, religious law will be heard speaking to them as well.

And we must take as our own the specifically Muslim questions about what guides and gives meaning to life; not so that we can propose answers we think we already know, but in order to discover alongside Muslims a God who answers questions we did not know we had. We must begin to let the Muslim expression of faith in God become our own so that we can discover, with Muslims, truths about Jesus (whom we believe is God) that have remained hidden in our necessarily finite religious tradition. It is not sufficient to risk, in dialogue, conversion. Rather we must actually be converted to a new kind of faith in Jesus as Christ. Such a conversion is not without precedent. Peter underwent a kind of conversion when he found that his Jewishness limited his ability to grasp the full meaning of Jesus who was also savior to the gentiles. And Paul's theology indicates that in living like a Greek, he not only adopted Greek customs, but learned among the Greeks the character of Jesus as the Christ in ways which could not be found in the most thorough exploration of the rabbinic heritage.

Such an approach has its dangers. If our own Christian faith is primarily an alignment with community expectations and values for the sake of psychological security, then the temptation simply to switch from the Christian to the Muslim community will certainly be acute. Syncretism, the confused blending of distinct and even contradictory beliefs, is also a danger. Our effort to hear Jesus speak from within Islam cannot diminish the contradiction between Muslim claims about Jesus and revelation and those of the Christian church. But our entry into *islam* is not to explore what Muslims believe about Jesus or the Bible, but to discover what they know about God that we have not yet learned, and in this to identify with Muslims a voice of Jesus they have not yet heard.

A Spirituality of Mission in the Twenty-first Century

This means first of all that Christian mission to Muslims must depend upon the Spirit of Christ to lead the way. The question of whether Islam is a preparation for the gospel is too abstract for the purposes of mission in the twenty-first century. The real question is whether the Spirit has prepared Muslims to hear Jesus. And we can know this only if we go among Muslims and find out. There is no denying that this approach to mission will entail deep losses for ourselves as Christians and Christian communities. For a community which breaks down the walls which define its boundaries and opens itself into and for the community around it there is the danger that it will simply be lost; diluted and assimilated into the surrounding religious culture. The individual who truly opens herself or himself to different questions, different ways of orienting life within the world and toward God, will certainly be caught up in a dizzying loss of any secure personal identity which comes from participation in a communal *weltausschauen* (outlook on the world) maintained by communal rituals and reassurances. The spiritual question is whether we, in risking these losses, risk losing Christ. And the answer must be no. We are not saved because we hold fast to Christ, but because Christ holds fast to us: "if we are faithless, he remains faithful — for he cannot deny himself" (2 Timothy

2:13). Thus ours must be a spirituality of *kenosis*, self-emptying, which in imitation of Christ holds most fast to God when it surrenders itself into God's hands. Such a spirituality depends not so much on the outward props of community and ritual, although these must not be abandoned, as on a life of prayer and diligent study of God's Word which are the channels by which Christ renews in us constantly his presence.

Conclusion

It is my own experience that the kind of mission among Muslims described above can take place only through the long process of developing both a theology which sees in Islam a place where Jesus may speak and in developing personal relationships in which it is possible to speak about Jesus. For this to happen I believe that Christians must undergo a kind of spiritual awakening in which they discover that God can love them, and the world, through faiths and communities which do not yet name Jesus as the Christ, although they clearly belong, like all things on heaven and earth, to Him. Mission is our hopeful surrender of self to these people and communities so that with us they may learn the joy of loving God through Jesus Christ.

CHAPTER 4

Women in Mission: A Philippine Experience
Elizabeth S. Tapia

> "To share Christ today is to ensure that justice, because it is central to the Gospel, is preached and demonstrated. To share Christ today is to be permeated with the understanding that without the advent of justice, there is no coming of God's reign."
>
> —SHARON JOY ROSE RUIZ DUREMDES[1]

I BELIEVE THE BASIC task of Christians is to continue the mission of Jesus Christ on earth—that of ushering in the total reign of God and giving life in all its abundance (John 10:10). Therefore, mission is, and should be, integrated in the life and witness of Christ's followers.

This essay aims to portray the contemporary role and contribution of Christian women in a developing country, the Philippines. It also identifies the impact of the women's movement and women's theologizing in the field of mission. At the end of the paper, some emerging trends in mission from the perspective of Philippine women will be offered as well.

I am writing from the perspective of one who was born and raised in the central part of the Philippines. I am an ordained United Methodist pastor serving as academic dean and professor of theology at Union Theological Seminary, an ecumenical Protestant seminary located within the Philippine Christian University, Cavite, Philippines. In the past twenty years, I have been privileged to work with various women's groups (both

Protestant and Roman Catholic) in the areas of ecumenical dialogue, Asian women's theology, human and women's rights, theological education, Christian education, and mission.

The Context of Our Mission in the Philippines

Christianity came to the Philippine shores through the Spanish ship, sword, and cross in 1521. The tidal waves of colonization swept the country: 333 years under Spain, fifty years under the U.S., and five years under Japan. After the 1898 Spanish-American War, the Philippines became a U.S. colony at the price of $20 million and thousands of lives. American Protestantism was planted, denominationalism was introduced, Americanization of education, and later on McDonaldization of culture, began.

It is said that during the precolonial times, Filipino women enjoyed an egalitarian status in society. Women were community leaders and healers. There were no stereotyped roles for either gender. Women before the colonial times had more mobility and rights. During the colonial period, the women's status became low and their participation was confined either to the home or to the convent alone.

Mariano Apilado, in his book *Revolutionary Spirituality*, writes, "To a great extent, the missionaries were instrumentalities of colonialism."[2] Both the Roman Catholic Spanish missionaries and the American Protestant missionaries supported the colonial rule of their countries in the Philippines.

Neocolonialism, patriarchy, poverty, and dependency characterize our present context. The context of our mission in the Philippines includes the following realities:

1. Economic crisis—increasing poverty (80 percent of Filipinos live in extreme poverty), unemployment, huge labor migration (there are Filipino contract workers in all nations of the world), foreign-controlled economy and import-oriented industries, "feminization of poverty," prostitution, rise of the global market, death of small industries, globalization, $47 billion foreign debt, etc.

2. Ecological crisis—overpopulation (72 million population in a land slightly larger than Nevada), water and air pollution (Manila is one of the most unlivable cities in the world), loss of rain forest, soil erosion as a result of excessive logging and strip mining, land conversion, etc.

3. Relational crisis—semifeudal relationships; breakdown of marriage

and families; regionalism; racism, sexism, and classism; HIV/AIDS epidemic; the health crisis, etc.

4. Spiritual/moral crises—quest for meaningful relationships, graft and corruption in private and public office, religious fundamentalism, widening gap between the rich and the poor, etc.

Given these realities, the greatest challenge that confronts the church in the Philippines today is to discern a vision and mission of justice and wholeness. To unmask the forces that enslave the people and to announce the good news of liberation to them are part of what it means to do mission, to be in mission in a developing country such as the Philippines. To paraphrase a leading Filipina lay theologian, Sharon Joy Ruiz Duremdes, to preach Christ today is to do justice.

The Mission of Our Contextual Theology and *Praxis*

Jesus' mission is to bring salvation that is total and concrete, in the here and now and in the ages to come. Jesus' mission is to do the will of God who sent him. I believe that the liberating witness of the Christian church today lies in the faithfulness to the message and mission of Jesus Christ.

The will of God in Jesus Christ is that all will have life. Jesus declares his calling in John 10:10: "I have come that you may have life and have it abundantly." When we participate in this mission, we become part of Jesus' family, for he declares, "Who are my mother and my brother and sisters? . . . Whoever does the will of God is my brother and sister and mother" (Mark 3:33,35).

Our unity in Christ enables us to break barriers in relationships. Our unity in Christ enables us to be partners in mission. We are all one in Jesus Christ (Galatians 3:26). I believe Christians do not have a monopoly of mission. Women and men of other faiths and traditions have mission, are active in their own way of expressing mission and vocation. We need to be humble enough to respect their sense and mode of mission. Asia, being the womb and home of many major religions, has much to offer to the world in terms of its religiosity and spirituality.

Our contextual theology includes a theology of struggle, women doing theology, theology of resistance and of "people power," mission of women empowerment, and mission of mutual and equal partnership. It also includes a mission of interconnectedness, as we learn from the indigenous peoples of the Philippines.

In the words of Sister Margaret Shanti, Immaculate Heart of Mary, of India: "The urgent task (of women in mission) is to awaken human consciousness to our interconnectedness in the web of life, and to fight not just for environmental protection, but for a renewed earth and a humanized community in communion with each other and with the earth."[3]

Furthermore, our mission in the Philippines today must embody what Apilado calls a "revolutionary spirituality." He writes, "In the larger context of Philippine history, Protestant Christians, in bonding together as the United Evangelical Church, had inherited the vision of the revolution of the 1890s. This was the vision of unity for independence and, in solidarity with the Filipino people, they had committed themselves to a revolutionary spirituality that would continue the struggle towards total economic, cultural, political, spiritual and social development."[4]

The Role and Contribution of Philippine Women to Mission

The Reverend Ruth Quiocho of the Philippines, Asia regional coordinator of the United Evangelical Mission, sees the role of women in mission as follows: "Women are the sustaining force for mission, they are nurturers of the missionary spirit through the voluntary work they did and continue to do in the churches, crossing frontiers and borders where men dare not tread."[5]

In the last thirty years, the Christian women in my country have been immersed in various mission involvements. When the martial law regime of President Ferdinand Marcos (1965–1986) brought untold sufferings to millions of the Filipino people, the women fought bravely alongside the men in the struggle for freedom and democracy. Many women were held as political prisoners, tortured, raped, and violated. Mothers of the disappeared and political prisoners organized themselves to ask for their release and humane treatment. Progressive churchwomen got involved in political work, aboveground and underground. One of my former students, Filomena Asuncion, was killed in a military encounter when her guerrilla unit was discovered. The mission focus then was how to minister to the victims of human rights abuses and how to work ecumenically to bring about national liberation.

In the nineties, the women participated in the campaign against the extension of the presence of the American military bases in the country. We were successful and the American military turned over the bases to

Displaced by war, a woman cooks in a camp for evacuees in Pikit, the Philippines. Tens of thousands of people have been displaced on the southern Philippine island of Mindanao since the military resumed attacks on rebel forces early in 2003. *(UMNS photo by Paul Jeffrey)*

the Philippine government in 1992. Now in an era of capitalist globalization, the mission focus of Christian women in the Philippines has included lobbying against the 1995 Mining Act, which is detrimental to the ancestral domain of the indigenous peoples. The increasing environmental crises and degradation pose a heavy challenge to the churches and civil society as well. Another immense problem is increasing poverty. One major phenomenon that is anti-life and anti-poor is the country's huge foreign debt, which amounts to $46 billion. Hence, the Jubilee Campaign was launched nationwide, and women are actively engaged in the campaign. Liddy Nacpil, a Protestant political activist, heads the Freedom from Debt Coalition, while Sharon Joy Ruiz Duremdes, the first woman general secretary of the National Council of Churches in the Philippines, is the national coordinator of the Ecumenical Jubilee Campaign Network. I am one of the twelve convenors of this ecumenical and national venture.

Mission in resettlement areas like Capas, Tarlac, and Pampanga is headed by women leaders. Those who had been displaced and relocated because of the eruption of Mount Pinatubo in 1991 are finding ways to get resettled. Bella Ramos of Santa Juliana, Capas, Tarlac, a graduate of our seminary, is the primary leader of her indigenous people in the mountains. She serves as the pastor, community worker, and teacher. Richard and Caridad Schwenk and other mission volunteers, with financial assistance from the General Board of Global Ministries (GBGM), have set up a water system. The Schwenks' term ended in the fall of 2000 when they retired as GBGM missionaries.

The new United Methodist mission partner-worker, Stephanie Crutchfield, works with the indigenous women and Bella Ramos in the areas of training primary health care workers and training teachers for children. Several women seminarians of Union Theological Seminary are also involved in weekend church work among the indigenous people. The Immanuel Bible School for the indigenous young workers was founded and managed by three dedicated women, headed by the Reverend Paz Macaspac of Pampanga.

One way to do mission with the urban poor in Manila is being carried out through social services of the Kapatiran Kaunlaran Foundation, Inc. (KKFI), a social service center of The United Methodist Church in the Philippines, based in Sampaloc, Manila. Founded in 1950, KKFI continues to be an oasis in the urban desert of human suffering. Its mission and vision are geared toward the uplifting of the lives of the poor and marginalized. Its programs include ministry with street children, therapeutic community for drug dependents (both women and men), job skills training, collaboration with indigenous peoples in that area (Aetas), and management seminars for church workers all over the country. It has recently acquired farmland in Pulilan, Bulacan, and its center is called Gilead Center. The center will offer learning and healing facilities to the very poor citizens in the area. The executive director of KKFI, Mrs. Priscila R. Atuel, is also the national president of the United Methodist Women in the Philippines.

The Impact of Women's Movement and Women's Theology

A big development in Asia in the last twenty years has been the emergence of people's liberation theologies, including Asian women's theologies.

Asian Christian women, including those from the Philippines, began to write how they do theology. In the Philippines, both the women's desks of the National Council of Churches in the Philippines and the Association of Major Religious Superiors (Roman Catholic) work hand in hand organizing people for women's rights, national transformation, church renewal, campaign for the cancellation of debt, and ecological concerns.

The Association of Women in Theology and the Ecumenical Association of Third World Theologians address the patriarchal bias in mission and theology. A critique of the traditional mission and missions reveals that they will not work now. A reinterpretation of mission and redefinition of missional thrusts and expressions are needed. For example, the proselytizing aspect of traditional missions has to go. Ecumenical dialogue and ecumenical *praxis* are needed now. In terms of method or approach, it needs to be a life-centered approach, issue-oriented, interfaith, interdenominational, interdisciplinary, participative, empowering, and celebrative.

The women's movement in Asia and in the Philippines that bloomed in the late seventies and early eighties have made us realize that the church can either hinder or help in the role of women in mission. Women's oppression is supported by patriarchal teachings of the church. At the same time, it is through the church that women can have the opportunity to lead, to do mission, and to network with women's groups for the uplift of women, youth, and children.

Christian women in the Philippines are presently involved in the following:

- contextualized ministry and mission, not abstract and absolute
- ecological concerns, economic justice, ecumenical work
- exposure of sexual and domestic violence
- struggle for equality in the church and society
- Bible-reading from women's eyes
- enlistment of women as young missioners in various parts of the world
- mission and ministry with the migrant women workers in Asia
- sensitivity and solidarity with the indigenous peoples
- theological education and training for women.

Sister Virginia Fabella, Maryknoll missionary, has said, "The aim of women's liberation and struggle for equality in the Church and in society is not to get even with men or to replace them as oppressors. *The true end of our struggles is a more just and human society for all, a society that reflects God's kingdom of Love, Truth, Justice and Peace"* (my italics).[6]

Mission Trends in the 21st Century in the Eyes of Women

Women in mission in my country are interested and committed to the following concerns:

- decentralization of power and authority
- critique of capitalist and imperialist globalization and governance
- increased roles of women and youth
- South-to-South exchange/solidarity and mission partnership
- nonhierarchical, more egalitarian structures
- ecumenical partnership in mission
- ecological concerns in mission.

At present, Christianity is more alive and vibrant in Africa, Asia, and Latin America than in Europe or North America. Asia will be supplying missionaries to Europe and America. World mission will need to integrate and interpret missional expressions coming from the South.[7]

The global market will influence the global mission. Those who control the global market are likely to control the religious and missional priorities of the people. Excessive consumerism and mammonization of cultures, if not curbed, will threaten the integrity of global mission.

In my observation, the appropriate approach to doing mission will be multisectoral, interdisciplinary, intergenerational, and interfaith. Theological education will need to be ecumenical, economical, and ecological. Missiology and ecology, ecclesiology and ethics, missiology and gender equality, and spirituality of mission, etc., might need to be added in curriculum.

The final statement of the Tagaytay (Philippines) Consultation of the United Evangelical Mission has identified emerging models of mission:

- new missionary training centers
- presence of young professionals in mission
- responsible use of electronic media
- exchange visits to mission fields for mutual learning and sharing
- member churches sharing financial responsibility for all joint mission ventures.

Carmina Teo, 10, a Muslim girl, holds a sign reading "Peace" in the Philippine language of Tagalog. Behind her are Muslim women and a Catholic nun. The women were waiting for the start of an interfaith peace march through the streets of Davao in the war-torn southern Philippines province of Mindanao after a bomb exploded in the Davao airport, killing 21 people and wounding more than 100. Action by Churches Together, the international coalition which includes the United Methodist Committee on Relief, provided emergency assistance to thousands of victims of the conflict. (*UMNS photo by Paul Jeffery*)

Moreover, an underlying principle to be observed in planning unified mission in the twenty-first century is that all programs, projects, and activities must be "flexible, innovative, and participative."[8]

Women will play a greater role as more and more women receive higher education, political consciousness, and personal confidence. The rise of indigenous and feminist spirituality positively contributes to this endeavor.

A holistic way of doing mission, not piecemeal, is necessary. Community organizing, basic health care, gender sensitivity, and ecological caring must be integrated in the missional priorities of the churches.

Ruth Quiocho names one important mission trend in the new millennium: "Mission work would require more women doing mission in war-torn countries. Their doing mission must necessarily take into consideration the concerns for health, refugees, peace process, conflict resolution and ecology."[9]

Asked what would be for her the mission trends in the new millennium, Hope Antone, a Filipina lay theologian of the United Church of Christ in the Philippines, has this to say: "The challenge of religious plurality in Asia will become a big issue to deal with, especially with the ongoing religious conflicts in different places. . . . Added to this of course will be the ongoing struggle against the ill effects of globalization, the ecological degradation, and gender inequality."[10]

Sister Nila Bermisa, dean of the Institute of Formation and Religious Studies in Quezon City and Maryknoll missionary, shares her feminist vision for a just society and world and her lens of indigenous spirituality. This is an important trajectory in doing mission in the Philippines in the new millennium. She writes,

> Feminist insight and ecology-based spirituality both serve to shape the future of spirituality in the Philippines. Feminism challenges the core of our structures and systems towards just and caring relationships. While ecology-based spirituality makes us rediscover and reclaim what has been ours all along. Both are needed for the future, for the betterment not only of our people but for the rest of our neighbors, the rest of the world and in the entire universe.[11]

Quiocho suggests the following implications for mission:

- to venture new forms of people empowerment
- to develop and strengthen ecumenical community and ecumenical relations
- to monitor the role and contribution of women in mission
- to recognize the voluntary work of women in mission
- to train women and men in overcoming violence through peace education
- to promote financial capability and political power of women through setting up income-generating projects and leadership training.[12]

What is seen as constitutive of mission in Asia today, according to Sister Mary John Mananzan, needs to be observed, namely, inculturation, liberation, and interreligious dialogue. She also comments that the challenge of the present mission does not consist in a triumphal aim of converting the Asian people to Christianity but is more a challenge to "witnessing and commitment, to sharing and dialogue, to mutual learning and mutual enrichment."[13]

Conclusion

In the Philippines and elsewhere, women play a very important role in mission. Women nurtured the family, supported the church, and participated in community events. Women have been engaged in mission throughout history, only the church has not recognized or nurtured their contribution.

The traditional society, colonialist rule, and orthodox theology have made women passive, apolitical, naive, and expendable. Today, in a proactive role, women in the Philippines have played a very strategic role in expanding the horizons of mission. Their prophetic vision, practical theology, and ecofeminist perspectives are rich resources in doing mission today and in the future.

In spite of economic hardship and patriarchal constraints, the Filipina Christian women hold up half the mission sky. They do mission in the context of their struggle for national liberation, gender equality, and personal struggle to survive and to have meaningful lives. Because of their prophetic, pastoral, and persistent acts, the women in the Philippines bring vision and dynamism into mission work.

Women contribute much in making Christianity alive and relevant in Asia. By giving birth to a holistic sense of mission, women, together with men, can and will journey towards the twenty-first century. This is enough reason to celebrate. But there is another challenge to the church. If the church wants to move forward toward a relevant and empowering mission in the twenty-first century, the perspective and contributions of women must be given high priority. Indeed, women bring dynamism and prophetic vision to mission. The journey has begun!

CHAPTER 5

The Future of Methodist Mission in Europe
James A. Dwyer

*F*ROM A EUROPEAN perspective, Methodism is a young movement, against a background of churches claiming their beginnings in New Testament times, drawing either upon the succession to the seat of Peter, or to restorationist reform of religion in the age of the Renaissance and Reformation. To understand the prospects for Methodism in Europe, it is necessary to look briefly at its short history and to project this history into the future. At its inception, Methodism, along with related movements, brought to England a different perspective from that provided by conflicts over religions, rationalism, and political and social philosophy. Whatever difficulties Methodism has faced in the European context, it is the contention of this author that Methodism has many gifts to offer the Christian church and society in twenty-first century Europe.

Twenty-first Century Europe and Methodism's Peculiar Gifts

However strong may be the tendencies of West Europeans today to withdraw from long-extant religious structures, we can also observe that at another level people are looking for significance in their lives and for deeper meaning. They do not expect to find this meaning tied up in institutions or hierarchies, nor by relinquishing individual autonomy to authority invested in officials of whatever religious or other body. A charismatic authority may be sooner recognized. But even this is a temporally limited assignment of authority over one's person to another.

A countertrend may be seen in the influx of individuals and groups of people with a different relationship to faith and spirituality, whether they are Christians from the eastern part of Europe or Africa, or adherents of Islam from the same regions or Turkey and Central Asia.

Although Methodism has never consciously claimed "official" authority over its members, Methodist structures, too, fall victim to tendencies to "clericalism" and to institutional will, often played out against individualist points of view. At root, this is, however, not a Methodist characteristic but an accretion from its social environment or simple human nature.

Rather, Methodism has a number of traits, which can and ought to free it from the usual inhibiting weight of traditional authority burdening other Christian religious bodies in Europe. At least five features of Methodism distinguish it from the lot of competing Christian religious bodies in continental Europe and may well be the contributions to the future of Christian mission in Europe which Methodism can and must bring.

Methodist Theology

One of the less obvious of our peculiar gifts may actually be our theology. Since we are often accused of having limited theological insight or interest in the face of our organizational drive, it is good to start here. As in most churches today, the actual theological heritage of Methodism is often a source of conflict, sometimes an arena of trivialization, and, now and again, one of our bubbling springs of brilliance. John Wesley and his successors have been less known for their systematic theology than for their pragmatic efficiency at defining the essential and organizing its implementation. This pragmatism may reflect either a lack of theological depth or an appropriate ordering of the task of theology in the living structures of human society.

My own view is that Methodism stands in stark contradistinction to, at least, the Protestant tradition in continental Europe (overlooking our mother in structure and sister in faith Anglicanism) by offering a "non-confessional" theology, which does not require theological agreement before common cause can be found. (Alternatively, some other groups may practice a disregard for traditional and current theological claims of their traditions in order to avoid conflict.) Many congregational structures start from the base of a covenant to which all adhere before work begins and to which all are held accountable until all have agreed to change it. Many hierarchical structures presume that all persons trained in appropriately accredited institutions will have been judged sufficiently orthodox in their thinking that they may work within the framework of a particular confession, whether of Augsburg (the basic confession of much of world Lutheranism), Westminster (basic Presbyterian faith), or Helvetia (the Swiss Reformed basis for faith). Similarly, both Orthodox and Catholic traditions tend to define faithfulness as loyalty to magisterial authority or a particular tradition of worship. Methodism assumes first of all that its leadership is called by God, evidences gifts and graces for that role, and has been tested by a process both democratic and connectional (or "connexional," as British Methodists would say). Once chosen, candidates agree, in a negative sense, to teach nothing directly contradictory to our doctrinal standards and, on the positive side, to administer their office in keeping with the requirements of the *Book of Discipline* of the church. Thus great freedom is granted each minister to find her or his own position within the church. Neither adherence to a strict interpretation of Scripture or doctrine nor personal loyalty or obedience to a superior church officer is implied in Methodist ordination, doctrine, or discipline.

(The so-called doctrinal standards have been defined differently at different times, harkening back to Wesley's "Model Deed" for Methodist meeting houses and its restrictions, or to the original constitution of the Methodist Episcopal Church [MEC] in North America, or to another variation in another part of our tradition. Doctrinal standards cannot be changed by General Conference. Provisions for exercise of ministry can and are changed, however, by each successive General Conference, speaking the mind of the church for the succeeding four years.)

While it may be true today that many annual conferences in United Methodism are focusing on disciplinary questions of how to behave when certain currently burning questions are asked, e.g., regarding sexual orientation and ministry, or blessing of same-sex couples, it is my own judgment that these efforts are based less on traditional Methodist doctrinal understanding than on specific, perhaps seasonal, implementations of the broad standards of Scripture, tradition, reason, and experience. These implementations frequently find themselves in divergence at the turn of the twenty-first century.

As in the past, issues of immediate concern to annual conferences in the U.S. (slavery, the U.S. Civil War, U.S. support of the League of Nations, U.S. entry into the world wars, or other issues of U.S. foreign policy, desegregation, and standard compensation for pastors) may leave many, if not most, conferences in Europe cold, perplexed, disappointed, or full of amazement that the issue is not clear already. Indeed, there is often a fervent hope that sources of conflict in the church's U.S. branches might not be exported to Europe. Of course, much with which the church in the U.S. must grapple appropriately has also already confronted or will confront Europe sooner or later.

Methodism does not, in the first line, require adherence to a body of doctrine but rather evidence of "gifts and graces" assumed to be given by God for the benefit of the whole, universal church, which gifts and graces may even at times stretch the church's previous understanding of itself. This is, in part, the genius also of its mission among people otherwise touched only by more hierarchical and authoritarian church and social structures.

Indeed, the experience of grace is at the core of Methodist faith and theology—grace which prepares us to hear God's call, which justifies us, who cannot find justification for ourselves, and which sanctifies us, who know the extent of our own unholiness. Grace precedes us, surrounds us, and uplifts us, even before we acknowledge its role in our lives. Grace given by God, and the flexibility that implies, is the foundation for Methodist theology.

A theology of grace can at times come into direct conflict with an expectation of justice—whether at the theological, sociological, or juridical level. Reliance upon grace may dull motivations both of fear and of gratitude, but it is nevertheless the universal offer of salvation, the overwhelming offer of love, grace, forgiveness, and restoration of the image of God in fallen human nature which lies at the root of our theology. This message of grace is, in the eyes of many who come to Europe from abroad, direly needed there. The Methodist message of grace, love, mutuality in Christian community, and acceptance of all persons as cocreatures of God needs to be heard and heeded. The message is needed, whether in the Europe of the European Union, or the Europe of the sometime Commonwealth of Independent States, or the Europe of those countries which find themselves aloof from either of these structures (whether hoping to get in, to get out, or to remain unnoticed by them).

Methodist Sociology

Methodism has always been a movement with a social consciousness and a social conscience. The founder John Wesley's message resounded especially in the hearts and minds of those who were the victims of the changes wrought by the Industrial Revolution in England. Although he could not be categorized as a progressive social thinker, Wesley allowed himself to be touched and moved by the social injustice of his day to reach out to individuals and groups of people who were its victims and to organize his followers to do the same. He justified his innovations in Christian community life on the basis of requests brought to him by persons in spiritual and physical need.

His status as the son of an Anglican priest would seem to imply a certain degree of privilege in England. His annual stipend as an unmarried priest without a parish (which supported him for decades until he broke its conditions by carelessly marrying) gave him great freedom to do what he considered appropriate without regard to ecclesial authorities. Yet his own family included nonconformists disadvantaged by English law and debtors who had spent lengthy times in prison for failure to pay minor or major debts, including his own father, the vicar.

Wesley knew firsthand from the English countryside the economics of using the nation's natural resources to increase profit while bringing the population to wrack and ruin. He opposed hard drink, not because he was opposed to imbibing alcohol, but because he rejected the conversion of grain into distilled liquor when the people were starving for lack of bread. The propensity of many peasant men and women to succumb to "the drink," as the Irish put it, led to the squandering of wages and the starvation of children throughout the English countryside, with circumstances reminiscent of those described in the twentieth-century autobiographical novel *Angela's Ashes*. Wesley was appalled by slavery (as well as other forms of trade in human misery) but left it to others to take the initiative in abolishing it, perhaps counting himself among those who thought less government interference was more!

On the other hand, like Luther in a previous century, he opposed those who went into rebellion and opposed the independence of the American colonies from Great Britain. Wesley's opposition to American independence did not go so far as to wish curses down upon them, as a Luther might have done. Indeed, when that independence precipitated the withdrawal of Anglican clergy, Wesley acted in favor of the colonists. He exercised the rights he believed belonged to every priest or presbyter innately in case of emergency, ordaining superintendents to establish a Methodist Episcopal Church in North America. This church was a substitute for the Anglican presence, established to provide the gospel and the sacraments both to the English and to others living there, even before the politically more neutral Episcopal Church of Scotland could move into the void left by the Church of England.

The "sociology" of Wesley was to support current forms and government until they were no longer applicable and then to respond quickly to perceived need with new arrangements to assist those suffering that need. It may not be Methodism's role to formulate political goals or ideals for the states or the regions in which it lives. Yet, in a Europe where change is rampant, Wesley's own attitude toward social change can help to position Methodism in a state of readiness to meet needs as soon as permission is granted and to seek permission as soon as requests will be heard.

While individual Methodists may well be able to take over a role in the formulation of a vision of a political or economic future for Europe, this may be secondary to the task of preparedness to meet needs as occasion, resources, and opportunity present themselves. A Methodist lay preacher, Dr. Ulrich Meisel, was among the first delegates from the former German Democratic Republic (GDR) to be elected to the European Parliament. (Unfortunately, these delegates lost their seats when the East German state was dissolved.) The president of the former Yugoslav Republic of Macedonia was, until his death in February 2004, United Methodist lay preacher Boris Trajkovski, whose brother, also a lay preacher, pastors one of Macedonia's United Methodist congregations.

Perhaps the church's vision of shared leadership between laity and clergy, between local leadership and more distant structures in an international partnership, has helped these countries to begin to grow productive new political cultures. Perhaps Methodist efforts at international understanding, both within Methodist structures and ecumenically, will benefit European decision-making in the long run. Perhaps the active commitment of a strong minority of Methodists to values of world peace will provide a resource for the Europe of the future.

Methodist Politics

Despite the lack of a normative political vision in Methodism, it can yet be determined that there is a political tendency to Methodism, which can be seen from its earliest days. Wesley, although himself an ordained clergyman of training and status in the Church of England and with an Oxford education and two academic degrees, found his mission in an appeal to the common populace of his day to renew their faith and seek nearness to God and to neighbor. The Methodist society was an early form of participatory democracy in a country where such was allowed to grow alongside hierarchical structures of episcopally ruled church and monarchically ruled state and empire. Although it is said of early Methodist conferences that the "conference considered and Mr. Wesley decided," Mr. Wesley could not be everywhere. His habit of structuring everything in local meetings, classes, and bands and identifying class leaders and society stewards laid the framework for a highly democratic habit of open and deep discussion, if not decision-making.

As opposed to some European traditions where both discussion and decision-making are reserved for the few, and not always the obvious few, this culture of openness is important for personal and social growth and for full development of Christian human values. Where, at times, this openness has not been apparent in Methodist structures, the sense of identification with its mission has also suffered. Intellectuals in German society could once only assert *Gedanken sind frei* ("thinking is free"), while many oppositional thinkers still had to make an *innere Migration* to survive, making sure not to share even their thoughts beyond an intimate circle of friends. Russia is well known for its secret police over many political generations and systems. The guillotine was a French response to varieties of opinion. "Byzantine" refers not only to the elaborate high culture of Byzantium but also to a tendency for untransparent decision-making and lack of open discussion known throughout the central and eastern parts of Europe. When Wesley had met the requests to set up new "societies," he was faced with the inevitable necessity of appointing lay preachers to minister to the societies thus formed. However much it went against his grain to do so, he was strongly urged by his advisors, including mother Susannah, that laypersons had as much access to God's grace as he himself. In another point of contention, his mother convinced him that women could be lay preachers just as logically as men. Thus the seed was sown which much later would lead to an almost universal assumption within Methodism that there was no rational basis for excluding women from positions of leadership in church or society or preventing their equal participation with men at all levels of the church.

Wesley's jump over the walls of his own narrower heritage was not limited to inclusion of unordained men and women in the leadership of the United Societies, the reins of which nevertheless remained close in Wesley's hands. His ministry also jumped the channels separating England both from Ireland and from continental Europe. He preached in

Ireland, as well as England, Wales, and Scotland. He visited Pietists in Germany, Holland, and elsewhere, learned German, translated German hymns into English, and drew both inspiration and confidence from his crosscultural experiences in Europe. In England itself, he sought to minister to French prisoners of war, having previously taken on the cause of those languishing in English prisons in general. Given the chance to go, with his brother Charles, to the North American colony of Georgia, he sought to undertake a mission to the colonists and the Native Americans living there, later to exclaim in despair, "I've come to save the Indians, but who will save me?" In short, the clear tendency in the life of John Wesley is to break down walls, to include, and to transcend narrowness in favor of a greater vision, a broader perspective. This aspect of Methodism's heritage can only benefit Europe in century twenty-one.

Modernity

Another of the attributes of Methodism, of vital importance to Europe today and central to a future of Methodist mission, is its modernity. In my own studies of European secular and church history and of Methodism, I have been struck by the fact that John Wesley may well be the first modern theologian to have successfully established an international structure for Christian faith with a world vision.

Wesley is "modern" in the sense that his theological activity occurs in the framework of the Enlightenment, simultaneous with much of the political and philosophical reflection and writing which gives reason its proper due as one of the gifts of God to human nature, or makes of it the supreme point of reference. The modern process of secularization had already begun as he began his own work. While rationalism brought atheism and agnosticism to some, and created both unspiritual leadership in some segments of Christianity and anti- and irrational reaction in other, conservative segments, Methodism embraced rational thinking as a part of the process of having and living out faith. Rather than chafe under this rationalism and secularism, Wesley found in it the challenge for a new and modern expression of inner faith and outward, faith-based commitment. If much has been said against "secular humanism" in some church circles, Wesley himself was a strongly humanist Christian in an already highly secularized age.

He is "modern" in the sense that there could no longer be any thought or talk of one religious point of view determining the life of all of society. England was among the first of the world's societies truly to tire of religious war and come to terms with pluralistic expressions of Christian faith. In addition to the established Anglican Church of England (in England itself), or the established Presbyterian Church of Scotland (only in Scotland), there was also a nonestablished Anglican "Church of Ireland," a Scottish "Episcopal Church," and a great number of legally acknowledged free church bodies (Congregationalists, Plymouth Brethren, Baptists, and Presbyterians in England, Scotland, Ireland, and Wales), and a mostly tolerated group of dissenting nonconformists. While Roman Catholics were not free to exercise their faith and to establish church structures at the time of Wesley, the debate was on. Wesley himself wrote his famous "Letter to a Roman Catholic" and his essay "Catholic Spirit," in which he propounded his conviction and invitation, "If your heart is as my heart, give me your hand."

Previous church foundings had been based on some variation of medieval scholastic distinctions. There was an "idealist" view of the church ("There is only one true church, and its manifestation on earth can only be a universal, i.e., Catholic Church," namely, the Church of Rome). There were "realist" views of church ("There is only one true church in heaven, and the nearest approximation to it on earth can be found in our provincial church structures," e.g., the Church of England, the Church of the Old Prussian Union, or a specific province of the Lutheran Church, etc.). And there were "nominalist" views of church ("The only church which exists is the one we have named and defined; there can be no other of which we can be sure on earth or in heaven," e.g., a strictly congregationalist church or a typical Baptist self-understanding). The Methodist pragmatic view took a new look: There is one true church in heaven; all earthly forms are but partial reflections of it and can only claim full participation in the true church as members of each show mutual respect and love for members one of another.

A part of Wesley's modernity may also be found in what has more recently been called the "Wesleyan quadrilateral," a self-reflective and self-critical standard of faith which calls upon not only Scripture and tradition, but also individual and scholarly reason, and individual and corporate Christian experience.

Personal Commitment

The final attribute of Methodism without which the others lose their significance altogether is the personal attribute. This attribute encompasses personal responses to God's grace, personal involvement in God's mission for God's people, and personal commitment to the vision of Christ to reach all with the good news.

It was, finally, a heartfelt, personal awareness of the presence of the grace of God in his own life which moved John Wesley to take upon himself all that he did for "the people called Methodist." It was Wesley's willingness to determine for himself the degree of commitment he would make and the structures he would need for his personal involvement in God's mission in Wesley's day. It was personal commitment which caused him to travel remarkable distances and to send out others to do the same for the sake of his vision—a vision of people joining together in mutual admonition and support to pray and to praise God, and to become "active in love" for anyone suffering need in their society. To this day, the necessity of personal commitment to Christ is one of the "Methodist distinctives" to which European Methodists cling.

Indeed, a fascinating "bone of contention" between German-speaking Methodism and developments in the U.S. United Methodist Church can be found in current discussion of baptism and church membership. German-speaking United Methodists feel that the move toward "baptized" and "professing" membership diminishes the Methodist free-church distinctive of volunteerist and committed membership. For them Methodist membership practice should stand in distinct opposition to the practice of the Roman Catholic, Lutheran, and Reformed understandings of a *Volkskirche* by which all members of the nation are claimed for their churches until death (or withdrawal of membership) through the sacrament of baptism within denominational structures. Indeed, in a worst-case scenario, these churches claim their due in the form of church tax even from those who simply err in filling in their tax returns or police residency registration.

In this regard, continental Methodists may be even more Wesleyan than Wesley himself, who believed that commitment can grow out of involvement, as well as involvement out of prior commitment. Barriers are often unnecessarily erected for those who are "almost persuaded," rather than encouragement given to them to practice the faith in growing commitment. Here the prerequisite for membership in Wesley's United Societies should inform us: they were open to all who sought after the truth and wanted to avoid "the wrath to come." (It was his continental spiritual guide, Peter Böhler, who admonished Wesley himself to preach faith until he had it!) Ideally, Methodism personally binds its members to one another and to a vision of common life which encompasses outreach to those who do not have such a bond. This vision stands in stark contrast to the mainstream of contemporary European culture, which at one level appears to feed the egotism of its diverse participants and to cultivate fractious development of opposing interests at the cost of society as a whole.

The Shoulders on Which We Stand

This author's own areas of expertise lie near the history of German-speaking Methodism. Although I will seek to find an inclusive focus for all of Europe, much of my anecdotal input may relate to Germany, Switzerland, and Austria, and to their central conferences, first of all. My apologies extend both to those sections of the church which might perceive themselves thus unfairly anecdotalized and to those sections of the church whose representatives may properly protest, "But it is not like that here." For the purposes of this essay, it was not possible to acquire the depth of experience or knowledge of all branches of European Methodism which might best serve our purposes.

The United Methodist Church (UMC) in Europe has roots in more than the four predecessor denominations which usually come to mind for Americans who look at the church's recent history. The UMC in Europe worships in approximately twenty European states, speaks even more languages native to those states, and is only one part of European Methodism. In addition to Methodist churches of Great Britain and Ireland, the Waldensian-Methodist Federation in Italy, and the united Protestant churches in Spain, Belgium, France, or the small Methodist Church in Portugal, Methodism in Europe is also represented by outpost congregations of the Methodist Church of the Caribbean and the Americas (MCCA), the Methodist Church Ghana, the Korean Methodist Church, and perhaps other national Methodist bodies native to continents other than Europe, as well as by a few isolated pockets of activity suffering "disconnection" when one of the Methodist bodies withdrew from one country or another, e.g., in southern France. Other related groups like the

U.S.-based Wesleyan Church, Church of the Nazarene, Free Methodist Church, African Methodist Episcopal (AME), or African Methodist Episcopal Zion (AME Zion) churches also look to play a role in some contexts. Methodist-founded or Wesleyan-inspired independent mission groups (World Gospel Mission or the so-called Mission Society for United Methodists) play their visible or invisible roles, as well, in the name of Wesleyanism. Many U.S.- and British-based parachurch groups active among youth, university students, or other defined groups may also claim the thought of Wesley as part of their parentage. For purposes of this essay, we will also include work in nations or contexts on or beyond the periphery of Europe in our survey: Turkey, Georgia, Armenia, Kazakhstan, and Azerbaijan are arguably outside the confines of Europe, yet clearly accessed through European "portals" of the former Soviet Union, western Turkey's relationship to the European Union, and neighboring countries. Political culture in these countries also ranges from reflections of modern Western Europe to hints of Asian despotism reminiscent of ages past.

In general, it could be said that Methodism found its roots most quickly in countries where the Protestant Reformation or one of its precedents had found widespread favor. Predominantly Catholic or Orthodox countries offered less fertile soil for a Methodist view of religion and society. Examples of the limited success of Methodism in Catholic countries may be found in Austria, France, Italy, Spain, Poland, and other Catholic countries in the eastern part of Europe.

German-speaking Churches

In Austria, Methodism relies heavily on its connection to the other German-speaking branches. Today, the church, administered between the wars from Berlin and annexed to Germany in 1938, is structurally more closely related to the Swiss church. In Italy, both British and U.S. Methodist bodies made mid-nineteenth century efforts to establish churches when democracy, republican guarantees of human rights, and nation-building seemed to be mutually supporting forces. The political and economic necessities finally caused the two Methodist bodies to unite, then to go into federation with the Waldensian Church. Currently, the Methodist-Waldensian Federation cooperates closely with the Baptists of Italy, in a collaboration known affectionately as the "fastest ecumenical structure in the world: BMW [Baptist-Methodist-Waldensian]"! In Spain, Methodists have been subsumed into the united Protestant church. In Portugal, efforts of two English Methodist laymen at mid-nineteenth century resulted in the first church construction and celebration of the sacraments of baptism and holy communion in 1868. Their efforts also led to the involvement of the London Methodist Mission Society, long years of literacy and educational work, and a period of strong growth 1920–1940, followed by crisis and decline. From 1954 onward, responsibility for leadership devolved upon the Methodist Mission Society once more; but from 1984 national leadership was again in place and in 1996 autonomy was realized.

The oldest Methodist work in southern Germany and Austria traces its roots to the missionary assignment by a British mission agency of emigrant butcher Christoph Gottlob Mueller back to his home village in the early nineteenth century. An existing network of religious societies marked by a quietist Pietism was languishing in a region near the Swiss-French-German border. Mueller, their former neighbor, had described his new religious experience from his refuge in England following the Napoleonic wars. The dissatisfied adherents of these south German societies saw in Methodism a hope for renewal and revitalization of their own bodies and persisted in requesting a missionary until, in desperation, Mueller was finally sent. After more than twenty-five years of patchwork effort under Mueller, without a single baptism or celebration of the Lord's supper, a British missionary, Dr. John Lyth, finally accepted the call to succeed him. Shortly, a seminary for training preachers took shape, and a mission strategy was developed which drew a beeline across the southern German states along the Danube and into Austria and beyond, with talk at one point of reaching Istanbul with new congregations. This beeline ultimately included the Stuttgart area, the Swabian city of Ulm, the Bavarian royal capital of Munich, and the Austro-Hungarian imperial capital of Vienna. At a later phase of the work, the by-then U.S.-oriented German Methodist Episcopal structures built upon these British beginnings were to include expansion into Hungary, Slovakia, Voivodina (now a region of Serbia), and other areas in the eastern half of the Austro-Hungarian empire.

A lesson of this British founding might be that Methodist mission flourishes when two elements are brought together successfully. The first is the desire and hunger of local people for a renewed faith. In this case it was faith based on their own previous experience with their dormant

Pietist societies and their hope for a renewal kindled by Mueller's reports on the depth and warmth of faith he was experiencing in English exile among the Methodists. The second is an intention and a strategy to respond to and build upon that local interest and employ it to enhance the mission of the church, which was supplied by Lyth and successors. Individuals renewed by the interaction of Pietist roots and the new infusion of Methodist vitality were eventually equipped and sent on to win others to a renewing relationship with Christ and fellow believers.

In a similar pattern related to the Evangelical United Brethren roots of The UMC, the re-immigrant Sebastian Kurz, who had been converted to vital faith as preached by the Evangelical Association in Pennsylvania (*Evangelische Gemeinschaft*), called for a missionary of that denomination to be sent to his hometown of Bonlanden, Germany. In 1850 J. C. Link and spouse arrived as the first Evangelical Association missionaries in Europe. Within a few years, the Swiss convert Gottlob Füssle was also active in ministerial leadership; in 1877 the still-extant seminary in Reutlingen was founded; and by 1880 and 1900, the work had spread to Switzerland and East Prussia, respectively.

Work in the German states of Saxony and Thuringia was begun by another re-immigrant whose American experience of Methodism had given him an evangelistic zeal still reflected two generations later in the work of his grandson, Bishop Friedrich Wunderlich. In the case of Ehrhardt Wunderlich, he began in his own family's estates and preached with evangelistic zeal to all who would hear him. Despite or because of a level of persecution unfathomable today, the number of people interested in experiencing the preaching of Wunderlich and others and the groups willing to offer temporary refuge increased.

Most petty states exercised a policy of quick deportation. Persons without local citizenship who were determined to be a nuisance in any way were sent to the next state, or sent back to their respective mayor. Indeed, the German word for mayor, *Burgermeister*, literally means, "lord of the citizens." This literal meaning was politically so understood by the plethora of German petty states. (Golo Mann claims, metaphorically, that there were 1,789 such states, "most [of which] consisted of a few castles and villages" in 1789, the year of the French revolution against the royal French centralist state!)[1]

We could speculate on whether Wunderlich's work would have had a durable influence if he had remained on his own. In fact, he had no assignment to preach for the Methodists and no support when he began. But within a short period of time, the new official missionary of the MEC in Bremen, Ludwig S. Jacoby, enrolled Wunderlich as a lay preacher in the Bremen Circuit and provided oversight and encouragement by correspondence from there. (Jacoby, a Jewish-German previously converted to Christianity and a convert to Methodism in the U.S., also spent years traveling as conference superintendent through what is now Illinois and Missouri.) Jacoby mirrored John Wesley's sense of responsibility to organize every effort into structures which would work to secure its success and which would identify the persons responsible and capable for the job and hold them responsible for both their performance and their moral well being. Just as the early class meetings helped build up their members and keep them on the "straight and narrow," so "our system of general superintendency" traditionally served to employ and deploy those called by God to service in our structures for greatest missionary effectiveness.

Although Mueller and Wunderlich are but two of a few dozen significant and colorful figures who shaped the future of Methodism in Europe around 1850, their examples suffice as we begin to shape a vision for Methodism's future after the year 2000.

A lesson for the future of Methodist mission in Europe not dissimilar from that drawn for Mueller's work may be drawn from Wunderlich's and related endeavors. Two elements are again involved. The first is the personal call of a woman or a man to service in which that person is willing to risk service without support or connection. The second is the willingness of church leadership, in this case Jacoby, to recognize the irregular work of the Holy Spirit and to incorporate that work into the official plans of the church. The call today is similarly one to acknowledge those who are drawn to serve and to incorporate them quickly into structures intended both to support and to kindle their missionary zeal while in an encouraging manner holding them responsible for the exercise of their calling.

Whether in the south German states or in central German Thuringia and Saxony, groups perceived as "sectarian" enjoyed more persecution than acceptance for their nonconformist religious views. In the Hanseatic cities of northern Germany the open and liberal administrations of the city-states, which were based on trade with the outside world, offered less resistance to Methodist presence. There were thus fewer "martyrs," so that Bremen became the seat of the first official Methodist structures set up by the North American MEC following the European revolutions of 1848.

The prospect of "Americanized" political and religious freedoms enticed American northern Methodists to Germany, where they stayed, despite a quick restoration of German petty state politics. The United Brethren in Christ and the Evangelical Association also moved to Germany in response to the hope seen in the changes of the day. Initial efforts were similar to those of the MEC. The developments of the Evangelical Association in the U.S. from a self-understanding of a religious society to that of a church (reflected also in the changes of name to Evangelical Church or, during its short schism, United Evangelical Church) had less impact in Europe, where the opportunity to develop as a full-blown church was circumscribed by the presence of an "official" Evangelical Church in almost every province and petty state. The work of the United Brethren in Christ Church, for various reasons, could not be maintained and was turned over to the Methodists. As a church whose U.S. history provided a strong element of German culture, the successors to Jacob Albright's "Newly Formed Methodist Connection" for German-speaking Americans grew with equal strength alongside the MEC work in both Germany and Switzerland until union in 1968, when EUB Bishop Reuben Mueller, also president of the Germany Conference of the *Evangelische Gemeinschaft*, led that denomination into The UMC in the act of union in Dallas, Texas. Whereas European Methodism was a relatively small portion of The Methodist Church at the time of union, the continental European work of the EUB Church was seen by many as coeval to U.S. work in that church.

By 1905 the work was consolidated into a Methodist Episcopal structure now including both British and United Brethren fruits, and a structure under the Evangelical Association, a.k.a. United Evangelical Church, a.k.a. Evangelical Church (before merger into the Evangelical United Brethren Church). In Germany, the name changes were not propagated — the church remained a "society" in the shadow of the state-related Evangelical Church, which itself was divided at the province level along confessional lines tracing back to Augsburg, Helvetian, or Prussian united histories. Indeed, until merger with the Methodists in 1968, many people remained puzzled by the relationships between the German branch of the EUB Church (*Evangelische Gemeinschaft*) and other societies or associations growing out of the state-bound churches, e.g., the *Evangelische Gesellschaft* or *Landeskirchliche Gemeinschaften*. In part, the confusion was not unwelcome.

In Switzerland, despite many commonalties with the rest of German-speaking Europe, the first Methodist work is usually traced back to a different set of British roots. Wesley's "designated successor" (who unfortunately died before him), John William Fletcher, and early efforts of the English to carry forth impulses for religious reform in Swiss Calvinism, especially in the Canton of Vaud/Wallis, can be cited. After working a number of years at Wesley's side in England and as vicar of Madeley, Fletcher returned to his native Nyon, where he lived from 1770 until his death in an epidemic in 1785. Current Swiss work traces its history more immediately primarily to MEC and Evangelical Association roots, while retaining edifices, such as the church building in Lausanne, Canton of Vaud, which bear witness to a second wave of early British influence dating to 1839–1840 in Lausanne and the Suisse Romande, where Charles Cook, James Hocart, and others began their work.

Hungary, Serbia, and Slovakia

As noted, the initial British mission work in southern Germany moved eastward from the Stuttgart area via Ulm and Munich (both in the kingdom of Bavaria) toward Vienna (capital of the Hapsburg Empire and the Austrian half of the "Double Monarchy" of Austria-Hungary). In response to waves of state persecution in the Austrian half of the empire, missionaries and preachers moved to the Hungarian half, at least for a time. As a result, they established work in Budapest, Hungary; Bratislava, Slovakia; and then in the regions of Banat and Baczka. The last are in modern Voivodina, a province of the Serbian Republic of the Federal Republic of Yugoslavia. Here the work spread among ethnic Germans but also among Hungarians and Slovaks living there and along the way. Methodism to this day bridges ethnic minorities in the central European countries where it is present. The Hungarian United Methodist Church harbors both ethnic Magyar and ethnic German Hungarians and has long sought to carry on a ministry to the gypsy tribes of the Sinti and Roma who move through and "settle out" in communities throughout central Europe each year.

In Serbian Voivodina, the recent political vacillations left Methodists at times voicing strong support for former dictator Milosevic. Since they were ethnic minorities themselves, this was necessary to express their belongingness to the Serbian-Yugoslavian state. The dominant Yugoslav religion in past decades, atheism, suppressed the national religion—Orthodoxy for the Serbs—leaving non-Serb Methodists as a "threefold minority," who are members of a religious movement quickly identified as "Western," if not specifically American, in a border region fraught with political danger.

The impact of the experiences of Methodism under Austro-Hungarian persecution upon the future of Methodist mission may, perhaps, be seen in the readiness of Methodist missionaries to move on, at least temporarily, to ethnic and linguistic groups they had not intended to serve as a means of diverting persecution. Accompanying this readiness is an attitude of persistence and perseverance, which may also cause groups to "dig in" and fortify themselves, rather than reach out and risk persecution. Likewise, the constant awareness of minority status may also help the church to look for other minorities needing to feel the love of God toward them and needing a sense of solidarity with and moral support from others in similar predicaments. This sympathy can also be found in the contemporary emphases of Methodists and Waldensians in Italy.

The most immediate situation of the Yugoslavian Methodists may also serve to remind us that expeditious political behavior does not separate us from the desire or the need to hear and respond to the message of God's love for all. (We need only recall that Wesley himself, while opposed to independence for the American colonies, moved quickly to allow Methodists in America to form a church structure separate from his direct oversight. He thus enabled them to further the mission he believed needed to be fulfilled among the colonists, whether in rebellion or not.) Central European Methodism and its ministries among the Sinti and Roma also remind us that settled peoples and migratory peoples need differing approaches with the gospel. Migratory peoples have other forms of social structure and discipline which provide other, perhaps less easily imagined, opportunities for the entry of the gospel into their individual lives and their social fabric.

Bulgaria

At about the same time that a widespread visible presence of Methodism in Germany was developing, the MEC began operating in Bulgaria in the 1850s. In many senses, this may have been a typical middle-class experience. Bulgarian Methodists seem later to have been marked by further education and professional advancement in a society heavily oppressed in many ways by the yoke of the Ottoman Empire and later distracted by Pan-Slavic and inter-Orthodox issues. At one point, some people speculated about Methodist ascendancy to state religion in Bulgaria. For nearly one hundred years, the work developed largely independently of work in the western part of Europe, only to be nearly completely extinguished by harsh antireligious measures of the Bulgarian Communist State, until liberalization began in the late 1980s. The only living Bulgarian with Methodist theological education at the time of liberalization had served years of harsh imprisonment for his faith and a ban on both work for and connection with his church upon his release. When the Reverend Zdravko Beslov became superintendent of a newly permitted Bulgarian Methodist church, only two congregations were still in existence.

In the meantime, eighty congregations have been raised up again within ten years. Bulgarian students are studying for the ministry in Austria and elsewhere. New church buildings have been planned and completed. Indeed, within the Central Conference of Central and Southern Europe the Bulgarian Annual Conference has displaced the Polish Annual Conference in second rank after Switzerland-France for number of congregations. (Poland still ranks second in number of pastors in conference membership.) In contemporary Bulgaria, Methodists also seek to work with the Sinti and Roma and have taken upon themselves a ministry with Turkish Bulgarians, a long-suppressed minority who were previously prohibited from bearing Turkish names or using the Turkish language. Perhaps work in Bulgaria may some day bear the fruit which British mission directors once saw for the march of congregations across southern Germany! By the year 2000 the Bulgarian church had managed to attain a high degree of self-support after only ten years under its new situation, something some other branches of the church, such as the Austrian, needed nearly fifty years to attain. (This independence may in part be attributed to the lack of a large influx of foreign missionaries, and to the low material expectations which the Bulgarian church has been able to accept.)

What lessons for the future may we draw from Bulgaria? Among others, we can conclude, "where there is a will, there is a way." Extremely committed Christians maintained their loyalty despite a half-century of severe persecution and grasped the first (and every?) opportunity to renew their church and their people's faith. They did not accomplish this alone, however, but by valuing and depending upon the connection, which faithful people in Austria, Switzerland, Yugoslavian Macedonia, and elsewhere had also worked to maintain by various and sundry overt and covert means during the period of imposed isolation. A second lesson might therefore be that Methodist connectionalism, when it takes itself seriously, works determinedly, if oft in secret, to prevent the isolation of those who hold to the faith, whatever their circumstances.

May we recall at this point that German Methodism was frequently on the brink of becoming "disconnected" under National Socialist (Nazi) rule in Germany, at points even desiring such disconnection for itself. Other powers finally won out, however. Similar pressures to disconnect The UMC in the German Democratic Republic from worldwide structures of the general church also met final defeat. (And unlike other German secular and religious institutions, where Eastern structures collapsed and the West assumed automatic, self-evident ascendancy, the two German central conferences made every effort—despite massive obstacles after twenty-five years of "separate development"—to negotiate as equal partners for a fair reunification.)

Many had worked to build up German Methodism as a part of the worldwide church. The world connection remained ready both to extend options for connection during the time of trial and to rush into an embrace with sisters and brothers who had survived when the trials of that period were over, even as they brought words of critique, as well.

Paradoxical as it may seem, a Bulgarian had been one of the last persons for whom German Methodism maintained its theological seminary in Frankfurt under Nazi pressure to close it. He was the only living theologically trained Bulgarian Methodist at the time the Bulgarian church's isolation was ended. There were no young German men left to study there because of the universal draft into military service, and as yet no tradition of woman pastors, except for deaconesses in emergency service. Yet Director Carl Ernest Sommer refused to turn over the seminary's last rooms to the Nazis by claiming he needed them for his student body (the lone Bulgarian, Zdravko Beslov). Despite isolation and the threat to their own existence, German Methodists had unawares prepared the way for the rebirth of a Slavic branch of Methodism. They did this even as the ethnic doctrines of National Socialism had sought to withdraw training and human value from the Slavic races, in general, as well as from Jews and Gypsies.

Here, too, we may find a lesson: Protest against injustice may not be apparent but may take the form of risking providing shelter for only one or two who suffer it. Those preserving the kernel of the church's moral stance may not even be acknowledged for what they have done. But their deeds may well have far-reaching consequences for the mission of Christ's church and for human dignity.

Macedonia

In Bulgaria's neighboring province of Macedonia, suffering under the same historical domination as Bulgaria, it was a ministry to the inmates of Turkish prisons in Thessalonika (Greek Macedonia) by Congregationalist Bible translators (the American Church Board) which resulted in a mission to Macedonians. This mission finally came under Methodist oversight for pragmatic reasons. True to its initial tradition, The UMC in the Republic of Macedonia has worked very near the grassroots of society. In Macedonia, a significant number of women played leadership roles in the face of a society dominated religiously by male-dominated Orthodoxy. Indeed, of the three current full clergy members of the Macedonia District of the Yugoslav-Macedonia Provisional Annual Conference, one is a woman nearing retirement age. Some of the more delightful anecdotes about Methodism in Macedonia center on her encounters with the Orthodox "popes" (local priests). The "popes" typically found themselves less well-trained and less able to argue their case than she, despite her peasant upbringing, which was, however, ameliorated by a Methodism which valued the training of its men and women for lay and ordained ministry.

Despite volatile interpersonal dynamics among Macedonian pastors and a constant competition of theological directions and viewpoints today, Methodism in Macedonia also has taken initiatives in dealing with the handicapped, the overlooked, and the marginalized in a society where conformity has long been highly valued and subordination to state authority demanded. Especially important is, perhaps, the training and enabling of women in their society. The question of finding an appropriate approach to the needs of Sinti and Roma women is also one which moves women leaders throughout European Methodism as they look at the Balkan region.

Albania

Albania remains today the most backward country in Europe. Many Europeans were startled to discover, once Communist oppression had ended there, that vestiges of Christian churches had actually survived, and that despite its great efforts at isolating its citizens, there were people of culture and education and high linguistic skills prepared to take up contact with the outside world. At one point near the beginning of the twentieth century, the king of Albania was ready to welcome a Methodist mission, but political circumstances interfered. Methodism has only just now begun to reach Albania since the fall of Communism there, in part accelerated by the displacements of the Kosovo struggles in rump Yugoslavia and by the United Methodist Committee on Relief (UMCOR) and other Methodist relief efforts there.

Poland and Czech and Slovak Republics

Initiatives by the Methodist Episcopal Church, South (MECS), following the First World War account for the presence of Methodists in Poland and the Czech and Slovak republics. Work there and in Belgium began in 1918 as Europe was seeking to rebuild from "the Great War." The intention was primarily to provide relief and no more, but the encounter between helpers without apparent ulterior motive and people in need who had not found the church to be their friend in the past created a demand for societies and congregations.

Following the lifting of Communist rule in Poland, Methodism there has participated in a blossoming which has included efforts to move to the aid of Polish populations in Ukraine and elsewhere in central Europe. Hopes of massive assistance from the West in this regard have not been fulfilled, in part as a result of a lack of clarity about priorities in the Polish church. Great self-confidence continues to buoy the church's efforts, however, and great things may yet develop. In Poland, as elsewhere, disappointment with the rapidity of support for Polish-initiated projects and the discovery that world Methodism is more pluralistic than Polish Methodists had realized in their isolation have provided an opportunity for conflicts present in the U.S. church to find expression in central Europe. A unit of the church cannot, perhaps, be faulted for finding help where it can get it, but help won on such a basis is often not the help one had assumed and may distract from longer-term maturation and integration.

Future in Europe [99]

This United Methodist church in Prague represents the many congregations who have recovered church property after the change from Communist-dominated societies. The Czech and Slovak republic churches are part of a central conference of The United Methodist Church of which the Polish church is the largest of the Slavic churches. *(Richard Lord photo)*

The Poland Annual Conference has, on the other hand, also built strong ties to British Methodists interested in the eastern part of Europe and to other United Methodists around the continent.

A fascinating trail of correspondence bears witness to the faithfulness of a U.S. deaconess, who insisted on staying behind in Warsaw when most other foreigners had left in the face of movements of German and Soviet troops during the Second World War.

One of Polish United Methodism's major forms of evangelism and public influence since its inception has been the English Language College in Warsaw at Mokotowska Place, site also of the church's general superintendency and its theological seminary. The building, provided for by the MECS in the period between the world wars, remained available to the church throughout the Communist era. During the Cold War, the college maintained a very high reputation for training Poles in English-language skills. Teachers from Great Britain, the U.S., and elsewhere were regularly a part of the staff. The superintendent of the church was, for a time, also director of the college. Because of its unique success, the English-language training program served as a model for many congregations.

Many Methodists have seen this as an appropriate way to enable their fellow Poles to live in the post-Communist Western world, while also helping them overcome the anxiety that central European Catholics typically have—whether active, "fallen-away," or only nominal—at the prospect of crossing a Protestant threshold. Such a "cultural evangelism" has a long gestation period. The results are not yet in as to the influence this work may have in the future. Will it preoccupy the church with questions of maintenance and business, or will it allow the church a new channel of growth and renewal? Certainly, educational institutions have at various times and in various settings been a prime force for mission within Methodist history and may well be that in the future as well, whether in Europe or Zimbabwe, where the Africa University has captured the fancy of many.

The Polish church views itself as a dominant force in Slavic Methodism, and rightly so. Polish aspirations to lead a Slavic unit of the church will continue to provide motivation for international conversations and may one day be an element in the formation of a new central conference in Europe. The other established Slavic units of the church are those in Bulgaria, Macedonia, Voivodina, and the Czech and Slovak republics. All of these are a part of the Central Conference of Central and Southern Europe with its episcopal leader, Bishop Heinrich Bolleter, headquartered in Zurich, Switzerland. More recent Slavic work in the Ukraine, Belarus, and Russia is largely under the administration of the Central Conference of Northern Europe.

The Nordic and Baltic Area of the conference includes the Scandinavian countries. Bishop Hans Växby was succeeded in 2001 by Oystein Olsen to serve as episcopal head of the area. The other area of the conference is Eurasia, which includes Russia, and over which Bishop Rüdiger Minor presides.

A lesson for the future drawn from Polish Methodism may be this: Mission based to a very large degree on material assistance from outside may retard the development of self-reliance and self-supported initiative, and generate, instead, the need for more assistance from outside partners and an accompanying dependence and frustration and sense of lack of power over needed resources. The same might be said of personnel assistance.

Russia, Scandinavia, and the Baltic States

Although Russian work draws its recent state-acknowledged legitimacy from prerevolutionary efforts, there is little or no continuity from that work to the current endeavor. A possible exception may be found in the fact that some of the current leadership of the Russian Orthodox Church may have been affected positively or negatively by international Methodist efforts to help structure Orthodoxy's theological education after the Revolution of 1918. It is difficult to draw a single lesson from Russian Methodist history for the future, except, perhaps, that even long-severed and forgotten traditions can serve as a steppingstone back into territories become unfamiliar through lack of contact.

Since re-entry of Methodism into Russia for humanitarian aid, dozens of new congregations and a seminary have been founded and many lay and ordained pastors trained. Recent figures show a hundred new congregations.

Like German work, Nordic Methodism in Denmark, Norway, Sweden, and Finland both Finnish-speaking and Swedish-speaking traces its origins in large part to re-emigration of native sons and daughters. Many had been embraced by Methodism in their new homes in England or North America and then returned home with new faith. British ministries to their expatriates there had more than a small role to play in introducing Methodist and free-church thought to the staunchest of Lutheran settings. As in South Germany, Methodist input into Scandinavian society played a role in a revitalization of local Pietist movements, even in the growth and development of Swedish religious renewal, but may also have given much of its impetus back to these movements.

Methodist work in Finnish Russia and Saint Petersburg predates the Bolshevik revolution, as Nordic missionaries made yet another incursion to the east in the late nineteenth century and the beginning of the twentieth. Methodism in contemporary Ukraine has roots in both Hungary and Poland. Baltic Methodism in Estonia, Lithuania, and Latvia finds roots both in the long-since-reversed German settlements in eastern parts of Europe and in Nordic endeavors, especially Finnish, among their ethnic and regional cousins. Each of the Baltic states, despite local Baltic and Finno-Ugaritic cultural memories, has a strong history of multicultural contact and crossfertilization. Estonian Methodism continued to eke out its existence, even under Communism, and was one of the first Eastern block Methodist units to develop a large-scale vision of what its role could be in the twenty-first century. The Baltic Mission Center in Tallinn is one result of that vision, as is the Agape Center in Parnu. Estonian Methodism has also presented its own candidate for the episcopacy in northern Europe. (Kaliningrad, a.k.a. Königsberg, since the Second World War a Russian enclave to the west of the Baltic region, lies today as an ongoing reminder of Prussian prominence in a previous era, while the Prussians themselves, a Slavic people who learned German, hint at the complexity of the region.)

Many of the countries which have experienced a strong emigration over the decades have also been graced with "favorite sons" and daughters who have met success in the U.S. or elsewhere and consequently established funds especially to support work of various kinds, including Methodist work, in their countries of origin.

In each and every case, the religious and ideological background against which Methodism had to work on the European continent did much to limit it or to open opportunities for it. Some parts of European Methodism live in societies still shaped by oriental intrigue. Others have to address a nationalist Orthodox orientation with strong mystical worship. Some have to find their place in a multireligious state where only age and tradition bring recognition. Still others face an ultramontane Catholicism and antagonism toward those not in union with Rome. Yet others have lived for decades under an atheist ideology and educational system. Others may live with more closely related Lutheran rationalism or pietism or with Calvinist strivings for diligence, order, and propriety. Each of these local histories has played its individual role in influencing both Methodism's past mission and in setting the framework for its future.

In short, Methodist Europe is in no sense unitary, and has never been so. Whether the MECS; MEC; London-based Wesleyan Mission Society; United Brethren in Christ Church; Evangelical Association; German-, Swiss-, or Scandinavian-based mission and evangelism to the East; social welfare work, prison ministry, tent meetings, and evangelistic efforts of many kinds; personality-based ministries; and institutional endeavors — each element has helped to create a potpourri of influences which have mixed with the various European "tribal" mentalities and traditions and the peculiar, often extreme, historical circumstances of each region.

Any close communication among the various parts of European Methodism left over from the nineteenth century was cut off by the First World War. Not until after the Second World War were the various elements given the opportunity to begin to grow together again—or for the first time. Not until the removal of the "Iron Curtain" dividing the Soviet block from Western Europe could this growth toward one another well be publicly described or celebrated. Church bodies whose parent bodies merged in 1939 only began to regularize relationships after 1945. Bodies merged in 1968 began only tentative conversations in their European structures in the 1980s. Bodies in all countries which felt a strong desire and need to be active in mission dared not look to the next country but looked instead, to distant continents—at least until 1990. Even before the political changes were rung, "Faith Conferences" for European Methodists from East and West were held in 1984, 1988, 1992, and 1997 in Hollabrunn, Austria, near the Czech, Slovak, and Hungarian borders, which provided informal opportunities for first contacts of laity and clergy not otherwise privy to East-West conversations.

The Future We Can Build

Against this backdrop we return to the question of the future of Methodist mission in Europe. I take this to be a question not of the future of European Methodist support of intercontinental mission, but rather a question about the status and direction of Methodist propagation of the gospel among the peoples and in the states of Europe.

Upon such foundations, Methodism is peculiarly fitted to respond to the needs of the twenty-first century in Europe. For almost two decades, the author has had opportunity to be in conversation with a large number of laity and clergy on the continent of Europe, both inside and outside Methodist structures. Subsequently, I have reached a number of conclusions about both the factors which may hinder mission in The UMC in Europe and those which further its cause and the cause of the Christian church in general. Recent conversations with the four bishops of the United Methodist Church in Europe have enhanced conclusions earlier drawn.

Since the massive changes in political circumstances beginning around 1989, the minority status of Methodism has not prevented Methodists from playing a disproportionate role in shaping Europe's political future. Regarding the GDR, it is relatively widely known that the churches—

Protestant and Catholic, formerly established churches as well as free churches—provided a "free space" in society. Within such "free space" thoughts, activities, and democratic practice of group organization not favored or directly opposed by the state and its central political party, the Socialist Unity Party of Germany, found their place. Among those most "practiced" in democratic group behavior and with the greatest opportunity to analyze critically both the political processes and the opportunities before them were a significant number of Methodists. Methodism can only claim a proportion of the population well below the 1 percent mark. Yet many local communities put Methodist lay and clergy leadership at the "Round Tables" when it was time to face down the ruling party in decline and to deal with issues of the abuse of power by the secret police. The "Round Tables" eased the opening of the society to its neighbors in East and West. Methodists often had a degree of courage to speak and be heard, a readiness which grew out of long practice in conversation with both the dominant Lutheran structures and with East German Methodism's international partners. This readiness was especially evident in areas where Methodists had been allowed a role, such as "trust-building measures" related to international peace and the "baskets" of the Conference on Security and Cooperation in Europe.

Unfortunately, the possibility of simple and easy emigration, which came for East Germans at the *Wende* ("Turning") of 1989, found reinforcement in the reality of economic collapse. As a result, many Methodist congregations in former East Germany have suffered a "bloodletting," which has only partially been a transfusion to congregations in the West. Indeed, the area of continental Methodism with the least clear cause for optimism today may well be German Methodism, perhaps including its German-speaking sister conferences of France-Switzerland and Austria.

The four annual conferences within the Germany Central Conference (and predecessor bodies) continue to lose members at an alarming rate. A straight projection of the losses can anticipate the date when the "last Methodist in Germany" should turn out the lights.

The Germany Central Conference of The UMC under Bishop Walter Klaiber with headquarters in Frankfurt-on-Main is the only European unit of the church which is not constituted internationally. What this means for questions of crossfertilization of ideas from one culture to another or for the sense of mission and responsibility for European Methodist mission as a whole is significant. The German branch of Methodism has suffered a series of complexes related to the creation of a separate unit for Germany alone in 1935–1936. The agenda following the fall of Communism in the last decade of the twentieth century called for restructuring. For many, it seemed a logical step to restructure on the basis of the status quo ante of 1935, i.e., Germany, Switzerland, and Austria could find their way together again into a common central conference. The smaller units in central Europe could be a separate mission. Or all of United Methodism in Europe could find a new form, including British Methodist units or not. It quickly proved to be a vision whose time had not yet come. Instead, the two German central conferences in the Federal Republic of Germany and in the former GDR negotiated a union into a new Germany Central Conference. Switzerland and Austria remained a dominant part of the Central Conference of Central and Southern Europe. While the two former German central conferences were left to perpetuate their respective positions of being single-nation-state central conferences even after restructure, both the Central Conference of Central and Southern Europe and what is now the Northern Europe Central Conference were faced with new outward-calling challenges. The infant work in Russia found its administrative structure in the present Northern Europe Central Conference, which, alone in Europe, was to elect a second bishop to meet the challenge. The Central Conference of Central and Southern Europe, already overladen with responsibility in a vast territory, which included newly propagated states as first Yugoslavia and then Czechoslovakia "devolved" into their member parts, faced increasing differentiation and new challenges. Likewise, the successor to the Soviet Union, the Commonwealth of Independent States, devolved increasingly into its constituent parts, some looking toward states in the Methodist area of Central and Southern Europe, others to the Northern Europe Conference for friendship and assistance. (For the complete list of annual conferences in Europe see the endnote.)[2]

Estonia, Lithuania, and Latvia declared their independence from the Russians. Lithuania even undertook a two-hour shift of its time zone to align itself with Western European capitals instead of Moscow.

Extant, "Indigenous" Work

Methodist work in many of the countries of the western part of Europe has a long history—but not long enough to guarantee the continuation of Methodist influence, whether in a separate church structure, or in some ecumenical form. Like the "mother country" of Methodism, Great Britain, both Germany and Switzerland show strong indicators that Methodism could eventually slide into oblivion in the near future. To some degree countermeasures have already been taken. The awareness that the age structures of the church will bring an even more rapid decline in both numbers and financial support worked for a while to paralyze the church and to put it on a course of institutional self-concern which viewed the purpose of evangelism to be institutional preservation. Fortunately, this initial phase seems to have passed.

Throughout German and Swiss Methodism, efforts are being made to identify the needs of people and to seek the church's appropriate response. After a longer period of uncertainty about its own identity and raison d'être as a separate structure, Methodism in Germany has finally begun to take note of the unique heritage it has. It has noted what would be lost to it in a united church dominated by either the congregationalist or Baptist ethos present in other German free churches, on the one hand, or by the culture Christianity which predominates in the regional churches of German Protestantism, where reliance upon church taxes collected from persons without a deeper commitment to the church stands in stark contrast to a Methodist vision of volunteerist commitment and support.

The church's leadership has made concerted, if sometimes unsuccessful, efforts to free resources for congregation-planting among young populations in various parts of Germany. Some of these younger congregations have become stable contributors to the overall life of the church. Others continue to struggle to find their way into Methodist connectionalism. Some continue to require more resources than they themselves can provide.

New Work among National Populations

In other countries where the wick of Methodism was only smoldering, new beginnings have brought more visible flame. The Baltic States come to mind. Lithuania may serve as one example. With only a very few persons left who survived the forced exodus of Germans during and after the Second World War, or the resettlement and the persecution under Soviet hegemony in the country, Lithuania could not be said to have an established Methodist church. Yet, an initial presence of U.S. missionaries, at first in administrative offices for a wider area, encouraged people to remember a former Methodist influence in the country. Then a missionary

University students in Smolensk, Russia, learn the concept of community service as part of a summer program at the United Methodist Christian Youth Center there. The program is part of a multipronged ministry pioneered in Smolensk by the United Methodist Campus Fellowship at Murray State University (Ky.). *(UMNS photo)*

couple, Kristin and David Markay, primarily concerned with helping young Lithuanians to exercise organizational leadership and to grow in Christian faith and understanding, helped create a vital new outreach to post-Soviet Lithuanians. The church in Lithuania today has, according to reports, a higher absolute number of lay workers willing to win disciples and organize congregations than any other area in the Nordic and Baltic area of the central conference.

A glance at Russian Methodism today reveals a burgeoning new work spread across the largest geographical territory imaginable and including new congregations and newly trained ministers being incorporated at an incredible rate and with accompanying risks into a United Methodist structure. While the Russian work may soon surpass other Slavic ministries in pure numbers, it is but a drop in the sea of Russian religious need, feeling, activity, and opportunity. Methodist re-entrance into Russia rested on agreements with fading Communist-related and Orthodox structures which saw an opportunity to tap the church's resources to meet crying social needs in hospitals, education, and other social institutions — not, however, in Methodist congregation-building. The opening for congregational work related, apparently, to ministry to foreigners in Russia. Some of the first work took place among Russian-born or immigrant Koreans. Initial Methodist congregation-building among Russian populations found support and sponsorship on the periphery of city partnerships between Russian and U.S. cities which also included active involvement of "tall steeple" United Methodist churches seeking a new motivation for missional involvement for their own people. Much of this initial "one-to-one" work has begun to find institutional expression. Among the first efforts were compassionate responses to the greatest needs of the hour. Soup kitchens and prison ministries, ministries of mercy, and actions to avert personal disaster in the first hours of economic crisis motivated many people highly.

Congregations formed and grew from these ministries. "Kitchen table evangelism" and training of local leadership by airborne missionaries has allowed the birth of dozens of house churches and Bible study groups around the country. The establishment of a theological seminary with the aid of United Methodists in Germany, the U.S., and other countries has offered the needed training for women and men feeling the call to the ministry. Provision for the translation of training materials, hymnals, and worship books from German and English into Russian, and the collection of Russian hymns texts, tunes, and translations has become a project which both catches the imagination and taxes the resources of the leadership of United Methodist institutions around the world.

A central motivation of the work has become leadership training and provision of working institutions in which committed Christians can exercise skills of discussion, decision-making, independent thinking, and initiative, aware of both potential costs and potential consequences of new effort.

Perhaps it is also a lesson to be heeded that the social and political skills implied by typical Methodist order, including both democratic processes and rules of accountability, may be the most useful byproduct of Methodist mission activity in societies like the Russian where deficits in these areas are most apparent. Time will tell if Methodism will tap deep

Russian emotional and spiritual roots in a fashion which will bring further renewal to the church—Methodist and non-Methodist—within and outside Russia.

Noteworthy in this regard is the German "Tent Mission Ministry"— an old German tradition of providing for tent meeting evangelizations with church-provided tents and local or conference-provided evangelists. This tradition finds little resonance among current German or Swiss Methodist congregations, yet the ministry has thrived since the political changes of the early 1990s. Methodists in central Europe have invited the tents to come to them, where appropriate public facilities for evangelization are either nonexistent or inaccessible to Methodists. The excitement of the tent has served many congregations in Poland, Yugoslavia, Czech and Slovak republics, the Russian federation, and elsewhere. Although Germans no longer find much local use for this style of ministry, they have been generous in providing for the periodic replacement and augmentation of the tents, transportation to the sites, and provision of professional help for the planners of such events. The German church has gained much through its people's involvement in evangelization for sister churches in central Europe. (The Tent Mission has also modernized with a large bus which provides a point of encounter when parked in a city center or on the edge of town, where discussions may be held, a coffee house ministry offered, or audiovisual and printed materials made available.)

Work among Immigrants and Foreigners

Methodism in Europe—perhaps in North America, as well—owes much of its first impetus to people who became Methodists while sojourning in a foreign land, usually Great Britain, Ireland, or the U.S. A clearer memory of this fact might have sooner brought Methodists in Germany and Scandinavia to the insight that it is an especially Methodist task to minister to sojourners and resident aliens among them. Unfortunately, Methodists in Germany, for example, spent long decades at the beginning of the last century proving that Methodism is as completely German as Lutheranism, and that being Methodist does not necessarily imply identification with any non-German ways of thinking or acting or with a dangerous "foreign sect." For decades, even the names of the church's founders had been Germanized. Books on the hymnody of Karl Wesley or on Johannes Wesley's perfection of Martin Luther's incomplete Reformation sought to demonstrate this fact.

More recently, however, German Methodists and those in other more established European Methodist church bodies have begun to see increasingly clearly the socio-political responsibilities of being a part of a worldwide church, as well as to reap its benefits. This insight may be coming a bit late, but it is coming. The other side of the coin is that Methodists, unlike more dominant groups, must act concretely and directly upon their convictions regarding social responsibility. They cannot rest on resolutions or proclamations calling upon government or society in general to act, since Methodist influence is too small and their voice too little heard to have much influence at this level.

Fortunately, the world has not been waiting on Methodists to found international ministries for foreigners in Europe or elsewhere. Early efforts of national church councils in Britain and North America, as well as some denominational initiatives, have established many "expatriate" congregations, as they are often called. Within the past several decades "national" ministries abroad, typical American Protestant churches, have taken note of the fact that these ministries have become international, with English-speakers from around the world finding a home in them. A recent listing of international congregations in Europe from *The Connection*, newsletter of Methodist English-Language Ministries in Frankfurt, Germany, reveals forty-four international English-speaking congregations. They range from Albania to Jerusalem, Helsinki to Madrid. Mostly ecumenically founded, several are Lutheran, some few are Methodist. Some are no longer Methodist, but were founded by Methodist bodies or workers. Besides the English-language international congregations, *The Connection* also lists four Ghanaian congregations in the Methodist tradition in Germany and the Netherlands.

Since the late 1970s some Methodist effort has been focused on identifying and meeting the needs of sojourners and resident aliens who might be Methodists but who find little access to local Methodist ministries. In part, language has been the issue. In part, it is a matter of piety, or as retired Bishop Franz Schäfer sometimes put it, "stall odor." Yet again, newcomers frequently find it difficult or impossible to break into the family groups, which typically form in a small fellowship that has not experienced much growth aside from biological growth for a few decades. (Here it may be important to reiterate that the forms the Methodist movement have taken in continental Europe are usually more uniform within a country than they are even in a limited geographical area in the U.S. parent church. Piety and mentality reflecting small groups of people without extensive worldwide experience or vision often have made it difficult for outsiders with divergent piety or mentality to find a home.)

In Austria, the Virginia (U.S.) Annual Conference and the Austria Provisional Annual Conference took cooperative steps to begin a new international ministry in 1978. The decision was made to allow Lee Varner, a retired pastor, and his wife Edith to act upon a vision to establish the English-Speaking United Methodist Church of Vienna as a separate charge conference within the Austrian conference. The vision had grown as a result of work caravans sent from Virginia and elsewhere to Austria to deal with the vast numbers of refugees arriving in and traveling through Austria and to help with postwar rebuilding after 1950. The establishment of Vienna as one of the headquarters of the United Nations, alongside New York and Geneva, Switzerland, had made the city an obvious choice for an international Methodist congregation. The congregation has always enjoyed the support of its bishops, first Bishop Schäfer, then Heinrich Bolleter (both in Zurich).

At the time, no support was forthcoming for the project from the United Methodist General Board of Global Ministries (GBGM). (United Methodism had already participated in founding the ecumenical Vienna Community Church some years before.) On its fifteenth anniversary, the United Methodist congregation experienced a serious challenge from parachurch groups appealing to the Mission Society for United Methodists, which had hired its former pastor when he departed from Vienna. But the congregation came through it more strongly and more self-confidently connectional than before. Meanwhile, after twenty-three years of existence, the congregation is well established but not yet self-sufficient, because of the high mobility of its fellowship. The growth of the international community in Vienna has justified many more English-speaking congregational foundings by various groups, and the English-speaking United Methodist congregation itself is considering beginning a "daughter" congregation in another part of the city.

Efforts by the same congregation to help in founding a Methodist international congregation in Bratislava, Slovakia, before the time of the dissolution of Czechoslovakia were discontinued when Baptists and Lutherans were more successful in meeting the needs of the immediately present international population.

For a time, Vienna was also the site of a Francophone African United

Methodist congregation, which shared facilities with the German-speaking and English-speaking congregations and ministered to people from the Democratic Republic of the Congo, Côte d'Ivoire, and other French-speaking African nations, as well as the occasional Francophone European. The Austria Provisional Annual Conference was unable to imagine continuing this work, however, despite the need, and the availability of a trained pastor. Efforts to continue a promising Yugoslavian and Macedonian congregation also met with insurmountable hurdles.

In Switzerland, Methodist facilities currently provide homes for both the ecumenical and nondenominational Zurich International Church and the International Church of Lucerne, although there is no specifically Methodist English-language work there. Methodists in the Switzerland-France Conference have also been active in work among asylum seekers and refugees. Work in Strasbourg and Paris among the Hmong people has had the wider effect of planting Methodism in Cambodia. In Geneva a Spanish-language Methodist congregation is developing.

In Germany, Bishop Hermann Sticher showed a strong concern for U.S. and British military personnel in the successors to the armies of occupation, many of whom were assumed to be Methodist. The Laity Abroad program set up "Points of Contact" between German Methodist congregations and English-speaking military and civilian personnel near the many foreign military bases in southern, western, and northern Germany. Additionally, his successor, Bishop Walter Klaiber of the Germany Central Conference, began to provide occasion for an annual retreat and consultation for Methodist chaplains in Europe and others in "appointment beyond the local church" (now "persons in extension ministries"). He has acted on behalf of the other European Methodist bishops, especially Bishop Bolleter of the Central Conference of Central and Southern Europe, who has occasionally also participated. Twice in recent years (1999 and 2001) this event has been extended to include GBGM missionaries in the administrative region which includes Europe.

Chaplain Ray Bell was the first director of Laity Abroad in the bishop's office in Frankfurt. The Reverend Dan Franks succeeded him. Under its third incumbent, the Reverend Sonja Waldmann-Bohn, the name was changed to Methodist English Language Ministries. By then it had become a missionary assignment supported by GBGM. The General Board of Higher Education and Ministry in its Section on Chaplains and Related Ministries has provided program money. The General Board of Discipleship has offered additional programming assistance.

The impulses brought back from these contacts into the German-American Committee and its successor, the International Council of The UMC in Germany, have born fruit in many ways, some visible, others less so.

Since 1984, one Bavarian point of contact has been the English-language congregation of the South Germany Conference of The UMC in Munich. Its founding pastor, the Reverend Cheryl Rhodes, at the time deacon on trial "trailing" her husband to his post in Europe, served only twenty-four months before departing, but the work continued. Since 1995 it is the first and only English-speaking charge conference in all of Germany. (It was also the first new charge conference to be founded in the South Germany Conference in any language for many years.)

Other English-speaking international congregations have also been founded. The former Wesley House ministry of the British Conference in Berlin—a sort of church-related "USO" for the British forces and civilians—found transformation into an English-speaking United Methodist congregation in Berlin-Charlottenburg under the leadership of British Pastor John Atkinson. A fellowship in Hamburg founded by an Indian-American couple studying there, Sharon and Romesh Modayil, and the Reverend John Ekem, a Ghanaian Ph.D. candidate in Protestant theology, resulted in two new United Methodist congregations in Hamburg. The Ghanaian society at Eben-Ezer Church in Hamburg-Eppendorf quickly grew to nearly three hundred members under the leadership of Pastor Isaac Amoah from Ghana, making it both the fastest-growing and one of the largest Methodist churches in Germany. Pastor Thomas Shaw at the international, English-speaking congregation at Christ Church, Hamburg-Fuhlsbüttel, has found a slower growth. In Düsseldorf, another U.S. spouse, the Reverend Linda Pliska, on leave of absence from her annual conference to accompany her husband in an assignment abroad, eagerly sought an opportunity to serve. Her initial efforts to found an international English-speaking congregation grew into something unanticipated—an additional Ghanaian congregation, which drew assistance also from Hamburg Eben-Ezer Ghanaian congregation. Not to be "defeated" by success, Ms. Pliska moved on to found a second international, English-language congregation in Düsseldorf, which she pastors with a Korean-

American retired pastor, whose wife brought him to Düsseldorf. Most recently, a successor to the first Ghanaian pastor in Hamburg has been assigned, along with a second Ghanaian pastor to work in Düsseldorf. Other fellowships with monthly services in English exist in Dresden or Hanover, for example. These, too, may at some point take on congregational structures.

Efforts to provide an overarching infrastructure for international work in Germany and beyond have not born clear fruit yet. Although the International Council has spawned a subgroup, the Network of International and English-language United Methodist Congregations, tendencies to want to assure German control of efforts to minister to international persons have frustrated much of the missionary drive of the international congregations themselves. Further handicaps can be found in the greatly divergent manner in which each of the ministries is structured and funded and personnel provided. The oldest such congregation stands in isolation within the South Germany Annual Conference, while all the newer congregations with assigned pastoral leadership are in the North Germany Annual Conference. The North Germany Conference has established a legislative group to hear reports of the work of these congregations at its annual legislative sessions. Oversight remains, however, in the hands of the various district superintendents and the German pastors who happen to be assigned to the charge conferences under which foreign pastors serve.

In the future it will be necessary to find structures to allow resident alien congregations to develop autonomous strategies for growth and outreach and to take increasing financial responsibility for themselves. The missionary impulse of the Ghanaian congregations to reach their kinspeople in other German and European cities needs self-determined channels to allow it to find full expression. The international, English-language congregations seek to join together in charting a strategy for expanded work with English-speakers across Europe. Together with the German church, the international and foreign-language congregations could identify other groups in need of ministry. In this regard, the New Europe, as it is sometimes called, will increasingly be home to people living outside their native cultures. Many of them will be speaking international languages other than English, i.e., French, Spanish, or Portuguese. Methodists from strong churches in Brazil, Mozambique, the Democratic Republic of the Congo, Argentina, and other countries of Africa and Latin America speak these languages, as well. Additionally, Methodism in the

Philippines and other Asian and Pacific Rim nations may have specific contributions to make in ministering to emigrants from their regions. It may also be possible and desirable to join hands with the Korean Methodist Church, already active among Koreans throughout Europe, in reaching out to other populations of Europe in their own languages. Currently, initial steps are being taken to provide a United Methodist-supported ministry to Vietnamese people in Germany. Here, too, the temptation must be avoided to assume that work among Vietnamese must be administered and overseen primarily by Germans, other Europeans or Americans, or that it must happen along known patterns.

Turning to the periphery of Europe, motivations of various kinds have recently engaged Methodist resources here. The Millennium Fund for Mission, a GBGM program using available investment returns to respond to new opportunities in Africa and the eastern part of Europe, has provided a vision and an opportunity for new initiatives and some innovative ministry in Europe. In response to other needs, UMCOR has been actively involved in meeting the needs of victims of natural catastrophe in the Balkans and in nearby Central Asian countries. As in the past, relief efforts often bring questions from their recipients, which may result in a welcome for Methodist input in local society.

UMCOR is assisting the people of Armenia as they work to build a democratic and market-oriented society. This help includes assisting in medical areas, personal hygiene, and health education; providing school supplies; training volunteers for self-help projects; doing health research into specific Armenian issues; helping to repair recent flood damage; and offering small loans to farms and businesses involved in food production.

Sometimes less focused on the long-term than the short, UMCOR's programs in Azerbaijan "focus first on meeting people's immediate needs. Then they support Azerbaijanis in developing ways to sustain and take responsibility for their own redevelopment," supporting

1. Vulnerable populations, who have access to free medicines and primary health care.
2. Preschool-age children who participate in educational programs to prepare them for school.
3. Women, who receive gynecological services, contraceptives, and invaluable information about their bodies and their health, as well as the health of their families.
4. Children in 32 children's institutions, who receive primary health care and medicine.

5. Young children, who have new opportunities to play sports and to interact with other children and adult role models.
6. Farmers who receive technical knowledge and skills that help them increase production, generate income, feed their families, and sustain their communities.
7. Medical facilities with needed supplies and equipment.[3]

In Turkey, UMCOR is working with international partners to assist in rebuilding after the devastating earthquakes of August and November 1999. Local community development groups are finding support in their projects to rebuild homes for residents. And UMCOR is working together with an Islamic organization to restore and improve a home for hearing-impaired children. Speaking for itself, UMCOR stated, "Operational since October 1999, UMCOR/Turkey is based in Istanbul with project activities in Gölcük and Düzce. In all of its programs, UMCOR establishes a close working relationship with the affected communities, focusing directly on the people most in need. UMCOR/Turkey communicates and coordinates activities with international humanitarian aid organizations, the Turkish Government and local NGOs. UMCOR implements programs in Turkey with funding from a variety of generous donors including Action by Churches Together, Catholic Relief Services, Episcopal Relief and Development, GBGM, and Tear Fund Netherlands."

Besides such relief and reconstruction work, UMCOR also supports community-building and peace-making in such places as Bosnia-Herzegovina, Albania, and Kosovo.

Methodism in Europe could enjoy an ever-expanding future, if it can overcome its current regionalism and provincialism to create international ministries across the continent, without unnecessary regard for national boundaries or current juridical distinctions.

In the Nordic and Baltic countries, too, response to the needs of international populations has been a source of hope in recent years, despite strong decline in the "indigenous" congregations. Most recently, following the mutual recognition of orders between Swedish United Methodism and the newly disestablished Lutheran Church of Sweden, Swedish Methodists have founded an English-language international ministry in cooperation with the Cathedral Church of Lund and the Lutheran university chaplaincy. A further and older English-language ministry exists in Copenhagen, Denmark, under African leadership. Leaders in the conferences of the Nordic and Baltic states have also undertaken other ministries among foreign populations, such as an Urdu congregation. Here, as in Germany, significant issues are raised by the questions surrounding the assimilation or nonassimilation of members of new ministries into the national church structures. Many Germans or Scandinavians or Finns may see work among foreigners as "their" ministry, which gives new meaning to their own congregations. Yet alien populations themselves will, in part, see a church congregation aimed at them as a safe place for their own culture and traditions, a place to determine their own fates without immediate regard for the wishes of their hosts in the foreign country.

Even in countries where there has not traditionally been a Methodist presence, there are today strong movements to found congregations intended especially for migrants into those countries. In the Netherlands, two different Methodist bodies are addressing the needs of two different population groups. English Methodists have, perhaps, individually found homes in some outpost parishes of the Church of England, just across the channel from home, and have participated in cooperative congregations there.

Caribbean Methodists, many of whom have the right to migrate to the Netherlands by virtue of holding Dutch citizenship, have nevertheless continued to speak English in a country which takes for granted that 90 percent of its own people will also speak English as a second language. The Methodist Church of the Caribbean and the Americas (MCCA) has been struggling to provide appropriate leadership to Europeanized islanders who have formed congregations in Amsterdam, Rotterdam, and Zoetermeer (near The Hague) over the past ten years. Attendance in these three congregations of the Holland Methodist Church may total 350 people on a typical Sunday, yet no arrangements have yet been made for them to enjoy ongoing pastoral leadership, except through superannuary or temporary supply arrangements. The Reverend Wilfred Hodge, a retired pastor, presided over the work for three years, but has since returned to retirement. In Rotterdam and Amsterdam, the MCCA congregations meet as guests in Moravian and Free Evangelical churches. In Zoetermeer, they meet in a multipurpose room in a community daycare and health center within earshot of other immigrant worshipers of other traditions.

Also in the Netherlands, the year 2000 saw the inauguration of official work by the Methodist Church Ghana in its Holland Methodist Circuit. Although Ghanaian leadership can also work in English, the Ghanaian populations in the Netherlands prefer to worship in one of the Ghanaian languages. Pastor Isaac Amoah, previously in the United Methodist assignment in Hamburg, is the first pastor to be assigned as leader of the Holland Circuit of the Methodist Church Ghana. About three hundred worshipers gathered in Rotterdam for a Sunday afternoon service of worship in 2001. A second congregation gathers in The Hague. Like many other African and Caribbean groups, the Ghanaian Methodists in Amsterdam meet in rooms provided by an enterprising charismatic pastor. They are temporary classrooms erected in the basement of a parking garage of an urban housing development.

At the root of the question of the future of Methodism in Europe among minority or sojourner populations lies the issue of new wine and old wineskins. Will Methodism be willing, and also able, to win people for faith and then to hand over to those newly won the reins of authority and financial autonomy which they need to build their own, peculiar congregations and church institutions? Or will sedentary European Methodist leaders feel that it is their first responsibility to make of their new, non-native Methodist brothers and sisters accommodated members of their own society? Can established leadership relinquish sufficient power to feed the motivation and ambition of new leaders from among the sojourners and resident aliens, so that they may make their own mistakes and book their own successes? There may be a strong temptation by leaders of existing church structures to replicate existing congregational forms. Yet it is not hard to imagine why people newly won to Methodist congregations seeking to accommodate their alien needs would want to avoid attitudes and methods of work which have brought such limited success to their hosts in various European countries!

In countries where there is no existing structure of note, the issue is one of winning disciples and training them as responsible leaders able to win and train others. As so often in the past, Methodism has resources from many countries which can be brought to bear to help inform and structure a mission which responds to the grace of God offered to all persons through the proclamation of Jesus Christ. Some of the persons who could provide leadership may already be "in country" — emigrants returned, or Methodist migrants just waiting for that opportunity to put their Christian faith into action again in the tradition of John Wesley. If new leadership can be kept accountable for wise use of resources and for an attitude of openness to the needs of the world around, there is much hope for Methodist mission in Europe in the twenty-first century, but it will most likely be a mission greatly different from that of the twentieth or the nineteenth centuries.

Resources Consulted

Wade Crawford Barclay, *The Methodist Episcopal Church, 1845-1939: Widening Horizons*, vol. 3 in *History of Methodist Missions* (New York: The Board of Missions and Church Extension of The Methodist Church, 1957).

Web Sites of Interest

United Methodist News Service provides current and archived press releases about work of The United Methodist Church at http://umns.umc.com.

The General Board of Global Ministries of The United Methodist Church provides current information on U.S.-sponsored mission projects at GBGM pages at http://gbgm-umc.org. Direct or indirect links to a vast number of Methodist-related sites can be found here. To reach smaller European UMC sites directly, one of the sites below is simpler.

Information on GBGM missionaries serving currently in Europe can be found at http://gbgm-umc.org.

The Central Conference of Northern Europe (Nordic and Baltic States and Russia) houses its own basic web directory at the GBGM site: http://gbgm-umc.org/northerneurope. The Central Conference of Central and Southern Europe provides a convenient web site with both a graphic linking to various regions in Europe and a text page linking to all the currently available European web sites: http://umc-europe.org. The Germany Central Conference site is located at http://emk.de.

The Methodist churches of Great Britain and Ireland likewise provide central web sites: Great Britain: www.methodist.org.uk (searching this site will also reveal links to autonomous Methodist churches around the world, including, e.g., Portugal); Ireland: www.irishmethodist.org.

CHAPTER 6

The Methodist Educational Mission in Latin America: History, Meaning, Perspective

Norman Rubén Amestoy and Néstor O. Míguez

Introduction and Exposition[1]

The activity and objectives of the Methodist missions in Latin America were marked by an emphasis (if not exclusive) on cultural development and education. This emphasis was not happenstance but rather the result of a specific intent and understanding that arose from the way in which the Methodist movement developed in North America, and the role Methodism could play to the south of the Río Grande. If the idea was to evangelize, there was also a political agenda—a specific way of understanding society and a purpose that would transform; its intention was not innocent or unconscious, rather it was made very clear through many of its projects, such as social reform. That continues to be the Methodist vision to "reform the nation," except that now it is applied to other nations and is part of the motivation for missions.

With that vision, the Methodist missionary effort in Latin America was, among other things, an educational mission. The liberal ideology, shared not only by the principal Methodist points of reference, but also by an important sector of the intellectual elite of the entire subcontinent, was to "educate the supreme authority," that is, the people (in the representative expression of D. F. Sarmiento, educator and, later, president of Argentina). Thus, it would be possible to overcome the anarchy and the leadership practices of the oligarchies that conditioned the people and kept the nations in backwardness. The Methodist mission found a favorable climate in sectors of the indigenous society that received it well and facilitated its inclusion in society. At the same time, it marked the development of the mission. Although, initially, Methodism did not remain in a certain sector and social scope, its search to "elevate" the people who came to the faith through its missions produced a resocialization similar to the values of the middle class. Subsequently, in general terms (there are exceptions to consider, as in the Bolivian case, with a strong participation of the original participants) the Methodist churches of South America have had great difficulty in including themselves in other social sectors and have only partially accomplished it.

It is certainly true that the continental area is very diverse. In what we currently call "the Southern Cone," the indigenous population was practically fenced in small territorial enclaves and numerically reduced to a very minimal presence, with little or no crossbreeding (with the exception of Paraguay and northwest Argentina). It is the opposite for the Andean nations, where the original population continues to be the majority (Bolivia), or where the criollos and mestizos constitute the basic substrata of the population (Peru, Ecuador), marked by strong characteristics from the numerous aboriginal groups who subsist in the region and continue their struggle for revindication of their identity and culture. On the Atlantic Coast, in northern South America and the Caribbean (as well as to a lesser degree in other areas), the influence of the African population brought over during the period of slavery is significant. Central America, the Caribbean, and México are a multifaceted mosaic in which these same components are combined in varying proportions by nation and situation, in some cases with significant Asian minorities.

Methodism developed in different ways in each one of these ethnic-cultural panoramas, with varying ideological and theological hues. In Bolivia and Peru, various sectors of Methodism entered the indigenous realm and developed into two almost parallel churches, creating tensions that still persist. In México, the influence of the nearby southern United States had a stronger influence on Methodism than it did in other nations of the subcontinent. The fact that the mission depended on the Methodist churches of the southern U.S., and the early autonomy of the Methodist Church in Brazil, made its own mark in the development of the mission in that vast country. In certain cases, internal theological factors produced other alternatives. Chile, for example, could have followed very closely the model of Argentina, Uruguay, and southern Brazil, yet, because of local characteristics, the irruption of an internal Pentecostal movement in the early decades of the twentieth century brought about a different history.

It is thus impossible to outline a history of Methodism in Latin America without lingering over these peculiarities. It is our understanding that although the initial intentions were all the same and the mission work was based on the same premise for all Latin America, the different realities found by the missionaries caused historic diversification, the development of different styles and types of missionary work, with the emergent churches taking on different characteristics. Yet, if there was something in common, it was the emphasis on education. The great Methodist schools that continue to be a presence in almost all the countries are testimony to that understanding and initial impulse which still exists to a great extent. In our opinion, it will be necessary now to evaluate, ponder, and to a certain extent assume, as a key to interpretation, the significance and purpose of the Methodist presence and mission in Latin America, according to their own history and style of being a church, based on the reference points of each place.

Our purpose in this essay is to study a case, which is both an exception and a paradigm. Exception, because Uruguayan society displays different characteristics from the rest of Latin America, which makes it a unique case: there, the genocide committed on the original inhabitants was almost total, to the point that hardly any nucleus of aboriginal people was left in the entire territory after the ambush at Salsipuedes (1831). It can be said without a doubt that it was the most rapidly secularized society in all Latin America, where positive liberalism became more strongly imbedded and was the most influential in the political and cultural realms.

It is also a paradigm, because in that setting the strategy for the Methodist evangelization and its relation to the educational project can be seen with greater transparency. There theological education was established for the first time in the subcontinent. It could almost be considered as a laboratory for the project and the manner in which the presence of the Methodist Church in Latin America was considered in that vein. If it did not develop further in Uruguay, it is because it could not develop any further anywhere else, much less in more complex and hostile societies. For that reason, to study the manner in which Methodism was brought to Uruguay (different, but with close ties to the sister project in Argentina) is to see the broadest expression of what the missionary drive of the nineteenth century wanted (and to what degree it was accomplished) in its effort to bring social transformation through education.

The Shaping of Missionary Mentalities

Church historians consider the nineteenth century as the great century of Christian expansionism and the century of greater Protestant missionary vitality.[2] This phenomenon can be explained by the confluence of various contextual factors.[3] The socioeconomic nature of a great many of these elements has led authors to be concerned about emphasizing the need to avoid a simplistic interpretation. Thus, for J. González: "Christianity's great geographic advance during that century had to do, without a doubt, at least partly with the political and economic expansion in Europe—and, later on, in North America. But the missionaries of the nineteenth century were more independent of the political interests and of the nations than those of any other period since the beginning of the Middle Ages."[4]

If, on the one hand, it is necessary to recognize that the effective drive of the missionary task for Río de la Plata was favored at least partially by the commercial development of the central countries, on the other, it came no less directly from the slow and progressive development of the Puritan mentality. This school of thought had arrived at the U.S. with hopes of creating a "new heaven and a new earth" related to the democratic ideal, the founding of the Republic and the resultant egalitarian aspirations.

In that regard, and in spite of a certain degree of anti-intellectualism felt by many supporters of the "religion of the heart," the religious societies reinforced the nucleus that more or less cultured families provided for the future development of both the social and spiritual life. Along that same line, it is necessary to assess the way the revivals that traveled the West from the late eighteenth century to the mid-nineteenth century continue to exert a notorious influence on the spiritual and intellectual life: defending moderation and morality, opposing slavery, and stimulating philanthropic initiatives in both the educational and social spheres. Some preachers related to the revival scene helped prepare the way for the development of intellectual values that they themselves sometimes scorned.

The advance of Methodism toward the western region of the U.S. ("the conquest of the West") was fundamental in the development of a missionary mentality marked by a strong spirit of optimism. After all, the results accomplished by "revivals" could very well be transformed into a similar experience in the missions that were starting in the American nations saturated by "idolatry" and the "Romanist" influence. In effect, the great majority of the Protestant missionaries who, as of 1840, came to Río de la Plata from England or the United States, all had this theological emphasis in common. However, this basic theological framework experienced considerable modifications from 1850 forward, with the resurgence of the "Second Great Revival." Some of the most significant changes occurred in the theological plane: a certain degree of free will, the emphasis on growth in holiness, the continuation of an individualistic nature that is highly subjective, and a close relationship between spirituality and social reform, where the missionaries related preaching the pure gospel to moral changes in society, including the abolition of slavery and an attack on poverty.[5]

These elements became a part of the missionary mentality that, once the Civil War ended in 1865, awakened the desire of expansion beyond the national boundaries. On the other hand, the nation itself was considered to have acquired an exemplary character. At the genesis of a developing industrial, urban society, a reform movement was happening which was worthy of imitation. The democratic faith which emerged in the mid-nineteenth century implied an inexorable faith in the eternal and universal supremacy of North America's republican and democratic institutions, as well as its suitability for all people, at all times, in all places, which in turn implied a commitment to assure its final success. At least that is how the Reverend Thomas B. Wood understood it. We will see later on his decisive performance in Río de la Plata, when he stated: "South America presents the most excellent opportunity for the North American evangelism to extend its dominion without competition; in order to fill this other great half of our hemisphere in the name of God and human wellness; transform that jungle of priestly practices and the power of the sword, and show the way to glorious Christian growth, to give the truth of salvation to millions who are already there and many millions in the future."[6]

The Uruguayan Case

In studying the insertion and diffusion of Methodism in Uruguay, we need first to explain the project for socioreligious reform spearheaded

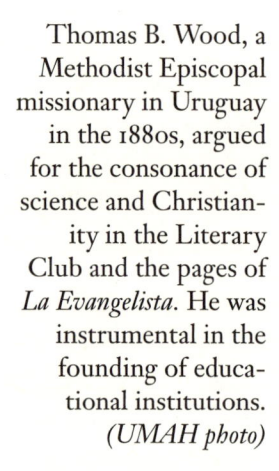

Thomas B. Wood, a Methodist Episcopal missionary in Uruguay in the 1880s, argued for the consonance of science and Christianity in the Literary Club and the pages of *La Evangelista*. He was instrumental in the founding of educational institutions. (UMAH photo)

by the Missionary Society of the Methodist Episcopal Church (MEC). However, it is appropriate to clarify that we are interested in analyzing the phenomenon, not only with regard to its social insertion, but also as a theologically and socially dissident ideology.

Methodist Missionary Societies in the Crisis of the Traditional Society (1868–1875)

The period from 1860 to 1890 was decisive in the formation of modern Uruguay, because, throughout these three decades, there were substantial changes in demographic, social, economic, political, and cultural matters which would allow the undermining of the old pastoral and tyrannical Uruguay and would cause the nation to be enrolled in a definite manner within the scope of influence of capitalist Europe.[7] It was indeed in that first decade when the missionary societies, their leaders, pastors, colporteurs, and supporters, made diverse efforts to spread their "pure and simple" Christianity to the "public mentality" and to settle down permanently in 1868. Hence our interest in investigating the context of insertion in those first years and the structural changes that occurred.

Beginning in 1860, social and economic transformations in the eastern society began to take place little by little.[8] These changes did not go unnoticed by the MEC Missionary Society in the U.S., which in 1851 had already emphasized the need to establish a mission in each major Latin America city—and, obviously, also in Montevideo—with the express purpose of:

> Taking care of the Protestant population in these Roman Catholic cities and countries . . . to attend to their spiritual needs and, thus, with God's blessing, save their souls . . . educate their children, especially in Sunday schools, on the Protestant Churches' principles and worship services, and thus raising a Protestant population within the Roman Catholic cities and states. . . . To present to the Catholic population an example of the pure and simple Christianity enjoyed by the Protestants, in order to gradually persuade them to adopt it. It is not the policy or the goal of these missions to interfere with South America's political or ecclesiastical institutions, rather to reach the point where the enlightenment and example of the mission might influence the public mentality.[9]

In 1856, the Missionary Society recommended "the reestablishment of the mission in Montevideo, with special reference to the native population; the initiation of religious freedom gave rise to an irrepressible desire to preach the Gospel to the Spanish population."[10] During his visit to Montevideo in 1860, Dr. William Goodfellow, the new superintendent for the Methodist mission, opened a prayer meeting, organized a "class," and finally reiterated an emphatic order to the Missionary Society: "We must spread the doctrine, we must follow our people who have dispersed; before a year is out we must have a service in Spanish in this city."[11]

The population of Uruguay almost doubled in the 1860s. Montevideo went from 58,000 inhabitants in 1860 to 126,000 at the end of the decade. It was a period of remarkable mercantile growth, sustained progress in the construction industry, intense activity at the ports and coastal trade. Through intermediary commerce, the mercantile capital of foreign traders of English, French, German, and Spanish origin grew. When we analyze Methodism's penetration in Uruguay, we can see the support the Missionary Society found in several of these men.

After some sporadic efforts of colportage, suddenly, in 1868, Andrés Murray Milne was transferred from the city of Rosario de Santa Fé to Montevideo.[12] Apparently, the main motivation the mission had for his transfer to Montevideo was the political instability in Rosario de Santa Fé caused by the civil war in Argentina. Once established, and after several months of work, he initiated gatherings to hear preaching and Sunday school at his home.[13] A year later, Superintendent Goodfellow visited him and held several gatherings among sailors and initiated preaching in Spanish. These gatherings to hear preaching grew significantly to the point that, taking advantage of the contacts he and Milne had with the Masons, they began to have meetings at the Mason Free School. The results reached during the conferences and the interest awakened among "the Uruguayans," were sufficient reason to decide that Pastor John F. Thomson, active preacher and polemicist from Buenos Aires as well as an active lecturer for the Masons, should visit. Stable and regular activity became possible because of the offer of "several gentlemen" — with whom Milne had made contact — to cooperate with the support of a minister, as long as it was the young preacher Thomson. Thus, the presence of Methodism in Montevideo is linked not only to the interest of the Missionary Society but also to the interest expressed by the Masons and foreign residents. The anti-Catholic controversy was not foreign to this situation.

In 1870, Thomson moved to Montevideo (1870–1877). The social atmosphere became unstable because of new civil unrest as well as a degree of commercial and financial paralysis. Nevertheless, the mission continued to take root and in 1873, the quarterly conference in Buenos Aires decided to give Thomson copies of the files from Montevideo so they could be maintained there.[14]

The Fundamental Goals of the Missionary Project

In 1873, the Missionary Society expressed its understanding of the purpose of its mission, which was "charitable and religious, conceived to spread the blessings of education and Christianity and to promote and maintain missionary schools and Christian missions throughout the United States, the American continent and foreign countries."[15] We cannot help but notice that, in this context, the educational task is mentioned before "Christianity" and "missionary schools" and before "Christian missions." It is not necessary to read through a list of priorities in order to see that this is an indicator of the mentality by which Methodism arrived on these coasts.

At the beginning of the mission, the task was centered on the development of new congregations, Sunday schools, and outreach activities to the areas around the capital and the cities in the interior, together with the dissemination of the Bible throughout the extensive missionary field that the colporteurs traveled in their "evangelistic tours." It is understandable that the sermons acquired a strong conversionary tone that questioned Catholicism. This does not mean that Methodism believed it would achieve a hastened massive substitution of the dominant religion; the goal was to create a split in the religious field, thus establishing its message of dissidence. In that way, it would be possible to break down the certainties of a nominally Catholic base and the prerogatives of exclusivity which it had monopolized historically.

Together with the message of conversion, the Methodist religious societies tried to offer their faithful a moral framework for their daily life. To that end, the insistent call to conversion implied for the wise individual the experience of breaking away from "worldly" values and traditional order. Thus, a demand fell to the newly converted to live a life of sanctity and perfection to include a full repertoire of habits and conduct that verified his/her testimony of faith, conversion, and new life.[16] An individual should have a rational and reflective character; therefore, there was an emphasis on virtue being "enlightened." In this sense, virtue, to be so, should have "as its aim, working for the good of humankind."[17] It is possible to see the preoccupation with prescribing an effective bond between the development of the believer's formation and his/her citizenship. Changing traditional society demanded that the modern order accept a moral model based on Pietism.

For the Methodists, however, religion had to stay away from public issues, political wheeling and dealing, and the exertion of influence over partisan legislation and opinions.[18] On the other hand, it functioned as a guide for customs and family life, thus working in favor of regulating the state. This outlook differed from those ideas that tolerance and freedom were strengthened as religiosity disappeared from the individual conscience. The "spirit of religion" and the "spirit of freedom" had to be intimately related. Emilio Castelar wrote: "Gentlemen, whoever wants religion, should not divorce it from freedom; and those of you who want freedom, do not divorce it from religion."[19]

With its intention of transformation, Methodism in Río de la Plata was between two fronts. At least that is how the evangelical poet Ramon Poza Blanco understood it, according to his representation of the Eastern Republic at the end of the 1870s: "there is a loss of confidence because of the transgression of divine moral laws, human laws, and also by the irreligious character that seems to desire to dominate the people." He called on the people to see how, in the unity among nations, the "happiest, more powerful and most free nations" were those that accepted the gospel as the cornerstone of their social order. For that reason, the confidence, the credibility and the true legitimacy of the social and political order disappeared when the religiously moral was scorned. It was thus placed in opposition to the Roman Catholics, but also to the "nonreligious rationalists." He criticized both when he affirmed: "Let those who exploit and mock religious beliefs, who soil the very pure Christian religion, blaspheme freedom, and those that spit on its very face say what they will. Some scorn what's good for society, promoting irreligiosity. Woe is unto the country that doesn't react strongly against this ill! If religiosity is lost, what can humankind trust? Religiosity is essential to the well being and development of the people. Its definitive formula is the gospel of Jesus the Savior."[20]

Missionary Societies and Popular Education for Social Changes (1879–1900)

From the virtues of this fundamental understanding that unites religious faith and citizenship, Methodism carried out an effort in favor of a popular democratic education and the diffusion from the civil society of initiatives to establish elementary schools, teacher's training colleges, libraries, school cooperatives, literary clubs, popular societies, religious leagues, etc. The massive spreading of elementary education was perceived as the most effective instrument in the process of social change and modernization. Education was not thought of as just an evangelizing tool; rather, it also proposed to create good citizens, according to Cecilia Guelfi de Bersiá.

Methodism proposed to bring about a religious reform capable of affecting a society permeated by Catholic tradition. As far as education was concerned: "Romanism has never worked to cultivate the intelligence of the masses, on the contrary, it has always tried hard to keep them ignorant, having exploitation as its most important aim." It is true that it had managed to teach "some of them," but with the intention of creating: "a caste ... in charge of thinking and acting for everybody. .. denying those who unfortunately had been rocked in the cradle of Papalism the right to think for themselves."[21]

Catholic traditions were counterproductive because, among other things, they created submissive men and collective and authoritarian societies.

After all, "Education makes a man free, independent," and the individual "aware of his worth and the mission for which he has been created." This view tied in with the religious sphere, where ignorance also produced devastating effects, because: "A man without an education allows himself to be led by those who have appointed themselves his teachers, obeying them blindly in everything they are ordered to do, without knowing whether it is good or bad or where it will take him."[22] In this context, education had a commitment to create an ordered scheme for the social system, spreading the new modalities of political order, offering a set of values and doctrines more in tune with modern times than those offered by an anachronistic Romanist absolutism. In this sense, we must understand the effective and ample educational apparatus created by Methodism in Río de la Plata.

The Development of the Scholastic Network (1879–1900)

The purpose of the Missionary Society was not restricted to attract members that would identify with their religious principles but also to offer its sympathizers the opportunity to learn and educate themselves. In 1872, with this goal in mind, the society had established that part of its work was: "To educate the masses, giving them all types of useful knowledge, human as well as divine . . . an essential condition for safety and progress."[23]

Around 1879, this pedagogical optimism was what motivated Pastor Thomas B. Wood to establish an exemplary educational network. For Wood, the educational system that began to develop had to shape the people physically, morally, and intellectually. To outline and shape the nation was part of the main challenge of the Methodist religious societies. The Methodist educational project was reciprocal with the Varelian educational reform that was orchestrated from the Uruguayan state. With this aim, starting in 1878, the head office, located in Montevideo, led to the establishment of elementary schools in various neighborhoods of the capital, where the religious associations enjoyed considerable growth.[24] Thus, between 1879 and 1886, an educational network was created in the center as well as the area surrounding Montevideo. While the schools were preoccupied with evangelizing, they were also considered to be "workshops where hundreds of souls were forged for the Saviour," and they had a moral obligation to create "good children and good citizens."[25]

A woman, Cecilia Guelfi, played a fundamental role in making this development possible. Guelfi, daughter of Italian parents, was born in Buenos Aires in 1855. Later, the family moved to Montevideo, where she became a teacher in 1872. She taught in public schools and participated in José P. Varela's reform. Converted to Protestantism in 1870, she became a member of the MEC in 1878. Summoned by Wood to initiate an evangelical school, Guelfi became interested in the project and began to correspond with the MEC Woman's Foreign Missionary Society (WFMS). When the society showed its support for the initiative, Guelfi resigned her position in the public school. She was offered funds and residence at the school if she continued in public education, tempting offers for a woman at that time; nevertheless, she declined the offer. In the "Statements of Accounts of the W.F.M.S. Work in Montevideo, Uruguay," dated August 1, 1887, Wood states that this proposal was "twice what the Society had offered her, with the possibility of promotion in her career, not only in honors but also monetarily. She preferred the scorned profession of a worker paid by the foreign heresy, working for less than what she was worth."[26] In the *Inspection of Education* of Varela for 1878, Guelfi is mentioned as a second-grade teacher with almost six years in public teaching.

On February 10, 1879, the Free Evangelical School (No. 1) was inaugurated. This school was "mixed," since it admitted "girls of all ages, and boys of up to 9 years of age," and registration was limited to forty students, according to the "order in which applications were received."[27] Given the growth of the day school and the development of the religious association, the ministry was transformed into an important outpost. The congregational work, carried out by Juan Escande and a Miss Davinson, summoned university students, who would get together to make presentations on doctrine and discuss it. Little by little, new types of schools were added, until a total of fourteen was established. Guelfi realized that she did not have enough trained personnel and opened a School of Educational Formation for the training of teachers. In 1882, in a newspaper item, the *Popular Tribune* expressed its recognition of Methodism's teacher training program: "The educational method used by the Director is at the level of instruction given at the best private educational institutions in Montevideo, and we have observed its examinations. . . . Showing, in general, the natural abilities the young women of our country have for learning, it is remarkable that they do not choose a teaching career which is so needed, committing one or two years to the study of the necessary knowledge, which is easy to acquire with such competent teachers as Miss Guelfi, who has already trained some young people for a teaching career."[28] In this regard, we should note the role that Methodism played in these countries in affirming the education of women and their place in education.

In his 1887 report on WFMS work in Montevideo, Wood, in referring to the Methodist scholastic network and Catholicism's opposition to it, stated that Catholics "fight them not only with all the resources of the clergy" but also with "education, mixing the religious fanaticism with competence." To this end, the tactics of the clergy were to use "Catholic teachers" to "control the families who are interested in the Gospel," and, on the other hand: "fighting the schools by means of other schools, with a well organized system, imitating ours in every possible way. The fact that our schools have merited this type of opposition speaks very eloquently for its growing power."[29]

As a result of Guelfi's premature death in 1886, her brother Antonio Guelfi succeeded her in her duties. The fine example of these schools is recognized in the reports prepared by Dr. Jacobo A. Varela, the national inspector of the Office of Public Education.[30] Through Wood's 1887 report to the WFMS, written the last year of his administration, we know that the Methodist scholastic network in the capital had 980 students registered that year. At the beginning of 1888, the minutes of the annual conferences indicated that in the capital's central area there were five day schools with 501 students registered. In Aguada and other outlying neighborhoods there were 450 students divided among nine schools.[31]

The evangelical schools established a complementary relationship with the state, taking responsibility for the neglected geographic areas, weaving their scholastic network through Montevideo's outlying areas. The priorities were public education at the primary level and the education of women, especially teachers.

The Methodist educational ministry was not limited only to the capital; primary schools were also established in the interior of the country. In many of them, most of the students were children from non-Protestant families. The hope was that their families would follow the evangelical principles, a hope frequently fulfilled. With this purpose, the itinerant preachers were spread throughout the towns of the interior. It is interesting to note how, in the establishment of similar congregations, schools, clubs, or other associations, there was a convergence of those "friends of progress" who represented liberals, Masons, and Protestants, all of them committed under the common banner of anticlericalism. In this sense, for the interior's liberal anti-Catholics, the evangelical schools represented in many cases the only scholastic network able to compete with the education offered by Roman Catholicism.

In 1888, in dealings with the Waldensian Evangelical Church, efforts were made to establish a secondary school and a theological institute. The latter was first established in Colonia Valdense but later on moved to Buenos Aires.[32] From that year on, the WFMS initiated a restructuring of the educational ministry. The death of Cecilia Guelfi, and the withdrawal of Wood from the superintendency and from Uruguay, had left the ministry without its fundamental pillars, so the mission, after the Antonio Guelfi period (1886–1888), named Minnie Hyde as the person in charge of the administration, aided by Mary E. Bowen.[33] In spite of their efforts, the educational network's expansion started to decline, and in 1889 three primary schools were closed.

To our knowledge, noticeable modifications began to take place in the Methodist educational project. In fact, with the change in the superintendency, then under the Reverend Charles W. Drees, and the naming of North American teachers to the administration of the schools, the evangelical schools ceased making the priority an expansive model of mixed public education at the primary level, in order to apply themselves to the establishment of a restricted educational model, separated by sex and with a new emphasis on university education. To this end, the WFMS, in agreement with Drees's opinions, advised the dispersed schools to concentrate on a central establishment, where graduate education could expand to incorporate teacher training for those students who would have reached certain levels in their studies.[34] In 1893, a structural reorganization of the educational ministry occurred: thus the evangelical schools divided into two educational centers, the Evangelical Grammar School for Girls, under the charge of Elizabeth Hewett, and the Evangelical Grammar School for Boys, under the charge of Antonio Guelfi, located on San José Street and Yaguarón. For reasons that will have to be analyzed at another time, the plan for a network of public education was taken to an increasingly elitist area which separated it more and more from Uruguayan culture.

The Scholastic Network and Its Pedagogy

In the Methodist scholastic network, national programs ruled and texts approved by the Office of Public Education were used. The principal distinctions grew from the incorporation of the Bible as a source of ethical-cultural values but emerged in a peculiar constellation of scientific education (geology, astronomy, physics), a renewed historical rereading, an educational training favorable to the emancipation of women, and the impulse of democratic and participatory pedagogical practices.

A high-priority goal of the evangelical schools was to shape the students through education.[35] In this vein, it is necessary to take into account that, for Methodism, education had "to begin with solid religious principles, as it prepares the soul for all virtues."[36] The gospel's function in the task of inculcating religious principles that molded the character was essential, because it constituted: "the most stable and most secure foundation for the prosperity of all peoples."[37] Consuelo Portea, a teacher trained in Cecilia Guelfi's schools, affirmed their ideal of emancipating women, and exhorted other women: "Ah! Let us shake off ignorance, to include these words in our banner . . . 'Learn if you want to be Free.'"[38]

Within the Methodist vision of offering a complete education, a particular emphasis was placed on musical education, an innovative and uncommon aspect in state schools. It was the same with the introduction of physical education, since gymnastics was "healthful, hygienic and advisable for the body."[39] Intellectual learning was not lessened by the emphasis placed on moral and religious values. On the contrary, within the framework of the religious struggle and educational competition established by Catholicism when it put "school against school," *The Evangelist* editorial staff made it clear that the evangelical schools were in tune "with the progressive currents of the century, spreading the knowledge by the most modern methods." For that reason, they struggled to "enlighten minds," because the endeavor was to spread "the light of true science" together with "pure knowledge of the Gospel."[40] Intellectual education did not consider the students to be simple receivers, so for that reason an education based on memorization was not the preferred method.[41] The hope was to establish thought processes and critical analysis. Thus, in 1879, the study program of the Evangelical School for Young Ladies (No. 2), included: "Object Lessons; Readings in Prose and Verse (printed and handwritten); Writing and Drawing; Grammar and Composition; Arithmetic; Geometry; Geography and History of the Republic; Rudiments of Astronomy; Rudiments of Physics; Natural History; Physiology, Hygiene and Gymnastic Exercises; Morality and Religion; Sewing, Sewing Machine Management, Dressmaking and Sewing." Although these last ones were expected in women's education, the emphasis in sciences at a school for women was not frequent in these parts during that period. In addition, special classes were offered in French, English, piano, and singing.[42]

To the extent that Methodism tried to instill individual and egalitarian values in its students, it differed more and more from Catholic education on its political and social point of view. Uruguayan Catholicism had a concept of society and state that was based on Pious IX's integral Catholic thinking, which is expressed in his conception of the world: "The universe constitutes a hierarchy which comes from God, the Mighty King, to the lowest beings. The Mighty One rules and uses the lowest for everything, in the same way that God rules over the world or the soul over the body." This concept explains the social order as an exchange of services for the common good, where each individual performs a function for the benefit of the community. The division of tasks is justified by the need the community has of each one of them. Likewise, this social order was sustained in a political order derived from a hierarchic conception of society. "In general terms, it is the obligation of the governing official to direct the activity of all classes in such a way that men can live a happy and virtuous life, which is the true purpose for man in society."[43] For that reason, every strata of society is subordinated to the other, in hierarchic order; and at the top of the pyramid, the governing official was answerable to God as the ultimate authority.[44]

Conversely, the theological, ethical, and political values of the Methodist pastors and teachers were the ideal liberal contractual thought. For that reason, the theological as well as the educational speech of Río de la Plata's Methodism was opposed to Catholic political and social order. When placed in the national context, this long-lasting controversy updated the controversial speeches and principles that had been used in the European context, from the Reformation in the sixteenth century to the burning disputes with the papacy in 1870. In the educational controversy, the teachers and pastors denounced what they understood constituted a traditional conception, which is corporate, absolutist, and authoritarian, and that opposed the principle of freedom of conscience for the individual.[45] In this vein, the evangelical schools struggled to educate students in the discipline of independent thought; the development of the will and the need to be civic minded and live a life of service. A graduate from the schools of Guillermo Tallon in Durazno said at the beginning of the century: "Educate the people, teach, instill in the child's mind principles, not fantasy, and you will have citizens conscious of their rights and duties. Only then will there be an end to hatred and factions that have darkened with their dark intentions the development of our nationality. Each one learns to respect the rights of others, that the political parties should be parties of ideas and principles and not just traditions. Then, very soon, the concept of democracy will become a beautiful reality."[46]

In this sense it is necessary to consider also the "pastoral" attitude of restraint toward needy children, which involved not only ministers and teachers but also a large group of collaborators and volunteers from within the congregations themselves. This was an element that differentiated them from the state schools. In a political context that systematically restricted participation and leadership in civic life, the policy of the Methodist schools was an effort to define pedagogical routines and practices exercised, understood, and accepted by the diverse actors in the educational process. In this respect, Methodists sought to rediscover functions for the civil society and give rise to a spirit of association in order to generate a new social consensus.

Methodism in the Academic and University Environment

In 1868 the creation of two institutions of far-reaching importance for the Uruguayan culture also occurred: the Society of Friends of Popular Education and the University Club, initiatives where it is necessary to emphasize the participation of prominent Protestant bodies. The polemic regarding the "religious controversy" and anti-Catholicism were considered relevant subjects by the learned generation of *The Literary Magazine*, the publication of the University Club. The club, founded September 1868 with the support of the teaching staff of the University of the Republic, became the first organic society of the university's intellectual movement.[47] Methodism, through Pastor J. F. Thomson and young people like him and Enrique Azarola, tried to get in the anti-Catholic controversy in order to reinforce it. If we consider that it was only three years from the time Thomson began his activities, it was surprising to see how quickly he and others participated in the debate taking place in the most prestigious academic environment of the country, and above all, in a role of leadership in the controversy between rationalism and Catholicism.

The first conferences reveal the predominance of rationalism within

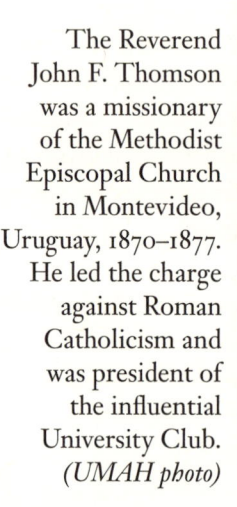

The Reverend John F. Thomson was a missionary of the Methodist Episcopal Church in Montevideo, Uruguay, 1870–1877. He led the charge against Roman Catholicism and was president of the influential University Club. *(UMAH photo)*

the institution. Thus, for example, Carlos M. de Pena did a partial translation of the work of Edgar Quinet, *The Genius of Religions,* and M. Arredondo — active militant of the club — offered a lecture on "Our Moral State and Its Causes." It seems that the lecturer identified moral decay as mainly responsible for the political situation in which the country found itself at that time, because, according to records: "Mr. Pena supported Mr. De María's ideas and fought Mr. Arredondo because the latter considered politics as the cause of our present state, maintaining that Catholicism was the evil that caused our present state and that to combat it, it was necessary to start a religious campaign and to preach Deism."[48]

In general, Methodism agreed with the characterization and the diagnosis, not so with the deistic solution. The "religious controversy" was fundamental in order to find political solutions. Roman Catholicism was the declared enemy of the modern order. Nevertheless, it was not enough to spread the "gospel" of natural religion, it was also necessary to adhere to and proclaim the "true gospel" of revealed religion. This was the discussion behind the opinions stated by both sides on the occasion of the first lecture of a Methodist follower, Azarola. The speech dealt with "Slavery and the Human Conscience," and the reactions from rationalists reveal an effort to debilitate the dissident interpretation while praising its own. In this vein, de Pena stated: "Christianity does not take a stand against slavery and that the destruction of slavery was due to the propaganda from some philosophers of the eighteenth century as well as in art and industry."[49]

Thomson, perfect spokesman for the dissident ideology, intervened in reaction and support of his coreligionist. For him, it was clear that the overcoming of slavery and its mentor, Catholicism, could not be achieved by replacing it with a school of thought which despised the revelation and denied its sacred condition but rather by the proclaiming of Christian doctrine. For that reason, Thomson "fought against Mr. Pena and declared that he considered Christianity as the only religion of divine origin and, therefore, the only true one." On the other hand, a Mr. Arechaga y Carvalho, as well as de Pena, "fought Dr. Thomson and declared themselves in favor of rationalism."[50] This simple debate synthesizes positions that would remain unbending during that time. If indeed there was a basic agreement in identifying Catholicism as their opponent, they still expressed their differences.

The Catholic press, through *The Town's Messenger*, confronted them. "Since the doctrines of E. Quinet, Bilbao, Renan, etc., are given value, we will try to refute them and to pulverize them with brilliant writings by men of stature. . . ."[51] The main ideology referred to by the Catholic church spokesman was the work of M. Guizot, *The European Civilization*, and Juan Donoso Cortés, *Essay on Catholicism, Liberalism and Socialism*. With the appearance of a magazine, *The University Club*, the spiritualist rationalism found one more consistent tool for the anti-Catholic controversy and an instrument for educating its militants.[52]

On the other hand, Protestantism was applauded for its concern for the development of new writings on civilization. In this sense, the University Club weighed the initiative taken by Thomson toward the middle of 1871, supporting the creation of the first evangelical Literary Association.[53] These gestures, which evidence the recognition already attained, were confirmed and strengthened during the last months of 1871. That year, on the occasion of the University Club's elections, Thomson appeared on the two slates of candidates, running on one for the vice presidency, and on the other as a member of the Supervisory Commission. Finally, the latter prevailed, with José P. Varela as president. In 1873, a group of members proposed the Methodist pastor to be the society's president. Thomson dominated the slate headed by Carlos María Ramírez and acceded to the presidency of the club.

In July 1873, a reading was done of an essay written by Juan Gil, an old rationalist who was now a follower of the Methodist Church and who wrote about "The Constitutional Right of the United States of America." During the subsequent debate, Thomson understood other inferences beyond the abundant praise received by the North American model: "Tonight, Mr. Gil teaches us a truth. The reason for the independence of the United States is found in the faithful observance of the precepts of the Christian religion . . . everything is not based on freedom and morality, because their necessary complement is religion."[54]

After these debates, it is necessary to wait until 1876 for the "religious controversy" to awaken again the interest of the intellectuals. In February 1876, Thomson offered a new lecture, "Protestantism and Catholicism as They Relate to the Social Aspects of People's Lives." In it, the dissident religious experience was presented as the fundamental cause of the progress of nations.[55] Between March and June of 1876, the Protestant participation continued growing in leadership within the University Club. Nevertheless, the main controversy had Catholicism as its contender. Later on, the "religious controversy" would be replaced with the educational debate and the first controversies between spiritualist rationalism and positivism.[56]

But it was not only in the theological-philosophical debate and controversy that Methodism became an interested actor in the social and cultural progress. Thomas B. Wood attempted to align Methodist teachers within the framework of the new pedagogy. He was the one who favored the learning and participation of students and supporters in the scientific-literary societies established by the denomination. In this regard, the Literary Club was founded in December 1877, the Christian Club of Montevideo in April 1884, and, under its superintendency, the Christian Club in Trinidad in June 1885, all of these creating space to sponsor a permanent education not limited to the classroom.[57] In disseminating scientific knowledge, Wood did not limit himself to lecturing at conferences; he also took advantage of *The Evangelist*'s pages to popularize among its subscribers the discoveries and advances produced in geology and astronomy.[58] His attitude was marked by the opening of and the search for a renewed relationship between science and faith, although, understandably, this position was not exempt from the scrutiny of the development of scientific advances, especially the Darwinist theory, and their consequences for the Christian faith.[59] For Wood, the sciences had to be accepted for their intrinsic value and in relation to the development of civilization and the republic's material progress. This was a "point of controversy" for the Methodist pastor, the manner in which "sciences . . . are making a powerful contribution to confirm the truth and eliminate what is false in the prevailing ideas about religion." Thus, not only did he welcome the sciences to Río de la Plata, he also gave his commitment to the creation of an appropriate environment to receive them: "As lovers and defenders of the truth, we can do no less than watch with interest the scientific developments which occur among us."[60]

So, without denying its particular place and articulating the testimony of faith by inclusion in the cultural world, Methodism in Río de la Plata, and we would say in all Latin America, demonstrated its understanding of the gospel. It was a dynamic and progressive conception of the faith, open to the reality of the surrounding world and scientific advances, concerned with social issues and committed to the people's well being. It could certainly be criticized, at a distance, for an excessive submission to the North American model and a lack of criticism for its imperialistic consequences. It is also possible to note a certain lack of understanding of the elements of popular culture within which North Americans did their missionary work and to attribute to "Romanism" all the problems encountered by the people of these lands. But it cannot be denied that it reached society with its attitude of service, calling for a vocation of the education of men and women who could contribute a renewed and a liberating vision to society. That is how the Methodist Church grew in this continent, and we believe that vision and task is still valid. Because that is how we learned to give testimony of the redeeming love of God in Christ and the freedom that the Spirit allows us.

Legacy and Meaning

The more-or-less detailed examination of the historical origins of Uruguayan Methodism obliges us to consider other issues. The relationships with the Anglican Church and other ethnic communities are important.

Among them, it is necessary to emphasize the aforementioned relationship with the Waldensian migration, established in Uruguay (although not in Montevideo) around that same time. The interaction between both movements is remarkable, since both churches (Methodist and Waldensian) established bonds from the very beginning. The evolution of these relationships, and the cultural and theological matters involved, allow different interpretations. What is certain is that when the theological educational activity begins during the 1880s, both testimonies coordinate their efforts. The intervention of Wood, along with Daniel Armand Ugon, the Waldensian pastor, was decisive in this sense. The Theological Institute created for both denominations, to which others would soon unite, still exists today at the Evangelical Higher Institute for Theological Studies (Instituto Superior Evangélico de Estudios Teológicos, or ISEDET) in Buenos Aires.

We have not delved into such important subjects as the dissemination of the Bible, the methods of approaching the social issues, or the manner in which the emerging congregations were organized. A total overview of these subjects would demand an effort that surpasses the intention and limits of this essay. On the other hand, more than a century has passed since the last facts we discussed, and things have certainly changed in Uruguayan society, in all Latin America, and in Methodism. Also, it must be noted that, later on, missions of other churches of Wesleyan tradition, as well as other denominations, were established on the continent.[61] The coexistence and interaction with other denominations, in minority communities, and in an often hostile environment brought about very significant theological influences.

However, upon reviewing this history, one has to recognize certain characteristics that have lasted beyond appearances and the manner in which they have developed. These characteristics, which left their mark in the formation of Latin American Methodism and its understanding of mission, include the location and manner of integrating into society, the sense of the missionary project, certain basic theological understandings, the positions taken in view of the cultural options, and collaboration with other evangelical groups, among other things, beyond the modifications that were taking place within the different contexts in Latin America and the different eras.[62]

Congregations and Institutions

An element that reinforces this interpretation is the fact that the Methodist mission understood its task not only as an evangelization aimed at establishing congregations, but rather it originated, whether directly or indirectly, a significant amount of institutions within its circle: schools, cultural clubs, service centers, to list those previously mentioned. In this area, the Methodist Church was most likely a pioneer in Latin America. This dimension was recognized in 1916 in the Missionary Congress in Panamá, where the Methodist model served as inspiration for the efforts of some other denominations in its mission on the continent.

This manner of developing the mission brought about a lot of tension between centripetal and centrifugal tendencies that occurred and continue to occur in the Methodist churches in Latin America. On the one hand, the institutions are understood to be a missionary extension of the church (and in many cases as a tool for evangelization and the securing of members). As such, they are expected to be subordinate to this function. On the other hand, the institutions acquire lives of their own. Their dynamics are molded according to the tasks, aims, and location of insertion in society: a school is a school and must fulfill the guidelines and objectives according to its social function and of the educational field to which it belongs. It is regulated not only by the church but also by the state system. The demands of an educational institution, as far as its economic requirements, qualifications, function, and autonomy of its personnel, etc., are concerned, are not always sensitive to the expectations of the ecclesiastical institutions that create and maintain it at its different levels. The same can be said of other service institutions. We know of no Methodist church in Latin America where this has not been a source of conflict concerning ecclesiastical projects, institutional power, and theological tendencies.

On the other hand, once established, the institutions tend to create their own power bases, acquire inertia to justify themselves, and become corporate forces that separate them from their first mentors. Or, even worse, the church can be used as a place to create institutions that answer to some of its members' personal or sectarian projects. When this happens, and the institutions become autonomous, their institutional vision begins to differ from the mission of the church as a whole, and it becomes more difficult to recognize in them the ecclesiastical projects for which they are answerable.

The Evangelical Popular Schools in Uruguay can be used as an example. Along with the fast growth we have indicated, there was also a rapid decrease of schools during the period immediately following. Why? A possible answer is given by the project itself. These schools were understood to have a supplementary and exemplary function to state public education. That supplementary function became unimportant when the Uruguayan state started fulfilling its function by extending general, mandatory, and free-of-charge basic education, according to the Varelian project, and was reaching all the districts and strata. The evangelical neighborhood schools, now replaced by state schools, concentrated on being establishments with an emphasis on quality education that would serve as an example. But that change in the institutional design brought about changes in the public and in the objectives of the new Methodist schools. For their part, the congregations, to the extent that they maintained themselves, continued to have their roots in the popular class. The schools were transformed into schools that reached a "more refined" sector of the population, losing touch with the sector of their own original membership. This change has caused tension between the educational institution and the church as a faith community that to date has left its own mark on the history of the Evangelical Methodist Church of Uruguay.

But along with the tensions brought about by this reality, it should also be noted how the existence of these institutions creates an area of interaction between the religious community and the civil society. In it, including the tension generated, there is emphasis on the elements of adaptation, and the social and cultural practices (even the legal and economic ones) that the church must assume in its testimonial task. One thing is to see policy from the church pew; another is to see it when the institutions must struggle with state bureaucracies that regulate them, to comply with labor laws with their personnel, etc. It becomes necessary to strike a balance in that the institutions can simultaneously meet the expectations that the church projects on them, as well as the social demands created by their environment.

Evangelical Faithfulness and Social Progressiveness

Another element that stands out in the Uruguayan experience is that the insertion of the Methodist mission in the social and cultural environment (with its clear derivations in the political arena) aligned itself with the sectors that have represented social transformation options and a positive attitude toward the renewal of ideas, science, and the arts. This identification with progressive sectors has been the case especially in those missions that have arisen from the MEC, although that is somewhat debatable in the case of the missions associated with the Methodist Episcopal Church, South.

But to the extent that the Uruguayan experience extends to the subcontinent's other realities, it demonstrates how Methodists are quick to take up the banner of causes supported by the sectors of society more concerned with the problems generated by poverty, lack of education, oligarchic controls, authoritarian regimes, and society's clericalism, restrictions on personal freedom, prejudices of race and gender, and in general all manner of oppression and social inequity. This does not mean that it has become a "popular" church. On the contrary, its requirements of militant attitudes, its creation of a critical conscience, and even style of worship—which we have not examined here—where a rational attitude and certain controversial rationality predominated, ended up appealing more to rising sectors of the working class and to the middle class. These qualities appealed more to the middle class than to those who are imbedded in the popular culture and are swayed more by the world of symbols that appeal to the emotions, to polysemic images, and to a certain syncretism which allowed the survival of traditions of persecution that the anti-Romanism of the first missions could not or did not know how to discern.

During subsequent years, this tension with the culture turned into the participation of pastors and Methodist communities in support of lay education, of union struggles, confrontation with dictatorships, movements of social liberation, organizations in defense of human rights, the vindication of indigenous people, and equality for women. These elements can be traced to almost all the Methodist churches of Latin America throughout the twentieth century. These involvements certainly generated internal controversies and certain divisions that, nevertheless, rarely became total breaks, although they often did result in clear internal divisions and very harsh confrontations. Occasionally, there was some exodus of some community leaders, but it can be said in general terms that the churches as such and the congregations remained united around their pastors and lay leaders who expressed the positions that were considered "forward-thinking."

Bishop Frederico Pagura is one of many Methodist leaders from the Southern Cone who protested against political repression there and who have also been leaders in the World Council of Churches. *(Photo © Peter Williams for the World Council of Churches)*

So it is this "ideological progressiveness," to give it a name, that provided the opportunity for the style in which the testimonial of faith was shared. As in those initial controversies, we are attempting to show that it is not necessary to renounce the faith in order to support the affirmations that have to do with liberation and justice. On the contrary, it can be the strongest support and foundation of lives dedicated to a testimonial task that demonstrates the social projection of the deepest evangelical affirmations.

A Theology Receptive of the Social Reality

This tendency can also be verified at the theological level. The political liberalism reflected in the Uruguayan case shows its affinity with the theological liberalism of the second half of the nineteenth century. In all South American Methodism there is a strong influence of the Masonic lodges. Their presence was felt in Methodism even beyond 1950. However, the contribution of the tendencies of the Social Gospel was also significant. At that time, the Barthian revision entered the continental Methodist leadership and allowed among us a break with liberalism, and it reinforced the participation of Christians in the civil society. In that regard, the Methodist churches in Latin America were, in general, an entry for a new theological trend. Let us also not forget the participation of related Methodists (along with Catholics and Presbyterians, the latter mainly in Brazil) in the emergence of the pastoral and theological options that brought the movement known as Liberation Theology to our continent.

Again, although we cannot ignore the fact that these theological concepts inform the church's internal elite much more than they do its members at large, it can be said in general terms (here we do find noticeable exceptions, as in the cases of Costa Rica and México), that the congregations have accompanied and supported their leaders who expressed themselves with these options. In the particular case of Uruguay, this has been especially significant. The Evangelical Methodist Church of Uruguay, as a result of the social and political commitments made by most of its pastors and many lay leaders, had to see a significant part of its more active members undergo persecution, jail, torture, banishment, and temporary or definitive exile during the last military dictatorship. This persecution was a significant blow to a church that already suffered from a lack of members. This pressure created a demand for a concerted effort to keep its testimony alive for those who could remain active in the country.

The inclusion of women in pastoral functions in the denomination began without great controversies, with no other resistance than the "machismo" in our culture. Female inclusiveness was, as it is everywhere, a slow process that went through various stages which we cannot discuss here. Without denying the decisive role played then and now by female theologians, pastors, and lay leaders in a process of female self-affirmation, it can be stated that, comparatively, the Methodist church in Latin America was more receptive to this process than most of the Christian churches in the continent and secular society itself. Another important point is the legacy left by the women who were pioneers at the beginning of the Methodist mission who raised the banner for equal rights for women. Nevertheless, it is probably on this subject where it is possible to show the greatest distance between leadership and congregations. Although at the structural and leadership level the female ministry in the Methodist churches of Latin America is not a controversial subject, a certain resistance to have "female pastors" still exists in many congregations. The prejudices come more from the cultural environment and social mores than from strictly theological reasons. In fact, the Evangelical Methodist Church of Uruguay has been the first in Latin America to ordain a woman, and has had women as presiding officers on several occasions (as it has today), even laywomen. (The Evangelical Methodist Church of Uruguay has not had an episcopal office since it became autonomous.)

In the biblical interpretation, the historical-critical trends enjoyed a mutual relationship with the physical, historical, and linguistic sciences; they were generally accepted in the theological formation of Methodists in Latin America. Later on, there were other trends on hermeneutic renewal. And although there are historical episodes where the presence of fundamentalist tendencies and the controversies that these unleashed can be seen, in the end, they have not been strictly imposed in any Methodist church. However, the indirect influence of other denominations cannot be missed, especially the influence these churches had on a very broad sector of evangelists in Latin America (and also some missionaries who joined in), the dispensational scheme and specifically Scofield's Annotated Bible. This vision subtly permeated certain interpretations and theological positions, which, without disclosing their particular origin, took this line as "the evangelical theology." The continent's Methodist churches have not been immune to these influences (neither have the immigrant churches). Nevertheless, it is necessary again to indicate that the established tradition of an open reading of the Scripture as practiced by Methodism since its missionary origins and the inclination to confront in a creative manner both revelation and science have prevented the bringing forth of exclusionary doctrinal positions in the denomination.

A detailed history will have to contemplate the subject of popular religiosity in Latin America, a very powerful and ambiguous phenomenon in our reality. Perhaps the closest to this is the Pentecostal/charismatic influence in Latin American Methodism. Since our study of its origins is limited to the nineteenth century, this element had not yet come into play. It will be in Chile, another country in the area of the Southern Cone, where the first Pentecostal expressions occur in the South American Methodist mission. This development brings about the first schism, with the creation of the Pentecostal Methodist Church of Chile. Curiously, it will be North American missionaries in Valparaiso, during the first years of the twentieth century, who are present at the beginning of this experience. Whoever visits the Methodist churches in Latin America today will see that there is quite a great diversity in the style, manner, and degree to which this expression of faith has had an impact on its members. Practices vary from sectors with a clear rejection of all styles related to this tendency (a minority), going through various degrees of integration of charismatic expressions by way of songs, prayers, and other spiritual expressions, to countries where the charismatic impact has been overwhelming and has threatened to divide the church. In some cases, the charismatic impact has modified the theological agenda of the Methodist churches, making several of these elements we have mentioned barely identifiable. But that does not mean they are not present one way or another and can possibly resurface, once the conflicts posed have been worked out, inasmuch as the churches continue maintaining a certain unity and internal dialogue.

In this way it is possible to see how, in the heritage received from the beginnings of missionary work, guidelines have been set that, because of changes according to time and events, continue marking the existence of this tendency to combine the testimony of faith in Christ with current social problems during each era and each reality. The appearance of an indigenous theology in the Methodist churches in the Andean zone is another example of this outreach. The incorporation of a whole new hymnology with songs whose music and lyrics reflect the native forms, the formulation of local creeds and liturgies, tied to ecumenical celebrations which accompany the Methodist participation in popular struggles, etc., reflects a different and probably unforeseen development by those first Methodists, and yet it is the fruit from seeds unconsciously planted by them.

An Intellectualism with Ecumenical Perspective

The manner and degree of participation of those pastors in the debates of their time, the groups of learned lay people created around them, the influence they had on their society, did not die with that first generation. The Methodist church in Latin America continued generating a leadership from within that was highly qualified in its theological formation, as well as theologically prepared lay people who became well known in the professional arena, especially at the university level. This characteristic of the Methodist mission was also shared by some other denominations that started immersing themselves in the Latin American reality, so it became an ecumenical undertaking. Thus, organizations took root with their own characteristics, such as Latin American Union of Evangelical Youth (Unión Latinoamericana de Juventudes Evangélicas, or ULAJE, "Ecumenists" as of 1970), and the Christian Student Movement (Movimiento Estudiantil Cristiano, or MEC). It is possible to see, when studying the origin and development of these movements, the broad participation of Methodist intellectuals in them. The same can be said of all the ecumenical movement in Latin America to date.

But this contribution of Methodism to the secular and ecclesiastic intellectual world remained not only within the narrow confines of the circle of the most compatible churches. Just as we have indicated that certain dispensationalist tendencies and fundamentalism have had an impact on Methodist communities, even if only collaterally, it is also possible to indicate how the Methodist church and many of its leaders became necessary resources for the entire evangelical world. The education of its pastors and the initiatives presented to the state, its support for the participation of the laity in society, and the historical coherence in their fundamental positions, have made them go beyond being, from the numerical point of view, a denomination of comparatively little development. It has given it a certain recognizable image valued by other evangelical groups, even if, for other reasons, their relationship is somewhat distant.

This consequence of the educational and cultural emphasis that Methodism had in its beginning in the continent is not separate from what we can call a broader ecumenism that includes all of society. The contribution of this thinking, which showed that it is possible to be intellectually solid and consistent in the faith while keeping current, had certain social repercussions. Social leaders who do not adhere to the gospel nevertheless recognize the influence that the education received in Methodist institutions, or the testimony of faith followed by Methodist organizations and believers, has had in their life and vision of society. The emphasis placed on developing a "good citizen," beyond its North American liberal coloring, showed a consciousness of the social responsibility that Latin American Methodism has generally preserved. In societies that have encountered a high degree of disintegration, as is happening in the continent now, it is an inheritance that cannot be squandered.

Perspective and Conclusion

It is not an acceptable excuse to say that "we are few but good." Yet we feel gratitude for those that preceded us in faith and left us such a significant legacy. It is, simultaneously, the awareness that, thanks to this past, we have a contribution to offer the connection. We have a responsibility to other brothers and sisters who have made their own contribution. It is to discover that what we have received and the projected future of the mission to answer the call of God in Christ is still valid today.

The Methodist churches in Latin America can find in these beginnings a source from which they can recreate their mission. For that, they can contribute the elements we have indicated in this essay: (a) the need to recognize each congregation's individual area and the service institutions working with them, the creative processing of tensions this generates, yet at the same time the meaning of social participation and evangelization the congregations have; (b) the possibility of maintaining the unity between evangelical fidelity and social progress, as a form of testimony in tune with the difficult times they face; (c) a theology which is receptive to reality, that helps people know how to think in order to face the new social and ethical challenges, where the tendencies to take refuge in theologies of evasion and neoconservatism end up justifying social exclusion or making the Christian message irrelevant; and (d) an intellectualism with an ecumenical vocation, which instead of becoming arrogant with its gains in order to differentiate itself from other ways to express faith, or to isolate itself critically from "Populism," accepts the idea of the church as one body, overcoming denominationalism and collaborating, with the specific talents and contributions of others, for the growth of the whole body of Christ.

Certain characteristics and institutions that came to our America with the growth of Latin American Methodism have not lost their applicability and can be revitalized. We thus consider the pertinence of evangelization through the congregational task with the aid of educational institutions and of service, where they have an auxiliary and exemplary role. Together with the Sunday school (and its extension into neighborhood mission work), these ministries occupy a place of distinction. These ministries continue to offer a workable scheme, especially at this time in which we face an uncontrolled urbanization of our continent.

But there is a significant place in the future for a function containing a gospel sensitive to human dignity, which is threatened by the new globalist oligarchies and the idolatry of the total market with its counterpart in the world of hegemonic financial power. In that sense, there is a need to recover the opportunity for citizens' power, the ethical sense to face the crisis generated by this late capitalism. This situation is also a theological setting which can serve to make the Wesleyan message handed down to us valid in today's world. A task that cannot be avoided is to give emphasis to the education of both pastors and laity, to have a creative answer to the multiple challenges presented by modernism and postmodernism, in that way helping other evangelical brothers and sisters with lesser opportunities and fewer intellectual traditions, so they can confront their problems. Today, the challenges of a new symbolism created from the computer science centers require a critical reading based on evangelical faith. It is not a manner of joining in defending a conservative traditionalism. But if the idea is to insert oneself in the cultural world and to find creative ways to symbolic building in agreement with a distinctively globalist world, let them be carriers of humanist options, messages of hope and justice that bring hope to the weak, to the marginalized. It is part of our heritage.

It is not up to us to develop the forms that this could take in each particular context, the priorities which could be set, or the transformations that this heritage should receive to become viable and useful in each specific situation. And certainly it is made clear in our own presentation that there are forms and attitudes which have imposed conditions on the Methodist mission and have restricted its area of service. With the passing of time, other Christian groups have corrected those defects, in their own way, and have filled those gaps. Now it is not a matter of recovering that time in a confrontational manner, to recreate the mission from its very beginnings, or to supply from the denomination the varied and multifaceted wealth that the Spirit of God has given and distributed to God's church. It is a matter of assuming our own role, which has been defined historically in time, in location, and by our own idiosyncrasies and theological tendencies, and to use it positively to do justice to the Word of God.

CHAPTER 7

Christian Mission in a Religiously Pluralistic Society
Sudarshana Devadhar

NEARLY TWENTY YEARS ago, a pastor invited a Hindu doctoral student, Nidhi (not his real name), to attend a missions dinner at a United Methodist Church. At that dinner, a missionary speaker challenged the congregation by saying that people do not have to go to faraway places to carry out missions; instead, they can go to neighboring universities to convert all non-Christians to Christianity. The Hindu student was angered by this comment. As much as he loved the pastor who had invited him to the dinner and respected the Christian institution where he had received his college education in India, he felt that it was wrong to use people of other faiths as objects of a Christian triumphalism. "Christian missionaries need to know that we, too, participate in doing God's will on this earth. We, too, believe that we will go to *Svargaloka* (Heaven) as Hindus," he said.

Three years ago in a different city in the same state, a Hindu young adult, whom I will call Sheela, was invited to attend a church by one of her friends. After attending the church for a few months and having been inspired by the Christian message and the love of the congregation, she decided to accept Jesus Christ as her Lord and Savior and took Christian baptism.

These incidents both took place in the United States in a state which may be called a bastion of United Methodism. They give a clear glimpse of Christian mission, though, as seen by people of other faiths. These attitudes in mission have existed for the last two thousand years, particularly during the years of great missionary expansion. Undoubtedly, the former

Christian Mission in the Third Millennium

In the United States, it is no longer unusual to find the spire of a Buddhist temple near a Christian church, like this scene from Santa Fe, New Mexico. In 2003, Santa Fe had more Buddhist centers than Baptist churches. *(Photo by Charles Cole)*

incident portrays the crusading attitude of Christian mission and the latter demonstrates the servant style of Christian mission.

Today there are increasing numbers of non-Christians in the U.S. Every city of any size, and many small towns, have a presence of a non-Christian community. According to one source, there are nearly 780,000 Buddhists, 1,285,000 Hindus, and 3,332,000 Muslims in the U.S. To these figures must be added a number of Jains, Sikhs, adherents of Native American religion and indigenous religions of other countries, Taoists, Confucianists, Jehovah's Witnesses, new age religionists, and of course, Jews.[1]

How can we be faithful to our call of making disciples for Jesus Christ without being offensive to our neighbors of other faiths? How do we invite the people of other faiths to participate in God's mission while we live in harmony with them? How do we reconcile the claims of our neighbors of other faiths that Jesus is a lord among lords, instead of "the Lord"? How can we participate in the extension work of the reign of God on this earth with our Native American friends, when there is deep pain among them, a pain caused in the name of the church? What should be the mission of the church in this millennium when Hindu temples, Jewish synagogues, Sikh gurudwaras, and Muslim mosques are found not only in our major cities but also in our villages? Is Christian mission a call to extend the Christian churches by extinguishing the religious centers of other faiths? What should be the heart and soul of the Christian mission in the religiously pluralistic world where we live?

The above questions challenge us to rethink our Christian mission in the third millennium. This is by no means a denial of all the wonderful deeds done in the name of missions in the past twenty centuries. If not for Christian mission, the ancestors of this author would not have become Christians. Performing missions in the context of the "Wesleyan quadrilateral" calls us, however, to affirm the good, correct the bad, and hope for the best.[2] Also, the scope of this article is limited to the rethinking of mission in relation to the growing number of people of other faiths in this country. Furthermore, this article is not at all intended to be an academic discourse but an attempt to offer practical signposts for clergy and laity as we lead our lives as children of God bearing the name "Christians" in the midst of all the other children of God who call themselves by different names. This paper is only a bird's-eye view of what is happening or what needs to happen in the third millennium, not a detailed sketch of all the discussions taking place in this arena. I hope these comments may serve as a tool to start discussions among people interested in this area. The rethinking of Christian mission in the new millennium, particularly in relation to people of other faiths, needs to take place primarily in three areas: (1) self-understanding of mission; (2) practice of mission; and (3) models of mission.

Self-Understanding of Mission

Self-understanding of mission needs to take place in relation to the understanding of Scripture, theology, Christian education, and pastoral care.

Scripture

If a survey were taken across our churches asking people why they would like to be involved in mission, undoubtedly the overwhelming majority would say it is out of their faithfulness and obedience to the Great Commission. Naturally, it would be ideal to start rethinking our mission by looking at the Great Commission as indicated in Matthew 28:19-20: "'Go therefore and make disciples of all nations, baptizing them in the name of the Father and of the Son and of the Holy Spirit, and teaching them to obey everything that I have commanded you. And remember, I am with you always, to the end of the age.'"

In rethinking our mission in relation to the self-understanding of the Great Commission, it would not be an exaggeration to say that many times, in the history of Christian mission, the Great Commission has not been taken in its totality. In our urgency and excitement to make disciples for Jesus Christ, we have failed to give any attention to the words, "Go therefore." In the original Greek, the word for "Go therefore," *poreuthentes*, literally means "to depart, to leave, to cross the boundaries." What it tells us is that before we start sharing the good news of Jesus Christ with anyone, we need to make an attempt to cross all our selfish, sociological, theological, cultural, racial, and mental boundaries. We need to have the mind and spirit of Christ. It is only when we have the self-emptying spirit of Jesus Christ in our mission that we will become effective disciples of Jesus Christ. Students like Nidhi will not have a problem with churches making disciples of Jesus Christ. They will have a problem, however, when an attempt is made to proclaim the gospel to them with a crusading mentality without understanding them. People like Nidhi do not want to be mere statistics in our missions; they want the church to know they are people with real names and identities. Naturally, they want to be understood before we reach out to them. Surely this is how Christ shared the good news with others.

To cite an example or two, in Christ's attempt to reach out to Zacchaeus (Luke 19:1-10), he not only called Zacchaeus by his first name, but he also made an attempt to share a meal with him. In that cultural setting, by sharing a meal with him, Jesus crossed cultural and sociological boundaries in order to reach out to Zaccheaus. In the story of the Samaritan woman (John 4:1–30), Jesus crossed the boundaries laid down by society in reaching out to her and asking for a drink before he helped her find salvation and become an evangelist for him.

Additionally, as we rethink our mission in the context of the religiously pluralistic world, we are also challenged to consider other texts in the Bible in addition to the Great Commission. These are texts such as the Nazareth manifesto of Jesus in Luke 4:16-19; Jesus' prayer for unity in John 17; and the Great Commandment: "'I give you a new commandment, that you love one another. Just as I have loved you, you also should love

Muslims pray at a 1 P.M. service at the Islamic Center of Southern California in Los Angeles. Many Muslims pray during the day not only in mosques and centers like this but also at work and in other public places where they happen to be. *(UMNS photo by Mike DuBose)*

one another'" (John 13:34). Can we carry out a mission based on only one text while overlooking the others, or do we need to take the words of Jesus in their totality? We need to take these questions into consideration as we proclaim the good news of Jesus to the people of other faiths, lest we repeat the mistakes of the past, mistakes which created animosity instead of harmony between Christians and people of other faiths.

Furthermore, Paul, in his attempt to share the good news with others, understood the people very clearly. Although these scriptural passages abound, the one that comes to mind immediately is 1 Corinthians 1:23, where Paul writes, "but we proclaim Christ crucified, a stumbling block to Jews and foolishness to Gentiles." Today, some of the neighbors of other faiths, particularly Hindus and Buddhists, do not see the cross as "foolishness." As a matter of fact, a prominent Hindu laureate, Manjeshwar Govinda Pai, who was touched by the crucifixion experience of Jesus, has written a powerful poem, "Golgotha," on this subject. What they do see as a foolishness is the Resurrection. This is where we need to reach out to them and ask them not only why the Resurrection is a problem to them but also need to explain to them the significance of the Resurrection. For a meaningful dialogue to take place in this arena, first we need to reach out to them, gain their trust, and be in conversation with them to help them understand the mystery and the power of the Resurrection. Jesus promised to be with us until the end of the age in our Christian mission, or as the writer of Hebrews reminds us, "Jesus Christ is the same yesterday and today and forever" (Hebrews 13:8). Christ challenges us to understand the people to whom we proclaim the gospel before we preach the gospel.

Additionally, self-understanding of the Scriptures is also of vital importance, particularly when we are involved with people of other faiths in relation to evangelism. Some of the people of other faiths who are well grounded in biblical knowledge challenge Christian missionary work by saying even Jesus Christ himself was inclusive, particularly when he said, "'I am the way, and the truth, and the life'" (John 14:6). Scholars of other faiths insist that Jesus did not say, "I am the only way, and the only truth, and the only life." It is very clear that obviously they leave behind the second part of this Johannine verse: "'No one comes to the Father except through me'" (John 14:6). Here we need to have serious Bible study and reflection with Hindus and Buddhists. The Hindu scholars challenge us with the fact that Jesus said, "'In my Father's house there are many dwelling places. If it were not so, would I have told you that I go to prepare a place for you? And if I go and prepare a place for you, I will come again and will take you to myself, so that where I am, there you may be also'" (John 14:2-3). Can it be overlooked that God used the Magi, the Zoroastrians, in the work of the reign of God on this earth? Would there have been a Christian mission today if the Magi had obeyed the directions and gone back to Herod to report all about the newborn baby Jesus?

Theology

Our self-understanding of theology is very important as we deal with Christian mission in the new millennium. Broadly speaking, the global church is divided between the camps of the ecumenicals and the evangelicals in terms of mission. Ecumenicals draw their insights from the World Council of Churches and its affiliated bodies, whereas evangelicals draw their insights from the Lausanne Covenant Document prepared by the 1974 Lausanne Congress on Evangelism and its affiliated bodies. One of the most important things that needs to be done in our mission in the new millennium is to hold a conversation between the members of these two camps so that there may be a common theological understanding of mission.

Any conceptualization of the theology of mission in the new millennium should be built upon a very strong trinitarian formula. One needs to be very clear that our mission is the mission of God, as introduced, modeled, and commissioned by Jesus, and achieved and directed under the direction of the Holy Spirit.

If one is willing to accept this understanding of mission, he/she also needs to raise some theological questions on either the topics or the issues connected with mission. These questions have been raised by Christians and peoples of other faiths as well. One needs to be very clear: Jesus' mission cannot be seen in isolation but must be viewed in the context of the entire biblical history.

First, is mission *theocentric* or *ecclesiocentric*? Theocentric mission is centered on God, and ecclesiocentric mission is centered upon church. Theocentric mission calls for a mission which is truly about participating in the extension work of the reign of God, whereas ecclesiocentric mission is about extending the church and extinguishing the other religious groups which are also involved in the mission of God. Theocentric mission is interested in the quality of mission, whereas ecclesiocentric mission is interested in numbers. Ecclesiocentric mission is interested in maintaining buildings with beautiful stained glass windows and beautiful fountains and fences around the church to keep away the unwanted people. Theocentric mission is centered upon God and God's saving grace revealed through biblical history, the mission of Jesus and that of his apostles. It constantly asks the question, "What can we do to transform the lives of the people around us and around the globe?" In carrying out its mission, theocentric mission invites people of other faiths to join hands with Christians. It does not matter whether the volunteers are Native Americans, Hindus, Muslims, Sikhs, or Jews.

The final question is: "Are we fulfilling the mission of God as modeled by Jesus and guided by the Holy Spirit?" This model is working well in some places in the world. There is a church in one of the cities of the northeastern part of the U.S. where Christians and members of a very strong Hindu group join other children of God, flipping hamburgers side by side in preparing meals for the hungry. At an ecumenical church agency in another city of the world, a Hindu and a Muslim stand side by side telling a group of youth and youth leaders from a church all about the mission of God and why they are working for this Christian agency. The answer is simple: to participate in the extension work of the reign of God on this earth.

This raises a question: Is mission the monopoly of Christians, or can other children of God, from other faith communities as well, participate in it? The prayer that is used by Christians across the globe which can also be said without any offense by Hindus, Sikhs, and Muslims is the Lord's Prayer, as taught by Jesus. This is a prayer people can say without using the name of Jesus. When Jesus' ministry and mission was so theocentric, why not ours in the new millennium?

Second, who is the model for our Christian mission? Is it Jesus, his ministry, passion, death, and Resurrection? Or is it a model interpreted by various Christian missionary groups? One needs to be very clear. Jesus' mission cannot be seen in isolation; one needs to place it in the context of the mission of God, the mission of the Holy Spirit. Mission needs to be built upon a truly biblical vision.

Third, what is one's understanding of the role of the Holy Spirit in our mission? Can Christians claim and curtail the work of the Holy Spirit only to and in the Christian domain? Can one truly believe the work of the Holy Spirit outside the Christian church and in all of God's creation? If one truly understands Jesus' promise of the Holy Spirit as outlined in John 14:15-31, one is very clear that the direction and guidance and dependence of the Holy Spirit are crucial in the work of Christian mission. Was not the Holy Spirit in the life of Mahatma Gandhi? Is it not true that if one reads Jesus Christ's Sermon on the Mount after watching the movie *Gandhi*, he/she sees the imprints of Christ's sermon very clearly in that movie? No one has given a better tribute to Gandhi than Pope John Paul II, who said that Christians could learn from Gandhi and that the pope also learned a lot from him.

Fourth, in the new millennium, the church has to deal with the question of conversion and baptism. Does conversion mean change of heart and mind, turning away from sin and turning toward God, or is it a change of religion? Does baptism call for acceptance of Jesus Christ as the Lord and Savior of one's own life, or does it also call for a change of name, giving up of one's own relatives, and living outside one's own community? People like Nidhi, who were raised in countries like India through their high school and college days, understand and support Jesus as a lord among lords; however, they have great difficulty in understanding Christian baptism. One reason is Nidhi's reaction to how baptisms were conducted in countries such as his. In his country, whenever someone was baptized, that person was stripped of all of his or her identity. He or she was given a new name (Krishna was changed to John, Kaveri was changed to Mary, for example), immediately taken out of the family, and placed in a separate area known as a mission compound. In many circumstances, mission compounds had solid walls built around them, with many houses, and a church and school within the compound. They were completely off-limits to people of other faiths, including the relatives of those who were baptized and placed in that compound.

This kind of attitude not only made Christians enemies of people of other faiths but also gave the wrong interpretation of Christian baptism. Sheela, who took baptism in the U.S., still maintains her original name, still goes to her house, and still talks and eats with her parents, brother, and sister. As a matter of fact, her brother and sister attended her baptism. Even though her parents were not excited about her baptism in the beginning, they later accepted it and presented her an icon of Jesus and placed it in her room after decorating it. Through this action, they were signaling to their daughter that they accepted her baptism and affirm that Jesus is one of the lords. Native Americans were in this country long before Columbus arrived in America, and most of the people of other faiths came to the U.S. as immigrants. Almost all of them have had exposure to Christianity in some form or other and they have a very clear understanding of what happened in the past in the history of Christian mission. In some cases, they painfully identify Christian missionaries with colonizers. Therefore, it is very important for the church to grapple with the issue of conversion and baptism. Is it acceptable for one to be a follower of Jesus Christ without taking Christian baptism? Is it possible for someone to be saved without being baptized? How would the church answer the question raised by the people of other faiths, "Is it not true that a thief on the side of Jesus (Luke 23:43) might have been assured a place in paradise without having been baptized?" Or how would the church reconcile the fact that there are a lot of "anonymous Christians" (in a phrase coined by theologian Karl Rahner) or "silent Christians" (as some others have called them) whose actions and deeds demonstrate clearly their Christian witness yet who have not been baptized? Any mission in the new millennium needs to have a fresh look at our understanding of conversion and baptism and needs to address some of the theological issues around them in order to be effective.

Christian Education

As indicated in the previous pages, our knowledge of Christian Scriptures and theology plays a vital role in our self-understanding of mission. One of the areas where it can be stressed very clearly is in the area of Christian education. Nearly 40 percent of the global population is under the age of nineteen. A key factor about this generation is that it is the internet generation and is constantly exposed to the teachings of other religions. When asked, most young people express an interest in spirituality and hate people placing labels on others. They also have friends and classmates whose faith practices are different from theirs. Therefore, our Christian education programs have to make room for learning about people of other faiths in order to prepare these youth for a mission of the church. It is very interesting that the people of other faiths, particularly Hindus, have started Sunday schools for their children to educate them not only about their religion but also about dealing with other cultures and people of other faiths. People of other faiths celebrate Christmas, for example. Not all cities and villages can have access to learning centers such as these, but in the cities where it is possible, it is wonderful to have interaction among various religious educational programs.

There are prayers and poems composed by people of other faiths which can also be said by Christians without diluting their faith. There are issues which are of vital interest to the global community which can be addressed by Christians and people of other faiths, which of course definitely fall under the agenda of God's mission.

A village church in the U.S. invited a practicing Jew who had a New Testament degree from an Ivy League university to conduct a Bible study in its adult Sunday school class. At the end of the series, the comments by some of the members of the class included, "We truly got a new perspective of the Scripture." On a sadder note, when a practicing Buddhist entered one of the local banks, a teller apparently made the comment, "Aren't you too early for Hallowe'en?" Apparently, this bank teller had not seen a Buddhist monk in his attire before. And when one of the major news networks televised a program on the Kumbh Mela, nearly 30 million Hindu pilgrims were televised taking part in a ritual bath at the confluence of the Ganges and Yamuna rivers. Upon seeing this, a respectable Christian made the comment to others, "Yukky!" Even though this person made a comment totally out of ignorance and without really understanding the significance of it, he was also making a comment that could easily have hurt a person of the other faith. Therefore, Christian education programs have a vital role to play in preparing people for the mission in the new millennium.

Pastoral Care

A district superintendent was meeting with a staff/pastor parish relations committee as part of the consultation of the appointment of a new pastor. In the middle of the consultation, a member of the committee asked the district superintendent, "I am a Christian. My husband is a Parsi. Does this pastor respect the people of other faiths and understand them as well?"

Comments like this compel us to say that we not only need to have pastors who are compassionate to people of other faiths but who understand them as well. Important in this area is the understanding of rituals. One question is: How would a Christian pastor participate in a Christian-Buddhist wedding or a Hindu-Christian funeral? When the only daughter of a parishioner decides to marry a devout Muslim and as a result has to convert to Islam, how would a pastor counsel this family? How would a pastor react in a situation when he/she is approached by a parishioner who wants a Hindu priest to participate with the Christian minister in a Hindu-Christian marriage? Can all pastors deliver a homily at a Hindu-Christian wedding, quoting both Christian and Hindu sources without compromising the Christian gospel? In the new millennium, Christian communities are challenged to answer these kinds of cutting-edge questions as we perform our mission. Are our seminaries preparing pastors in these areas? This is a serious question that needs to be answered.

Even though these may sound like pastoral concerns rather than mission issues, the very nature of the issues places pastors within the larger framework of Christian mission. Pastors are also being called upon more and more to say a prayer in ecumenical settings, where the participants are from all faiths. Is it acceptable for a Christian pastor to say a prayer composed by people of other faiths? Recently, a Christian pastor said a prayer composed by a Hindu at a particular function. A devout Christian who was at this gathering did not see any problem in that prayer. Another did.

What is the answer? Can one use a prayer composed by a person of another faith in a Christian setting?

Practice of Mission

Based upon our history, and in an attempt to offer a responsible Christian approach to people of other faiths, consider the following proposed guidelines for the practice of mission in the new millennium.

First of all, as Christians and as United Methodists, we need to have a strong missional understanding, based upon the Wesleyan quadrilateral: Scripture, tradition, reason, and experience. The writer would like to proceed in this area without explaining what these are but will indicate why they need to be linked to any meaningful mission in the new millennium, particularly in relation to the people other faiths.

Scripture lays a solid foundation, linking us to a mission of God our Creator, Jesus Christ our Redeemer, and the Holy Spirit our Sustainer. Additionally, Scripture gives various models for our Christian mission in the new millennium. Though one can use all of them, the one which is particularly appealing in the post-Christian era, the one in which we live, is a model based on the Acts of the Apostles. This style may be of great help to us because the atmosphere in which post-Christian churches find themselves is similar to the atmosphere of the Christian communities found in the early days of Christianity.

The church in its ministry and mission has in the past incorporated traditions outside the Christian faith, as long as these traditions have been successfully judged and scrutinized by a scriptural base. Many times, traditions help us to rediscover our biblical witness. For any meaningful communication of the Christian gospel in the new millennium, other faith traditions have to be seriously incorporated into our mission as long as these traditions are judged in relation to the Christian gospel before they are incorporated.

Our experience, particularly in the area of Christian witness, ministry, and mission, helps us not only to understand the nature of God's forgiveness, grace, and power but also helps us to prepare for future ministry and mission. One of the understandings of grace, as explicated by John Wesley, is that prevenient grace will help us as we collaborate with people of other faiths in our mission.

Reason has to play a vital role in anything we do in the area of Christian mission. With reason we need to read and reinterpret our Christian Scriptures and reflect on our Christian witness. As we perform our mission in the midst of people of other faiths, we need constantly to ask the question: Should our mission in this new millennium be only a proclamation of the saving knowledge of Jesus Christ, or should it include the saving action of Jesus Christ in the wholeness of life as well?

Second, mission needs to be carried out in the spirit of a servant rather than that of a crusader. For any mission to become powerful, God has to be glorified, Christ has to be affirmed, and the Holy Spirit needs to be acknowledged. The only way to fulfill this is by performing the mission with a spirit of Christian servanthood. Partners in mission need to understand that all are the children of God, created equally by God, and all are searching for the true manna from God. When one participates in the mission with a spirit of a Christian servant, he or she is aware of the fact that our mission is *with* people of other faiths, not just a mission *to* people of other faiths.

Third, a true mission cannot take place unless all involved in the mission are identified. As much as the writer is reluctant to borrow from a secular model, one has to acknowledge that no franchise would survive unless it knows the needs of its clientele. Likewise, any mission in the new millennium needs to identify the people before they are invited to participate in the mission of God. Some common questions about the people of other faiths include: What is their history? Where do they come from? What is the vocabulary they use? What are the phrases and terminologies they use in their conversation? What do they mean in that particular context? In the past, missionaries were successful in reaching out to people of other faiths when missionaries had identified themselves with those people before they preached the gospel to them. In situations such as this, they were not only successful in reaching out to the people but were also well received and appreciated.

Fourth, any mission in the third millennium has to be a boundary-free mission. All the boundaries, whether they are sociological, cultural, racial, or religious, have to be crossed in order to reach out to others. One of the ways to cross boundaries is through dialogue. Even though the word "dialogue" may have been overused during the last forty years of ecumenical discussions, we still need to use it because of its early Christian use. Even Paul used it in his missionary work. Scholars like Stanley Samartha argue that dialogue should not be used as a tool for Christian mission. Even though one may not disagree with that assumption, one should accept the fact that dialogue would open an opportunity to challenge another to become involved in the extension work of the reign of God. Even though the discussions around dialogue have gone through various stages of interpretation in scholarly circles, one of the best understandings of dialogues comes from Thomas Thangaraj:

> The Roman Catholic document "Dialogue and Proclamation" lists four types of dialogue.
> (a) The *dialogue of life*, where people strive to live in an open and neighborly spirit, sharing their joys and sorrows, their human problems and preoccupations.
> (b) The *dialogue of action*, in which Christians and others collaborate for the integral development and liberation of people.
> (c) The *dialogue of theological exchange*, where specialists seek to deepen their understanding of their respective religious heritages, and to appreciate each other's spiritual values.
> (d) The *dialogue of religious experience*, where persons, rooted in their own religious traditions, share their spiritual riches, for instance with regard to prayer and contemplation, faith and ways of searching for God or the Absolute.[3]

Expounding on these four types of dialogue, Thangaraj argues that such dialogue would encourage solidarity and mutuality, encourage participation in societal-transforming activities like building houses for Habitat for Humanity, deepen the understanding between various faith communities, and encourage participation in the religious practices of others without losing the values of one's own faith.

Fifth, any mission in the new millennium is a ministry of innovation. Challenged and nudged by the Holy Spirit, people involved in mission have to look continuously for innovative ways of performing that mission. If a mission is like a well without an ever-flowing spring, the water of the well becomes stale and unusable. Likewise, any mission in the new millennium has to depend on the Holy Spirit to blow the new winds of Spirit into mission endeavors. It should always listen to the voice of the Holy Spirit and should carry on mission courageously.

One such endeavor that is taking place in The United Methodist Church is in the Northeastern Jurisdiction. Each year the Northeastern Jurisdictional Council on Youth Ministries takes youth to different parts of the world on a "Mission of Peace." Wherever it can be arranged, youth have the chance to visit with and to eat with people of other faiths and to get to know them and understand them. Many times after such exposures, the youth have commented on the gifts of the different children of God and expressed their appreciation for the contributions of each human thread in the tapestry of God. Youth have admired the devotion of the Buddhist monk, the eagerness of the devout Muslim in prayer on the busy streets of a city, and the hospitality of Hindus to strangers. Youth have raised their eyebrows and said: "Why can't we partake in a mission with them without losing our Christian identities?" These young people, the leaders of today's church, have an understanding about the people of other faiths which is completely different from the generation before them. Is the church able to practice its mission today meeting the understanding of our youth?

Model for Mission

Would it be possible to perform our mission in the new millennium, in the midst of the people of other faiths, without losing their respect, yet remain faithful to the Christian gospel? Would it be possible to offer a model for Christian mission in the new millennium, taking into consideration the issues raised and guidelines offered for the practice of mission in the previous pages? Would it be possible to offer a model for mission, which would certainly be a helpful model in making disciples for Jesus Christ, yet a model which would command the respect of people of other faiths?

One model which is based on Christian witness could be "Silent Evangelism." This model was, in fact, successfully used by Mother Teresa. Even though she launched her mission in a part of the world that was not congenial to Christian missionary work, her mission was supported by Christians and by people of other faiths as well. Her life was eulogized by Christians and people of other faiths and walks of life at her funeral. Interestingly, she was the only nonpolitical person in India who was ever given a state funeral. She did not preach to others, but whenever people asked for her advice, her answer was, "Love Jesus." These words, along with the actions of her missionary work, encouraged others to realize that when there is a deep love for Jesus, when one is a follower of Jesus, when one affirms the Lordship of Jesus Christ, one truly tries to become "salt of the earth" and a "light of the world" (Matthew 5:13, 14) and invite others to follow Jesus Christ. When one becomes a true follower of Jesus Christ, he or she makes Christ's ministry and mission the foundation of his/her witness, based on the models offered by Christ. It will be a mission glorifying God in all creation, built on the love, justice, and peace of Christ, and trusting in the power of the Holy Spirit. Once this becomes the nucleus of the mission, the rest of the things will take place.

Sheela, who is mentioned in the beginning of this article, the newly baptized Christian, shared that she continues to visit her parents, brother, and sister. She does not preach to them. She does not try to convert them. She loves them, demonstrating her love of Jesus. She now feels that her sister may soon become a disciple of Jesus and be baptized. Again, one can give several illustrations where people have become the disciples of Jesus Christ and taken baptism through the silent evangelism of others.

Christian mission in the new millennium, a millennium which begins as a post-Christian millennium, wants the church to hear very carefully the words of Jesus, who said, "'But you will receive power when the Holy Spirit has come upon you; and you will be my witnesses in Jerusalem [home], in all Judea and Samaria [country], and to the ends of the earth [world]'" (Acts 1:8). The Lord of the church wants us to be silent and to wait for the Holy Spirit to empower us to be strong witnesses for justice, peace, and reconciliation, where we are placed in life, as faithful disciples of Jesus Christ.

Once the power is upon us, we need to be courageous to use whatever model or method the Holy Spirit challenges and empowers us to use to witness to our Triune God — God the Creator, Redeemer, and Sustainer. In this Christian witnessing, we also need to bear in mind: "Always be ready to make your defense to anyone who demands from you an accounting for the hope that is in you; yet do it with gentleness and reverence" (1 Peter 3:15*b*, 16*a*).

CHAPTER 8

The Future of Native American Ministry
Marvin B. Abrams

Introduction

This chapter will attempt to forecast, in a limited way, the exciting potential for Native American ministry in The United Methodist Church (UMC) during this third millennium. For this potential to become a reality, however, we must explore an essential conviction that affected the past and continues to affect present Native American ministries. Simply said, this conviction is a desire to integrate a rich cultural and spiritual Native American heritage with Christian ministries. Perhaps a simple way to express this is to share what many traditional Native American religious leaders have shared with me: "Native Americans see that every event in life has spiritual significance."

I would further define this spiritual perspective by sharing words that are reported to have been spoken by Chief Seattle: *"The earth does not belong to man, man belongs to the earth. All things are connected like the blood that unites one family. Man did not weave the web of life; he is merely a strand in it. Whatever he does to the web, he does to himself."*[1] This belief pervades the everyday spiritual experience of many Native Americans. If encouraged, this underlying conviction could emerge as one force that could shape, in a positive way, the future of Native American ministry within The UMC.

If this conviction becomes a reality, two things can occur that will enrich future Native American ministries. First, Native Americans will be able to share, with our non-Indian Christian brothers and sisters, the richness of our unique walk with God. Second, Native Americans can share,

Native American dancer Sandra Roye performs the shawl dance during a powwow of five United Methodist congregations at Oklahoma City University in 2002. The Oklahoma Indian Missionary Conference has more than six thousand of the 18,000 members of Native Americans in The United Methodist Church. (UMNS photo by Mike DuBose)

with non-Christian Native American brothers and sisters, how we perceive the amazing love of God known through Jesus Christ.

In this chapter I will use my ministry journey as a way of exploring the consequences of integrating this conviction with present and future Native American ministries. This method will enable us to understand conflicts that, I believe, have blocked Christian Native American ministry in The UMC. This exploration will lead to recommendations that may not eliminate the conflict between traditional Christian practices and traditional Native American spirit ways, but will, I hope, help us to understand the conflicts. It is my hope that this may lead The UMC to begin a process that will help Native Americans to see that this is not just a "white man's church."

Personal Journey

I am a member of the Seneca Nation. The Seneca Nation is one of six nations within the Iroquois Confederacy. The Iroquois have reservations both in New York and Canada. I was born on the Allegheny Seneca Indian Reservation, which is one of three Seneca reservations in western New York State. As a child, I attended a Free Methodist Church on the reservation. My grandparents had been converted to Christianity by Free Methodist missionaries. My father was, however, a member of the Longhouse.

The term "Longhouse" refers to the type of home that once housed Iroquois people. Longhouse also refers to the place where Iroquois practice their spirit ways (religion). One of the ceremonies of the Longhouse is a naming ceremony held during the midwinter ceremony. My maternal grandparents, influenced by missionaries, viewed the Longhouse as pagan and refused to let my father take me to the naming ceremony. Therefore, I never received an Indian name. Though not crucial to my sense of identity, it still leaves me with the impression that something is missing.

I am sure that most missionaries were sincere in their intentions that the Native American "come to Jesus." Unfortunately, most missionaries felt this meant the Indian must give up indigenous culture and language. (Throughout this essay I will use the terms "Indian" and "Native American" coterminously.) Consequently, Native Americans were forced to embrace foreign cultures and values. Because of this compulsory acculturation, many Native Americans have come to view the church with mistrust and see the church as a "white man's church."

When I was six years of age, our family moved to Buffalo, New York, and began attending the Asbury Delaware Methodist church near our home. I grew up in this church and carry many wonderful memories of it. In 1953 I entered the U.S. Marine Corps. Upon discharge, I began attending the University of Buffalo with the dream of becoming a doctor to help my people. At that time I also returned to worship at my childhood church. In 1958, my wife and I were married in this church. We continued to attend there. One day as we were leaving worship, the pastor asked my wife and me if we knew anyone willing to be the pastor for a small Indian church on the Cattaraugus Reservation, one of the other Seneca reservations in western New York.

I knew that the pastor was not asking me to serve but wanted to know if I knew of an Indian who might be interested. We went home and after much prayer, it seemed as if God was saying, *"This is something you should be doing."* Now keep in mind there were no voices and no writing in the sky, just an awareness that God wanted to use a tongue-tied, simple Indian, with limited public speaking experience, and his wife. So we volunteered. I say "us," because my wife has been a partner in this journey. This is how I began my service with The Methodist Church (and subsequently The UMC).

I am thankful the people in that first church had patience with me. I remember sharing with the children a story which used a mallet to make a point. As I swung the mallet the head came off and went hurtling to the back of the church, where it glanced off the head of the lay leader! Fortunately, he took it in stride. The members of this church endured many such things. Many of these experiences have had value for my ministry journey, especially the need to make sure that mallet heads are screwed on tightly.

While at this church I went on to study and complete the church's five-year course of study at Wesley Theological Seminary in Washington, D.C. Completing this course enabled me to become an associate member of the Western New York Annual Conference. After serving seven years on the reservation, I was appointed to non-Indian churches in Jamestown, Kennedy, and Rochester, all in New York.

In 1978, Bishop Charles Golden of what is now the California-Pacific Annual Conference called and asked if I would be interested in helping to develop a Native American ministry in Southern California. Consequently, I moved my family to Southern California. While serving and developing this new ministry, I received my elders' orders under a *United Methodist Discipline* paragraph entitled "exceptional promise." I continued my studies, however, and received my Master of Divinity degree and my Doctor of Divinity degree from the Claremont School of Theology. My doctoral dissertation was a study on Native American spirituality.

The Native American United Methodist Church that was created initially was located in downtown Los Angeles. In addition to a Sunday service, the ministry offered Bible study, personal fellowship, and crafts. The people so enjoyed being together that at three o'clock on Sunday afternoon we had to urge them out the door. It was because of this desire for community that we developed our gathering ministry.

When the church was located in Los Angeles, it was very active. Programs included Head Start, a crisis and caring center, and a food program for senior citizens. In 1983, the ministry was forced by the Los Angeles Building and Safety Commission to move from downtown Los Angeles to Norwalk, California. This forced move occurred because the downtown church building did not meet the earthquake codes, and it would have been prohibitively expensive to retrofit the church. We shared these facilities with the Norwalk church for thirteen years. Some of the thirteen years were exciting and others were simply difficult. Exciting, because we were able to focus on a geographically scattered people. Difficult, because we faced some racism. During this time we prayed for and searched for our own facility.

Trinity United Methodist Church was an elderly congregation, declining in members, in Anaheim, California. In May 1996 the members of Trinity asked if the Native American UMC would join them in worship on Easter Sunday. Two weeks after the joint service, the Trinity members asked, "Are you willing to become a multicultural church?" They added, "If so, some of us are willing to stay and merge with you." We were and they did. The members of Trinity UMC and the Native American UMC voted to merge. On May 26, 1996, the merged churches became the Native American United Methodist Church of Southern California. At last, after twenty years of sharing facilities with other churches, the Native American UMC had its own church home. We had prayed for this for twenty years, yet we were still amazed. We have since developed an endowment as part of our plan for the future. We serve as proof that multicultural experiences can work.

The stated mission of the Native American UMC of Southern California is "to enable Native Americans and others to become aware of and experience the reality of God's presence, power, love and purpose for their lives." This church, as it has carried out its mission, has attempted to be a bridge between those who support Christian church beliefs and those who practice traditional Native American spirit ways. In doing so, the church has worked jointly with Southern California Native American organizations to develop cultural programs that enhance the self-esteem of Native Americans. For example, an intertribal dance workshop for Native American children and youth is jointly sponsored with the Southern California

Indian Center. The goal has been to teach Native young people their Native culture and to inspire pride in their heritage. Another joint venture has been an after-school tutoring program. This program is designed to help Native American young people succeed in school. In 2002 we were working to develop a preparatory school for Native American children in grades six through eight. The curriculum of this charter school will place an emphasis on Native American culture.

Insights

In 1978, when I first came to California, the largest population of Native Americans in the U.S. was in Southern California. This population was, however, scattered geographically. Historically, this was the result of a United States Government policy, the goal of which was to relocate Native Americans from reservations to urban areas for jobs and schooling. The consequence of this policy has been that nearly 70 percent of Native Americans live in major metropolitan areas. Because Native Americans in Southern California are scattered and often have limited access to traditional extended families, they often feel isolated. The church has attempted, through its gathering programs, to provide some elements of the extended family. Because of limited resources and great distances, these families cannot, however, always come to the church in Anaheim. It soon became evident that we would have to develop a plan to go to them. So, in addition to Anaheim, we "gather" in Los Angeles, Riverside, and San Diego, with an eye to other locations as God leads and the opportunity presents itself. We have trained laypersons to be "Gatherers," the Circle of Life leaders, who gather other Native Americans for worship, fellowship, outreach, and service. We use the words "gather" and "gatherer" because it is reminiscent of the lifestyle of earlier tribal days. Native people want to be together, to experience what they had in their tribal settings, the extended family. This extended family, in the reservation setting, helped to build a tribal family in which members helped each other to survive. The church in Southern California attempts to be this family.

Originally, our Los Angeles Circle of Life was housed at Echo Park UMC. One of our members was excellent at obtaining food from various food banks and stores, so we were able to distribute food twice a week. Because this food distribution program was successful among the Hispanic population in the Echo Park area, it enabled that church to develop Bible study and other programs for this Hispanic population. Its very success, however, forced the Los Angeles Circle of Life to relocate. It moved to the Robert Sundance Family and Wellness Center, a Native American social services organization. The Riverside Circle of Life meets at the Sherman Indian School in Riverside, a boarding school operated by the Bureau of Indian Affairs for Native American high school students. The San Diego Circle of Life meets at the Normal Heights UMC in San Diego.

In 1985 Native people suggested that there should be a model for developing Native American ministry in other urban settings. The General Board of Global Ministries (GBGM) of The UMC developed a board-wide Native American Urban Initiative which used some elements of this "gathering" ministry model. There are now similar gatherings of Native Americans in other cities such as Seattle; Fayetteville, N.C.; and Grand Rapids, Mich. There are others, and some that were started have since closed. I believe these closings were due, in part, to the lack of leaders trained in urban ministry and the lack of a strong spiritual foundation. Another problem was that annual conferences were unwilling to provide a strong, intentional, and long-term financial and spiritual commitment to these gatherings.

Native American Spirit Ways

While serving on the Cattaraugus Seneca Reservation, I visited the Longhouse and listened to the teachings there. Later, I read more about the work of Handsome Lake. His prophecy and teachings became the spiritual foundation for the Longhouse. The teachings brought about the rebirth of spiritual elements that enabled the Seneca Nation and other nations of the Iroquois to survive. As I read and listened to the teachings, I found myself thinking: This is like reading and listening to the Bible. I began to see that traditional Native American and Christian Native American theologies were not hostile to one another and have many things in common. This realization was further confirmed during my doctoral work on Native American spirituality.

The doctoral work focused on the steward as caregiver. We usually think of stewardship as applying only to money. In Native American spirituality, however, stewardship means caring for:

- ourselves — mentally, emotionally, and physically;
- our families — including the elders;
- creation — including land and creatures; and
- the spirit ways — including traditional spirit ways and our own walk within the Christian church.

Caring for the family fosters a communal element within Native American spirituality that is sometimes missing from mainstream Christian teachings. In the Native American setting, the individual is to care for self and the community.

Caring for creation includes the identification of the earth as earth mother. The belief that earth and all of its creatures are related leads to a sense that all of creation is sacred. As a result, Native people feel that the land and all the creatures are part of their family, a feeling which includes a desire and responsibility to preserve the natural world. Integrating this relatedness into their spirit ways, many Native Americans sense that every event has spiritual significance and that the individual, the family, creation, and church/spirit ways must always operate in harmony.

There are 557 tribes in the U.S., including Alaska, collectively regarded as Indians, American Indians, or Native Americans. They are diverse tribally; their cultures are diverse; yet they share many commonalities. They are the only people in the U.S. who are required to prove their identity. For example, when I say I am Seneca, this has special meaning for me, for it speaks of the tribal family that gives me my Indian identity. Seneca children are taught that they are more than members of a biological family. They are also members of a tribal family. In that tribal understanding of family we have responsibility for every other member of the family and beyond that to the seventh generation. In the Seneca language the term "warrior" identifies someone whose responsibility is to care for the family.

Racism and Oppression

For more than five hundred years, Native Americans have struggled with oppression. It is interesting to note that, during the 1800s, the U.S. Government passed legislation that provided funds to churches to Christianize Native Americans. This policy is now seen by Native Americans as an attempt, not to Christianize, but to "civilize the savage." This action came about because Native Americans were considered by some Christians, during that time, to be subhuman.

When Native Americans first wanted to develop their own ministries here in Southern California in The Methodist Church, they went to the episcopal office and asked for support. They were told, "We have all these Methodist churches you can attend." The general church still did not understand *the need to worship as Native Americans.*

Racism, even in The UMC, is alive and well today. During the time we shared facilities with a UMC in the 1990s, prejudice, accompanied by *oppression*, reared its ugly head in many forms. For example, when Native Americans prayed in their own language in church, some members of the dominant culture objected because they found it offensive. Once, when Native Americans from downtown Los Angeles sat on the lawn after church school waiting for worship to begin, one of the ushers came out and said "these people" had to leave or he would call the sheriff to have them removed. Why? "Because they are in the way!" he said. The truth was it was because they were different. They were not middle-class whites like those that made up the host church's congregation.

For some in this congregation, it was not acceptable to use fry bread and one cup for communion. During joint communion services, the host church insisted that if we chose to use fry bread and a single cup, we must also use wafers and individual communion cups. Also, after sage was burned, as part of a blessing ceremony, a "no smoking" sign was put up on the sanctuary door. Yes, prejudice with its accompanying oppression is still alive and well.

Rediscovering Our Heritage

Many Native American youth, however, are not willing to remain consumers of European-American culture and are going back to their traditional roots. That is why a lot of young people participate in the powwow, a growing force in Southern California. Nearly every weekend during the summer there is a powwow—a semireligious gathering of Native Americans celebrating the richness of their culture through art, music, dance, storytelling, food, and spirit ways. Native people are beginning to take responsibility for their own well being, their spiritual health, and their spiritual ways.

Many Native American leaders believe that God is central to all cultural experiences and that faith and culture are connected. The church must begin to affirm what is good within the spiritual culture of Native Americans. The goal of the Native American UMC of Southern California is to incorporate into worship Native American cultural and spiritual symbols and ceremonies that will enhance our Christian worship and have spiritual value. They are not used simply because they are Indian. For example, acolytes carry not only the light but a prayer pipe into the service. The pipe, as a symbol of prayer, is placed on the altar. We have a Native American naming ceremony, when the family wishes, as part of the sacrament of baptism. At the close of communion in the sanctuary, the elements are taken outside. The people gather in a circle as the contents of the cup are returned to the earth and the bread is scattered for the other creatures. In this way, the church reaffirms its commitment to care for all of God's creation.

Incorporating/enacting these cultural customs in an authentic way, not simply because it is Indian, begins to speak to our young people of the richness of our heritage, to rebuild self-esteem, and to instill pride as a people. Again, we see no hostility between most basic traditional spirit beliefs and most basic Christian beliefs. We believe that the church can become the extended family empowering Native Americans to reconnect with their traditional spirit ways as an expression of their Christianity.

The Gift of Survival

One of the gifts that Native Americans can bring to Christian mission is an understanding of how their spirituality helped Native Americans survive as a people. The church has never really talked about the holocaust among Native people in America and how the church was part of it. One Native American group in California developed a video, *The American Holocaust*. It is a protest against the Roman Catholic missions in California. The United Methodist General Conference of 1996 made an apology for the Sand Creek Massacre in which Colonel John A. Chivington, a Methodist minister, led a predawn attack on a Cheyenne village, killing and mutilating two hundred people, two-thirds of whom were unarmed women and children. Chief Black Kettle had been promised protection from any American aggression by the territory of Colorado as long as he

Many Native Americans have turned to casinos as ways to gain income for their tribes. Some Christian Native Americans are opposed to casinos, some of which employ Native Americans while others do not. Studies in New Mexico, where this casino is located, showed that gamblers are predominantly older adult Anglos and blue collar workers. *(Photo by Charles Cole)*

flew the American flag over his village. The church has not done anything to follow the apology of 1996. Shouldn't an apology be followed by some concrete act of repentance? The churches were sometimes given land on reservations to build churches. There are places where the land is no longer used for churches. Shouldn't it be given back to the tribes? These kinds of injustices have caused bitterness, and a great many Native people are saying we cannot let this happen again. Other Native people say these events took place yesterday and we have to move on.

Recommendations

What can the church do to help Native people regain their cultural pride and enable them to "become aware of and experience the reality of God's presence, power, love and purpose for their lives?" After forty-three years of service and much learning and experience, I have many thoughts.

1. The church can support the integration of the underlying conviction, expressed in the introduction, into Native American Christian ministry. The UMC can encourage Native Americans to determine their own spiritual future by supporting the petition submitted to the 1988 General Conference. The resolution simply asked the church to "let Indians be Indians."

2. The church could work with the tribes on economic development. The Supreme Court has called Native American nations "dependent nations." Many Native tribes developed gaming, or gambling, as a way to help their people. The church wagged its finger at them but did not offer an alternative. Some people think all Native Americans are benefitting from gambling, but in actuality only a small percentage are. Gambling succeeds when the site is next to a major metropolitan area or a freeway. Many Native American nations are isolated and like real estate, success comes from "location, location, location." If you are isolated, what can you do? Economic development means not just giving money but finding ways to create self-sufficiency.

3. The church has mission interns who go to other countries. The question might be: Why not send mission interns to sovereign tribal nations within the U.S.? A few years ago the Native American International Caucus (NAIC) asked the World Division to recognize the sovereignty of tribal nations.

4. The United Methodist Committee on Relief (UMCOR) has programs to help people coming to the U.S. from other countries. Native Americans ask, "Why not include Native Americans who migrate from their nations to a U.S. city in UMCOR programs?" A satisfactory response has never been received. The church needs to include Native American nations when we provide resources for mission in or to other nations.

5. Diversity can be an advantage or disadvantage. On the positive side, many different tribes are working together in Native American organizations to bring reconciliation between The UMC and our Native brothers and sisters. Organizations such as NAIC, the National United Methodist Native American Center (NUMNAC), the Southeastern Jurisdiction Association for Native American Ministries (SEJANAM), and the Western Jurisdiction Center for Native American Ministries (WJCNAM) are working to help the church reaffirm the value of Native people and wel-

come their unique gifts. NAIC was instrumental in developing the Native American Comprehensive Plan, first approved by General Conference in 1996 and reaffirmed at the 2000 conference.

NAIC has accomplished a great deal in its role of advocacy. It encourages the development of a Native American jurisdictional structure in all five United Methodist jurisdictions. It also advocates that there be a committee on Native American ministry in every annual conference. Each committee would have the responsibility of overseeing Native American ministry in its annual conference. Many Native American leaders feel that The UMC also needs to assist Native Americans in their efforts to deal with poverty (with unemployment being 90 percent on some reservations, and the average 45 percent), health care (e.g., tuberculosis is 7.4 times greater among Indians than non-Indians), suicide among Native Americans (one in six adolescents has attempted suicide, a rate four times that of other teenagers), alternatives to gaming, economic development, and other issues.

6. What we do now as a church is not reaching the majority of Native Americans. According to the U.S. Census Bureau, there are 1.9 million Native Americans in the U.S., with another 6.7 million who claim a Native American ancestor. There are only about 17,000 Native American members in The UMC. We have many good ministries but there is much more to be done. The next development must be a national mission ministry that is intentional about Native Americans being in control of their spiritual destiny. There must be a commitment to develop a four-tiered, ten-year strategic plan that focuses on the self, the family, creation, and the church. It must begin by analyzing strengths and weaknesses of past and present ministry and then bringing together Native Americans and resources to support a plan that is constantly changing and evolving. The plan must capitalize on the gaming window of opportunity and create alternatives to gaming that will be the basis for long-term social and spiritual development.

As Native Americans, we can no longer be divided. The U.S. Government made promises through treaties that were never kept. This policy promoted the growth of a dependency psyche. Native Americans themselves must develop a healing process that nurtures networking and interaction. We can no longer depend on the benevolence of the church to meet our spiritual and social needs. The dominant society has its own problems and tends to take no responsibility for the wrongs of the past. The answers for Native Americans are education, political unity, and economic development.

Summary

Through it all, I remain an optimist about Native American ministries. There is a renewed interest in Native American cultural and spiritual traditions in our nation. Sometimes the focus is, however, on the Indian of the nineteenth century. A valid plan must encourage the church to keep the essence of old applicable traditions and blend them with new traditions. Perhaps this is how the church can begin to be a bridge between traditional Christianity and traditional Native American culture. So often the church has mirrored what the dominant culture sees as the so-called *true ways to minister*. I believe, however, the church is the place where transformation can take place. If the church will intentionally support Native American Ministry, society would follow. The only way that significant change will happen is for Native people to be assertive. No one else can act for us. The time is past when Native Americans think of themselves as victims. Native Americans must begin to take responsibility for finding ways to support their churches and ministries.

Both the church and the federal government have determined what Native Americans needed in the past, an approach that did not work then and will not work now. The church needs to avoid imposing a structure on Native peoples that does not speak to their needs. Native Americans have to develop their own ministries. Though it is threatening to some people, it is time to support Native people leading the way in ministering to Native people. Native Americans need to rediscover how to honor their cultural heritage and reclaim their cultural pride. The Native American UMC of Southern California has developed "foster" communities so that Native people can come together as families and celebrate their heritage as they become aware of and experience the reality of God's presence, power, love, and purpose for their lives. It is our hope that other cultures will open themselves to experience our rich spirit ways where communion with God is an integral part of our daily life.

CHAPTER 9

The Future of African Americans and Mission

Anthony J. Shipley

*S*INCE MUCH OF my ministry has been in urban settings, most of my reflections on the future of the church's mission with, by, and for African Americans will consist of comments on urban ministries. But I also want to put these reflections in a global setting and in the context of United Methodist belief and practice.[1]

The United Methodist Franchise

Too often mission has been done out of paternalism. That discussion has gone on long enough that I don't need to get into the major part of it, but there are some subtleties I would like to address. Often in transitional churches, the white remnant that is left says, "Yes, we want to be in ministry to this community." They focus on the African Americans moving into the community who are poorer than they, less educated than they, and whose lives are shattered and splattered. So they take the theology of Methodism, which is middle class, and pass it on to people who are not middle class at all. They want to continue to sing anthems and keep a style of worship which is appropriate for a Eurocentric middle-class lifestyle, but they expect people who are Afrocentric and poor to buy into it.

I like to say that in order to get a United Methodist franchise and hang out a United Methodist cross and flame, you must be able to take care of your building, pay your pastor, pay your apportionments, and pay for a pension. People who are welfare mothers with three children, or who are the working poor, earning less than $6,000 a year on a minimum wage, cannot afford to take care of a "white elephant" United Methodist building and all the other things. That is simply a franchise they cannot afford to buy. It's like saying to someone who can afford a Volkswagen, "You must have a Cadillac."

The way racism works is that we take this middle-class system and impose it on people who cannot afford it. To impose apportionments on the poor is another form of exploitation. But that's how we see mission in The United Methodist Church (UMC). We're going to start a church in a poor community, and it is going to look just like The UMC in a rich community. It is going to have a pastor who has four years of college and three years of seminary, because in the UMC you have to be trained. I think it's fine to bring all those resources to poor people, but we must do that in a way that is not an imposition on the poor. If you make $60,000 a year, paying a pastor and paying apportionments is appropriate; but if you make $6,000 a year, it's an imposition. So I think there is a moral question about how we are in mission to poor communities. And in America, if you are African American, your chances of being poor are much greater than the rest of the population.

Entrepreneurship and the Church

Another issue: In the African-American community, the church is the seedbed of entrepreneurial action. The Reverend Floyd Flake, pastor of Allen African Methodist Episcopal Church in Jamaica, Queens, is the quintessential example of this. But let's be clear that when African Americans think of a middle-class church, like the African Methodist Episcopal Church (AME) or the Christian Methodist Episcopal Church (CME), or Hope UMC in Southfield, Michigan, they are thinking of churches that started out looking specifically for middle-class African Americans. We call them "silk stocking" churches.

Almost two decades ago when I was on the cabinet in the Detroit Annual Conference, we did a demographic study and discovered that 85 percent of the people moving into Southfield were African Americans. Southfield has one of the highest per capita incomes of any African-American community in the country. Essentially you had these affluent African Americans moving into a community where the only UMC congregation was an all-white church. It had been white for a hundred years, and the people there had no desire to be different. Edsel Ammons was the bishop at the time, and after we did the study, I suggested we place an African-American pastor at that church. The cabinet's response was, "Why would we do that? We have a church of two hundred members that pays its apportionments, that has paid for its building, and is a thriving institution. That's no place to send an African-American pastor." We prevailed on the cabinet and persuaded them that if we looked down the road about ten years we would have a huge African-American population there. The cabinet's response was, "If you can find an African American who is qualified to serve Euro-Americans [and of course, the normal qualifications of college and seminary would not be enough], go ahead."

So we looked around the country to find someone who was qualified. We found Carlyle Fielding Stewart teaching at Garrett-Evangelical Theological Seminary, so we prevailed on the cabinet to make him the pastor. He left the seminary and came to the church. After about two years all the Euro-Americans left. Stewart had quite a struggle in building the church, but it has grown and thrived and has several thousand members now. By the year 2000, Stewart had stayed eighteen years, which raises another question about mission. In the African-American community pastors come and stay.

We have lots of examples: Hartford Memorial Baptist Church in Detroit, where the pastor has been for thirty years, Tabernacle Missionary Baptist Church for forty years, and the list goes on. Wherever you see a strong African-American church in an urban center, you will see a pastor who has been there a long time. The way we do business in The UMC, moving pastors every few years, you cannot possibly build a strong church.

Family the Paradigm

In the African-American community, the church is your extended family, and if you want a really dysfunctional family, change the father and mother every three years. In the African-American community you need a pastor who can come and stay for a long time, you need a system which does not exploit the people and take their money away, and you need to appeal to people for whom the United Methodist system of thought, theology, and intellectualism is appropriate. So if we're serious as United Methodists about doing ministry and church extension and mission, then we need to be clear that we're a middle-class denomination and we should be trying to build middle-class African-American churches. Everywhere

Windsor Village United Methodist Church near Houston, an African American church, was originally founded as Southmont UMC in the 1960s. Its name was changed in 1968, and it has become the largest UMC congregation, with more than 15,000 members. *(Photo by Ricardo Merendoni)*

in the country where we've had a successful African-American church in The UMC, like Hope church in Michigan or Windsor Village church in Houston, where Kirbyjon Caldwell is the pastor, or others in Texas, the Southwest, or California, these great churches are middle-class institutions. I don't know of an example of a strong UMC in the middle of a poor African-American community.

Community Economic Development

For two hundred years, mission in The UMC has been the way Euro-Americans took care of their responsibility for the poor and needy. I don't want to belittle that, because that is what Jesus did. Jesus said, "I come to bring life and bring it more abundantly." He hung out with the pimps and the prostitutes and the poor and the lepers, and really was an advocate for the downtrodden. But the way that plays itself out in The UMC, we who are affluent help ourselves to feel good by doing something for people who are poor. We see poor people as the objects of mission rather than as the subjects of mission. We need now to begin to talk about how to empower the people who are poor to be in mission.

Some examples: We have had across the country city societies (in Detroit we call it the Methodist Union), and these societies really got started initially when city churches closed and sold the property, and we took the money to build in the suburbs. These city societies say, "If your church has an endowment, you have to spend it all and become absolutely poor and when you demonstrate to us you have no financial resources of your own, we will fix your boiler or your roof, and you'll have to be beholden to us." We *should* say: "We have a church in the city and what we must do is build an endowment under it, so when it has a $2 million endowment, then it will be able to generate the cash it needs to operate in a poor community, since the people in that community cannot afford to be in ministry." So if The UMC wants to see mission as empowerment, we would say here is a place where we need to be in ministry in the city. It takes $200,000 a year, so we will create an endowment of $2 million which will generate the $200,000 for basic costs, and whatever additional money comes in the offering plate will be used to enhance mission and ministry. We would create a financially stable church that is empowered to do ministry in the city.

Every congregation needs to be endowed. Foundations related to The UMC should be developing strategies to assist local churches in building these endowments. In addition to endowments that consist of investments in stocks and bonds, there are insurance products that provide important opportunities to leverage small donations and create significant capital.

The Bethel AME Church in Detroit created a Community Housing Development Organization (CHDO) and built the Bethel Towers senior citizens apartments. These apartments generate a substantial income for the church. In The UMC we won't let a pastor stay long enough to do a project like that. If you are going to get into economic development in the city, you had better plan to be there for ten to twenty years so you have time to do it.

At ordination, United Methodist pastors are asked to care for the temporal and spiritual needs of their people. It is important that clergy understand that God loves the forest, not just the trees. The church must be on a mission of redeeming communities in addition to saving individual souls. In the Old Testament, Moses and the Hebrew children were told to go up and possess the land. It is critical that the church control as much land in cities as possible. Every day the cost of land in the city goes up, and the opportunity to purchase it inexpensively dwindles. An aggressive program of land acquisition in the city is needed.

In order to make community development work, the church must form for-profit corporations that earn significant income, which can then be contributed to the nonprofit ministries of the church. The community development efforts of the church could focus on housing projects which purchase, rehabilitate, and then sell houses to people who become first-time homeowners. Becoming an integral part of the revitalization of businesses in the city is crucial for the church. Such revitalization will create individual financial stability and the opportunity for individuals to contribute to the church.

Although these ideas apply to all churches, not merely African-American churches, they are especially pertinent to African-American churches because a large number of them in our inner cities are economically disenfranchised. During the twenty-first century the church must focus on building wealth for both individuals and institutions. For the individual this means home ownership. The church should assist people in understanding the difference between appreciating and depreciating assets and help people acquire appreciating assets. For most Americans, their home is the place where they first learn to have an appreciating asset. The church is in a unique position to create the opportunity for people to own their own homes and develop their own businesses.

Charter Schools

One of the opportunities that is staring the church in the face is charter schools. In 1996 Christ UMC in Detroit, the church I pastor, started a charter school—Chandler Park Academy. Michigan has one hundred and fifty charter schools, which is more than most states. They are public schools, so any child who applies can enter. They are not religious schools. Any concerned group of citizens can organize a board of directors and apply for a charter. We have only twenty-four students in a class. In other Detroit public schools they have thirty-five students per class. We have a fully functioning computer lab with internet connections. We can structure how we relate to parents. In our school we do not send report cards. Parents must come get them. Our teachers stay at night and meet with parents between 5 and 8 P.M.

When we opened our school, we started with sixth-graders reading on first-grade level, with math scores on second-grade level. In May 1999, these children left our eighth grade and applied for public schools. We received 123 certificates out of 192 students with outstanding scores on tests of the Michigan Educational Assessment Test (MEAT).

Our teachers are at-will (nonunion) employees. If a teacher does not perform, we fire him or her the next semester. We have been at this for three years, however, and have never fired a teacher. These teachers come to us because the environment is one that allows them to teach. Our salaries are less than those in public schools overall, although the salaries are higher per student than in the public schools.

We claim as United Methodists that we care about education. Yet there is not a single staff person in any general church agency whose job is public education. Higher education and theological education, yes, but there is no one on the general church level who gets up every morning saying, "Children are important, schools are important, what is the church's relationship to public education going to be?" I think The UMC should use its money and its power to be supportive of quality public education, and right now the easiest way to do that is with charter schools.

Multicultural Coalitions

As we think about urban ministry, multicultural coalitions are essential. A group of churches in the Detroit East District have formed a cooperative parish, which consists of racial, economic, theological, ethnic, and gender diversity. Tiger Woods has said he is black but more than black. His mother is Asian and his father is part-German and part-Irish. He is a mixture of cultures and genetic makeup. The problem is our categories are too small. The time is past when we could divide the world into white folks and black folks. The problem of racism is not over. But in reality the advent of the internet, the number of people who fly every day, and other changes mean that all of us live in the whole world, and that means when you talk about change and development, coalitions are the only way to go. One of the wonderful things about The UMC is that we really do have a cultural diversity. We don't even understand what it means in this time in history to be a connectional church. We don't see its power.

Right now I am working on a project to make it possible for United Methodist churches in the inner city of Detroit to have economic development programs. A typical United Methodist church cannot do that because of the appointive system. No bank in its right mind is going to trust a pastor who says, "I was appointed a year ago, and I might be moved in three years, will you lend me a half-million dollars?" But if The UMC comes along and points out this church has been on this corner for a hundred and thirty years, and it has had a number of pastors in that time, but we, The UMC, are standing behind this, and we are asking for a half-million dollars and our combined assets are almost a billion dollars, then the bank would say yes. We have not even thought about that aspect of connectionalism. I am working now with people in the city mission society which has banking relationships, and with that coalition we should be able to create an economic development program that a single local church could not consider.

In the Lord's Prayer we pray, "Thy Kingdom come, thy will be done on earth as it is in heaven." If God's will is to be done on earth, the church must be that spiritual force in the community that participates with others to ensure that God's agenda is achieved in the city. The church's presence will cause a synergy making it possible for Christian values to be included in the process of urban redevelopment. These values can be integrated into the community by moving beyond the traditional partnerships with institutions like the Boy Scouts and United Community Services. We can form new partnerships with community development corporations, banks, insurance companies, developers, and major corporations. The church can partner with public servants like mayors, governors, state senators, and city council members.

African Americans as Subjects of Mission

As we think about the future role of African Americans in mission, we are beyond the point where we simply conceive of African Americans as objects of mission. We are now active subjects of mission; meaning, we participate in the way mission is done and we carry out mission to the world

Members of Ben Hill United Methodist Church in Atlanta erupt in praise during a dedication service for the new residence hall they financed at United Methodist-related Africa University in Mutare, Zimbabwe. The church, the second-largest African-American United Methodist congregation in the United States, made the commitment in 1999 to construct the two-story dormitory after learning of the need for more student housing at the school. *(UMNS photo courtesy of the United Methodist Board of Higher Education and Ministry)*

along with the rest of the church. The phenomenal growth of the black middle class since the 1960s means there are African Americans with the resources to provide the people and the money to support mission projects. But I think a more important reality in America today has to do with the divide between the rich and the poor. I agree with Cornel West that "race matters," and if you are an African American you are much more likely to be placed in the caste called the permanent underclass.[2] There is clear linkage between being black and being poor.

The serious problem about poverty is not that you have no money but that you have no control over your life. When I was a council director I would say to Euro-Americans, "Let's meet." They would say, "Two o'clock in the afternoon is fine. I own the company. Of course I can meet with you." When I'm in a community of the working poor who work on assembly lines, they may agree to meet with me in the evening, but if the boss says the firm is running a double shift tonight, they don't show up for the meeting. Or if I'm dealing with a single mother with children, she may agree to come to a meeting, but if one of the children gets sick, there is no one else to care for that child, so she doesn't show up. It's not because she's lazy and shiftless, it's because she has no control over her life.

This dimension of poverty, which is absolutely destructive, goes hand in hand with racism. If you're racist you make sure that black folks are poor and then you can exploit them in all kinds of interesting ways.

The Diversity of African-American Churches

African-American churches are not all alike. They have diverse ways of going about their mission work. Let me mention a few examples here in Detroit. There's Hartford Memorial Baptist Church, which built a Kmart. It has become the fourth-most profitable Kmart in the country. Tabernacle Missionary Baptist Church and Hope UMC are excellent models of African-American churches in mission. Second Ebenezer Baptist Church has a pastor, the Reverend Edgar Van, who is probably the most powerful black pastor in Detroit.

Across the country we have Glide Memorial UMC in San Francisco, which the Reverend Cecil Williams, an African-American pastor, established as one of the most innovative and open congregations in the country, and which the Reverend Douglass Fitch, another African American, pastors today. Glide has been noted for its inclusion of the poor, gays, and ethnic minorities in its membership. It has also combined theological sophistication with a mission to the hungry and the homeless.

Then there is Windsor Village UMC in Houston, which Rev. Caldwell changed from a struggling 25-member congregation into a congregation of 15,000 members with 120 ministries that range from job placement and financial planning to weight loss and alcohol rehabilitation. In Atlanta, Ben Hill UMC was a congregation of 400 when Cornelius Henderson, later a bishop, became pastor in 1975. By the time he left in 1986, it had become a congregation of 4,000. The Reverend McCallister Hollins has continued that kind of leadership.

The common thing we are learning is that if you have a strong African-American middle-class community and you put a strong pastor in that community, then the church will do extremely well. If you have a good pastor and put him or her in a depressed community without financial resources, it doesn't work. The idea is to put strong African-American pastors into vital, middle-class African-American communities, and then we can do serious new church development.

Gifts and Resources of African Americans

When we think about the gifts and resources of African-American churches, we need to think about the global village. Global leadership needs to be bicultural. Leaders who understand only one culture are severely handicapped. The theory of the "dumb-ups" suggests that the people in power know less about people who have no power than vice versa. For example, women know more about men than men know about women, because women have had to learn about men in order to survive. Men didn't have to understand women, because women did not have much power. Children know more about their parents than the parents know about their children. The whole business of growing up is understanding your parents and managing them. Blacks know more about whites than whites know about blacks. Television and other media are norms of white culture, and blacks are privy to that. Black culture however is something not available to whites without whites working to understand it.

Leaders who are bicultural are valuable—people who speak two languages as opposed to one, who understand two or three different cultures. In management circles, companies want to hire people who are flexible and who know how to think and solve problems in more than one way. Bicultural leaders have at least two systems of thought and two ways of doing things. One of the things African-American leaders bring to The UMC is this biculturalism. They understand African-American culture *and* Euro-American culture.

When it comes to working in the African-American community itself, what African Americans bring is an understanding of the culture. If they go to Euro-American churches, they understand the culture. If Euro-American pastors are appointed to African-American churches, the pastors are lost; they don't understand basic stuff because they have never been exposed to it and have had no need to know it.

African Americans also bring the gift of patience and forgiveness. Clearly African Americans have been the most forgiving people on the planet and have sincerely and earnestly forgiven people so that life could move forward. The whole church can learn an important lesson from that.

African-American churches and pastors really do understand their ministry as service. We understand that it's not a we-give-you-this-you-give-me-that fair exchange proposition, but that what the love of God is about is a covenant. And in a covenant it's a one-way street in which God gives everything and will not alter His commitment based on our sinful behavior. When we sin, God continues to keep the covenant and loves and cares for us. That's what the whole story of the New Testament is about. It's hard to understand that message when you are rich and believe your riches are the result of your hard work. But for people who are poor it's a very important message that here is a God who loves me and cares for me no matter what my circumstances are. These people feel that the world may be raping them and taking away life, liberty, and the pursuit of happiness, but God will bless them no matter what.

In the old days the bishops of Liberia were elected in the United States. U.S. bishops were then appointed to Africa. Today that process is turned around, and now in many annual conferences of The UMC there are persons who were born in Africa who are serving as pastors, district superintendents, and conference staff. The rich gifts of the brightest and best of African culture are here doing service to U.S. churches. In one sense it is part of a brain drain that these persons who need to be in Africa contributing their wisdom, gifts, and talent to that culture are here enriching, enabling, enlivening, and empowering the Euro-American culture. That's the downside. But on the upside these persons from Africa are having the opportunity to have a broad experience and enrich their learnings and growth so that if and when they return to their own countries they will bring a wealth of knowledge and skill which they could have never gained by staying where they began. The primary flow of gifts is that persons born in Africa and other persons of color from around the world are now giving their gifts to enrich The UMC in the United States.

Global ministry means a profound respect for the individual cultures of various peoples. In addition, we need to acknowledge that biblical truth transcends culture, and even though religion is both specific and global, we have to understand that the truth transcends those individual cultures. We have to be both immanent, that is, respecting everyone's culture, and transcendent, understanding that the blindness that comes from our particular culture prevents us from seeing the whole truth of God. We all have to understand that we see through a glass darkly. The way to get out of the darkness and into the light is to let the cultural bias of someone else intersect with your cultural bias so that you can begin to determine what is culturally biased and get a little closer to the truth.

The interface of cultures in the global village is a tremendous theological asset, because the way we think about God has now been enhanced and challenged by other people who think differently from the way we think about God. I think the problem with the Western mind is that we have been so accustomed to thinking about life from our arrogant standpoint that we think the only other choice is to think about it from another arrogant standpoint. What we need to realize is the truth that everybody's standpoint is biased and limited and that we have to continue to function out of our partial blindness in order to find truth. Stephen Covey, the management author, says we do not see the world as it is; we see the world as we are. That is also true about God. We do not see God as God is, we see God as we are. If we are male, we see God as male; if we are female, we see God as female; if we're WASP, we think God has blue eyes; if we're Asian we think God is Asian; if we're black we think God is black. Finding ultimate truth is a matter of transcending the limitations of our eyesight.

African-American Missionaries

In this regard, we need to recruit and deploy as many African-American missionaries as we can. One reason is that it is very important to provide that international opportunity to African Americans. There are African Americans who, if they grow up in a place like Los Angeles, never "cross the river" or have a chance to go to China or Borneo or India. If they could it would broaden their experience and give them a whole different approach and understanding of what life is about. So in terms of advantages to those persons, it would broaden their lives and the impact would be monumental. More importantly, it would enable them to develop leadership skills and have experiences that would qualify them to make even more contributions to the rest of the church.

The second reason is that sending African-American missionaries is a way of transporting African-American culture to other parts of the world.

The images that people in other parts of the world have of African Americans is likely to be what they see on television news, which is not very pretty—body bags and the like.

But if we send more African-American missionaries, we must do it with some cultural sensitivity. If you're affluent and have parents with two incomes, you can afford to spend two years as a missionary. But if you have grown up in South Central Los Angeles and manage to get through college, you have piled up so much debt that the chance to spend two years as a missionary is not something you can afford. An example is a camp we had in New York, and the members of the camping commission decided they wanted to make the camp available to African Americans. They did that, and the kids tore the camp up! So I said what you have to do is have some staff in camp that the African-American kids can identify with. You cannot have a camp with all-white staff and expect these kids to come out of the ghetto and treat the place properly. So we recruited African-American college students to work in the camps. They wanted to serve but said they had to earn enough to pay their tuition. So we paid them the same kind of minimum wage we pay everyone else, but we also provided substantial scholarships out of a scholarship fund that we had. So some people complained, "You mean, if a white kid is washing dishes in the camp we are going to pay him $100 a week, but if a black kid is standing beside him, we are going to pay him $100 a week *plus* we're going to give him a large scholarship?" They said it was not fair. I responded that it was fair because this black kid brings a special resource that we desperately need if we want to achieve our goal of integrating the camp. Therefore from a management standpoint we are buying the talent we need. But be clear the scholarship money is coming out of the scholarship fund. They finally agreed, and the next summer we had African Americans in camp and a successful program. So if you are going to recruit African-American missionaries, you must do what is necessary to make it possible.

African Americans have a special affinity for mission in Africa. I am very proud of The UMC. I don't know of any other denomination that has built a university in Africa. That says something about us. Until institutions have people of color leading them, there are certain kinds of decisions they cannot make. The paternalism of missionaryism says, "Yes, let's feed people, let's bring them up to a certain standard of living," but it never thinks about helping the people who are the objects of mission to become smarter, brighter, and richer than we are. It's only when you get African Americans and Third World people giving leadership to the decision-making process and some sense of influence over the resources of the world that those resources can be allocated fairly. Clearly The UMC has not done all it should do in Africa, but equally clearly we have done an awful lot more than many in the Christian world.

I think the most important thing now in relationship to ministry to Africans is the number of Africans now in the ministry in the U.S., and the free exchange of people across the ocean coming here to study and learn and be in ministry and return to Africa. This exchange also involves Americans going to Africa to be in ministry. That ongoing process of exchange is thrilling and will make an enormous difference in the long run in terms of what will happen to the church in Africa as well as the church here.

Racial Justice and Mission

I think we are coming to the realization that justice is a global issue. If people can be hired for a dollar a week in México, then people are going to move their factories to México, and labor unions who fought for a wage of $10 an hour will not have a place to stand, because not only will there not be $10 an hour, there will not be a job at all. The global economy means that justice has to take place everywhere if we are going to have justice anywhere. So the claim, "I am my brother's keeper," is coming to us in ways now that are very graphic and very unmistakable. We can no longer say only, "Let's make things good for Americans," because things cannot be good for Americans unless they are good for everybody.

Someone has said that if you live in a First World country and have a Third World education, you'll make a Third World salary. That is very true. Each person's destiny is tied to my own. We're beginning to learn that because it's inescapable. The parts that go into American cars are made all over the globe. The lines are blurred. With the coming of the internet, people on the other side of the world can talk to people here. When we watched on television the celebration of the year 2000 and waited for the Y2K crisis to materialize, which of course it never did, we got a glimpse again of how the whole world is tied together and how you could be sitting in your living room in New York watching what's going on in Malaysia and seeing in graphic detail what the difference in time zones really means. We live in a global village all right, and justice means more than "just us," taking care of ourselves, but justice for everyone.

I believe the issues of racial justice and equality are at the heart of mission. Christ gave his life for the poor, the needy, and the downtrodden. He lived his life as a revolutionary, railing against a system of injustice that was so debilitating to his people. If you study carefully the anthropological evidence regarding the life of Christ and the historical time in which he lived, it's very clear that he was an advocate for the poor and the homeless and the marginalized. If we don't do that, then we're not Christians. Unfortunately, many of us have practiced the religion *about* Jesus and know nothing of the religion *of* Jesus. When you get clear about the religion Jesus himself practiced, then clearly justice is at the heart of it. If you practice the religion about Jesus, then liturgy and ritual and wealth and stained-glass windows are at the heart of that.

I remember a story about Jesus who took people to a window and said, "I want you to look out this window so you can see God." That was the religion of Jesus. He said, "I and my Father are one. If you know me, you know my Father. I want you to know God and spirituality so you can have life and have it more abundantly." But we took stained glass and put a picture of Jesus in the window, so we started worshiping the window because we couldn't see out of it to see through to the spirituality that Jesus was taking us to, which was really what God was about. So you cannot practice the religion of Jesus without having justice and equality issues at the center of your faith.

It also means there is no such thing as individual Christianity. The Kingdom of God is a corporate Kingdom. It is a Kingdom you cannot get into all by yourself, nor does the Kingdom have any meaning as a single, solitary thing. There is a sense in which individual salvation is an illusion, because whole cultures need to be saved. Dr. Mauiana Karenga, who gave us the gift of Kwanzaa, said that to free a black man into a capitalistic society with no capital is like freeing a goldfish into a bowl with no water. To think you can be saved into a world that is unjust, destructive, and hostile is an illusion because it's like being a goldfish without water. You have to be saved in a community where there is sustenance and support and nurture for the continuance and development of your Christian life. Without that community of nurture, salvation has very little meaning.

African Americans understand that people of color have been mistreated all over the world, and therefore we are not simply concerned about African Americans, we are concerned about the whole African diaspora in Latin America and the Caribbean and in other parts of the world, even in India and Bangladesh. There are very few places on the globe where people of color have not been discriminated against or mistreated, so we understand our destiny is tied to theirs and theirs to ours, and our concern is really global.

Now from the standpoint of white racism, Africans, Asians, Hispanics, and others are insignificant minorities in the white church. The truth is the first Methodist societies founded in the New World were black. It is common knowledge that the first societies or classes were formed by John Wesley in England in 1742. The first societies in what is now the United States were formed about 1766. But Nathaniel Gilbert, a Methodist layman, had formed classes in Antigua in 1759.[3] So we can say with some justification that blacks were the first people in the Methodist movement in the New World; therefore, The UMC is our church. As we expanded we allowed whites and Euro-Americans to be part of it.

One of the serious symptoms of the disease of racism is the arrogance to believe that you define the world by starting with yourself and making everything else subsidiary. People of color have been in The UMC from the very beginning. That means we are not going anywhere. Others may choose to leave, but we'll be here. If the Christian church and The UMC get serious about being Christian and understand the true origins of humanity and the true origins of Jesus, then it will be very clear that the minority in the church are Euro-Americans. As the population of Christians continues to grow around the world, that becomes a statistical fact. Euro-Americans are fast becoming a minority even in the U.S.

Rather than thinking about insignificant ethnic minorities, all of us are going to have to become clear that we are the children of God, and all of us have been created equal. There is no place for terms like minority or majority in the Kingdom of God. To the extent that we are ready to become a part of the Kingdom of God we need to remove those categories from our language.

The guaranteed appointment needs to come to an end. UM pastors need a high standard of performance with the ability to succeed or fail. The question of member retention will be equally serious among African

Americans as it is among other groups in the church in this country until The UMC can change and function in a way that is compatible with the world in which we live.

Contributions of African Americans

If we consider the contribution that African Americans can make to the church, I would rather discuss the poor and the rich, since so many African Americans are in the ranks of the poor. I think right now The UMC is still a middle-class institution in terms of its polity and practice, and if it wants to serve poor people, then it has to move from its middle-class assumptions about the church, its ministry, and its constituents. For example, we need to assume that if we are serving people who are poor, they cannot give the kinds of money that will pay for the ministry they need. That is basic.

Two, we need to confess our sin as a denomination that we have profited, and continue to profit, at the expense of the poor. As long as our pensions are invested in the worldwide stock market that sells nongerminating seeds to other countries, and we through our pension investments commit other atrocities that cause people to starve to death, I have to be held accountable for my sinfulness. We as a church need to be mindful of that sinfulness and figure out how to sin less and take responsibility for the people who are the victims of our sinning. We have to be clear that the reason there are poor black people dying in cities all over this nation is because we have contributed to the possibility of rich white people in suburbs. The process that makes some people rich also makes some people poor. We have not been opposed to that system. We keep investing our pension moneys in it. The recent allowance for an option that enables pensioners to invest in socially responsible funds is a step in the right direction, but we need to analyze the effect of all church funds to be sure our money is contributing to the right things.

If we are going to live in a capitalist world, and I think that is the only choice we have, we had better figure out how to make the capitalist system serve the poor. That means we have to endow urban churches, or create economic enterprises which build cash streams around them, and be clear that clergy need to be prepared to serve well, which means we have to create the economic resources to pay for first-class leadership. We also have to be sensitive to pastors who serve in urban areas. We should be clear that after we put them through four years of college and three years of seminary and send them out to be of service, they will expect to live in a way that is consistent with their sacrifice and debts from education. Therefore, they will have to be paid salaries to pay their debts and support their families. When pastors choose to live in urban areas where education is not available to their children, we will have to be sensitive to the need to make education available to them. There are a variety of issues where the church needs a different level of sensitivities and a different set of policies. In the past we have had the policy that if a church could not afford to pay a pastor enough money, we would put the church on a three-point charge, or we will put the church on welfare and give the pastor salary supplement and make her or him feel like a welfare victim. Those are bad policies. We need policies that take care of the whole economic health of a congregation so the pastor can be there as a healthy part of a healthy church, not as a part of a church that is bankrupt and trying to survive with welfare assistance from the denomination.

Another change that would make a difference is for white people in The UMC to stop picturing black people only as poor black people. Since 1960 there have been hundreds of black millionaires created in this country. The UMC does not have a single strategy to invite those people to be United Methodists. These are people whose lifestyle is consistent with our theology. We should have an intentional program of church extension that would specifically do the demographic homework to target affluent African Americans as the next group of people we are going to invite to become United Methodists. Then we should train the appropriate African-American leadership to start new congregations in affluent suburbs, or "edge cities," where there is a predominance of African Americans and start African-American congregations there.[4] That would make a huge difference. Those would be the easiest people for The UMC to evangelize. Where we have done that, and there has been an entrepreneurial pastor with the courage to step out and break the rules and do it, we have had great success. Kirbyjon Caldwell, Carlyle Stewart, and Zan Holmes, a pastor from the North Texas Conference noted for his preaching, are all examples.

I also think the way The UMC has dealt with African-American leadership is disgraceful. White pastors who serve on the cabinet and then leave usually get major churches. Some African-American pastors have left the cabinet and gone to churches of seventy members. Someone needs to do a study of African-American district superintendents in The UMC, the kind of appointments they left when they went on the cabinet, and the kind of appointments they went to when they went off the cabinet. It is one of the great horror stories of the denomination. If we could take twenty-five African-American superintendents and compare them with twenty-five white district superintendents, we would find that it is a terrible story. It is not a story that encourages young African Americans to be United Methodists. We might also document the legions of African-American pastors who are now serving in other denominations because of the racism in the church. Some of those changes would make it possible for The UMC to become beneficiaries of the talents and skills of African Americans.

I believe the future of The UMC among black Americans can be awesome. But we must clarify our two separate and distinct strategies.

Number one: Focus on the expanding black middle class and build strong megachurches for them.

Number two: Create adequately funded, endowed mission churches in poor communities with well-trained, committed leaders who will be compensated appropriately for their commitment to serving the poor.

CHAPTER 10

"Looking Forward Inwardly": The Future of the Korean Mission in the United States
Stephen S. Kim

Introduction: "Looking Forward Inwardly"

This essay as part of the United Methodist History of Mission project of the General Board of Global Ministries (GBGM) addresses the prospect of the Korean-American mission and ministry in the United States in the new millennium. Emphasis is on the role of Korean culture in the practice and theology of the United Methodist mission in the new century. And the present task is, on the one hand, to analyze and articulate how Korean culture, including social and religious precepts and practices, influences Korean-American immigrants and their children in their views, ideas, and practices of Christian faith in the new cultural context of the United States. On the other hand, perhaps there are habits and patterns of Korean religious and cultural life that need to be adjusted or transformed so as to facilitate the inculturation process. While our endeavor in both terms is required, I propose to "look forward inwardly" in this paper so that we understand how the Korean mind works and how Korean views, ideas, and values change in the context of the immigrant life in the U.S. in general and in the context of The United Methodist Church (UMC) in particular.

My suggestion is that Korean-American United Methodists need to turn their attention inward to nurture their inner selves in self-reflection and meditation even as they look forward striving to advance the Kingdom of God in all arenas of their life. Such an introspective critical reflection (I want to call it an "inward" look) will, I hope, afford us an opportunity to contemplate the ways in which Korean-American United Methodists can participate meaningfully and faithfully in the ongoing ministry of The UMC in the new century. Implicit in the suggestion is a critique of the Korean-American spirituality that has, it seems to me, concentrated on the "external" things such as membership growth, connectional issues, and political aptitude. This is not to say such "external" efforts are any less important than the internal. It simply refers to a view that, compared to other faiths, such as Buddhism, Protestantism in general, and United Methodism in particular, has not paid as much attention to "spiritual discipline," that is, self-reflective, meditational self-discipline to be wholly emptied of selfish desires and attachment so that the Holy Spirit might fully occupy the self.[1] In fact, the purpose of this paper is to advocate for the need to "look forward inwardly" in meditation and "self-negation" so God may find in us a space for continuing creation and transformation. This is to say that this article for the most part is part of a self-reflective, self-critical visioning process by a Korean-American United Methodist author, which is in itself a call for the larger United Methodist community to embrace the Korean-American self-critical reflection as its own.[2]

Plans for the Korean-American Mission and Ministry

Before proceeding to critical self-reflection, however, I want to survey the plans being made by various agencies and committees in the Korean-American United Methodist community for their mission and ministry in the new millennium. There are only a few published records of these plans. Here I have consulted two primary documents published in the last decade or so. One is an ambitious symposium planned and carried out by Korean United Methodist Church of Greater Washington in McLean, Virginia, under the leadership of the Reverend Young Jin Cho, held November 7–10, 1991. At the symposium, with the title of "Roots & Wings: An Invitational Symposium on the Future Ministry for the Korean-American Community," many competent researchers, teachers, and ministers representing a variety of perspectives, including a sociologist, mission executives, pastors, transgeneration ministers, clergywomen and clergymen, and lay leaders, were invited to present their views and a highly sophisticated dialogue resulted.

The other document I consulted was the report of the General Conference Task Force on Korean American Ministries, chaired by Bishop

Hae-Jong Kim, to the 2000 General Conference of The United Methodist Church. The task force presented, after long, careful study and analysis, a comprehensive plan of action to advance the ministry of, with, and by Korean-American United Methodists in the coming quadrennium. It purports to show the "growing consensus about future directions for the United Methodist Korean American ministry as it seeks to serve faithfully in the mission of 'making disciples for Jesus Christ'."[3] The report identified three broad areas that The UMC needs to address: clergy and lay leadership development, ministry with and for the next generation, and development of new "mission congregations," including strengthening the ministry of all congregations. With an authorized budget of nearly $3 million, the National Committee on Korean American Ministries launched its work in December 2000.[4]

The report, in my view, is solid in its research and analysis, and the imaginative and creative ways it proposes to achieve the goals are truly comprehensive. It is only with hope of fulfilling the mission to the fullest that I offer an explicit suggestion through this critical self-reflection on the report, which is in part already implied and assumed in the report. For successful implementation, the goals and action plan, I claim, must be predicated by the discussion articulated below in terms of "the glocal" identity, global ethic, and "a journey forward inwardly."

The Mission and Ministry of the Korean-American UMC

Although the General Conference task force report shows by far the most comprehensive planning, other documents along with numerous newsletters and reports of the caucuses and committees, including the National Association of Korean-American United Methodist Churches and the Transgeneration Ministry, reflect similar views. And they can be summarized in two large categories, leadership development and congregational development. The former includes the development of lay leaders, clergywomen, clergymen, next-generation pastors, formal education (seminaries and the annual conference board of ordained ministry's process for ordination), and informal education that happens in various official and unofficial contexts.[5] The latter involves supporting existing congregations, investing in establishing new congregations, and resourcing mission and ministry by securing buildings and publishing culturally sensitive and relevant materials. Claiming the most urgent needs for the denominational attention were

[206] *Christian Mission in the Third Millennium*

A sculpture, symbolizing arms reaching up to God, is on display outside Christ United Methodist Church in Honolulu. The artwork was unveiled in 2003 as part of the centennial for Korean American Mission in America. *(UMNS photo by Kathy L. Gilbert)*

(1) identifying, enlisting, and supporting the next-generation leaders (transgeneration and second-generation leaders), (2) mainstreaming clergywomen, and (3) contextualization of the resources of mission and ministry. Since the report has been adopted and the budget granted, and the work of the National Committee on Korean American Ministries has been launched under the leadership of Bishop Hae-Jong Kim, I will forgo a detailed discussion of these goals and action plan. Instead, here I briefly offer a critical reflection on the ongoing effort to advance the Korean-American United Methodist mission and ministry in the new century.

"Asian Transcendental Pragmatism"

The operating assumption here is that the theologies and practices of many Korean and Korean-American Christians, including Methodists and United Methodists, are heavily influenced by century-old religious and cultural ideologies, patterns, customs, and habits, primarily those of Confucian, Taoist, and Buddhist traditions which have thoroughly pervaded the entire Korean culture and spirituality in the past five thousand years. These theologies and practices are characterized by what I call "Asian transcendental pragmatism"—a peculiarly Asian way of relating oneself to the teachings of different religious/spiritual/cultural traditions, such as Confucian, Taoist, and Buddhist views and values. These traditions are regarded, not as three distinct sets of orthodoxy, among which the best or the truest would be chosen for devotion and commitment, but as complementary "teachings" (which is translated as "religion").[6] This Asian way of relating weighs, in my view, significantly in the daily life of Korean Christians wherever they live. In post-Cold War era America, Korean Americans, like many people in the global village, must deal with at least three "contending forces in the global arena"—globalization, communitarianism, and military industry rivalry—as Professor Jan Love expertly articulated. These forces bring with them opportunities as well as threats. And the Christian mission is to put them "to use for life-sustaining, open, and diverse communities that promote a better world for all."[7]

This paper considers the three themes of "Asian transcendental pragmatism" ("familyism," fatalism, and latitudinarianism) from the *Chung-Yung* perspective[8]—the idea of balance and harmony—to see how the worldview predicated upon these ideas and views interacts with the social, ethical, and spiritual forces of the new world thickly conditioned by the "contending forces in the global arena."[9] Such a critical analysis will help us understand the cultural and spiritual heritage of Korea and perhaps will render some guidelines for the future mission of Korean United Methodists in the U.S. And I propose to name three guiding lights for the missional vision, namely, the "glocal" identity,[10] global ethic, and "a journey forward inwardly." To wit, the future of the Korean-American mission and ministry depends on the faithfulness of Korean Americans to sojourn with a God who journeys with them and to maintain a keen sense of who they are as members of the global family, an ethical imperative of interdependence and global solidarity, and the inner, contemplative life that was so characteristic of Jesus of Nazareth.

Widening of the Horizon: Mission as Transformation toward a Global Faith[11]

Korean spirituality undoubtedly is part of "Asian transcendental pragmatism," heavily influenced by animistic/shamanistic supernaturalism, which permeates all Asian religious/spiritual sensibilities. Shamanism has survived the onslaught of foreign faiths by effecting a subtle change in the very essence of the invading foreign spirituality (such as Confucianism, Taoism, Buddhism, and Christianity) in such a way as to assert decisive influence in slightly altering a consciousness and eventually in changing a worldview.

The explosive growth of Christianity in Korea in the late twentieth century did not alter the situation much.[12] My claim is that the Korean church has yet to achieve reflective rationality that is characteristic of personal and prophetic consciousness.[13] As the Buddhist teaching of devotion to *Amitabha* in its content is closer to a *gut* (shamanistic ritual), praying for the spirit's favor, than to a Buddhist prayer in meditation for self-negation, much of the Christian practice remains prereflective and prerational.[14] Animistic/shamanistic supernaturalism is ubiquitous in the history of religions in Korea down through the ages, from the Dangun myth in the Three Kingdom period (fourth century C.E.) to Buddhist Shila and Korea (from eighth to fourteenth centuries), to the Confucian Yi Dynasty (from fourteenth century to early twentieth centuries), and to the Christian modern period in the twentieth century. In contemporary Korean society, Christians make up more than one-quarter of the entire population owing to the unparalleled success of mission and evangelism which began with devoted missionaries in the late-nineteenth century, primarily from the U.S.[15] In Christian rituals in contemporary Korea, for example, many remnants of animistic/shamanistic supernaturalism can be found. These remnants include *Tongsung Gido*, loud public prayer of petition in a worship setting, which is mostly a series of loud pronouncements of a wish list or even a shouting match with "God" to influence God's will in the petitioners' favor, a practice that resembles shamanist *gut* both in form and content. These supernaturalistic remnants also exhibit characteristics of "other-worldism" peculiarly confused with juvenile impatience demanding immediate gratification. The themes of salvation, eternal life, and material blessings in return for devotion and donation dominate the contents of prayer, worship, and "faith," which shows much shamanistic influence imbedded in the Korean psyche, including the Christian.

Such a syncretic and shamanistic tendency has subtly yet thoroughly infiltrated Korean spirituality to produce the characteristic modalities of Asian transcendental pragmatism, of which three major themes are selected for a brief discussion: familyism, fatalism, and latitudinarianism. At issue is the fact that all of these themes have often been embraced by the Koreans to limit, rather than to expand, their horizon and vision, owing to the historical vicissitudes. Thus, the concern for the welfare of the family, small and large, becomes "familyism" (which could be styled "familialism," but which I prefer to call "familyism" to be clear), an exclusive conservatism that keeps concerns outside the immediate family at bay or even antagonistic. The insurmountable adversities the Koreans had to endure throughout history led them to "blame" them on fate rather than to face reality. The "wise" attempt to embrace both extremes in balance becomes a flunky attempt to dupe the situation by saying "yes" and "no" in the same breath, that is, latitudinarianism. My claim is that before we can accomplish leadership and congregational development,[16] we must learn how to turn this around and make these age-old Korean characteristics widen our horizon and expand our vision so that we may embrace the world as our family, face reality with faith and courage, and be truly inclusive for the advancement of the dignity of creation and the Kingdom of God. In addition, my claim is also that all of these must be predicated by "religious," "spiritual" discipline of the "seekers" in the solitary encounter with God in quiet meditation. To our woe, many of us in the Protestant tradition simply assume the spiritual aptitude of our ministerial candidates to be engaged in God's mission in the world, when they have only begun their spiritual journey with little preparation. Buddhists, in contrast, and many other traditions for that matter, consider preparation of the self so essential a preparation as to require a certain level of spiritual aptitude; they consider preparedness an absolute prerequisite to any work in outreach mission. This is why the quality spiritual training of the leaders (which is a top priority in most plans for the future mission) must be taken seriously, since these leaders are going to be the agents of God's transformative work in the world. Such transformation is the goal of mission, including the Korean-American United Methodist mission in the new millennium.

Familyism to "Glocal Identity"

The contention here is that Korean/Asian familyism is a communitarianism — a basic human need — that needs to be liberated from its parochial parameters. As Love illustrates, communitarianism works both ways: it works like glue to solidify the members of the community — its best example being religion — but at the same time it can and often does distort religious commitment and twist the group identity, pitting one group against another, as has been seen in numerous occasions in our history, most poignantly in the "ethnic cleansing" in the former Yugoslavia. Familyism as communitarianism needs to be nurtured to go beyond the traditional boundaries of "conservatism . . . communism, tribalism . . . identity politics, global fragmentation, and clash of civilizations."[17]

Originating from the Confucian teaching of filial piety, the concept of family is arguably the most consistent and influential character in Asian spirituality. Koreans, like most other Asian peoples, operate around the axis of family in their personal, social, political, and spiritual life. Every activity revolves around the family, which, as a basic cell of society, is believed to be the center of life and thus acquires a sacred character. Parents and ancestors who are the origins of our life in the family are venerated with such reverence as to equal closely our devotion to deity. In the Confucian teaching, children are to pay homage to their parents and ancestors as if they were indeed "gods." A folk belief (which is clearly shamanistic) is that the spirits of departed parents and ancestors are accessible through rituals such as *gut* and *gosa* (rituals designed to pacify the spirits by offering food and devotion). The spirits not only accept our devotion (material as well as spiritual) and return favors with practical prizes (such as healing of diseases or achieving success in business, etc.), but they also take revenge if their wishes are not met. This custom survives the long Buddhist reign and even Christian iconoclasm, primarily through its shamanistic metamorphosis. So we saw the mayor of the great city of Seoul (who holds a Ph.D. from a prominent university in the U.S. and had been a professor in Seoul National University, a cabinet member before he was elected to the mayoralty, and a presidential candidate) falling on his knees paying homage and offerings to a cooked boar head, asking for blessing and safe operation of an underground tunnel in the middle of the metropolis. This brief description of the process shows that every means is called into service to protect, sustain, and nurture a community in the family.

The chief familial value of *Hyo* (filial piety) is considered high enough in its importance to cause confusion in ethics when *Hyo* is in conflict with one's faithfulness to the imperial king. When Yoon Ji-Choong and Kwon Sang-Yeon of Jinsan, Cholla Province, buried their family tablets (which are deemed sacred as records of ancestors) in 1791 to confess their conversion to the Catholic faith, they were beheaded for the charge of treason and insubordination to the king. The chief opposition to Christian faith in Yi Korea in the eighteenth century was its iconoclastic attitude toward "ancestor worship."[18] The underlying fear for the government in its persecution of hundreds of missionaries and Korean converts was its disregard for the family as the most fundamental unit of social and political order and the consequent chaos in the hierarchical social and political structure based on the concept of family. Such a family-centered social and political structure has given strong cohesive power to Korea as a nation "born of single blood," but it has also been the source of much corrupt crony and party politics, as well as parochialism and regionalism in all aspects of Korean life that have often disturbed the Korean society.

Such a parochial familyism has been a dominant pattern in family and church life for most Korean immigrants. The majority of them cite the education of their children as the single most important reason for their emigration in the first place, and in most cases a family sticking together for better or worse helps them survive the harsh reality of immigrant life in a foreign land. Finding stability is the highest priority for them both at home and in church. All its scandals and sins notwithstanding, the Korean immigrants' churches have been centers of stability in their social and spiritual life. And the houses and the church buildings are two items the Korean immigrants invest in with the utmost urgency, as Professor Jung Ha Kim pointed out.[19] But it has also been a concern for many leaders that Korean families and churches find it difficult to go beyond the boundaries of their small, parochial families to find their identity invariably linked with that of other families and churches. And to help Korean immigrants achieve what I call "the glocal identity" is, I argue, one of the most urgent missions of the church in the new millennium.

Koreans are peculiarly parochial when it comes to matters relating to the welfare of their family and the sense of identity as members of the family. The notion of family itself for many Koreans is limited to their immediate relatives living under the same roof eating out of the same rice cooker. The more "family-oriented" they are, the fiercer they become to protect and isolate "the inner circle" of their kinsmen and relatives, thus putting the larger family of society and the world at bay. Such parochialism, of course, has a social and ethical value. It provides them a sense of community and accountability in the communal life of a family. So in a difficult time, such as the hard days of the Korean War in the 1950s, they stick together and push and pull for survival in wartime. When things go well, however, it is not easy for them to extend attention and care beyond their small family circle. They feel little, if any, responsibility for the welfare of the larger family of Koreans and even less of the world community. Nevertheless, such a close-knit community gives them a sense of identity and thus stability, and it often is contradicted when they are pushed to open themselves to the global arena, which it is increasingly becoming urgent for them to do, in the era of multiculturalism that is commonplace in the U.S.

This conflict between the safe haven of the "local" identity of Koreans and the challenging "global" identity as Korean Americans living in the new world might perhaps require us to learn how the old ways can be commensurate with the new in a changing context to produce "creative transformation,"[20] which constitutes the mission and ministry of Korean United Methodists in the new millennium. That is, it is necessary to articulate a new "glocal" identity for Korean-American United Methodists to capitalize on the themes of "old" Korean spirituality that will help them to be members of the global family without abandoning Korean identity and heritage.

From Fatalism to Global Ethic

The themes of Asian transcendental pragmatism are predicated upon a worldview that assumes an ultimate unity, namely, the Confucian principle of *Li* (propriety), which holds everything together in family, society, and the cosmos. A long history of foreign aggression and feudal oppression, compounded by escapist religious philosophies, created, however, fatalistic folk beliefs such as the Korean obsession with the notion of *Pal-ja* and popular religious practices that led the people either to seek refuge in an otherworldly haven or long for the return to nature, such as the Taoist notion of longing for (or escaping to) mother-nature.

In her article "Faith, Fortune-telling, and Social Failure," Professor Dawnhee Yim Janelli of Indiana University (Bloomington) shared a penetrating insight into the Korean psyche revealed in the Korean fascination

Korean United Methodists in the United States have raised $100,000 to build an information and training center in Mongolia that will supplement the work of mission churches like this one in Ulaanbaatar, Mongolia. The United Methodist General Board of Global Ministries will contribute another $100,000. *(UMNS photo by Sang Yean Cho)*

with fortunetelling.[21] The article is a critical analysis of Korean beliefs and cultural values surrounding the notion of *Pal-ja* and *Pal-ja-so-gwan* (literally, eight characters, referring to the fate a person is born with, but metaphorically referring to fatalism and escapism, "blame it on the fate" — *Pal-ja-ta-ryung*). In order to obtain some measure of belief in the validity of fortunetelling, she interviewed seventeen Korean women who frequently visited fortunetellers. According to the study, many Korean women tend to explain all failures in their lives as *Pal-ja*. They see the failure in their social relationships (or lack of them) with their husbands and children. Her data showed women between the ages of thirty and fifty held a greater faith in fortunetelling and had a lower degree of skepticism. A thorough analysis of the data also showed that women with low familial and social responsibilities (no children to take care of and with daughters-in-law to help them) were socially anomalous. They occupied social positions which did not belong to the expected life cycle of a Korean woman. Many of them were divorcees, lived alone, had husbands but no children, were unmarried "old maids," and were widows living with old unmarried daughters. So her hypothesis was that fortunetelling is especially appealing to socially anomalous women because it explains their social condition in such a way as to relieve them of personal responsibility for failing to attain what is customarily expected of Korean women.

This customary expectation comes from the powerful Neo-Confucian ideology of social order, of which the family is the basic unit, and women were customarily forced not only to give birth to new family members but also to serve them. A Korean woman's first and most important duty is to give birth to sons, and the failure to do so is one of seven "evils" which can be legally used by her husband to expel, not divorce, her. She is left with no recourse but to blame *pal-ja* and resort to fortunetellers' comforting words and accept her fate. That is how *pal-ja* is the most fundamental concept of fortunetelling.

The word *"pal-ja"* literally denotes "eight" in Chinese and represents the year, month, day, and two-hour period of one's birth which, according to ancient Taoist/shamanist beliefs, determine the fate of a person. It has six major characteristics which betray strong influences of Neo-Confucian ideals of balance and harmony of family and the state, ideals which are sustained by women's perseverance.[22] Therefore, women's failure to produce sons and to serve men is tantamount to treachery against the state as well as the disruption of familial and social, and even cosmic, unity and harmony. Conversely, it meant the pivotal role and place of women in the sustenance of Asian existence, which Confucian men would not admit.

The theme of interdependence in *pal-ja-so-gwan* (attributing to *pal-ja*) is particularly significant in a Korean woman's relation to parents as a young woman and to husband as a wife. Less often, a child's *pal-ja* influences the lives of parents; but becoming a widow and expulsion from home, that is, social anomaly, are particularly felt as serious misfortunes for which only fortunetelling can provide a relief. To have a good *pal-ja* is to have a harmonious and complete family life. An expelled woman, a widow, an unmarried girl, a second wife, a concubine, a woman without a son, or a woman whose husband keeps a mistress — all are considered to have a bad *pal-ja*.

In short, going to a fortuneteller as *pal-ja so gwan* is a way of dealing with frustrations, failures, and anomalies in life because life is expected to be whole, to be balanced and harmonious, to be just and peaceful. The family, in its best sense of the word, is a model of wholeness, justice, and peace and is the basis of the great social and cosmic order envisioned by the Confucian scholar-statesmen. They assumed a world of unity, harmony, and peace. But just as familyism can easily be turned into exclusivism for those who are not in the family, women who were forced to sacrifice themselves to sustain such a family or the world were ignored.

Such fatalism must be transformed to a "global ethic"[23] to affirm the interdependence of all creation in God's care, and Korean-American United Methodists shall have to help Korean Americans move away from the fatalistic and escapist mode of existence to a life with accountability and a sense of solidarity with the entire human family.

Latitudinarianism to Holism

Historically, Koreans have had to depend on the whims of conquering nations, such as Mongolia, China, the Soviet Union, and Japan, for their peace and any chance of happy and meaningful life, which made the people of Korea quite flunky or latitudinarian for survival. This dependence is a tragedy, but a fact; Korea, situated in the geographical crossroad of multinational rivalry of power and hegemony, developed highly sensitive antennae for survival. Religion also has functioned as a means of survival, if not meaningful life. And religion, particularly Christian faith, has given the poor, tired, and despairing Koreans a power of hope, and the Christian church helped the Korean people survive the brutal Japanese colonial exploitation thirty-eight years. After the Korean War (1950–1953), the nation struggled to recover from near bankruptcy; the Christian faith along with other religious faiths provided spiritual resources in rebuilding the nation to rise above all adversities. Such a history was thought to be one of the reasons for Korean flunkyism. Thus, a happy life in the next world meant a great deal more than the present award for religious devotion, and on such an elusive promise, the Korean people have been preyed upon by many political and religious entrepreneurs.

Highly susceptible to eschatological "other-worldism," Korean Christians, and perhaps shamanists, Taoists, Buddhists, and Confucians too, have shown their flunkyism to the gods of materialism, this-worldliness, and temporary powers. In the *parvenu* economy of the late 1980s and 1990s, many religious groups, particularly Christians, sang praises to God for the promise kept in bringing the material blessing and explosive numerical growth. But as they got used to worldly success and comforts, their praise subtly changed to self-admiration and self-indulgence. Even as the preachers shouted the promise of a better future in the other world for those who contributed more, worshipers contributed more in expectation for more in this world. There is an interesting dynamic in the relation between "other-worldism" and "this-worldism": Korean Christians fervently pray for the success of their business, family's health, and children's passing the entrance exams, and they back up their wish list with fat contributions, just as they would do for a shaman. And if the prayers are not answered to their satisfaction, they move to another church or even to another faith, since the god of that pastor or of that church did not deliver, and there surely would be a church whose pastor has more spiritual power to deliver than this one. This is the same old shamanistic ritual of *gut*: coaxing the spirit to come down and give blessings. If the offering is not sufficient, more will be given. In this sense, Korean pastors are compared to shamans. (Kim Il Sung, by the way, is considered one of the most able shamans by the North Korean people.) It seems as though the Korean people, Christian or not, are out to beat with vengeance age-old defeatism, foreign domination, and empty promises for a better future. Secularism has taken over religious institutions, which are now in the business of building churches and retreat centers for profit. Money and vainglory, having now taken the place of devotion and sacrifice, are new masters for many flunky Korean Christians.

Looking back, perhaps shamanist and Confucian teachings in Korea have always had pragmatic, practical, utilitarian (not necessarily public), material expectation in return for devotion. Koreans have fallen down to their knees before the altar of materialism and secularism. Success, material success, becomes more urgent than principle, at times, even more urgent than life. It may bring wealth, but such intense cupidity causes an intense competitive lifestyle which endangers holistic community living, which must be a major missional objective of Korean-American mission in the new millennium.

Chung-Yung as a Guide to the Journey toward Spiritual Maturity

An underlying principle for the Asian transcendental pragmatism illustrated above is the ubiquitous hermeneutic of harmony and balance, influenced by the Neo-Confucian ideal of *Chung-Yung* (the Middle Way, or balance and harmony, ultimately pointing to the reality of unity in diversity; it also means sincerity), which was suggested as a way of perceiving reality in a complementary perspective.[24] It also meant to nurture a true humanity, a sage. Prof. Sung-bum Yun proposed a theology of sincerity (*Chung-Yung*) based on the idea of sincerity as the foundation of reconciliation in family, society, and even in the ecosystem.[25] His notion of *Sung* (sincerity) is extended to harmony between revelation and reason, the spiritual and the material, law and gospel, the sacred and the mundane, the church and the world, and even the unification of North and South Korea and peace between the West and the East.[26] Family is its prime example; each member of the family complements other members to sustain a community by faithfully fulfilling one's own station. When any one of the members fails, the whole family suffers, and conversely, when any one member has a joyful occasion, the whole family rejoices. There is a dynamic and organic relation among the individual members of the family: the patriarchs take the responsibility of maintaining harmony and balance in various relations in the family. In many cases, this concept of small family is extended to include a village, or a town, or the entire nation, or even the global village.

Harmony and balance are also major concerns of the Buddhist faith as well as the Taoist. As social, political, and cultural critics in opposition to the Confucian statesmen-scholars in the Yi Dynasty, the Taoist hermits sought transcendence by removing themselves from the society (which fragments) and by attempting to find unity (harmony and balance) with nature. Equanimity, eternal bliss, and immortality would be the blessed results of such efforts. The chief motif of many Buddhists, particularly Pure Land and Son Buddhists (two extremes of Mahayana faith), is to return to the original Buddha nature or Buddhaland, a blissful state of nothingness or emptiness (the unity of *samadhi* and *prajna*, according to Chinul), which is an ultimate expression of harmony and balance.[27] Harmony in heaven and earth is also a core concept in shamanism.[28] The ideal humanity of a person is sustained in the harmonious and balanced relationship between heaven and earth, which is the foundation of the Dangun myth. This myth is also an expression of the creation of the cosmos, and the birth of a nation as the center of the cosmos, according to Professor Dong-Shik Ryu.[29] Professor Kwang-Shik Kim interpreted Yun's *Sung* and Ryu's *Poong-ryu* (a man in full harmony with nature and the cosmos) as the continuation and the maturation of the ideal humanity theme in Dangun myth. As such, a strong motif of harmony and balance remained a distant hope and vision for Koreans, since the reality has always fallen short of their aspiration.

The idea of *Chung-Yung* is also related to Korean reluctance and hesitancy to break cleanly with what seems initially untrue and unjust because things from the perspective of *Chung-Yung* always have within them the potential to be transformed and become true and just, whereas the true and the unjust can always become opposites. But this is not to say that the Koreans do not have a clear sense of true and just. It is only that the Korean temperament is not to make a hasty decision. This hesitance or reluctance, however, is often mistaken for unscrupulousness, and for a good reason. It is not duplicity, but rather dubiousness, or careful suspension of judgment until such time as everything becomes crystal clear. Such dubiousness, though no harm may have been intended, caused havoc for the Koreans and their neighbors in a multicultural context. Harnessing the energy "wisely" (that is, for the welfare and dignity of the larger family of God's creation), however, is intended to maintain balance and harmony in life, and a vigilant attendance to sustain the balanced life is the art of life in tranquillity and detachment. Mission and ministry, thus, is an art of keeping God's people in a faithful journey toward God's presence in a world of constant flux. It is an inward journey looking forward to spiritual maturity.

CHAPTER 11

A Latino Perspective
José M. Fernández

Introduction

The United States Latino population in 1990 numbered 22,428,749 — almost 23 million.[1] The U.S. Latino population today is approaching 30 million.[2] The projected Latino population for 2030 is 52,765,870 and is expected to account for 25 percent of the population.[3] The U.S. Census Bureau reported that Latinos represent 16 percent of the population under the age of eighteen, compared to 15 percent of African-American youth. By the year 2020 Latinos will represent 20 percent of the youth in the U.S.[4]

Two emerging facts get our attention from the projected Latino population trends in this new millennium: first, the Latino population will be the largest minority group in the U.S.; second, the Latino youth group will represent 20 percent of those under eighteen years of age.

In view of these projections, General Council of Ministries President J. Woodrow Hearn said, "We must learn new ways of relating to persons who represent a variety of cultures, languages and traditions. To have a wider selection of all God's people in the Church can enrich us as we share with each other."[5] These words spoken by one of our bishops can well be a challenge to our own United Methodist Church (UMC).

This essay will endeavor to do four things:

1. Present the Latino as a positive ingredient in the U.S. population.
2. Introduce a new paradigm for dealing with Latino issues.
3. Present the National Plan for Hispanic Ministry as a vital tool for missions.
4. Summarize and list recommendations for mission.

The Latino in the United States

Early Explorers and Founders

Writing about the Latino in the U.S. runs the risk of being repetitious in telling our story. In recent years Latino writers have been retelling the Latino experience in the U.S. by writing books, articles, and essays. The Latino has been in the territory now called the U.S. before the British founded their first American colony in the area now called Virginia. Spanish settlers living in Cuba founded the city of Saint Augustine in Florida. Twelve years before the Pilgrims landed on Plymouth Rock, the Spaniards founded the city of Santa Fe, New Mexico.[6] Latinos were explorers and founders of cities throughout the area that now comprises the U.S. This diffuse presence can easily be seen as we look at a map of the U.S. and find cities named Los Angeles, San Diego, Sacramento, Las Cruces, and El Paso. We also see states with names like California, Colorado, New Mexico, and Florida which reflect the Latino influence.

Some of these explorers, such as Fray Marco de Niza (killed in what is now New Mexico, 1539), Francisco Vásquez de Coronado (exploration of 1540), and Alvar Nuñez Cabeza de Vaca (stranded in the present Texas, 1528) had large contingents of men in their exploration trips. Many of these men settled in various places of the territory explored. These men and others not mentioned in this essay are the ancestors of the present-day Latino.

The Emergence of the Term "Latino"

Historians writing about the Spanish-speaking people in the U.S. have used different terms, most of which have come about by bureaucratic and political needs, and most of the time these were not the choice of the Latino. Allow me to walk you through the several stages of the Latino experience in this country and see the terms used by historians in writing about these Spanish-speaking people.

The first stage: Spanish explored the territory now known as the Southwest. These people were known as *Hispanos*. The term "Hispanic" (English for *Hispano*) was used to identify those persons coming from Spain, which in early European history was known as the Hispania Iberian Peninsula. Many of these early pioneers settled, especially in New Mexico, and up to the present some of these people prefer to be called

Hispano. Because the present Latino population in the U.S. is made up of many subgroups who have come from countries other than Spain, the term "Hispanic" does not truly reflect all present subgroups, and not all Spanish-speaking persons accept the term.

Second stage: Mexicans migrated northward during the early years of the twentieth century. These Spanish-speaking Mexicans migrated into the U.S. and settled not only in the Southwest, but throughout the U.S. These people were identified as Mexicans, but because they were in "America," their children were called Mexican-American.

Many residents in the U.S. think that the term "America" means only the country known as the U.S. In all of the countries south of the U.S. border, people consider themselves "American." The term "American" is not used by these Americans for identification purposes; they just say, "I am a Mexican," or Nicaraguan, Argentinean, etc.

Still others wanted to called these Mexicans "Chicanos." As was expected, not every Spanish-speaking person of Mexican origin liked to be called a Chicano.[7]

Third stage: Today the Spanish-speaking group in the U.S. is composed of several subgroups, such as Cubans, Puerto Ricans, Mexicans, and Central and South Americans. This group, then, is ethnic in the sense that all subgroups within the whole are bound together by similar customs, social views, and especially the Spanish language. These subgroups are very nationalistic, and no one wants to give up national identification, yet there is a common term preferred by most and that term is "Latino." This term is probably a shortened term for *Latinoamericano* and appeals to the majority of this ethnic group.

Northward Migration of Latinos

Humans and animals have two basic needs in common—the need to survive and the need to procreate. Both species go about meeting these two needs in very similar ways. In this analogy I will deal only with the issue of survival and let the other be dealt with in the reader's imagination. Living in a border town presents different experiences and calls forth different reactions from various people.

Allow me to share with you the way I experience life in a border town named Douglas, Arizona. My first pastoral appointment was to this same town in 1958, to a small Latino Methodist congregation which was faithfully serving the border area, including Agua Prieta, Sonora, which is the town in México across from Douglas. The Phelps Dodge Corporation was the only source of industry for both cities.

A company town has certain idiosyncrasies, and Douglas was typical in every sense of the word. The city and business leaders were of European or Anglo descent, as were the managers of the copper smelter, while Latinos served as the main labor source. These European descendants had their own civic clubs, ate at their own restaurants, and worshiped in their own churches (including Methodist). We jump ahead to the year 2000, and this is what I see in Douglas. The copper smelter is gone: literally all physical traces of this large enterprise are gone. Only a large mound of black waste called "slag" remains to remind us of the Phelps Dodge legacy. Today as you walk down the main avenue you see signs on businesses that say "El de Todo," "El Major Precio," "La Familia," etc. The personnel of all businesses, including the Safeway and Wal-Mart, are Latino and bilingual. Douglas has seen a complete transition from Anglo to Latino in all levels of the city. The Anglo churches have not kept pace, however, with the transition and are almost empty on Sunday. Projections indicate that The UMC, along with congregations of the other mainline denominations, is going to die soon!

At night as I lie awake I can hear the barking of dogs about a mile to the south side of the city; this barking wave is moving northward until it stops on the north side. What is causing this wave of barking? It is the wave of immigrants jumping the border fence and moving northward. The last vehicle I see at night as I check the door and peer into the darkness is a white van with a green stripe on its side telling me it is the Border Patrol. The first vehicle I see in the morning as I go for the newspaper is another white van with a green stripe on its side.

As I drive to any other city away from Douglas, I see dozens of Latinos being rounded up like cattle and put into Border Patrol vans and buses and taken back to the port of entry. Let me put this into perspective using table 3 at the end of the chapter. The number of apprehensions of undocumented aliens (almost all of them Latinos) for fiscal year 1999 was 1,599,606. The question that arises from this fact is: How many are getting through the Border Patrol forces? Estimates made by knowledgeable people like Ray Borane, the mayor of Douglas, and others show that at least 10 percent of the number of apprehensions make it through.

Referring once again to the analogy of humans and animals having the common need to survive, we see the survival of both depends on food; in this analogy food means jobs. In the animal kingdom we see herds like caribou, wildebeests, etc., migrating from one area to another depending on the food source. Hunger forces a herd to migrate even long distances to find food. The migrants going through Douglas are moving northward to meet the basic need for food and jobs. Humans in their effort to "save" land or property from migrating herds put up fences and employ large number of personnel and equipment to patrol their land. Sometimes humans will devise methods of controlling the herds, like the wild horses in Nevada, by building barriers in a funnel formation and, using helicopters, herding horses into the corrals. This analogy can be seen in the Border Patrol tactics of using the funnel systems. The two extreme points of the border between the U.S. and México have been fortified, and the neck of the funnel is the Tucson sector. This sector reported 470,252 apprehensions of undocumented aliens in the fiscal year 1999. In reviewing the breakdown of the Tucson sector, note that the funnel system is again used, and the Douglas port of entry is the neck of the funnel. Of the total Tucson sector apprehensions, Douglas reports almost one-half of them, 202,868.

Another interesting fact in table 3 is the nation of origin of those apprehensions. With the exception of thirty-three persons, all were Latinos. A constant wave of undocumented aliens is migrating northward, a phenomenon which adds to the projected population growth of almost 53 million for the year 2000.

The border-city issues are a common scenario in all U.S.–México border communities. The immigration issue has become a volatile political issue in both countries. This essay is not meant to deal with the immigration issue, rather to point out some of the subissues resulting from the fact that there is a northward migration of Latinos.

My personal experience living in Douglas leads me to say that this station looks like a police state. The number of armed Border Patrol is frightening: twelve thousand agents for the Tucson sector, four hundred agents for the Douglas station. Under the label of Operation Safeguard the Border Patrol has increased its visible equipment along the border—stadium lights, both portable and stationary, remote control video cameras, infrared cameras for night patrolling, electronic sensors buried in the ground, imagery movement cameras, and a steel bar fence twelve feet high.

Some negative subissues resulting from this migration have developed. For example, there is a wide-scale people-smuggling problem. The *pollero*

[224] *Christian Mission in the Third Millennium*

These undocumented immigrants were apprehended by the U.S. Border Patrol in April, 2003, as they sought to enter the U.S. through the Tohono O'odam Reservation in southern Arizona. Eighty-five of the 145 immigrant deaths recorded by the U.S. Border Patrol in Arizona for the year ending September 30, 2002, occurred in this area. The flood of undocumented immigrants, some 1,500 a day, has created a severe problem for the reservation, which is already struggling with poverty, unemployment, and a high diabetes rate. *(Photo by Jack Kurtz © Phoenix Newspapers, Inc.*, Arizona Republic, *April 27, 2003. Used with permission. Permission does not imply endorsement.)*

(a person who lives in México and smuggles people; from *pollo*, or chicken) and the coyote (a person who lives in the U.S. and smuggles people) are both earning large amounts of money. The average amount paid by each migrant to the *pollero* or coyote to get into the U.S. is $600. Not only is this an exorbitant amount, but the smugglers many times leave migrants stranded in the desert or mountains where they die from the heat or the cold. Many of them alert the Border Patrol about the whereabouts of their *pollitos* (chicks).

Another problem which has arisen is that of drugs. On both sides of the border there seems to be a network in place where drugs are being imported to the U.S. The drug traffickers (*narco-traficantes*) pay large amounts of money to the "mules," who are not drug users nor traffickers but are the ones literally carrying on their backs sacks filled with blocks of marijuana. "Mules" are the poor, hungry migrants coming northward. Then there is also the problem of border bandits who operate on both sides of the border. These bandits prey upon the migrants, for they know they probably have some money to pay a smuggler to get into the U.S. These bandits are ruthless and violent. They not only rob the men but sometimes rape the women traveling north. The Mexican government has responded to this problem by creating Grupo Beta, a paramilitary group of men to protect the migrant while in México. The U.S. has not created any program to respond to this need.

Where Do Latinos Live?

The majority of the 7.3 million Latino households in the U.S. live in urban areas within the states of California, Texas, New York, Florida, Illinois, and New Jersey. The average number in Latino households is 3.6 persons; this number reflects the high birth rate and the extended family of Latinos. Those of Mexican origin make up 63 percent of the Latino population. This group is the fastest-growing segment of the U.S. population. Those of Puerto Rican descent make up 10 percent of the Latino population, while those of Cuban descent make up 5 percent. The remaining 22 percent of the Latino immigrants come from countries in Central and South America.

The Spanish language is an integral factor in the Latino culture and is the mortar which holds the different subgroups together. Spanish is the first language of approximately 93 percent of Latinos and of these, 96 percent first learned the language in their home and 46.4 percent of their children speak Spanish. Today the U.S. is the fifth-largest Spanish-speaking country after México, Spain, Argentina, and Colombia. Projections are that by 2010 the U.S. will be the second-largest Spanish-speaking county after México.[8]

Since this essay is intended to be read primarily by United Methodists, let me point out that there is not one jurisdiction in The UMC which does not have a large concentration of Latinos. Please refer to table 1 and notice that in 1990 there were a total of 22,428,740 Latinos in United Methodist territory and that the projected Latino population for 2020 in that same territory will be 52,765,870.

Latinos in the Mainstream United States

The chart at the end of the chapter under this title is a list of Latinos who have made contributions in their respective fields to make the U.S. what it is today. These and many other Latinos have mainlined into the U.S. culture but have not assimilated. Assimilation requires a person to give up his/her culture and to adopt a new one. In the Spanish-language programs for television or radio there is a highlighting of Latinos who have excelled in their fields and are referred to as an *orgullo* Latino, meaning, "this Latino makes us proud." Some Latinos have assimilated to the degree of denying their roots and culture; usually they are not taken seriously by the Latino population. The list is a good indicator that the Latino is integrating well into the mainstream; notice also that this list reflects the Latino of Mexican origin.

One of the major contributions of Latinos to the U.S. is to the economy. Latino-owned businesses comprise almost 40 percent of all minority-owned firms. The U.S. Census Bureau in 1992 reported that Latino men owned 42 percent of all minority-men-owned businesses. Today there are more than 1.5 million Latino-owned businesses in the U.S. Seventy percent of them are in Los Angeles, New York, and Miami. Latino-owned businesses are in the U.S. Latino Chamber of Commerce.[9] The (often wrongly used) label that the Latino immigrant is a negative in the economy does not hold true. Latino migrants keep our cars washed, our tables supplied with fresh vegetables, and our restaurants and hotels operating. The established Latino is mainstreaming in a positive manner.

In Douglas, this town which was supposed to have died after Phelps Dodge Corporation took its copper operation elsewhere, the economy is bolstered by the great number of border crossers coming to shop at the regional stores like Wal-Mart and Safeway. The downtown stores which were vacant at one time are now busy with Mexican citizens. I am sure that what happened in Douglas is happening all along the U.S.–México border. There is a symbiotic relationship between the border towns in the U.S. and their counterparts in México.

The Latino in The United Methodist Church

Statistics showing the Latino in relation to religious organizations/churches in the U.S. are not in yet. This issue could be good arena for a doctoral thesis. The data briefly showing the Latino in The UMC is not very encouraging. Allow me to point out a great gap between the Latino population in each of the jurisdictions within The UMC and the number of Latinos reported to be in The UMC. (More complete statistics are in tables 1 and 2 at the end of the chapter.)

Jurisdiction	UM Latino Members, 1998	Latino Population, 1990
North Central	2,299	1,536,220
Northeastern	4,086	3,937,220
South Central	25,453	5,330,820
Southeastern	6,618	2,054,930
Western	4,793	9,569,550
Totals	43,249	22,428,740[10]

Where are the Latinos attending church? Which church is reflecting the greatest number of Latinos? Are all Latinos Catholic? The most important question is: Where is The UMC in relation to the Latino in the U.S.? I am not going to try to answer this last question; rather I will try to present the Latino as a person who expresses the faith in a very cultural manner. In the section on the need for a new paradigm, this issue will be dealt with in greater detail.

Let us look at one ingredient of the Latino culture which is expressed in worship. This element is one of celebration, or the fiesta spirit. Latinos typically like motion, emotion, music, and song in their way of worship. This means that handclapping, arm-raising, and body movement are integral for Latino worship. The traditional organ and piano music is being replaced by string, wind, and percussion instruments. Traditional hymns are being replaced by simple songs of faith; these usually are presented using overhead projectors. Some congregations have even gone to the point of replacing the traditional altar and chancel furniture with a choir or ensemble of musical instruments that looks like a rock concert platform. Traditionalists bewail the shrinking attendance at Sunday services and a decrease in membership. There still are some strong traditional congregations, but the number is decreasing.

Where are Latinos worshiping? Many of them are still attending the Roman Catholic Church, but even in some Catholic churches where the traditional order of worship is observed, there is a noticeable increase in the use of mariachi music and the singing of the cultural songs, *coritos* or *estribillos*. Although there are no official statistics which show where Latinos are worshiping, a nonprofessional observance is that the pentecostal-type churches are the ones getting the larger number of Latinos. These pentecostal-type churches are not limited to the Assembly of God, but are even found in mainline Protestant churches, including The UMC.

Another element in worship favorable to Latinos is conservative theology. Latinos are still very conservative in family values, for example. Acceptance of divorce, homosexuality, adultery, etc., are not part of the conservative element of Latinos and their religious expression. Another example of this conservative theology is the belief in salvation of the soul and the belief in Jesus as the means of salvation. It seems that the elements of liberal theology along with the emphasis on social (service) involvement as practiced by the modern-day non-Latino Methodists have not been appealing to the Latino.

As a retired clergy member of the California-Pacific (Cal-Pac) Annual Conference and as the author of a doctoral dissertation on Hispanic Methodism in the Southern California-Arizona Conference, I will analyze my own conference to show the difference between being a United Methodist church with the freedom to be culturally Latino and the present church.[11]

	1941–1955 Latin American Provisional Conference	1998 Latino Churches, Cal-Pac Conference
No. of churches	41	45
No. of members	3,004	934

Table 2 shows that the number of Latinos in the Cal-Pac Conference in 1998 is 1,741; this figure must be a preacher's count. I personally researched this in preparation for this essay and the total is 934. Allowing for the figure of 1,741 to be correct, that means that there are 807 Latino members in non-Latino churches. It seems unrealistic that almost one-half of the total Latino Methodists are in non-Latino churches.

Notice in table 2 that the Río Grande Conference reflects a respectable number of Latino members, 15,067. This size has been the result of maintaining the Latino culture to a great extent. There was a time when Río Grande was being pressured by some to be integrated into existing neighboring annual conferences, but it refused to go that way. One of the strong arguments against integration of the Río Grande Conference was that its members did not want to see their conference undergo a tremendous change (a negative one) as experienced by the integration of the Latino American Provisional Conference into the Southern California-Arizona Annual Conference.

Table 1 indicates that the Western Jurisdiction Latino population in 1990 was 9,569,550, and the projected population for 2020 will be 20,912,060. The 1998 total of Latino membership in this jurisdiction was 4,793, as shown in table 2. As can be seen, the church is not keeping pace with the population growth. This is a challenge for the church as a whole but particularly for The UMC. In the early years of the twentieth century, Methodists were pioneers in mission outreach, and Latino Methodist work was being looked upon as a model by other denominations. Today we see that the California-Nevada Conference has surpassed the California-Pacific Conference in Latino membership. (To be fair to this assessment keep in mind that the California-Pacific Conference at one time included what is now the Desert Southwest Conference. The Latin American Provisional Conference included the Latino Methodist work which is now in the Desert Southwest Conference.)

One interesting and positive trend in Latino membership in The UMC is the figure for the Florida Conference. After the Río Grande Conference, with 15,067, Florida Conference shows 4,352. Why? In Florida Conference there are many Latino Methodists who are of Cuban, Puerto Rican, and Caribbean descent. In comparison to the Latino United Methodist on the West Coast, those Latinos in Florida are relatively newcomers and have not assimilated into the U.S. way of worship. These Latino United Methodists are the ones reflecting the Latino culture in their worship.

The Need for a New Paradigm

In 1996 La Trinidad United Methodist Church of Los Angeles celebrated its centennial anniversary. This congregation was the first established Latino Methodist church on the West Coast. The branch of Methodism under which La Trinidad was organized was the Methodist Episcopal Church, South. The history of La Trinidad is like a textbook lesson of how to and how not to do mission in the third millennium.

It was my privilege to be the pastor of La Trinidad when the centennial was celebrated and I researched and wrote a brief history of La Trinidad. Without going into technical aspects of the stages in the history of this congregation, I will list major stages and important issues.

First stage was the establishment of a mission by Anglos doing mission work in the East Los Angeles barrio. This work went well in the establishment and organization of a Methodist Latino mission, which at that time was named La Primera Iglesia Metodista Mexicana. The church programs and outreach into the barrio were well established à la Anglo-Methodist style. In 1939 when the unification of the several Methodist branches came about, La Trinidad was well on its way to being a strong congregation numbering close to five hundred members. In 1956 at the time of the integration of the Latin American Provisional Conference a change was taking place.

Second stage was marked by the beginning of the decline in numbers and prestige of La Trinidad. Why? The main emphasis of the integration movement was to transform the Latino churches into Anglo-like churches. The use of the Spanish language, for example, was discouraged and even forbidden at annual conference meetings. The women's group, known then as "La Sociedad Femenil," had to comply with conference rules, and the name was eventually changed to United Methodist Women. The youth group underwent the same transformation and the results were the same. The congregation began to disintegrate. Latinos who were active at this point in history were saying, "instead of integration, disintegration has taken place." Integration had taken place on paper but not in reality.

Third stage was the building of a new sanctuary and the division of the congregation. There was a strong group of members who felt that being a replica of the Anglo church was not acceptable, while the other group felt that continuing to be a Latino model of the Anglo-type church was the way to go. Using the excuse that because neither group could agree on the altar arrangement or the placement of a large cross, the congregation divided. As a loss for Methodism the departing group represented the power block, both in economics and leadership. This block bought a nearby church building and continued as a nondenominational church and named it "La Trinidad." The group remaining at the original La Trinidad is the

The murals in Chicano Park in San Diego illustrate the way Chicano culture expresses itself in public works of art. The land beneath an interstate highway was to be used for a highway patrol station, but residents and others objected. Government officials withdrew their plans, and the site has been transformed into a symbol of Chicano pride and self-determination. *(UMNS photo by Tom McAnally)*

one that celebrated the centennial in 1996; however, it was never able to recover from the split and the membership in 1997 was fifty-seven.

The Anglo model of being a United Methodist church is very expensive. The future of La Trinidad under the present model is not very promising. Questions that arise from this experience are many: Why was this allowed to happen? What can be done now with other Latino churches in the Cal-Pac Conference which are in the same situation as La Trinidad?

This section will try to answer some of these questions. Let us begin by saying that there is a need for a new paradigm. In Webster's dictionary, paradigm is defined as "a philosophical and theoretical framework of a discipline within which theories, laws and generalizations and the experiments performed in support of them are formulated." I do not know if the Cal-Pac Conference leadership was aware of the paradigm which was in effect in establishing Latino churches. As recorded in my dissertation, there is evidence that some theories were being implemented; for example, the intentional Americanization process. This process was one where time, money, and effort were employed to Americanize the Mexicans. When this process was not working up to the Anglo standards, the Mexicans were looked upon as "the problem." The Americanization process meant, in effect, doing away with this Latino culture, and the result was that many Latinos became pseudo-Anglos in order to be accepted and not to be considered a problem. This change contributed to the noticeable decrease in the Latino church membership.

Another example of the Anglo paradigm being practiced was the integration of the Latino American Provisional Conference into the now California-Pacific Conference. As with the La Trinidad saga, integration was done on paper rather than in reality. The beginning of the demise of the Latino Methodist church was the implementation of the integration process, a development I reported in my dissertation. The figures to support this assertion have already been given.

Another way of explaining a paradigm is using the analogy of a window. Every person or organization (church) looks at the world through a given window. What we are, what we think, how we look at things as we look through that window will determine what we see. The UMC has been operating with a window (paradigm) formed and reinforced by European/Anglo values and insists in looking at the Latino church and Latinos as a whole through that paradigm. The UMC continues doing mission among the Latinos as it did one hundred years ago. It does not work: that is one reason for the disparity between the Latino population and Latino church membership as we go into the third millennium.

This Anglo paradigm is reflected in the form of worship, including the theology undergirding it, in the typical Anglo UMC. I suspect that the decrease in The UMC membership might be that even some non-Latinos are feeling the need for a new paradigm.

Dr. Justo L. González lists four important characteristics for a new theological paradigm.[12]

First: "theology is always contextual." A particular theology in order to be good and useful must always be in the context to the recipient of such theology. "The central doctrine of the Christian faith is the doctrine of incarnation." We believers accept that one characteristic of our faith is that God reveals Himself to us by becoming one of us. The "us" here does not mean a generic us or generic nation; it means the incarnation (taking on flesh) of theology in each culture and situation, in each time and circumstance. As important as it is that the Christian faith is one, it can be experienced in many ways according to the time and circumstance. This experience is where the nature of contextual theology is found. González argues that the theology taught in our seminaries and courses of study, the theology handed down to us even from our ancestors, was good at the time, but it was not ours. This new paradigm calls for a theology that must be ours without ceasing to be universal.

In speaking of a pastoral *praxis*, González says that the Latino theological paradigm requires:

A new corps of leaders "who know the tradition of the church as well as the theology that has shaped and continues shaping it," a new group of leaders who know the church well enough so as to witness the universality of it.

A new "corps of leaders who are able to relate the gospel to the concrete situations" of the barrio and to be able to contextualize these situations into the universal arena.

The theological education required for this new paradigm is not easy. New Latino pastors must learn the traditional subject matter taught in our seminaries, but in addition they also must learn how to contextualize theology to the Latino experience. If the Latino corps of new leaders does not understand this new approach of theologizing, the result will be the same as we see today. Present seminaries are producing good pastors to do pastoral work in an Anglo-type setting but not able to do creative pastoral *praxis* among the Latino. This failure is evident as we again see the disparity between the Latino population and the Latino United Methodist membership in the U.S.

Second: Latino theology must be affirmative. Once we understand that theology is contextual, then we are ready to say it is ours. The theology which has been handed down to the Latino has come from a European/Anglo context. This contextual theology from the dominant culture may very well be affirmative for those within that culture. This theology tells them that their culture is good, and so is their way of living, and we agree that for them this is good. But it is not good for those outside the dominant culture. Latinos are constantly told directly or subliminally that their culture is not conducive to democracy, that the Spanish language is not American, that the Latinos have much to learn from the dominant culture and that they are poor through their own fault. Are we still seeing the

Americanization process going on today? This sounds a lot like what was happening to the Mexicans at the turn of the century.

The theology coming from the dominant culture is not working and is even counterproductive in the Latino barrios. The good news being preached by some televangelists and from some pulpits today is that human beings are "nothing but unclean worms, who are not worth anything," as González wrote. This same message was being preached, and is still being preached, by some Latinos. These preachers are reflecting the theological tradition that says the best way to exalt God is by degrading the human being, as if to say God will be greater the more worthless we become.

Another aspect of this dominant theology is that of blaming the victim. Some Christians have little tolerance for those living in squalid situations, where their apartments are overrun by vermin. In Douglas like any other town the migration of Latinos into the U.S. has become a very negative political issue, and those not tolerant of these migrants are becoming vigilantes. This reminds me of the post-Allende era in Chile. When I went to Chile on a study tour I witnessed a military state in full force. Militia with carbines stood at almost every street corner. Some people were also disappearing; they literally vanished from their homes or from the streets. These were the ones suspected of plotting against the government. Then there were the *sopladores*, who were turning in even their relatives to the authorities. It seemed to give them great pleasure in doing what they called their civic duty. I returned from Chile with three new words: *carabineros* (riflemen or soldiers), *sopladores* ("blowers," or deceivers), and *desaparecidos* (those who disappeared). When I see some of this happening in my own town it makes me nervous. We are blaming the victim. The victim in this case is the poor, hungry migrant coming north to try to survive. González says, "And we still claim that it is 'good news' to tell them that they are worthless!" The new paradigm calls for telling the oppressor, the violator, the one who undervalues the human being, that he is oppressing, violating, and undervaluing the very image of God, because we are created in the image of God.

According to González, the dominant theology also believes that "the most important element of the human being is its intellectual life." It seems to say that the major goal for life is to sustain that life. This is the reason we in the U.S. place more worthiness on the computer programmer, the CEO of a large enterprise, or even a professor of theology than on the person picking lettuce, washing cars, or making beds in a hotel. Let us keep in mind that even these are in the image of God. The theology of affirmation must affirm the value of every human being. No one human being created by God in His own image is worth more nor less than anyone else, regardless of economic or social status.

Third: A theology of solidarity is needed. Christian theology has become hostage to an individualism which contradicts many values of the Bible and traditional cultures and "forgets the *communitarian* element, not only of faith, but also the very purposes of God." (Italics in original.)

González explains this by pointing out why we speak of "my salvation," of Jesus as "my Savior," and of what God has done for *me*. Salvation is important, but when we limit this relationship to God and me, we are forgetting a fundamental dimension of the gospel of Jesus Christ. When Jesus was asked by his disciples to teach them how to pray he told them that to pray saying, "Our Father," a title that implies that we are not alone, *not even with God;* we are with God in our community. The dominant theology emphasizes the need for the church but with the agenda of nourishing the individual only. God does nourish the individual Christian, but this view mistakenly assumes that "what God wishes is to create a large number of individual Christians," which make up the church, which in turn supports and strengthens the faith.

In contrast, González wrote, "The church is the body of Christ. The church is the manner in which Christ exists in the world. First is the body, then the members." And: "The body does not live for the members, but vice versa." The understanding of the essence of community/solidarity is important in order to understand that God wants us as a community as opposed to our individualism.

Similarly, in the dominant culture the understanding of family is different from that of the Latino. In the dominant culture the family has very well-defined borders, and members operate as individuals. In the Latino culture the family is not that well defined, for we can see fluidity or extension. In the Latino culture, family is not limited to the immediate blood relatives, but it goes beyond, and we hear the saying that the church is the family of God. Individualism is overcome in the concept of community and solidarity.

Fourth: An eschatalogical theology is required. Webster's dictionary defines eschatology as being concerned with the final events in the history of humankind. The dictionary also explains that Christian eschatological theology includes belief in death, ultimate destiny of mankind, resurrection of the dead, the second coming of Jesus Christ, and the last judgment. This kind of theology seems to be absent from the dominant culture.

In some Latino churches there seems to be a trend to follow the dominant culture, and eschatological sermons are becoming rare. Latinos must understand that this theology is not one of fear but one of hope. A theology of hope is one that, in spite of all the indications that there is no hope, there is hope! We must understand that we must live life, not in the past, but in the future which is our hope, which is what gives life meaning and purpose. Our hope is that the future will be different from what we see today. The future will be an order of justice and peace—an order where there will be no more wars, when we shall have no fear. It is in that future of hope that as Latinos we shall live the life as children of God, as heirs of the Lord's Kingdom.

Is The UMC willing to help the Latino in the third millennium?

A Model for Latino Ministry

Latino United Methodist mission work in the Southwest has been carried out faithfully by dedicated and consecrated pastors and laypersons. Río Grande Conference is a candid example of this ministry, which can serve as a model for other conferences. Latino Methodism on the West Coast, which was started at about the same point in history as the Río Grande Conference, has had a different journey and at times has served as a laboratory for other areas of Latino ministry. Let us look again at the integration era of the Latin American Provisional Conference into the now California-Pacific Annual Conference. As was pointed out earlier there were several factors why integration did not work out favorably for the Latino. Integration looked at through the Anglo paradigm meant complete assimilation of the Latino into the Anglo culture.

It did not work. As a result there was a need to find an alternative to the frustration felt by the Latinos. In secret (underground) meetings Latinos began to share feelings and especially to support the elder pastors who could not accept integration as it was being carried out. The main idea was to begin strategizing and planning how to go about seeking a way to tell conference leadership that integration was not working. This point in history was the emergence of the civil rights movement in the U.S. and the emergence of the caucus phenomenon. I was present at a meeting of the few Latinos who dared to go against the status quo, and the Latino caucus in the conference surfaced with the name Latin American Methodist Action Group (LAMAG).

LAMAG started to organize as a visible force on the conference level, and several victories were achieved. One of these was the formation of a conference-level committee to begin to deal with Latino issues. Other conferences began to organize their own caucuses, which led to the formation of a national Latino caucus known as Metodistas Asociados Representando la Causa Hispano-Americanos (MARCHA). Under MARCHA other committees were formed to continue strategizing for a national Latino plan of action. In the early 1990s a consensus emerged called "National Plan for Hispanic Ministry," which was presented to General Conference and adopted in 1992. In 1996 the General Conference again approved the National Plan, which listed five specific tasks:

1. Interpreting and advocating
2. Planning
3. Training
4. Securing and providing resources
5. Supporting, monitoring, and evaluating.

The National Plan for Hispanic Ministry called for a Committee on Hispanic Ministries to oversee the implementation of this plan, and the Reverend José L. Palos was selected as coordinator. The following data is gleaned from the report to 2000 General Conference. Mobilization of annual conferences for Hispanic work utilizing the process called *acompañamiento*, or "walking with," was undertaken.

The following was reported by mid-1999:

- 64 new chartered Hispanic churches in 30 annual conferences
- 208 Hispanic missions and fellowships (congregations not yet chartered) in 46 annual conferences
- 32 Hispanic ministries (smaller groups) in 8 annual conferences
- 538 faith communities in 51 annual conferences
- 263 church school extension programs in 30 annual conferences
- 63 revitalized congregations in 25 annual conferences
- 839 outreach ministries in 47 annual conferences
- 17 commissioned missionaries in 11 annual conferences. (Note: This data has not been included in table 2.)

The plan called for teams of pastors/mentors and lay missioners to form faith communities for Bible study, worship, and prayer, as well as to serve in various kinds of outreach ministries. The report lists several missioners and their respective places of action.

Another aspect of the plan calls for committed persons to be trained and commissioned as missionaries to help conferences within their boundaries. By the end of 1999 there were 19 lay missioners working in eleven conferences, and a total of 25 were expected to be in ministry by the end of 2000.[13]

The National Plan for Hispanic Ministry, in its report to the General Conference, called for The UMC to recall and reaffirm the report as approved by the 1992 General Conference. The commitment of the church as a whole to this plan must go beyond the present moment. It will require the commitment of an entire generation. Rev. Palos lists two important reasons why this ministry must continue:

1. The Latino population continues to grow dramatically in the U.S., including Puerto Rico.
2. The ministries already started and those which are still needed will continue to need the mobilization, nurturing, and resourcing provided by the National Plan.

This plan is one model of Latino ministry in The UMC; others will be offered in the summary section of this essay.

Summary and Recommendations

The Latino population of the U.S. will grow during this century until it constitutes the largest minority group in the country. Many different terms have been used for this population, and we are using "Latino" as the most comprehensive. Although the immigration across the U.S.–México border has many negative aspects, we need to appreciate the many positive contributions the immigrants are making, particularly to the U.S. economy. Most Latinos in the past have been Roman Catholic, but today we are seeing a change, even in Latin America. Protestantism and pentecostal forms of religion are gaining adherents among Latinos. This context raises some hard questions for The UMC with respect to its Latino mission.

The words found in the order for confirmation and reception of members in the church state:

> The church is of God,
> and will be preserved to the end of time,
> for the conduct of worship
> and the due administration of God's Word and Sacraments,
> the maintenance of Christian fellowship and discipline,
> the edification of believers,
> and the conversion of the world.
> All, of every age and station,
> stand in need of the means of grace which it alone supplies.

I am sure that every time we as pastors lead the new believers into the membership of the church, our faith is affirmed and we rejoice when the congregation receives the new members into the fellowship of God's church. But statistics will confirm that The UMC in the U.S. is still decreasing in numbers, although by smaller amounts each year; perhaps it is reflecting the trend that is evident in all of Protestant Christianity. The problem of decreasing membership is multiplied when those within the church accept this as a matter of fact. There seems to be an air of resignation among church members who find themselves in churches that are about to die.

These are some of the things The UMC must do in order to do mission in the new millennium:

1. Be prophetic. The UMC pulpit must become again what it used to be in earlier years. The words of Saint Francis of Assisi can well be the basis for prophetic preaching:

> Lord, make me an instrument of thy peace,
> where there is hatred, let me sow love;
> where there is injury, pardon;
> where there is doubt, faith;
> where there is despair, hope;
> where there is darkness, light;
> and where there is sadness, joy.

The UMC must return to the time when the word "Protestant" meant just that—to protest—against the evil in our society. There is a very serious drug problem in the U.S. The reason the drug cartels in South America exist is that there is a demand for the product. The UMC must become alarmed at this serious problem. Crime, violence, and children killing children at school and at home are other serious problems in the

Bishop Juan Vera Mendez of the Methodist Church of Puerto Rico inspects the remains of a U.S. Navy attack jet used for target practice on the island of Vieques, Puerto Rico, in 1999. He and other United Methodists objected in a series of protests, and the navy withdrew from the island in 2003. "This is a very special day for me and for the people of Vieques and Puerto Rico," Mendez told members of the United Methodist Council of Bishops after the navy announcement. *(UMNS photo by Mike DuBose)*

U.S. The UMC, along with other religious agencies, must become prophetic in order to do mission in the third millennium.

2. Be evangelical. United Methodist congregations in every area of the U.S. are surrounded now, or will soon be, by Latinos who want to hear the prophetic voice of John Wesley and the earlier Methodists. To be prophetic means to be evangelical. The UMC must recapture the zeal and the untiring, working spirit of the circuit rider. The church needs to understand and contextualize the Wesleyan theology. Justo González is saying that there is a need for the Latino pastor to contextualize theology. This need is also evident in the non-Latino church as well.

The Latino wants to worship, wants to belong, wants to be ministered to, wants to help others to know Christ. The UMC must return to its evangelistic fervor of the early times in order to reach out to the Latinos who are moving into our communities.

One of the dangers for The UMC is to continue thinking and operating as if the ultimate goal is to perpetuate a system which worked up to a degree but is not working very effectively today. The mainline denominations are undergoing a decrease in membership, while the evangelical, less-structured, churches are growing. There is a need for the church to be prophetic and evangelical in order to continue its journey into the new millennium.

3. Use radio and television to communicate. The new immigrant is not ready to join the organized church, yet has a need to be nourished spiritually. In Douglas, Arizona, and Agua Prieta, Sonora, México, Spanish evangelical radio programs are very popular. Radio stations are becoming aware of the wide listening audience and are even offering free radio time to the pastors willing to do this type of ministry. I am sure this type of ministry could be undertaken in any area in the U.S. The growth of Latino evangelical churches in Douglas, including the United Methodist one, is due to radio evangelical programs. Television is also being used as an effective tool for reaching the unchurched. Television has been used for non-Latino audiences, but it has not worked for the new immigrant. Perhaps the non-Latino television and radio programs can be modeled after the Spanish programs. The church should explore this type of ministry and invest money to see it come to fruition.

4. Use new models for mission. In this essay the model being used by the Latinos is the National Plan for Hispanic Ministry. This is an effective program which has proven itself.

Another model which has been implemented on a smaller scale but has proven effective is the central church concept. This model was first implemented in South America. I attended a midweek service at the central church in Santiago, Chile. At least two thousand persons attended on the main floor of a large, box-like building. The balcony on three sides of the building could accommodate at least another one thousand persons. The front contained no traditional church furniture, just a high platform for the musical instruments and the preacher. The order of service was very simple—lots of singing and, surprisingly to me, no handclapping or body movement. It was a quiet, solemn spiritual experience for me. At a given time a choral group from the balcony would sing accompanied by string instruments. Out on the yard and even on the sidewalk there were vendors selling finger foods and passing out church programs.

After an interview with the pastor and his leaders, I discovered this is the model:

Have an organized church be the central focal point. This congregation must be well organized. It must be a training center for those going out to all the *colonias* (barrios) to organize prayer cells, similar to the early Wesleyan type of ministry. These cells will join other cells in the same geographical areas, but they will not become an organized church. These cells take turns coming to the central church during the week. In order to accommodate all of the cells there are several meetings in the evening during the week. The total membership of the central church on Jotabechi Street, including the outlying cells, was twenty thousand and growing.

The secret to the success of this model was the worker-priest concept. This concept calls for a person who is totally committed to God and the Kingdom without receiving monetary compensation for doing God's work. This person is employed in the secular arena but invests a good portion of his or her life in ministering to people. This model for ministry has proven to be very effective in South America; that is the reason why Pope John Paul II went there to see for himself why the Catholic church is losing so many members to the evangelical church.

While I was pastor at La Plaza UMC in downtown Los Angeles, this model *was* implemented on a smaller scale. A Latino United Methodist congregation had been dissolved by action of the annual conference. The church building was sold, but the congregation refused to die, and it rented the building from The UMC. This congregation asked me to be its mentor and a retired pastor became its leader; members came to La Plaza for special services. A new congregation was started in another area of Los Angeles under my leadership. This new congregation functioned as a cell under the central church concept. In both cells the worker-priest concept was in effect.

Multiple staff is a requirement. This central church concept calls for a strong leader who is totally committed to God's work; it calls for a corps of worker-priests and calls for a central office for administrative work. This concept can be used not only for Latino work but for the church as a whole. Because of the lack of reaching out to the people in the community, many churches are going to be vacant. Some of these pastors could undergo some training to be able to minister in a culturally changing community. The church facilities could be used for training and for a central office.

The problem with the present system in The UMC is that the structure and philosophy of being a church is more like a secular corporation that exists for making profit. To do mission in the third millennium will require a radical restructuring of the system which we now call the church.

5. Develop a new academy. González is alerting Latinos to the need for a new pastoral *praxis*. In essence he would like to see a corps of new pastors who are Latino in the true sense of the word, i.e., in culture, theology, and lifestyle. He acknowledges that there is not such a corps yet, but it could come about with intentional changes in the church structure we now have. Although González did not spell out exactly how this corps of pastors can come about, it is obvious to some of us that the present system of training pastors is not preparing present pastors to do effective ministry among new Latino immigrants. This assertion is backed up by the gap which exists between the number of Latinos in the U.S. and the number of Latinos in The UMC. Something radical must be done, and perhaps this can begin by having a specialized academy for training laypersons and pastors for mission in the third millennium.

An experiment which was put into effect by Israel was the kibbutz. The philosophy for this experiment required families, parents, and children to go away from the cities to live in a communal style in specially selected areas. To those outside of Israel this philosophy was too radical and, some argued, not conducive to a positive lifestyle. It was my privilege to visit two kibbutz settlements in Israel, and I found that those living there had a very good experience. The garden and farm products were of superior quality and were not only used for the self-sufficiency of the settlement but were also being sent to the cities as well. The persons from the kibbutz were exceptionally pleasant and well-educated, and they very much reflected the best of the Israeli culture. Some of these young men and women were involved in the six-day war of 1967. Israeli pride was evident in all aspects of not only the kibbutz, but in the cities as well. The concept of the kibbutz, as radical as it may sound, could well be used as a model for development of Latino leaders.

Another experiment which has been put into effect is the approach some African-American leaders are taking even today. These African-American leaders select children who will be trained in the African-American culture. There are special academies where these young children are educated and trained to be the leaders among their own people. I know that some people in this country frown upon this approach that teaches children in their own culture, but whether we like it or not, some of the most articulate, well-educated African-American young leaders have gone through some of this cultural training.

Perhaps the time has come for Latinos to begin training young children in their own culture. These young trainees would be excellent candidates for any field of study or vocation they would choose for themselves.

The UMC could begin looking at this radical approach by gathering Latino leaders who have the vision of a new world order. The Latinos in the U.S. can help in the creation of a new world order.

Rev. Palos wrote in his report to the 2000 General Conference: "At the beginning of the millennium, The National Plan for Hispanic Ministry has called The United Methodist Church to a strategy of hospitality, evangelism, social justice, and service, remarkably similar to the early Methodist movement."[14]

It is my wish that this essay will serve as a statement for thought and as a catalyst for action by The UMC as we move into the third millennium.

[Chart 1]

Latinos in Mainstream America

These are Latinos who are easily recognized by mainstream America for their contributions in their respective fields.

Name	Field	Expertise
Federico Peña	Government	First Latino secretary of energy
Lee Trevino	Sports	Golf
Edward James Olmos	Arts	Film industry
Jaime Escalante	Education	Youth motivator
Placido Domingo	Music	Opera
José Hernández	Mariachi Music	Director, Mariachi Sol de México
Diego Rivera	Arts	Muralist
Soledad O'Brien	Television	Broadcast journalist
Elias Galvan	Religion	First Latino bishop, United Methodist Church
Joel Martinez	Religion	First Latino elected president of a United Methodist program board (General Board of Global Ministries)
Justo González	Theology	Writer
Ellen Ochoa	Space science	First Latino woman astronaut
César Chávez	Labor relations	Organizer
Alfred Rascon	Military	Recipient Congressional Medal of Honor
David Maldonado	Religion	First Latino seminary president in United Methodist Church (Iliff School of Theology, Denver)

[Table 1]

Population Trends in the U.S. in Jurisdictions of The United Methodist Church

	1990 Population and % of Total Pop.	2020 Population Projection	1990–2020 Percent Growth
North Central Jurisdiction			
Latino	1,536,220 3.0%	4,713,640 8.0%	207%
Northeastern Jurisdiction			
Latino	3,937,220 6.7%	7,296,570 11.3%	85%
South Central Jurisdiction			
Latino	5,330,820 14.2%	12,929,370 25.6%	143%
Southeastern Jurisdiction			
Latino	2,054,930 4.0%	6,914,230 9.5%	236%
Western Jurisdiction			
Latino	9,569,550 18.6%	20,912,060 27.5%	119%
Totals	22,428,740	52,765,870	

Source: UMC News Service, "Racial/Ethnic Population Trends Challenge United Methodists," August 21, 1998.

[Table 2]

Latino Membership in The United Methodist Church (U.S.) 1998

CONFERENCE	LATINOS
North Central Jurisdiction	
Dakotas	13
Detroit	252
East Ohio	45
Illinois Great Rivers	163
Iowa	142
Minnesota	152
North Indiana	160
Northern Illinois	834
South Indiana	84
West Michigan	170
West Ohio	156
Wisconsin	128
Total	2,299
Northeastern Jurisdiction	
Baltimore-Washington	368
Central Pennsylvania	115
Eastern Pennsylvania	628
New England	227
New York	1,520
North Central New York	62
Northern New Jersey	512
Peninsula-Delaware	47
Southern New Jersey	430
Troy	69
West Virginia	22
Western New York	(not reported)
Western Pennsylvania	51
Wyoming	35
Total	4,086

CONFERENCE	LATINOS
South Central Jurisdiction	
Central Texas	735
Kansas East	90
Kansas West	173
Little Rock	15
Louisiana	108
Missouri East	36
Missouri West	110
Nebraska	83
New Mexico	1,339
North Arkansas	84
North Texas	983
Northwest Texas	677
Oklahoma	408
Oklahoma Indian Missionary	19
Río Grande	15,067
Southwest Texas	2,846
Texas	2,680
Total	25,453
Southeastern Jurisdiction	
Alabama-West Florida	125
Florida	4,352
Holston	95
Kentucky	69
Memphis	16
Mississippi	21
North Alabama	22
North Carolina	94
North Georgia	806
Red Bird Missionary	0
South Carolina	94
South Georgia	93
Tennessee	324
Virginia	351
Western North Carolina	156
Total	6,618

continues

[Table 2] *continued*

Latino Membership in The United Methodist Church (U.S.) 1998

CONFERENCE	LATINOS	Recapitulation	
Western Jurisdiction		North Central	2,299
Alaska Missionary	27	Northeastern	4,086
California-Nevada	1,855	South Central	25,453
California-Pacific	1,741	Southeastern	6,618
Desert Southwest	691	Western	4,793
Oregon-Idaho	81	1998 Totals	43,249
Pacific Northwest	203		
Rocky Mountain	188	1997 Totals	40,652
Yellowstone	7	Increase	2,597
Total	4,793		

Reported ethnic membership as percentage of total membership of The UMC: 0.16 percent.

(Ethnic membership includes Latino, African American, Asian American, Native American, Polynesian, and others.)

These figures exclude The United Methodist Church in Puerto Rico and outside the U.S.

Source: National Plan for Hispanic Ministry, General Board of Global Ministries, The United Methodist Church.

[Table 3]

U.S. Border Patrol Apprehensions of Undocumented Aliens, Fiscal Year 1999

Sector	Number of Apprehensions
Marfa	14,589
Yuma	76,195
Laredo	103,433
El Paso	125,035
Del Río	131,058
McAllen	204,257
El Centro	226,695
San Diego	248,092
Tucson	470,252
Total	1,599,606

Breakdown of Tucson sector for 1999

Stations	
Sonoita Station	3,320
Ajo Station	21,300
Casa Grande Station	28,616
Willcox Station	28,962
Tucson Station	35,240
Naco Station	63,417
Nogales Station	86,529
Douglas Station	202,868
Total	470,252

Nation of origin	Number of Apprehensions
Pakistan	2
China	4
Yugoslavia	4
Iran	8
Bulgaria	15
Honduras	413
El Salvador	519
Guatemala	579
México	468,708
Total	470,252

Source: The Arizona Daily Star, *January 4, 2000.*

CHAPTER 12

Women, Mission, and the Future
Peggy Halsey

Forty heads are always better than one. When I was asked to reflect on how the participation of women in the mission of the church has changed over the past two decades and to identify trends for the next twenty years, I knew I needed to do a typically female thing: consult and collaborate. I interviewed, individually and through a focus group, approximately forty women who have been deeply involved in mission, both professionally and as volunteers. Their wisdom, insight, and voices are woven through these paragraphs, and occasionally I have quoted some of them.

Laywomen in The United Methodist Church have always led the church in mission education, support, and involvement, and continue to do so, through the organization of United Methodist Women. An article about women and mission must necessarily give significant attention to the contributions of that extraordinary organization. The focus here is broader than that, however, and encompasses all women of the church who care about and engage in mission, as well as women in the United States and around the world whose lives form the context for mission.

The Context: Women at the Turn of the Twenty-first Century

The lives of women in the United States have undergone tremendous change in the past century and will continue to do so in these early years of a new millennium. There is much to celebrate. Women can and do own property. Women vote and in larger numbers than men. Most professions are open to women, although there are still barriers to their rising to the top in many of them. Women have, on average, two children (compared with seven in 1900). Women's life expectancy is almost eighty years—seven years longer than men's. Yet challenges remain. Most women continue to work in sex-segregated, low-paying occupations. Whether women work outside the home or not, homemaking and caretaking are still primarily understood to be "women's work."

Today's young women carry a burden that earlier generations did not. Society expects a woman to do a full-time job and also give her children adequate time and attention—and to do both jobs well. To compound the problem, women expect it of themselves as well. Women remain caught between a world of work which presumes that behind every worker is someone to take care of family needs, and the presumption that women assume primary responsibility for children and household.

The ratio of women's to men's earnings, which had been narrowing for some years, widened slightly after 1993; in 1996, women made seventy-five cents for every dollar men made. The college-educated proportion of women has been increasing faster than that of men; the U.S. woman between twenty-five and thirty-five years old has, on average, more education than her male counterpart. Yet higher education still does not pay off as handsomely for women as for men.

Politically, U.S. women have come through a massive upheaval since the Second World War and find themselves on entirely different terrain. Politics in the nation will never be the same; the personal is political, and women have discovered their voice. At the end of the 1990s, fifty-nine women served in the 105th Congress. It is important to note, however, that this is only 11 percent of Congress, while women account for more than half of the U.S. population.

News on the health front is mixed. Women's death rates from heart disease have dropped significantly since 1970, while death rates from cancer have increased. Women's lung cancer death rates increased fivefold between 1960 and 1990. Breast cancer is more common among white women than black women, but deadlier for black women. The incidence of AIDS among black and Hispanic women and teen-age girls is far out of proportion to its presence in the population as a whole.

Violence against women does not appear to have lessened; in fact, there is some evidence that it is increasing. An estimated three to four million U.S. women are battered each year by their husbands or partners; more than 50 percent of all women experience some form of violence from intimate partners. The number of women who are victims of rape is nearly one in five; more than half of the victims report that they were under seventeen when they were first raped.

At every age, but especially in adulthood, females are more likely than males to be poor. Black, Hispanic, and Native American women have by far the highest poverty rates. As Cynthia Costello has noted:

"Many women—especially those with adequate incomes and good educations—will continue to thrive, and it is likely that women's representation in better-paying jobs will continue to increase. Those less fortunate because of their race, lower incomes, or other disadvantages will probably continue to fall through the cracks. Whether women's futures are bright or shadowed, in short, depends on the borders where they stand—borders of income, race, occupation, class and family responsibility."[1]

Globally, the picture is even more contradictory. A June 2000 report from the United Nations reviewed developments since adoption of the Beijing Platform for Action in 1995. The following benchmarks give a glimpse into the global context for women and girls at the turn of the century: (1) The percentage of girls enrolled in secondary education actually decreased in twenty-four countries. (2) Women's share of paid employment increased in most regions, with the exception of parts of Eastern Europe, but women still provide more than 70 percent of the time spent on unpaid care work within the family. (3) While the economic inequality between women and men has widened, some specific strategies like microcredit and other financial instruments for women have been successful. (4) Insufficient attention to the role of social and economic determinants of health leaves women and children unequally vulnerable to diseases like HIV/AIDS and other infectious diseases as well as to the effects of poor sanitation, water quality, etc. Rates of maternal and infant mortality remain unacceptably high. More than 100 million women continue at risk for female genital mutilation. (5) While rates of violence against women do not appear to be decreasing, there is some evidence that societies and governments have begun to accept that violence against women and girls, whether occurring in public or private life, is a human rights issue.

Women and Mission: Changes and Trends

To talk about mission in The United Methodist Church (UMC) is to talk about women—active women, knowledgeable women, laywomen, organized women. It is widely accepted in the denomination that mission happens because women make it happen. That is the way it has been for so long that shifts in any facet of that reality are barely noted. A new millennium offers the opportunity to reflect on changes that may have already begun to affect the picture and on trends that may suggest significant change in the future.

The Nature of Women's Involvement in Mission

In the year 2000, participation by women of the church in its mission is an increasingly intentional choice, made from an ever-widening array of choices. In the not-so-distant past, church women who were seeking meaningful involvement, intellectual stimulation, and community with other women saw mission as a logical, appealing arena for activity — and it had little competition. Women today face more demands on their time, more pressure to "do it all" (and do it all well), more emphasis on personal development and physical fitness, more approaches to join more organizations. Mission no longer stands out as one of a very few outlets for their participation.

Young families with two working parents tend to be quite deliberate in deciding how they will spend their time and their resources; choices about involvements outside work and family are made consciously, judiciously, and jointly. Professional, service, and self-help organizations court these women for their limited time; church and mission organizations are having to learn to do the same. As one mission agency staff person said, "We're having to find new ways to package and sell mission. Mission will increasingly have to go seeking women because they will not come looking as in the past."

The spheres of influence and involvement of women have widened. Most women are now in the workforce, which is both global factory and global marketplace. Women workers, who were once the objects of mission, through such projects as homes for "working girls," are now themselves the agents of mission and participation in the world. Daily routines bring many women into contact with new ideas, with technological, social, and political developments, and with opportunities to influence, in small ways and large, their communities and their world.

Women's lives are vastly different and bigger in scope. A much smaller percentage of a woman's life is now spent being mother and wife. In addition, developments in contraception and reproductive rights have forever changed how women view their options and their future, with significant numbers of women choosing singleness and/or childlessness. Women once used their personal sphere of influence (as wives, mothers, sisters, daughters) to press for social change. They are now more empowered themselves in the public sphere and tend to view mission through their own roles as architects of social change.

For increasing numbers of church women, mission is less about supporting the church's programs and more about exemplifying traditional Christian values in their work worlds. One woman interviewed for this article told of her young secular colleagues in a nonprofit organization who are intrigued by her participation in community worship, her insistence on ethical behavior in the workplace, and her volunteer work for social justice. For her, mission is witness in the world, embodying respect for people who differ from her economically, culturally, and racially.

A desire for "hands on" involvement in mission service is one of the defining trends that has emerged over the past decade. Women have never been satisfied simply to give money for mission, though many have given generously and consistently. They have seldom hesitated to become personally involved, often through missionary service. What is new appears to be a preference for short-term local activity, for more individual local control of mission, for face-to-face encounters, but not necessarily ongoing ones. There is much to be said for this trend. Vast amounts of essential goods, such as disaster relief kits, are being supplied. Women are going in record numbers as volunteers in mission, not just to cook for the men who wield the hammers but to offer their own unique knowledge and skills to communities in their own regions and around the world. The danger lies in seeing mission as essentially individual rather than communal and in failing to engage in the systemic analysis and social change efforts with which women organized for mission have traditionally accompanied direct service. Increasingly, the church will need to offer opportunities of varying duration that combine the learning environment of "schools of mission" with the chance for "hands on" work across lines of culture and class of volunteers in mission. Some mission volunteer programs will need to be redeveloped so that they intentionally focus on root causes and offer opportunities for community organizing before young women will throw their energies into them.

Bigness for its own sake seems to have nearly run its course. This change will manifest itself in coming years in a number of ways. There may be fewer large, assembly-type gatherings. (If this is so, and if other ways to be together and connected emerge, one question is that of quality control.) It is not likely that huge mission structures will still be with us fifty years from now. The trend may be away from overarching, global, highly centralized efforts, and toward more discreet efforts at mission, with a sharper focus and the potential for increased impact. One possibility is that the church will find a way to do less but do it more excellently and thoroughly in fewer places.

A New Environment for Mission

Women have never engaged in mission in a vacuum. World events, secular culture, and new discoveries have shaped mission as surely as have current theologies and the status of women in church and society at any particular time. In the last two decades of the twentieth century, change rushed at the church and its mission from every corner of the denomination, the ecumenical community, the nation, and the world. A number of developments, events, and movements have had particular impact on the way women in The UMC are understanding and engaging in mission.

Feminism, or the "women's movement," has profoundly changed the ways in which women view themselves and their place in the world. Women of faith and women committed to mission have experienced dramatic shifts in consciousness and role. They have moved steadily and in ever-greater numbers into key leadership positions in the church. The use of inclusive language is widely expected, though still resisted in some quarters. Women are increasingly comfortable with doing theology out of their own experience. Many diverse women, working both separately and together, are appropriating religious language and symbolism in new ways, creating a spirituality that is uniquely female.

Inevitably, a backlash has developed in the wake of feminist gains in the church, particularly the emergence of women's spirituality. The ecumenical "Re-Imagining" conference in 1993 has come to be viewed as a watershed event and will no doubt continue to be cited as the "tipping point" when women committed to shaping a new way of being the church reached a critical mass, and traditionalists felt compelled to react and restrict. For a number of years following the event, the chill of the backlash was noticeable, with many women hesitant to speak up, fearful of being targets, deferring to men for leadership. Yet many also agree with one interviewee: "Anyone afraid of following through on the implications of Re-Imagining for the future of the church and its mission will miss out. . . ."

And another: "In the future, many women will take the church seriously only if it addresses issues the Re-Imagining event was raising. While many others currently oppose dealing with such issues, their numbers will gradually decrease."

The widespread movement in society toward spirituality has not yet peaked and will continue into the early decades of the new century. Mainstream Christians have tended to downplay the importance of the trend, with the result that they have left cutting-edge religious turf to new age practitioners who, according to one observer, "are plucking whatever fruit they want from the branches that have been planted and tended by the churches, without getting to the roots." When the Women's Division created a task force on Christian mysticism in the 1970s, it seemed "way out" to most United Methodist Women (UMW). Today, mysticism is widely embraced, but questions are being raised about its depth. Is it in the stream of Christian mystics across the ages, or is it a shallow invention, using the words without the meaning?

As women enter male-dominated, high-pressure fields, they are finding in themselves a deep hunger for balance and are looking for spiritual centeredness. Ironically, some report that they are not finding it in their churches or women's mission organizations and are forced to turn to other organizations and resources to fill the void. A woman who has long provided leadership both in UMW and as a conference lay leader suggests that the church and the organization must begin doing a better job of helping women balance interior and exterior faith needs. She suggests that as much effort should be given to providing excellent spiritual renewal experiences and resources as is given to mission education and "hands on" mission involvement.

Isolation by class appears to have increased in the U.S. in recent decades. The affluent, which includes much of the membership of The UMC, are more likely to live in gated communities, more likely to send their children to private schools, more likely to attend church in class-segregated neighborhoods. Unless intentionally sought, there is less chance for children and families to experience diversity, especially across class lines. For many United Methodists, the workplace and the connectional church (beyond the local church) remain among the few places where people from different classes, cultures, and races may encounter each other and form alliances and relationships.

Racism remains alive in the church and its mission despite decades of campaigns, charters, covenants, and curriculum that sought to eliminate it. Every achievement, such as an increase in the diversity of young adults participating in mission programs, seems followed by the awareness of an area where progress has been too slow, or gains have been lost. Several persons who were interviewed cited the uncomfortable reality that, when leadership roles are being filled or elections held, women of color are openly or subtly forced to compete for a few "ethnic" slots. Others spoke of the subtle but pervasive nature of racism today and the declining willingness of people, including church people, to talk about it.

Much of the focus on racism at the turn of the century, at least in the church, is on hate crimes — a welcome effort. But there is little attention to "garden-variety" racism, the kind that lives in each of us, not just in hate-mongers and white supremacists. Reclaiming this area for attention and action takes on added urgency in light of population and demographic predictions. If the days of white majority in the U.S. are numbered, and if Hispanics and perhaps Asians are soon to pass African Americans in percentages of the population, it becomes critical that the inevitable reactions be anticipated and dealt with by the church and by women's organizations.

The mission "wing" of The UMC has long been one of its most diverse and colorful; in order for this dynamic to be maintained and strengthened, much more intentional work must be done on racism and multiculturalism.

Globalization has crept up on us. The mission of The UMC and the purpose and work of the UMW have long been so thoroughly international that larger political, economic, and social movements toward globalization may not have seemed as remarkable as they clearly are. The impact, however, reverberates in every corner of every life on the globe — including life among women in mission, and all those touched by that mission. Not surprisingly, the impact has both negative and positive aspects. It appears that, in response to the increased diversity and pluralism accompanying globalization, people have pulled inward, seeking likeminded and like-appearing groups, some with fanatic edges. Issues and concerns loom so large in scope that they are difficult to comprehend or tackle, so the tendency is to do nothing. One manifestation of globalization in the U.S. is the dramatic rise of faiths other than Christian and Jewish. The challenge is how to be in mission responsibly in a multifaith nation as well as a multifaith world. One person interviewed wondered: "How will Christianity and other faiths be chatting and shaking hands in the next decade?" Several observed that Christian triumphalism must be replaced by a more respectful, dialogical relationship with other faiths.

Technology is revolutionizing the lives of women and the way they engage in mission. Traditionally, women tended to react adversely to technology because of lack of access, but the instant, uncensored communication of the computer, especially the internet, is different. Its use appeals to women's affinity for interactive communication (as did the telephone from the very beginning, and as television and radio did not).

The use of the internet for mission purposes holds yet-untapped potential. E-mail messages, as a replacement for missionary letters which took months from writer to reader, and mission web pages make it possible for local church members and leaders who care about mission to know immediately when something happens and to have instant access to the best thinking about mission. People and projects engaged in similar mission and social justice work can share ideas and best practices, chat about what works and what does not, and learn in a timely fashion about available resources and training opportunities. These things are happening but are still in the "catching up" mode. The level of expectation is rising and may be the push the church needs in coming years to bring to bear the best technology has to offer on the mission enterprise. Working women are being exposed to top-notch training methods and resources, which in itself raises expectations regarding the level of excellence. As one national mission executive said, "Women don't want to see overhead transparencies at schools of mission when they see Power Point presentations at work."

Mission is personal; technology is impersonal. There is the danger of isolation in a high-tech environment. While technology will be increasingly critical to communicating mission concerns, there will remain the need for experiential learning and face-to-face encounters. The challenge for the future will be resisting overreliance on technology as the only answer, in favor of a stance that embraces new technologies as significant tools among many, including the time-honored ones of visits and voices.

"Mission" is a loaded word, with the baggage of centuries. It used to call up images of the other, the exotic, the mysterious, the different. While United Methodists in the U.S. still tend to think of mission as "over there," there has emerged an intensified interplay between how the news is delivered and how concepts of mission are formed. News now comes through headlines, snippets of information lacking depth and study. We now know too much of too little. The CNN instant-news phenomenon makes the world and its people and crises seem almost *too* familiar, too close, without offering any understanding of what is seen. The result is often less caring and more immunity to pain and need. In addition, public media tends largely to pay attention only to the Roman Catholic Church and the religious right. Progressive Protestant Christian voices, particularly of women, are missing. In coming years, women must find effective ways to use both technology and the media to communicate their truths about the world, its peoples, and the role of faith and mission.

Mission is no longer in the sole purview of mission agencies like the General Board of Global Ministries (GBGM). The language of religion has been secularized (we speak now of "marketing mission") and the language of government has been "religionized," relying on concepts of mission and charity to convey meanings far removed from their religious origins. And it is not just about words. Evidence of a softening of the separation of church and state in the last years of the 1990s is seen in faith-based groups being allowed, even encouraged, to do much of the social welfare work of the state without having to curtail religious content. At the same time, government agencies are taking on the rhetoric of values and morality, with related public policy changes. Implications for women and for the church of this sea change in the way "mission" is popularly understood are far-reaching. One woman asked rather plaintively, "What will distinguish Christian women in mission from progressive, justice-oriented women working for a better world?" Then she murmured, "Maybe it doesn't matter."

United Methodist Women: An Evolving Organization

If the UMW is a niche organization, and that's a big "if," it may for some time find itself looking for a new niche, or, more likely, doing extensive remodeling of the one it has occupied for so long. Women may not be feeling the same degree of need for a women's mission organization, which functioned so well in the past as "university" for women who would otherwise have little exposure to continuing or higher education, or to the best thinking regarding the world and its peoples. Outlets for study and action, for voluntarism and service, are suddenly too many rather than too few. Within the church, women are not only finding many roles open to them but are actively seeking them, so they are less focused on mission as their primary expression of faith in action. For today's busy, well-

United Methodist Women is intentionally seeking to recruit young women for its membership. Here Shermain Daniels, on the left, participates in an event sponsored by the Women's Division of The United Methodist Church for young women.
(*Jim Stocker photo for Women's Division*)

educated and employed women, UMW is no longer the only game in town.

As UMW members work increasingly in coalition across gender, denominational, ecumenical, and secular boundaries, their work as "women in mission" becomes less easy to identify and less visible as the work of the organization. Opportunities for women to participate in mission are not limited to membership in UMW; serving as volunteers in mission is a major alternative, but not the only one. It can no longer be assumed that women who seek mission involvement will choose to express it through the organization. Speaking of the increase in women serving in leadership roles in every corner of the church, one UMW member said, "It's what we have hoped and worked for, but we still find it somewhat disorienting."

While the Women's Division and the UMW continue to enjoy programmatic health and institutional strength unparalleled in any other denominational women's organization, there are signs that aspects of the old formula for success need revision. It is increasingly difficult to secure leadership for all levels of the organization, especially local. This problem accompanies a decline in membership of about 15 percent from 1994 through 1999, despite the organization of more than six hundred new units during the same period and membership increases among specific constituencies such as younger women, newly retired women, and Korean and Hispanic women.

When a formula has worked well, it is difficult to let it go or even to change it significantly. The Women's Division organizational formula for UMW has been phenomenally successful. The lives of the women it serves and seeks are, however, changing. Women are less inclined to a traditional line-officer model and have less time for meetings, schools, and conferences. Women are increasingly resistant to joining an organization that expects ongoing attendance and participation but are willing to take on one-time commitments. There is some evidence that women are becoming less communal and more individual in working on tasks and projects, a change which challenges the old operational style. Short-term leadership of a specific project is seen as more attractive and manageable than taking on a year-long office with attendant responsibilities. The time women have for mission activities is greatly reduced, and what time is available is in small time segments, not the large blocks of the past. Any women's mission organization that expects to survive and thrive will need to offer a variety of individual and group opportunities for learning, service, spiritual growth, and social action on a short-term basis. More of its events will have to be short, focused ones, and its structures and leadership roles will need to be flexible.

Women organized for mission will increasingly be forced to share "their" issues with the church at large. The track record is mixed. In 1980, the Women's Division actively encouraged GBGM to take on issues of women in crisis, particularly domestic violence and sexual assault, as mission concerns of importance for the whole church. It celebrated and supported the former National Division in its development of a program to deal with these issues. Years later, however, when the Bishops' Initiative on Children and Poverty was introduced to the church, and the initial distress in some UMW leadership quarters, expressed in the question: "Where have they been all these years while we supported ministries with children and the Children's Campaign?" soon gave way to welcoming this new effort and acknowledging it as a successful widening of the circle of concern and action on behalf of children. The UMW may be called upon to embrace as one of its primary functions the pioneering of cutting-edge mission which it then offers to the whole church.

Despite a growing intolerance for being challenged and asked for time, energy, and financial commitments, women are hungry for meaningful experiences. Participation in the mission organization represents a rare arena for diversity and inclusiveness, for exposure to antiracism work and social justice struggles. Unlike most of the plethora of options available to women, it offers depth and purpose.

Mission education has been at the heart of UMW's genius. The magnitude and quality of annual mission studies and the network of Schools of Christian Mission have been the envy of professional adult educators for years. Some observers are suggesting that a new model may be needed to replace the old approach to mission studies; one woman cited the collapse of Friendship Press as symbolic of an antiquated dependence on a text. What is needed, some say, is learning that is more experiential, more interactive; learning that takes advantage of more than the printed page and relies less on large, extended time gatherings. The educational offerings need to include both intellectual and action models.

With respect to age, the growing edge for membership in the UMW appears to be with youth (teens and college women) and with recently retired women. Women's Division efforts in the 1997–2000 quadrennium to recruit young women and especially to organize units on college and university campuses have paid off with encouraging gains in all regions of the country. Increases among teen women seem linked to a new effort by conference organizations of the UMW to offer programming for children and youth at Schools of Christian Mission. The importance of these developments is clearest to older members of UMW, who remember the close pre-1964 relationship of the organization to children, youth, and students. Many mourned the thirty-year void in mission education and the fact that a generation of young women grew up in the church without a solid grounding in mission. One person interviewed observed that, now that the Women's Division has re-established itself with this young constituency, it can begin to concentrate on mission issues affecting youth and students, such as the rise in the number of youth being targeted for membership in hate groups.

Increasing numbers of women are taking early retirement; at that pivotal point in their lives, many seem ready to embrace the challenge of mission through the UMW. At least three jurisdictions reported membership increases in 1999 among newly retired women. Many of these women are looking for opportunities, individually and as part of retired couples, to engage in paid or volunteer mission work related to their work or professional fields. Traditionally, church and mission organizations fulfilled needs of older women for socialization and fellowship as well as study, service, and worship. With full-service retirement communities now offering all of these, including worship in some cases, the congregation and its related unit of the UMW may have a lesser role in the lives of many older women. A number of units have been organized at retirement communities and centers.

Changes in The UMC and GBGM

Declining denominational loyalty, combined with a shifting understanding of mission with little regard for denominational sponsorship, has created an entirely new climate for mission. Few youth or young adults know or care about "the connection." Many more women than in the past did not grow up in The UMC; indeed a significant number have no church background. Especially in suburban areas, new members seem to be seeking churches that can provide programming for their children and families. The result is that fewer women understand or value the connectional nature and mission history of the denomination. It is less likely that such women will exhibit a natural tendency to embrace mission and outreach.

The breakdown in commitment to connectionalism and the simultaneous tilt toward congregationalism endangers support for a worldwide denominational program. Many clergy contribute to this movement, not because they are necessarily anticonnection, but because they simply do not see a need for it and thus ignore it. This shift away from interest in mission can be seen in declining subscriptions to *New World Outlook*, the mission magazine of GBGM, and in the failure of most seminaries to offer substantive education for mission. The institution itself bears responsibility. Mission programs in the U.S. and around the world are hampered by the wheels within wheels and unrealistic expectations of restructured agencies. Large churches are rewarded in a variety of tangible ways even if they are insular; very small churches that are heavily involved in mission and outreach do not feel similarly recognized.

Some see a "fractured church" on the horizon, with the specter of mini-churches emerging within the larger denomination. They wonder what this means for a coordinated, connectional mission effort. The focus in many local churches has moved from mission and outreach to membership and the life of the worshiping community. Many congregations see themselves as islands in hostile communities rather than ones who gather in order to move out into the world.

With the growth in resources and the sophistication in communications of the conservative branch of The UMC, which often opposes views and actions of GBGM, controversy about how mission funds are spent has heightened. The extent of conflict at any given time depends in large part on which issues have been highlighted in the media. Women tend to be aroused by the heightened rhetoric and spend enormous energy on the controversy of the moment at the expense of the larger mission.

Yet there are hopeful signs in denominational life as well. There is more emphasis on "mission with" rather than "mission to," and a growing appreciation for partnership and for mission as both giving and receiving. People are more willing to be recipients of mission from others. Enthusiasm for new mission enterprises such as the Russia Initiative and Africa University remains high.

The climate for mission is shifting in some subtle and some dramatic ways. New expressions of mission involvement are emerging in unlikely places, such as units of the UMW in women's prisons. A "cookie-cutter" approach to mission will not work any longer, if indeed it ever did. Mission leaders are learning that they must bend the rules some, shaping programs to the needs of specific constituencies. A "regular" pattern of officer roles and terms will not work at a prison-based unit. Summer young adult missioners have traditionally been assigned outside their own communities, but that "rule" has been set aside to meet the needs of young interns in Native American and other communities of color.

Some "old" forms of mission have been resurrected and remodeled to meet new needs. In the U.S., orphanages have been considered for some time to represent an antiquated approach to ministering to children. In the wake of the AIDS pandemic around the world, as well as civil wars and regional conflicts, mission once again includes establishing orphanages to offer care and safety to children whose families have been lost to disease and violence. In the Philippines, the traditional "Bible woman" role has been reinstated but with a new emphasis on empowering women as leaders and teacher.

By the late-twentieth century, the mission enterprise had shifted from a purely denominational activity to one with a more ecumenical focus. In the twenty-first century, the approach is increasingly interreligious. Christians now interact in their communities and workplaces with persons of many faiths. This interaction calls for a different approach to mission, one that embodies profound respect for all faiths and seeks partnership wherever possible. There is no denying that this is a point of tension in The UMC. Members of the 2000 General Conference struggled with, and finally rejected, several pieces of legislation that emphatically stated belief in Jesus as "the only way." A concern for theological integrity combined with interfaith openness will continue to challenge the church and its mission in coming years.

Mission will also have to navigate between old images of mission that have not kept pace with new realities and the tendency of younger members to want mission to be contemporary, instantaneous, attractively packaged, "cool," and "in." Mission education will always have the task of playing catch-up with a rapidly changing world without succumbing to fads and trendiness. Women are traveling more widely than in the past. They are more savvy and more aware of opportunities for involvement. Mission must be prepared to compete at this heightened level of challenge and expectation.

Old missionary stereotypes, particularly of women missionaries, are still prevalent in public and church consciousness but no longer fit the reality. Missionaries today are more likely than not to be on the cutting edge of what is happening in their region and the world, to have both a global perspective and a progressive social analysis, and to be committed to peace and social justice. Women missionaries, in particular, bring different skills to their work than in the past. Women used to be mission generalists or, if there were any focus, it was likely to be in the social services, teaching, or nursing. The majority now bring specific skills to mission: in technology, political action, community organizing, financial and legal services, etc.

Women are more likely now to enter mission service in their middle years and as a second career, especially if they are single. Career-long professional women missionaries or mission staff are fast becoming a "remnant." There appears to be an increasing number of women willing to give up high-paying careers, including ordained ministers on a fast career path, at or near the peak of their status, in favor of engaging in community-based mission for small salaries. Women also tend, perhaps more than men, to start projects, train young local leaders, then turn program leadership over to the next generation. They see mission leadership in terms of enabling others.

At the same time, some observers have noted an apparent lessening of a sense of adventure. While women have remained courageous in dealing with the unknown, younger women are likely to do so through the internet, and older women to "go" in groups. Persons are more private and cautious; they seem to need permission to cross borders. The challenge may be to reclaim a sense of ease in participating in mission.

As recently as a quarter-century ago, married women missionaries typically went as helpmeets and were seldom expected or encouraged to engage in their own mission work. Today, when a missionary couple is commissioned, each partner gets her or his own job description and appointment. Women go out to new communities with their own skills and gifts.

In 1995, a survey of women missionaries found startlingly fewer single women serving outside the U.S. than a generation earlier. Prior to 1964, hundreds of Women's Division institutions around the world had women in positions of top leadership. Once those institutions merged with ones related to the former Methodist/United Methodist Board of Missions, men (usually clergymen) began appearing in top positions. Now, in many parts of the world, few schools or other institutions that primarily serve women and children are headed by women. An example: of six schools in Brazil founded by the Women's Division and traditionally headed by women, only two had women at the helm in 2000.

As a result of the 1995 survey and other reviews of developments in mission since 1964, an aggressive effort has been made, and continues to be made, to strengthen the deaconess program. Growth has been phenomenal. From 1980 to 1996, a total of 39 women were commissioned to the office of deaconess in The UMC; between 1996 and 2000, 22 women were commissioned. The future looks even brighter. Forty women were in process of applying for the office of deaconess as of summer 2000, and another 40 were scheduled for a discernment retreat to explore the possibilities. An exciting new aspect of the deaconess movement is the new Deaconess Cutting Edge Ministries, which enables deaconesses to be employed directly by GBGM and be available for placement in nontraditional ministries.

The personal relationship between commissioned missionaries and the constituency in the U.S., both congregations and units of the UMW, has eroded significantly. The result is a decline in comprehensive support, particularly emotional and moral support, for women missionaries with intensive and difficult assignments. The internet should offer some creative solutions, limited only by imagination and, for now, lack of access to computers at both ends. Growing participation in mission volunteer programs puts some people in at least short-term relationship with missionaries. There will always be a need for face-to-face opportunities to give and receive reports on mission trends and on specific projects, locations, and challenges. In the past, this exchange has happened during mission itineration visits to local churches, at mission conferences, and schools of mission. Teleconferencing is an emerging method that is almost, but not quite, face-to-face.

Without a doubt, one of the most dramatic changes related to women in the church has been the emergence of significant numbers of women clergy. The nineties saw women moving into leadership roles such as district superintendent and bishop in numbers that were no longer simply symbolic. This development has been of massive significance for every facet of denominational life. The mission of the church, which has always been a primary arena for participation of and leadership by women, cannot have been untouched. The question posed to persons interviewed for this article was: "In what ways has the emergence of women as pastors and as clergy leaders at every level begun to affect the mission of the church?" Not surprisingly, the responses were immediate and passionate.

"The women's ordination movement has turned the focus of women's energy inward toward the institution rather than outward toward the world." That statement was among the strongest, but it is consistent with a widespread sense of disillusionment among women whose lives have been lived out in mission more than half a century. The perception is that, with rare exceptions, neither female nor male clergy are sufficiently mission-minded and need to be sensitized to mission beyond the local church. There is a feeling that "clergy are clergy are clergy," and that the hope that women would bring their historic commitment to mission with them into ministry has not materialized. The professionalization of mission and ministry can send a message that being "just a layperson" is a lesser calling.

Some see positive signs, particularly as ordained women have moved into higher positions of power. Some women bishops have helped get concern for the lives of women and children and commitment to social justice, once the purview of the Women's Division, into the church at large. While this is seen as a welcome shift, it is acknowledged as having perhaps contributed to a backlash against progressive women's issues. Women clergy who had been doing cutting-edge ministry have felt marginalized and cut off within the church structure. Some have chosen to carry out their ministry outside the church and its appointment system in order to remain faithful to mission. It could be characterized as coming full circle, from lay mission to ordained ministry and back to mission, but as neither fully lay or fully clergy.

The relationship between ordained women and the organization of the UMW is fraught with complexities. In an earlier era, the women's mission organization attracted a number of women who wanted to be leaders in a church where the clergy route was effectively closed. The Women's Division and its predecessor organizations took leadership in the struggle for ordination rights in the denomination. Once women clergy gained sufficient strength in numbers and positions to be a force in the church, it seemed to observers that many began to work, perhaps unwittingly, against the very sisters who got them there. The other side of the coin is that some women clergy appear not to have made the transition from no longer being laity and have exerted inappropriate influence over the laywomen's mission organization and even insisted on their "right" to be officers. As a result, the Women's Division has enacted specific policies to preserve the lay leadership of the organization—something few would have anticipated as necessary only a few years ago.

New trends are emerging. One is an increasing number of women moving from holding office in the UMW to filling pulpits as local pastors, a change due primarily to a growing scarcity of ordained clergy in some annual conferences. Another, resulting from a growing number of clergywomen who grew up in another denomination without an appreciation for the unique purpose of the UMW, is women pastors who block the mission activities and giving of the organization and attempt to redefine it as an "altar guild" or a women's auxiliary or responsible for providing only food and decorations. Other women clergy, committed to mission and trained as leaders, tend to see themselves as the ones to do all the mission themselves on behalf of the congregation, rather than as supporters and catalysts for mission by laity.

There appears to be a new stream of young women who have worked as community developers and as young adult missioners who are entering the ordained ministry and carrying their mission commitment and experience with them. If they are able to sustain that focus and offer support to laywomen in mission without usurping their leadership, the learnings could be valuable. The missing link appears to be an intentional effort to help women clergy understand mission and appreciate the unique history, purpose, and role of the organization of the UMW.

Women and Mission in 2020: Some Predictions

The forty women whom I interviewed for this article seemed, almost to a person, taken aback when asked to make "one prediction about women and mission in the year 2020." It's not an easy thing to do. Change has come so fast, and so unimaginably in some areas like technology, that we are aware we could not have accurately predicted in 1980 how women would be involved in mission in 2000. Yet there is much we did know, and much that does not surprise us in the least. My own guess is that the picture drawn by the following composite predictions will largely be true twenty years from now:

> Women will continue to be in the business of mission, addressing some of the same issues: children, health, education, the empowerment of women. The purpose of mission will be unchanged, but the institutional forms it takes will be so drastically different that we cannot predict them and might not recognize them.
>
> Women will still be the primary deliverers of mission and will also continue, with children, to be the neediest recipients of mission. As more and more women committed to mission assume top leadership positions in the church, mission will be less about conversion and soup kitchens and more about enabling leadership and doing justice. Yet general church structures, which have not taken seriously the need for ministries with women and children in the past one hundred years are not likely to do so in the next twenty, ensuring that women, particularly laywomen, will still have to press from the margins and work through the women's organization.
>
> Definitions of and language about mission will be greatly changed. Women who use technology, especially the internet, will be those who lead. By 2020, technology will be taken for granted, but it will be ac-

companied by a longing for face-to-face communication, for recreating community around the kitchen table. There will be fewer huge mission gatherings and more small, focused ones. Women active in mission will claim leadership in the debate on gay and lesbian rights, refusing to be frightened into silence. Tensions in The UMC over theology will have escalated in the first quadrennia of the new century but may be beginning to lessen.

Women will continue to be in mission in an organized, purposeful way. The women's mission organization will be smaller but more streamlined and focused, more intense and less expansive. The age range will be wider, and retired women will be doing mission more actively than their sisters in 1980. Membership, both in the church and the organization, will reflect demographic trends in the U.S., with more Hispanic and Asian members. The trend toward women's mission units in unlikely settings (campuses, retirement homes, office buildings, prisons) will continue but probably will have peaked by 2020. Study and giving will remain benchmarks of women in mission, but more women will be involved in "hands on" volunteering in communities around the globe. Women organized for mission will do more networking and collaboration with women's groups internationally, forging organizational partnerships and working together to support and expand women's power and influence in the world.

At the risk of ending on a female chauvinist note, I quote one interviewee: "Women will continue to be the ones who keep mission alive, who address critical issues in the world from a faith perspective, who 'get it' before our brothers. It is a special role God has given us, and thankfully we embrace it like Esther rather than running from it like Jonah."

Finally, though, it is what is not said, what simply cannot be imagined, that is the wild card and that will remind us, once again, that we are not in charge. It is God's mission today, it was God's mission in the middle of the twentieth century, and it will be God's mission in the year 2020. By God's grace, women have had, and will continue to have, a unique perspective and role in that mission.

CHAPTER 13

Youth and the Future of Mission
John O. Gooch

YOUTH WILL BE, indeed, already are, an important part of mission in the twenty-first century. In 1999, probably 40 percent of the world's population was under the age of nineteen.[1] That's as many people as were alive in 1950! The demographics alone suggest that youth will have a major impact on mission, both present and future. Then we add the expanding definition of youth—in most of the world, including the United States, adolescence begins somewhere around age ten and ends around age thirty. This expanded definition means that more than half the world's population (at least) fits into the category we call "youth." Major corporations have already adapted their marketing strategies to target these youth. Mission strategy will also have to take account of their numbers, their needs and expectations, and their commitment (or lack thereof) to service and compassion.

In this essay, we will look first at a theological understanding of youth as a part of the people of God. Then we will look at some of the characteristics of youth as we "round the turn" into a new millennium. Third, we will look at some ways youth are in mission today and identify some trends for the future. And, finally, we will suggest some other ways in which youth will influence the mission of the church in the twenty-first century.

Youth as the People of God

What does it mean to be a part of the people of God? Specifically, how do youth participate in the people of God? United Methodist theology says that one becomes a full member of the church in baptism, yet one of the struggles in developing that theology was the issue of how children and youth participate as full members. The struggle continues in both the General Conference and in theological debate across the denomination. One practical way that question emerges is, "Should these members (children and youth) be allowed to vote in church conference?" There is a large gap in both perception and practice between our official theology and the everyday life of the church. Would it be a major disaster for the church if baptized children and youth were allowed to participate in decision-making about building programs, major changes in church life (such as the time of services of worship), and budgets?

The same issue is expressed in the oft-heard phrase, "youth are the church of tomorrow." This continues to be one of the great myths of American Protestantism. For the most part, youth do not represent the future of the local church where they are growing up. They represent the present, the now, of the church. So even the title of this essay is misleading: youth are not the future of mission — they are the present of mission. If they are not allowed to participate as full members in the present, they may not care to participate at all in that nebulous future. So how does the church open itself to shared ministry with youth? How does the church invite youth to become the church of the present in all its fullness? Our profession is that we want to emphasize youth and youth ministry. In the denominational press, there are more "help wanteds" for youth ministers than for any other position in the church. We have a denominational emphasis on youth. But what happens in practice? We have separate youth ministries, with separate budgets often raised by youth themselves, and separate ways in which youth participate in mission. Youth raise funds to go on work camps or other mission trips, work in soup kitchens and homeless shelters, local food banks and other mission opportunities, while "the church" does its mission thing in a parallel track. We do allow "youth representatives" to sit in decision-making bodies in the church but often either ignore or patronize them.

Youth are a part of the people of God. They are not "people-of-God-in-training" or "future people of God." They are God's children, called by God and given the name of Christian. Certainly they are not yet fully mature Christians. (The same could be said of many of the adults in our congregations.) But they are a part of the people of God, and the church ignores that reality at its peril.

Our theology reminds us that we are called by God to ministry in our baptism. Every baptized Christian (every member of the church) is called to ministry. United Methodists refer to this as the "general ministry of all Christians." All those youth in our congregations are called to ministry in the name of Jesus Christ. We have already seen some of the ways in which youth are in mission in the world. We will see other ways later in this essay — and there are hundreds of other ways in which youth are in ministry that will not be mentioned. They are responding to the call to ministry. They are living ministry as part of their walk with God.

Who Are These Youth?

We will attempt to answer that question in two parts. The first part will deal with youth in the U.S. and, to a lesser extent, in Canada. The second part will deal with youth in other parts of the world, with special attention to differences from the U.S., and how these differences affect the view of mission for the world.

Youth in the U.S. comprise what sociologists call the "millennial generation." This generation includes all persons born between 1982 and 2002 (with slightly different dates given by other sociologists). The high school graduating class of 2000 represents the first wave of the millennial generation. This is the largest generation in American history, with a greater population even than the "Baby Boom" generation. In the year 2000, there were 75 million millennials, ages one to eighteen, in the U.S.[2] The oldest youth in this generation were just graduated from high school; the youngest are just being born. By the year 2008, the staggering number of 54.3 million members of this generation will be in school. This population will put tremendous pressure on the education system. Public schools will need to expand, colleges will set new records for enrollment, and 2.2 million new teachers will need to be hired in the next ten years. This suggests that one important new field for mission by the church is support of public education.

The millennials are the most diverse generation in American history. There will be more Hispanics, Asians, and Pacific Islanders in the population. The black (non-Hispanic) segment of the youth population will increase by only about 1 percent, and the white (non-Hispanic) segment will decrease dramatically, from 74 percent in 1980 to 59 percent in 2010. Asians and Hispanics are identifying themselves by national origin (e.g., Korean, not Asian; Guatemalan, not Hispanic). These trends indicate that a key component of mission with youth will be an awareness of the rich diversity of cultures in our midst. We also need to be aware that the "melting pot," the dream that all immigrants would sooner or later become "like us," is long gone. The new image is more like a patchwork quilt, where each culture continues to keep its special identity and makes a unique contribution to the mix of cultures that makes up the U.S. Mission/ministry with youth will increasingly call for proficiency in languages other than English, which will also help move mission in a direction of openness to other cultures.

The writer spent an hour in the local shopping mall while writing this essay, doing a highly unscientific survey of religious backgrounds and preferences. In that hour, he talked with a Sikh, two Muslim families (where the women were covered from head to toe, with only their eyes showing), and four different individuals who were Hindus, in addition to Roman Catholics and a wide variety of Protestants. The bakery where we had morning coffee is owned by a Buddhist, and just around the corner is a huge new Hindu temple. All of this in Nashville, Tennessee, one of the cornerstones of conservative Protestant faith and culture! Youth today will not just read about other faiths and cultures; they will encounter persons from those faiths in their daily lives. As a result, they will either learn greater openness to other cultures and faiths or have the prejudices of their communities reinforced. Where an earlier generation studied "world religions" in order to find ways to "convert the heathen," this generation will need to learn to be in dialogue with persons of other faiths in order to understand differences and work toward mutual understanding.

Family life is not, and will not become, simple for millennials. Thirty percent of this generation will be born outside of marriage. By the time the youngest millennials reach eighteen, 35 percent of them will have gone through their parents' divorce. For this generation, there is an emerging new definition of family, based on relationships rather than biology. The important adults in a young person's life may not be the ones who brought her into the world. Stepfather or uncle may be more "family" than biological father, for example. Or foster parents, clergy, or other caring adults may operate *in loco parentis* for many youth and be more of a real family than biological relatives. In other parts of the world, huge numbers of orphans mean that "family" will be determined by an understanding different from the nuclear family concept. "Family values" will continue to be important, even as the understanding of what constitutes a family is changing so dramatically that it threatens traditional family values (based on a stable nuclear family). Family will be a broader concept, embracing both biological and relational extended families.

For millennials, there is no "safe place." Theirs is the generation that entered kindergarten the year the shuttle Challenger blew up (1986). Millennials have lived through Rodney King, the Oklahoma City bombing, Waco, Columbine and other school shootings, and shootings in churches. In fact, the shooting at Columbine High School is almost certainly the "defining moment" for this generation. It marks the millennial generation as the Kennedy assassination marked an earlier generation and helps to determine who they are and how they react to life. What used to be almost guaranteed safe places (school, church) now remind youth of just how unsafe they are. In fact, in the light of Columbine as the defining moment for this generation, it is significant that youth (on their own) are beginning to work out theologies of martyrdom! For ministry and mission with youth, this suggests the need for increased skills in theological reflection. It also suggests the need to introduce youth to some of the accounts of martyrdoms in the history of Christianity. Such a study might not only help youth develop a theology of martyrdom but also help them discover ways in which Christians have been insensitive, oppressive, and rigid to both other Christians and persons of other faiths. This, in turn, could lead to reflection on the importance of openness, honest discussion of differences, and ways to be honest about our own faith without putting down the faith of others.

The age of the millennials is also the age of electronic communication. Thirteen million of them have access to the internet and use it regularly. They are at home on the world wide web and often prefer to "get together" electronically, rather than to "get together," or "hang out," as previous generations did. They are in the process of inventing an entire electronic culture, and we can only guess, at this point, what form that culture will take. But we can expect, for example, that those in mission will be linked electronically around the world, and that persons of different cultures will be in mission together, perhaps without ever seeing each other. Web sites and chat rooms will become increasingly more sophisticated and provide access to more information and more possibilities for relationship. In spite of the promise that the internet and the information highway offers for the future, however, many youth in this generation have no access to the technology that is touted as the key to the future. If the only contact with information technology a child has is an hour a week on an outdated computer in a crowded classroom, that child is not going to be able to participate fully in the electronic future. Poverty (either in the family or in the community and school system) is a major reason for the lack of access to technology. Lack of access to technology, in its turn, helps deepen poverty. The gap between the haves and have nots in our culture is growing, and there is no easy solution in sight. The technology that promised to bring us closer together may drive us farther apart. That has implications for knowledge, communication, economics, and mission. Missouri United Methodists, for example, are in partnership with the Mozambique Conference and have developed a rich ongoing relationship between the two areas. Missourians offered to provide laptops to churches in Mozambique to facilitate communications between the partner conferences. To use a computer one needs a reliable source of electricity, a modem, and a reliable telephone system. None of those are available in Mozambique. The same is true in many other areas of the world, where "the people called Methodists" try to be in partnership in mission.

Millennials, as a generation, exhibit certain other characteristics. They are postmodern in that they confirm truth through personal experience, not through scientific method. For them, the power of mission and the motivation for it does not come from logical arguments. Rather, motivation and power come from stories of real people and real communities. A sermon on Matthew 28:16-20 may leave youth totally unmoved. Tell them stories about pastors in another country who are struggling to live on the equivalent of $900 a year, and whose congregations cannot afford that much, and they line up to offer help. The future of mission with this generation (in the U.S.) lies in the power of stories, in the power of direct contact with other persons and other cultures, and in "hands on" mission and service. Millennials are not content to give money to mission boards to use however the boards see fit. They want direct contact with people, at least through stories, and direct giving in response to those stories. They want to be able to participate directly with others. They also want to be partners, and not patrons, in ministry. They are willing to give money and other resources, but they want to give in response to needs identified by the recipients. They also want to work together with partners in receiving congregations, to develop relationships, and see the results of what they

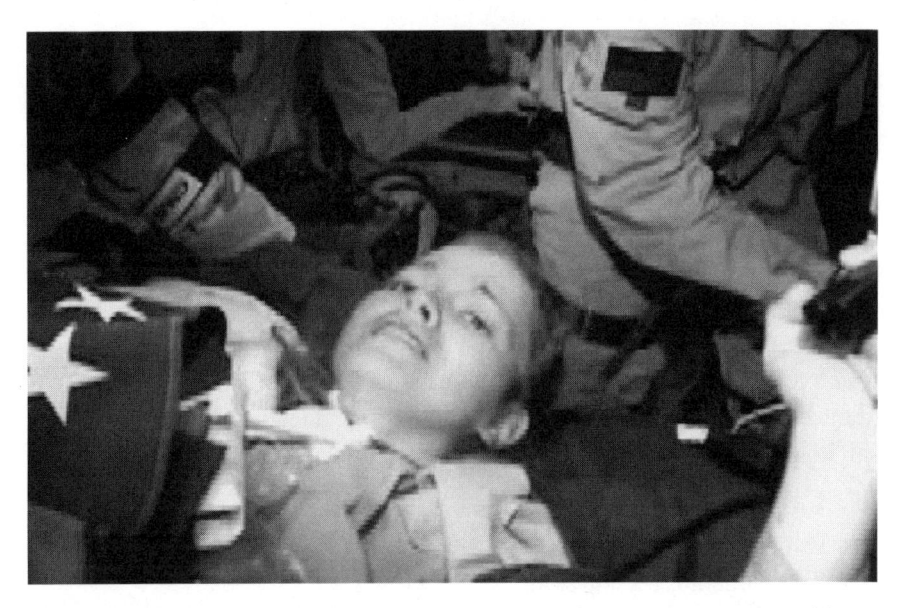

Army PFC Jessica Lynch, age 19, shown in this video image, was carried by U.S. special forces after she was removed from Saddam Hospital in Nasiryia, Iraq, during the U.S. war on Iraq. Although the stories surrounding her rescue were criticized as untrue, Pvt. Lynch illustrates that some U.S. youth are willing to place themselves in harm's way to serve their country.
(AP/Wide World Photos)

do. Mission, in the future, will need to pay careful attention to this need for relationships and partnership.

Millennials are more connected with nature than their predecessor generations and see that "we're all in it together" when it comes to survival on this planet. They are concerned with issues about peace and peoples getting along together. They continue to volunteer for the Peace Corps and other similar organizations, as well as for church-related mission projects. They volunteer for work projects that directly benefit persons in need. They are concerned about the quality of the air we breathe and the water we drink and are willing to work for ways to clean up the environment. They are not as obsessed with conspicuous consumption as their parents, particularly because they know the cost of their consumption to both persons and the environment. That does not mean all of them take vows of poverty and that the economy will collapse. It does mean they do not need as much "stuff" to satisfy them. And yet, in a totally contradictory statistic, youth in the U.S. spend an average of $84 a week (which means some youth spend a lot *more*). A growing minority of youth has its own credit card, or cards, which these youth use regularly. Advertising campaigns are increasingly aimed at members of this generation — they are a primary target for consumer goods and services. Because this generation is so large, its consumer choices can make or break products. Its choices can also make or break ministries and mission projects.

Craig Miller, staff member of the United Methodist General Board of Discipleship, has identified some short-term (2000–2005) and long-term (2006–2010) needs of the millennial generation.[3] Healthy relationships and spirituality appear in both lists. In addition, short-term needs include:

- strong families
- security
- discernment tools and skills
- coping skills, and
- advocacy.

Other long-term needs include:

- access to technology
- asset development
- exposure to different cultures, and
- leadership development.

All these needs suggest new avenues for mission and ministry with youth — perhaps in all cultures. We see, for example, all through this essay, the changing nature of the family and the need to help children function in strong families. This need for family security is as characteristic of the affluent teenager in middle America who cannot talk to his parents as it is of the millions of orphans in Africa. Whether we talk about school shootings in Colorado or forced military service in Rwanda or Colombia, youth need security in order to develop as human beings. The other needs listed also are challenges for mission and ministry with youth.

What does that have to do with the future of mission? Youth, along with other members of the people of God, need healthy relationships, spiritual formation, a sense of personal security, and so on, in order to be in mission and ministry in ways that are healthy both for themselves and for their partners in mission.

Another characteristic of the millennial generation is the emphasis on experience-based faith. To some extent, this has been true of every generation, but it has particular relevance for this generation. "Experience-based" means that truth is not found in abstract ideas but in the crucible of living. Is the faith true for me, in the world in which I live? Does it make sense? Does it help me be a better person and live in more meaningful ways? In terms of mission and ministry, experienced-based faith suggests that mission be planned and carried out on the basis of the question, "What do we want persons to experience as a result of this ministry, and how will they be different because of it?" "Persons," in that sentence, means both ordained ministers and those to whom they will be ministering. Obviously, youth need to be full partners in identifying the experiences and outcomes of ministry—or else it will be someone else's experience they are living.

In terms of faith, we are beginning to see the resurgence of the religious revival among youth. At times this takes the form of a born-again personal relationship with Jesus Christ. In other cases, it takes the form of group confession, emotional bonding, all the signs of the traditional revival—but without a specific religious content or a church context. U.S. youth are interested in spirituality but not necessarily in the church or in traditional religion. This indifference may be, in part, because for so long they have not been able to function as full participants in the people of God. They are looking for a different lifestyle from that created by either aging Baby Boomers or "Gen Xers."[4] They can be challenged to be "better than they are," to grow in faith and understanding. Some questions about the religious revival are obvious: Will youth seek to embody their search for spirituality in the church, or will their search become a series of individual quests? Will this new spirituality be an internalized, personal relationship with Jesus, or will it embrace outreach, justice, and mission themes as well? Is the church prepared to work with youth in their quest for spirituality and encourage them to become an integral part of the community of faith? The answers to those questions are critical for the future of mission with and to youth.

Generational theory suggests that when a generation is age seventeen to twenty-four, it begins to find its "voice" and to make an impact on its culture. For millennials, those key years will be 2006–2012. In that period, we can expect that millennials will begin to shape the culture in which they live, both electronically and in other ways. They will begin to speak with a clearer and a louder voice about their own vision(s) for the future and what they are willing to sacrifice for the sake of those visions. The emerging electronic culture will begin to show a clear outline during those years, and those of us who are older than the millennials will struggle to adapt to that culture.

All that we have said about the millennial generation is true for the U.S., and perhaps for Canada. European colleagues in youth ministry say that while the generational concept is an interesting one, it has no relevance for the youth in their countries. So even in the Western world, we need to be cautious about generalizations about youth and their culture. Generational theory may hold for youth in the U.S., but we probably cannot describe youth in the rest of the world in those terms.

For many parts of the world, adolescence may not even be a valid concept. In economies where a person earns less than $1 U.S. per day, adolescence is a luxury. Children move from being children to being wage earners, taking on adult responsibilities at younger and younger ages. In many instances, child labor is a matter of sheer survival for families. Without the money children can earn, the family would starve. There is no adolescence, and visions of mission are limited to obtaining food for tomorrow and, perhaps, an education.

In many parts of the world, youth are conscripted into the military and become adult soldiers at an age when their counterparts in the U.S. are concerned with acne and skateboards. Child soldiers are being used in more than thirty countries around the world, according to Human Rights Watch. Some 300,000 are serving in current armed conflicts (as of January 2000).[5] They carry assault weapons on the front lines, serve as human mine detectors, carry supplies, and act as spies, messengers, or lookouts. Many of them are kidnapped or recruited by force and made to follow orders under threat of death. Others join voluntarily, seeking to escape poverty, to avenge family members who have been killed, or simply to survive in a society that has broken down. Under the Convention on the Rights of the Child, a child is any person under the age of eighteen. Article 38 of the convention, on children and armed conflict, defines fifteen as the minimum age for recruitment into the military. This minimum age is ignored in many areas as children are forced into military service. There is an international movement to raise the age of conscription to eighteen, but this is opposed primarily by the U.S. and the United Kingdom, who continue to accept sixteen- and seventeen-year-olds in the military.

Another factor in the fate of children and youth is the AIDS epidemic. *Children on the Brink*, a report from the U.S. Agency for International Development, says that by the year 2010, the total orphan population in Africa, Asia, and Latin America will reach 44 million—two-thirds of those orphans because of AIDS.[6] These are children up to age fourteen—all of them part of the present generation. Already in 1999, the total number of AIDS orphans had reached 13.2 million, with 12.1 million of those orphans in sub-Saharan Africa. At the Durban AIDS conference, Nelson Mandela said the total number of African AIDS orphans will reach 30 million. We can raise questions about which statistics are accurate, but that is "fiddling while Rome burns." The reality is that even the most conservative estimate is appalling—and raises serious issues for mission to and with youth. Never before in the history of the world has there been such a widespread child-care crisis. The traditional approach to orphans has been to build orphanages, but this crisis is beyond orphanages. One adviser to the U.S. Agency for International Development says that Zimbabwe, for example, would have to build an orphanage a day for ten years to care for all the orphans left behind. Then how does the world—and the church—handle 30 million orphans? Some have suggested that families adopt large numbers of children. Adoption does put the children back in a family structure but also creates a financial strain for the families. How does a family, perhaps already struggling economically, handle the added financial burden of adopting homeless children? How does the rest of the world help families who are willing to adopt large numbers of children find money for food, clothing, medicine, and education? Even to raise these questions suggests a major restructuring of the economic systems of nations in order to meet the crisis.

And the crisis goes beyond orphans. In Kenya, the education minister reported that 20 percent of school pupils in the fourteen- to seventeen-year age bracket are HIV-positive. An editorial in a Nairobi paper, *The Nation*, said in January 2000:

> The one-liner to sum it up is that we stand to lose an entire generation to AIDS, period. The age-groups mentioned form the core of our youth. Given that ours is a youthful population—with over 70 percent of the entire population below 25 years—one can see that the minister was literally talking about tomorrow's Kenya. The import of the grim statistics is that AIDS is stealing Kenya's future.

In June 2000, Reuters News Agency reported that there are currently 350,000 orphans in Mozambique, and that AIDS will raise that total to one million by 2004. In Rwanda, as many as one in ten persons are HIV-positive. The *Zimbabwe Standard* reported at the same time that one in four adults in Zimbabwe is infected with HIV. The statement that AIDS will cost sub-Saharan Africa an entire generation may not only be accurate but perhaps conservative!

The implications of the AIDS crisis go beyond orphans, of course. In rural neighborhoods, the two immediate impacts of illness and death are (1) loss of time, and (2) increased debt. When family members take time from the fields to care for the sick or to mourn, crops go untended and the food supply suffers. Expenses for medicine and funerals add to the debt burden and eat into the capital that could be invested in agriculture. Add to that the effects of drought, floods such as the one that devastated Mozambique in early 2000, erratic markets and government programs, and the loss of agricultural production, and the crisis begins to assume alarming proportions.

What does this have to do with youth and the future of mission? First, it is a grim reminder that there is no future for many youth. The future of others may well depend on developments in these areas: sex education, care of millions of orphans, the upheaval in the agricultural economies of many countries devastated by AIDS, and economic development, including creative ways to deal with the burgeoning debt of developing nations. None of those areas fits easily into traditional understandings of mission. But today's youth in the U.S., for example, could easily become missionaries who lobby Congress about not withholding foreign aid funds from countries that have strong, active programs of sex education. Youth with MBAs could become missionaries working with the governments of both developed and developing nations to reshape debt structures, reshape national and global economies, and build an entirely new economic system for the world. Still others could work with the child-care crisis, or with rebuilding shattered agricultural systems. Because youth are more open to partnership, they could work with persons in developing nations, learning from those persons what works and does not work in a given culture, instead of simply imposing a Western notion of how to improve the situation.

In still another arena, we see the rise of fundamentalism in nearly all faiths, all cultures, and all religions of the world. All these fundamentalist groups, whether Christian, Jewish, Muslim, or one of the Eastern faiths, have similar aims. They want, first, to control the thoughts and actions of others. They want to impose their own ethical and cultural practices on their coreligionists, and they insist on rigid conformity to a literal interpretation of passages in their Scriptures. They interpret the Scripture in a way that fits the political, cultural, and ideological aims of their own group. Their stance is something like this: "What I do is God's will, and so God blesses whatever it is I do. How do I know it is God's will? I read it in Scripture." These interpretations often lead, in practice, to the insistence that women take a subordinate role in the family and the culture. They lead to insistence on strict enforcing of moral law, often with swift punishment for those who refuse to conform. Control is also related to the exclusivist mentality of the group and their scriptural interpretations. "I'm right and you're wrong, because I'm on the inside and you're on the outside, and that's what God said," is a simplistic, but not inaccurate, summary of this attitude of exclusivism.

The challenge, for both youth and missions, in confronting the reality of fundamentalism, is the challenge of openness, inclusivity, and dialogue versus a closed system, exclusivity, and a reliance on "sound bite" manipulation of texts. Where persons of the same religious faith cannot carry on a conversation because of the radical differences in the way they interpret Scripture, there is little hope for dialogue with persons of other faiths, or no faith at all. This challenge is an important one for the future of mission. Beyond questions of conversion, there are basic human questions of dignity, equality, love, compassion, and openness that are integral to the future of mission. Those same basic questions are often threatened by fundamentalist interpretations of faith, with their insistence on being right.

Youth Involvement in Mission Today

For at least some youth, "hands on" involvement in mission is almost a rite of passage. The model for mission as rite of passage is the Church of Jesus Christ of Latter-day Saints, which sends young men for two years as missioners. These youth/young adults travel to a specific site, somewhere in the world, and spend two years talking to persons about the Mormon faith, seeking converts. They are often rebuffed but are unfailingly cheerful and always respond with enthusiasm whenever anyone shows an interest in their work. Other denominations also engage in evangelism/mission with youth, but these are usually adults seeking youth, rather than youth seeking adults, as in the case of the Latter-day Saints. Urban street evangelism programs such as Teen Mania or Acquire the Fire! are found in various places throughout the U.S. These are forms of mission that are in the traditional model, that is, one based on evangelizing those who are not a part of the faith.

Other youth commit themselves to serious service/mission projects that do not involve evangelism. These service/mission projects are also a rite of passage for many youth. The "first mission trip" involvement moves youth into an "in group" among the youth and near-adult status in their own minds. Participation in such programs as Volunteers in Mission, Appalachian Service Project, Mountain TOP (Tennessee Outreach Project), and so on, becomes a marker on life journeys for many youth. Some of these programs are specific to an area or a nation; others involve work outside the country. For example, youth from one local church in Tennessee have been involved in service/mission projects in Latvia, the Bahamas, Appalachia, and a local Habitat for Humanity project, all in the past two years. These programs call for an extended period, usually a week, of hard work on a project that directly benefits a person, a family, or an institution with whom the youth can enter into personal relationships. The work is done in a context of worship, study, and reflection on what it means to be involved in mission with other persons. The keys to these programs are (1) "hands on" service, (2) personal relationships, and (3) immersion in both work and reflection.

Let's look at some specific examples. The Society of St. Andrew Harvest-of-Hope project involves gleaning in fields and orchards, rescuing fresh foods that would otherwise be wasted, and channelling those foods to the hungry. Gleaning is a biblical practice which the Levitical law enjoined as a way of caring for the poor (see Leviticus 19:9-10). It is familiar to most Christians through the story of Ruth, gleaning in the fields of Boaz. As practiced through the Society of St. Andrew, it involves youth in gleaning specific foods at specific times, education about world hunger, biblical and theological understandings of gleaning, and how it can be a powerful tool for dealing with world hunger.

Habitat for Humanity, founded by Millard Fuller and made famous by

President Jimmy and Rosalynn Carter, is a growing ministry to the homeless, or to those who live in inadequate housing. The concept is simple. Habitat provides building materials and skilled craftsmen to oversee a project. Volunteers, including many youth, come to do the actual building of a home. Persons who will one day own a Habitat house provide "sweat equity" on their own home and on those of other families as a part of their participation in the program. Many United Methodist churches are "Habitat Partners" and regularly give time, skill, and money to the project. Youth are active participants in many Habitat projects. Youth work camps regularly work on Habitat homes, either in the local community or in a different region.

An entirely different kind of mission is Global Justice Volunteers, a short-term mission program of the General Board of Global Ministries (GBGM). Global Justice gives young adults, ages eighteen to twenty-five, the opportunity to live and work in an international setting. Participants live in another culture, immerse themselves in the language and culture, and explore links between faith and justice. U.S. volunteers are high school graduates with at least one year of college or work experience. They commit themselves to:

- live and work in grassroots communities
- show respect for and a willingness to live among people of different faiths, cultures, and traditions, and
- be involved in the experience of linking faith and justice.

They work for two to six months with church-related agencies, nongovernmental organizations, or community groups. Structure and support come from the GBGM. These are international events. A young woman from Montana and a young man from Ghana worked together in Armenia with 4-H clubs, for example. Other groups worked in Brazil with street children and in Liberia with a United Methodist project aimed at reconciliation in a nation that has been torn by war.

Missioners of Hope is designed to work with children and families in Africa, the victims of war, famine, flooding, and AIDS. It is a partnership of the African central conferences of The United Methodist Church (UMC) and GBGM. Missioners must be at least eighteen years of age (twenty-one if working internationally) and willing to serve for two years. They work with children and families to restore ministries that "care for the physical, social and spiritual well-being of children."

College students can participate in mission as summer interns, working in United Methodist partner agencies in the U.S. In addition to the important work through these ministries, these students explore the relationship between faith and important social issues.

A much older mission program, US-2s, focuses on direct service and leadership development in the U.S., including Puerto Rico and the Virgin Islands. Young adults in the program work with local organizations struggling with hunger, homelessness, HIV/AIDS, illiteracy, at-risk children, and so on. They work in community and church centers as partners/learners/fellow strugglers with faith and society.

The Bishop W. T. Handy, Jr. Young Adult Missioners program is an emerging ministry. Called a model of mission "from everywhere to everywhere," it will place youth/young adults from every country in mission/service. The "everywhere to everywhere" concept appeals to the sense of partnership among youth and young adults. It also helps the worldwide church move beyond the idea that mission is something done by people from the West to the rest of the world. Imagine the impact of young adult missioners from Africa or southeast Asia working in Missouri or Texas!

What about mission/service projects not directly related to the church? At the end of 1999, there were seven thousand volunteers and trainees active in the Peace Corps. Not all of these were youth or young adults, but their median age was twenty-five. The mission of the Peace Corps, begun in the 1960s under the leadership of President John F. Kennedy and Sargent Shriver, is to help people of interested countries meet their need for trained men and women and to promote better understanding across cultural and national boundaries. Currently, the Peace Corps is at work in seventy-seven countries around the world. The volunteers are working in the following fields:

- education — 40 percent
- health — 18 percent
- environment — 17 percent
- business — 13 percent
- agriculture — 9 percent
- other — 3 percent.

The Peace Corps continues to tap the idealism and commitment to service of people who want to make a difference in the world.

Another key service organization is Interact, the youth arm of Rotary International. One of the aims of Rotary is international service. A key example of this international service is PolioPlus, a Rotary program which spearheaded the drive to eliminate polio from the world by the year 2005. Interactors all over the world served as volunteers for this project. In addition to major projects such as PolioPlus, Interact clubs work in service both to the local community and around the world. In local projects, a club in Bhuj, India, planted trees as part of a movement to protect the environment. On the international level, the Interact Club of Madera, California, travels each year to Ensenada, México, for a four-day service project. In recent years, club members have built two playgrounds. They purchased, repaired, and painted used playground equipment with their own funds, in addition to the work on the site. Other groups work in community centers, in Habitat for Humanity projects, with at-risk children, in tutoring programs, and in a host of other activities.[7] The motto of Rotary International is "Service Above Self," and Interact clubs live out that motto. On the surface, there is little difference between what church groups and groups such as Interact do. The key difference is in the reflection on one's faith and how faith relates to social issues and human need.

Another interesting phenomenon at the end of the century is the increasing number of school districts that are requiring some kind of community service for graduation. This community service is not some form of judicial punishment but a recognition that educated citizens have a responsibility to serve their community. While one can argue with the idea of service as a graduation requirement, one still has to credit the understanding of the importance of service for both individuals and the community.

Back within the structure of The UMC, we find the National Youth Ministry Organization (NYMO) and its Youth Service Fund (YSF). NYMO provides a forum in which youth can plan and direct their own involvement in mission, living out their status as members of the people of God. The biennial Legislative Assembly sets priorities for youth ministry in the church, passes resolutions about the relationship between faith and social issues, and calls youth to live in response to those resolutions. It functions as a sort of "General Conference" for youth. Many resolutions from the Legislative Assembly actually find their way to General Conference in the form of petitions, and thereby affect the entire church. YSF is a mission arm of NYMO. Money raised by youth for mission is channelled through YSF, primarily to projects that benefit children and youth.

Grants are made to individual projects on the basis of criteria developed by youth. Youth also make the decisions about which projects receive money and how much each receives. In this way, youth help to shape the environment for mission and ministry. They assume both control and responsibility for mission to/with youth. They empower youth to live and act as full members of the people of God.[8]

Since 1966, the Women's Division of GBGM has renewed its outreach to youth and young adult women by offering full membership in United Methodist Women (UMW) as active partners in mission. The goal of this outreach is (1) to rekindle the organization's long-standing relationship with younger women, and (2) to empower younger women through leadership development, spiritual growth, "hands on" mission opportunities, and involvement in social justice advocacy and action. Young women ages twelve to twenty-five are being challenged to take an active role alongside their older sisters in the organization of UMW. Since UMW has historically been a driving force for mission education and advocacy in the denomination, this effort has the potential for raising mission-consciousness among young women and, by extension, among all United Methodist youth.

Finally, United Methodist Campus Ministries provides an avenue of direct mission and service for young men and women in college. Most campus ministries work through Volunteers in Mission offices to identify and relate with mission projects; some still choose to work directly with communities where they may have been serving for years. Mission projects range from building or repairing homes, churches, and schools to helping drill wells and install water systems (particularly with teams from engineering schools!), working with children and youth, or other needs that have been identified by the church and community in a given area. Some campus ministry projects are in the U.S., others are far beyond our borders. The mission projects are carried out by student volunteers, who pay their own way and often provide materials for the project on which they are working. In The UMC, campus ministries are a part of the General Board of Higher Education and Ministry.

Several themes have emerged in these accounts of youth in mission. First, there is the idealism of youth, wanting to make a difference in the world. Second, there is the desire to serve others and to learn from them as a part of the process. Third, there is personal involvement in mission. Youth are not in mission to anonymous masses or to big projects that want

A wind-blown Jonathan Meier, senior religion major at Iowa State University in Ames, walked down Illinois Highway 67 during his 1,050-mile journey to Washington for a peace rally leading up to the U.S. war on Iraq. Meier heard his pastor, the Rev. Cindy McCalmont, preach at Collegiate United Methodist Church in Ames, Iowa, on Mary answering God's call. Meier, like many U.S. youth, not only believes in peace but is willing to "put his body on the line" in supporting it.
(UMNS photo © Eric Rowley/Iowa State Daily)

only financial contributions. They want to be in mission where they can be face-to-face with persons they serve. They want to be a part of the decision-making process, determining in what projects they are to be involved and what form their ministry will take. Fourth, nearly all the forms of mission we have examined deal with service to others. Fifth, there is a challenge to youth to immerse themselves in another culture or to relate on a personal level with individuals who live in different social and economic circumstances. The goal is to understand and appreciate others for who they are and for how they cope with their world. Sixth, there is an attempt in nearly all these forms of mission to help youth to explore the relationship between their faith and the social issues with which they struggle. Finally, there is a sense of community that develops between the youth involved in mission and the people with/for whom they work. These themes will all continue to be important for the future of mission.

And What about the Future?

What can we suggest about youth and mission in the future? First, we can expect more of the same, only that it will be different. Many of the forms of mission in which youth participate today will continue to be effective means of service for them in the future. There are, however, some specific areas which will be important for the future of mission in the church.

First, international and intercultural mission/service/work projects will continue to grow. Youth will not only work side by side with persons from other nations and cultures but will demand the opportunity to do so. International understanding will be a key component of mission in the future.

Second, the interlocking of mission and spirituality will be crucial for the future. Youth are looking for a different lifestyle. They want to be challenged to be better than they are. It will be crucial for the future of mission that this challenge be deeply rooted in the Christian faith. If one is a United Methodist Christian, how does one live out one's faith in practical, everyday terms? How does a United Methodist Christian relate to overwhelming social and economic issues and respond in the name of Christ? Mission/service projects will need to include more time for in-depth study of the Bible and theology, of the Social Principles, and of the *Book of Resolutions*. Youth will need to be challenged not only to help build housing for the homeless but to develop a personal theology that relates driving nails or wielding a paint brush to the foundations of their faith. The words "United Methodist Christian" were deliberately chosen. Important studies by Boys' Town, among others, tell us that an important part of spiritual life (and protection against engaging in high-risk behavior) is *identification with a specific denomination*. For youth, "generic Christianity" is not enough. Christian faith must take on a specific identity and heritage for them. Relating the United Methodist heritage to ministry and service will be an important component of mission for the future.

Third, youth will be concerned about global justice. We suggested earlier that new forms of mission might include lobbying Congress to write laws that help support justice for all the world, or working with banks and other economic institutions to help rebuild and reshape national and global economies. One future for mission is the creative development of recruiting and training persons for mission in secular employment. Bankers, corporate decision-makers, government officials, and lobbyists, among others, will be shaping the economic and social future. What if they did that shaping with a sense of mission, rooted in their United Methodist faith? This is a possible future for mission that needs careful, creative study and planning—followed by a challenge to youth to be in mission in creative new ways.

Fourth, action against violence will be an important new future for mission. In the U.S., the Columbine shootings are seen as the defining moment for the millennial generation. Worldwide, violence against children and youth is almost endemic. When the millennial generation begins to find its voice and to make its impact on the U.S. and the rest of the world, it may well begin with campaigns against violence. This work against violence could change both the face of mission and, if successful, the face of the world. It would certainly be "countercultural" for most of the world!

Fifth, this generation of youth may very well evangelize its own generation. There are some signs of that, as we have already seen. If this is one future for mission, the church needs desperately to be helping youth know more, and more deeply, what their biblical, theological, and ecclesiastical heritage is—and how that heritage shapes their reaching out to others.

Sixth, the future of mission involves the integration of the experiences of youth (both present and hoped-for) with programs/ministries that enable them to live out their vision for the world.

For some, the "golden age" of missions is in the past, when missionaries fanned out all over the globe, carrying the gospel to persons who had never before heard of Jesus Christ. That was, indeed, an important era for mission, even when the gospel also carried the baggage of Western culture and trade. But I suspect the golden age of missions for United Methodists is still ahead of us, perhaps beginning when today's youth begin to find themselves and to reshape the world.

[Notes]

1. The Future of Christian Mission in Ghana

1. "As missionary and settler parted, settler and Maroon and settler and receptive likewise—all without any abandonment of the Methodist name, polity or practice." Andrew F. Walls, "A Christian Experiment: The Early Sierra Leone Colony," in G. J. Cuming, ed., *The Mission of the Church and the Propagation of the Faith* (London: Cambridge University Press, 1970), pp. 125–127. Churches existed side by side. This makes it inexpedient for one "outside" American Methodism in Africa to presume to deal with the knowledge of Methodism even in West Africa alone.
2. Most of the West African Methodist churches participated in the inauguration of episcopacy in the Methodist Church Nigeria (MCN) in 1976 and at the January 2000 parallel event in Ghana, where the prelate of MCN was the key officiant.
3. Walls, p. 108; see also pp. 107–129. Compare Stephen C. Neil, "The History of Missions: An Academic Discipline," in Cuming, pp. 149–170.
4. Walls, p. 121.
5. Mercy A. Oduyoye, *The Wesleyan Presence in Nigeria 1842–1962: An Exploration of Power Control and Partnership in Mission* (Ibadan, Nigeria: Sefer Books, 1992), pp. 6–7.
6. Oduyoye, *Leadership Development in the Methodist Church Nigeria, 1842–1962* (Ibadan, Nigeria: Sefer Books, 1992), pp. 34–53.
7. Sarpong, "Emphasis on Africanising Christianity," in Teresa Okure and Paul Van Thiel et al., *Incarnation of Christianity in Africa* (Spearhead: AMECEA Gaba Publication, 1990), pp. 103–111.
8. Sarpong, p. 80.
9. Okure and Van Thiel, p. 5.
10. Sarpong, p. 110.
11. Okure and Van Thiel, p. 69. Compare Romans 6:1–23, Acts 9:2.
12. S. K. Odamtten, *The Missionary Factor in Ghana's Development 1820–1880* (Accra: Waterville Publishing House, 1978), p. 48.
13. Odamtten, p. 24.
14. Odamtten, p. 37.
15. J. S. Pobee, *Religion and Politics in Ghana* (Accra: Asempa Publishers, 1991), p. 51. Gas, Fantes, and Asantes are people with distinct ethnic languages. "Ga" is sometimes referred to as "Ga-Adangme" or "Ga-Adangbe."

16. Pobee, *AD 2000 and After: The Future of God's Mission in Africa* (Accra: Asempa Publishers, 1991), pp. 1–7.
17. Oduyoye, *Leadership Development*, pp. 1–8.
18. Oduyoye, *Wesleyan Presence*, pp. 39–40.
19. Neil, p. 150.
20. The *Padroado* was: "An ancient principle of the crown of Portugal of naming bishops for vacant sees in certain missionary countries wherein Portuguese subjects were settled." Donald Attwater, ed., *A Catholic Dictionary*, 3rd ed. (New York: Macmillan, 1962), p. 363.
21. Leslie E. Shyllon, "Aspects of the Dynamics of Methodism in Sierra Leone: A Reflection," in Ogbu U. Kalu, ed., *African Church Historiography: An Ecumenical Perspective* (Bern: Evangelische Arbeitsstelle Oekumene, 1988), pp. 95–114.
22. Oduyoye, *Wesleyan Presence*, pp. 59–62.
23. K. A. Dickson, *Uncompleted Mission: Christianity and Exclusivism* (Marymount, N.Y.: Orbis, 1991). Also see Shyllon, p. 103.
24. Shyllon, p. 108.
25. Pobee, *Religion and Politics*, p. 57.
26. Pobee, *Religion and Politics*, pp. 57–59.

2. Asian Mission to Asians

1. The major exception would be those areas under the control of imperial Japan.
2. T. Dayanandan Francis, ed., *The Christian Witness of Sadhu Sundar Singh: A Collection of His Writings* (Madras, India: Christian Literature Society, 1989), p. 2.
3. See Sundar Singh's publication, *With and Without Christ* (New York: Harper Brothers, 1929), with the informative subtitle, "Being incidents taken from the lives of Christians and of non-Christians which illustrate the difference in lives lived with Christ and without Christ."
4. It is not clear when Sundar Singh died. He left on his last missionary tour to Tibet on April 18, 1929, and was never seen again.
5. Bishop Azariah, along with K.T. Paul and others, started the National Missionary Society at Serempore in 1905. This was the first all-Indian missionary society which was interdenominational. Four years after participating in founding the society, Azariah accepted a call to Dornakal in Hyderabad under the slightly older Tinnevelly Missionary Society (1903). This work among the very poor would become one of the greatest Christian movements in India in the coming decade.
6. It would also be helpful to study the love-hate relationship these Asian pioneers had with Western learning. John Sung, for example was quite brilliant, finishing undergraduate, master's, and doctorate degrees in chemistry in six years in the United States. He then went off to Union Seminary in New York where, in the midst of a dramatic conversion, he repudiated all Western learning and returned as a missionary of one book.

7. Peter Brierley and Heather Wraight (Nashville: Thomas Nelson, 1998). See page 41 and the charts at the end of the volume (pages not numbered). Justin D. Long of the Global Evangelization Movement mentions that there are 4,500 Indian missionaries working outside of India (Roman Catholic and Protestant only) and an estimated 114,500 evangelists. Many of these evangelists are, technically speaking, missionaries: crossing linguistic, cultural, and geographic boundaries to witness to the gospel (gem-werc.org/).
8. India Missions Association, *Directory of Member Missions*, April 1995, p. 2.
9. *Operation World* (Grand Rapids, Mich.: Zondervan, 1993).
10. These numbers are all a little slippery, so reader, beware. The 1993 *Mission Handbook: North American Protestant Ministries Overseas* (S. Wilson and J. Siewert, eds., [Monrovia, Calif.: MARC Publications, 1993]) listed 44,713 missionaries sent from North America. This number goes down every year. In January 1997 David Barrett estimated that the total number of foreign missionaries in the world grew from 240,000 to 403,000 in twenty-seven years. Foreign missionaries are growing dramatically in the non-Western world as those from the West slowly decline.

    Another perspective may be helpful. In 1900 it was estimated that there were 4,600 Western missionaries working in India. This was at the height of the "Great Century" for Christian missions. Sherwood Eddy, *Pathfinders of the World Missionary Crusade* (New York: Abingdon, 1945), p. 141. David Barrett estimates that there were 62,000 foreign missionaries working in all of the world in 1900. Nearly all of these would have been westerners. *International Bulletin of Missionary Research* 21 (January 1997): 24 ff. See Barrett, George T. Kurian, and Todd M. Johnson, *World Christian Encyclopedia*, 2nd ed. (New York: Oxford University Press, 2000).
11. Missionaries were working in Hong Kong, Fiji, Tasmania, Senegal, and Ghana.
12. Brierley and Wraight estimate five hundred Protestant missionaries from Singapore today.
13. This complexity confronts us with slight variations in every Asian country. In Myanmar there are around seventy Presbyterian missionaries working in the country, and this from one of the smallest denominations. These missionaries are all working with newer indigenous structures. Korea has more than twenty-three hundred missionaries serving around the world through many different societies, many of which are local churches.
14. In each of these stories the geography is accurate, but names have been changed because much of this mission work is very sensitive politically.
15. This story is from an unpublished paper (by M. Zau Yaw, dated 1981) which I received in 1987 in Rangoon. I have still changed the names, even though the evangelistic mission is fairly well-known among Baptists in Myanmar.
16. Nepal was added later.
17. *International Bulletin of Missionary Research* 24 (January 2000). See also "Global Evangelization Movement" web site for February 27, 2000: gem-werc.org/index.htm.

18. This context is easily documented through the many speeches and writings of the BJP. "Bharat" itself is the ancient word for the "motherland of the Hindus." To be Indian is to be Hindu.
19. Statistics come from "Jane's Defence Spending Worldwide: 1997–98" (Surrey, United Kingdom: Jane's Information Group, 1998). See also Uk Heo, "The Political Economy of Defence Spending Around the World," vol. 10 of *Studies in World Peace* (Lewiston, N.Y.: Edwin Mellen Press, 1999).
20. First published as *Methods of Mission Work* (New York: Foreign Missions Library, 1886).
21. As Allen D. Clark notes (*A History of the Church in Korea* [Seoul: Christian Literature Society of Korea, 1971]), Nevius's notes are a little different from those of the missionaries. Both the self-support and the focus on biblical knowledge seem to have been emphasized.

3. The Challenge of Christian Mission in Islamic Southeast Asia

1. *Ummah*, or *umma*, is a Muslim term for community: "The Muslim umma is worldwide and one, not divided by sect, doctrine, or ethnicity, in the Islamic worldview." Jonathan Z. Smith, ed., *The HarperCollins Dictionary of Religion* (New York: HarperCollins, 1995), p. 1108.
2. Voglar was a colleague on an international team working on a Pew Foundation project, "Christian Theological Education in Muslim Contexts," headed by David Kerr. Voglar represented the context of U.S. theological education in areas with large immigrant and black Muslim populations, and I coordinated the Southeast Asia team.
3. Pancasila, or "Five Principles," refers to the ideology first enunciated by the Indonesian leader Sukarno in 1945, subsequently incorporated in the Indonesian constitution: "The belief in one God, just and civilized humanity, Indonesian unity, democracy under the wise guidance of representative consultations, and social justice for all the peoples of Indonesia." "Pancasila," *Encyclopaedia Britannica*, 23 vols. (Chicago: Encyclopaedia Britannica, 1998), 9: 108.

4. Women in Mission: A Philippine Experience

1. Keynote speech, Ninety-third Union Theological Seminary Anniversary and Church Workers' Convocation, November 22, 2000.
2. *Revolutionary Spirituality: A Study of the Protestant Role in the American Colonial Rule of the Philippines, 1898–1928* (Manila: New Day Publishers, 1999), pp. 256–257.
3. "In God's Image," *Journal of Asian Women's Resource Center for Culture and Theology* [Kuala Lumpur]19 (September 2000).
4. *Revolutionary Spirituality*, p. 271.
5. Author interview with Quiocho, February 13, 2001, in Dumaguete City, Negros Oriental.
6. Talk at the Asian Meeting of Religious (AMOR), Seoul, Korea, October 1985 (Manila: Socio-Pastoral Institute, 1987).

7. These views are reflected in Kenneth L. Woodward, "The Changing Face of the Church," *Newsweek* (April 16, 2001): 46–52.
8. Final statement of the Tagaytay Consultation, United Evangelical Mission, May 18–22, 2000, pp. 11–12.
9. Interview, February 13, 2001.
10. Author interview with Antone, July 19, 2000.
11. Bermisa letter to author, December 18, 2000.
12. Interview, February 13, 2001.
13. Mananzan, "Mission Yesterday, Mission Today," *Pintig-Diwa* [journal of Scholastica College, Manila] (June 1995): 38.

5. The Future of Methodist Mission in Europe

1. Mann, *The History of Germany Since 1789*, translated from the German by Marian Jackson (New York: Friedrich A. Praeger, 1968), based on *Deutsche Geschichte des 19. und 20. Jahrhunderts* (Frankfurt am Main: S. Fischer Verlag, 1966), p. 6.
2. The General Council on Finance and Administration reported the following list of European central conferences as of April 2001:

    Central and Southern Europe Central Conference,
    Bishop Heinrich Bolleter
        Annual conferences:
            Austria Provisional
            Bulgaria Provisional
            Czech and Slovak republics
            Hungary Provisional
            Poland
            Switzerland-France
            Yugoslavia-Macedonia Provisional
    Germany Central Conference,
    Bishop Walter Klaiber
        Annual conferences:
            Germany East
            Germany North
            Germany South
            Germany Southwest
    Northern Europe Central Conference
    (bishops noted below)
        Annual conferences:
        Bishop Oystein Olsen
            Denmark
            Estonia

        Finland-Finnish Provisional
        Finland-Swedish Provisional
        Norway
        Sweden
    Bishop Rüdiger Minor
        Russia

3. General Board of Global Ministries web page, http://gbgm-umc.org.

6. The Methodist Educational Mission in Latin America

1. This is an abridged version of a more extensive work that abounds with quotations of the period, details the arguments, and lingers on the particulars of many discussions. To obtain the longer article, the authors may be reached at ISEDET, Camacuá 2828, 1406 Capital Federal, Buenos Aires, Argentina.
2. Huber Jedin, *Manual de Historia de la Iglesia* (Barcelona: Herder, 1978), pp. 343 ff. Also, see Kenneth Scott Latourette, *A History of Christianity* (New York: Harper & Bros., 1955), pp. 1063 ff.
3. See, for example, J. Dillenberger and Claude Welch, *El Christianismo Protestante* (Buenos Aires: La Aurora, 1958), p. 160.
4. Justo González, *Historia de las Misiones* (Buenos Aires: La Aurora, 1970), pp. 230, 212–13, where he affirms, "The nineteenth century is characterized by Protestant colonial and missionary expansion. Several Protestant countries, but especially Great Britain, extended their economic and political power to different regions of the globe. . . . As far as the United States is concerned, it continued its work of expansion towards the West, sometimes by colonization, other times by the purchase of territory, and other times finally by means of armed conflict. . . . It was to be expected that all this would awaken a new missionary interest in England and in the other Protestant countries. This was, in effect, what happened, but it is necessary to indicate that the Protestant expansion of the nineteenth century, particularly that which started from the United States, was much more independent of the political and economic colonization than the Roman Catholic one of the previous centuries."
5. The specific theology of Methodism, according to K. S. Latourette, favored the growth of the denomination toward the border, inasmuch as: "Arminians in theology and not sustaining the doctrine of choice like the Presbyterians, Congregationalists, and many Baptists, the Methodists proclaimed that the love of God is for all men and that all could repent and be saved" (Latourette, p. 427). In this vein, Donald W. Dayton writes, "the Arminian and perfectionist motives of Methodism, as much explicit as implicit, were a background that was compatible with the desire to express and even nourish the optimistic expansionism of the region." *Raices teológicas del pentecostalismo* (Buenos Aires: Nueva Creación, 1991), p. 427 [published in English as *The Theological Roots of Pentecostalism* (Peabody, Mass.: Hendrickson Publishers, 1993)].

    However, it is worth indicating that the influence of the Wesleyan beliefs and practices progessively traversed the North American Protestant religious field and led to a growing "Arminianization of North American theology," as

James Hamilton indicated in "Academic Orthodoxy and the Arminianizing of American Theology," *Wesleyan Theological Journal* (spring 1974): 32–33. These developments permitted Dayton to affirm, "This impetus, which culminated in the emergence of a spiritual enlivening, merged with the flourishing Methodism to establish the foundations of the evangelical religious and cultural synthesis which would dominate the atmosphere in North America before the Civil War" (*Raices*, p. 38). In his terms, the evangelical synthesis in regard to theological thought was "an alliance of Calvinism with 'revivals' and evangelical 'Arminianizing.' That is to say, a combination in which Methodist ideas dominated, including the doctrine of Christian perfection" (*Raices*, p. 38).

6. Wood, "South America as a Mission Field," in *Protestant Missions in South America* (New York: Student Volunteer Movement, 1900), pp. 213–214.
7. José Pedro Barrán-Nahum, *Batlle, los Estancieros y el Imperio Británico*, vol. 1 of *El Uruguay del Novecientos*, Ediciones de la Banda Oriental (Montevideo: n.p., 1990), pp. 19–21.
8. For information, see José Pedro Barrán, *Apogeo y Crisis del Uruguay Pastoril y Caudillesco (1839–1875)*, in *Historia Uruguaya*, vol. 4 of Ediciones de la Banda Oriental (Montevideo: n. p., 1992).
9. Missionary Society (Methodist Episcopal Church), *33rd Annual Report*.
10. Committee on Missions in South America, *Actas de Sesiones*, November 7, 1856.
11. *Journal of the Proceedings of the Quarterly Conference of the Methodist Episcopal Church in Buenos Aires (S.A.)*, book D 4, Minutes of Proceedings, April 4, 1862.
12. The original intention of Andrés M. Milne had been to establish the agency in Montevideo, but the disturbance that fittingly brought the revolution of V. Flores (1863–1865) led to the city of Rosario being the final choice. Likewise, the efforts of colportage continued in Uruguay where he placed a considerable sum of New Testaments, not only in homes but also in some private schools for their use in reading classes. In mid-1865 he was detained in Pando, accused of selling "false books." Milne suspected that the commissar had acted according to the advice of the parish priest and some women who supported him. As a result of this incident, Samuel LaFone interceded before the president of the republic and obtained a license that held the signature of the minister of government. This license permitted Milne to sell Bibles more freely and to face new endeavors with the collaboration of the colporteur George Schmidt. In a letter, he noted that in Montevideo the common people had fewer prejudices, and he speculated that the reasons could be: "God had a special purpose of mercy for these people," or "they are more intelligent," finally concluding that in the end, the fundamental reason was that he "was more familiar with the language." Manuscript, Cartas de A. Milne a la Sociedad Biblica Americana, Montevideo, June 16, 1865.

Milne was born August 12, 1838, in New Deer, Aberdeenshire, Scotland, converted in 1858, and came to Buenos Aires in 1862 as an employee of Roberto Begg, an established businessman in Greenock and Buenos Aires with whom he worked for two years. In 1864 he was named an agent of the American Biblical Society.

In his colportage work between 1864 and 1873, Milne was able to place 8,636 Bibles, 10,597 New Testaments, and 21,041 biblical portions for a value of

$10,544.76. Ines Milne, *Desde el Cabo de Hornos hasta Quito con las Biblia* (Buenos Aires: La Aurora, 1944), p. 263.

13. Concerning the beginnings of the preaching ministry, Milne informed the American Biblical Society: "I have been seeking to obtain a few of those who have shown interest in order to gather on Sunday evenings to read the Scriptures and pray, but as of yet, I have not been successful. I trust that this place is ripe for the preaching of the word, as difficult as it may be to arrange the first meeting, and I will continue to invite them." Cartas, letter of Milne to the American Biblical Society, Montevideo, July 14, 1868.

    In another letter he wrote, "Daily, I encounter people who seem interested, and apparently they listen with great attention when I speak of the path of salvation; not a few have promised to meet with me on Sunday evenings to read the Scriptures together, but none have come as of yet." Cartas, Montevideo, October 14, 1868.

    The Sunday school began in September 1868 in an area far from the downtown and directed toward children of Scottish origin, but from the very start Milne was able to attract Uruguayan children.

14. *Journal of the Proceedings of the Quarterly Conference*, book D, Record of Proceedings, February 10, 1873.

15. *54th Annual Report of the Missionary Society of the Methodist Episcopal Church for the Year 1873* (New York: Printed for the Society, 1873), pp. 10, 12, and 14. Also see Robert T. Handy, *A History of the Churches in the United States and Canada* (New York: Oxford University Press, 1979), pp. 174–175.

16. Jean Pierre Bastían, *Historia del Protestantismo en América Latina* (México City: Cupsa, 1990), pp. 126–127.

17. *El Evangelista* 3 (June 19, 1880): 236.

18. *El Evangelista* 7 (September 27, 1884): 309. The editor states: "There are eras in which religion can add to its characteristic influence the artificial power of the laws and the support of the material powers that direct the society. One has seen religions that are tied to the governments of the land, dominate souls by means of terror and of faith at the same time, but when a religion contracts such an alliance, I'm afraid to say, it conducts itself as a man would conduct himself; it sacrifices the future in view of the present, and by obtaining an undeserved influence, it jeopardizes its legitimate power. . . . By forming an alliance with a political power, religion increases its strength over some peoples of the Plata, and loses the hope of reigning over all of them. . . . Religion could not divide the material strength of the governing without exposing itself to some of the hatreds that the governing provoke."

19. *El Evangelista* 1 (May 11, 1878): 314. In this line, E. Castelar felt pity for "those that believe that religion can be a reactionary tool; but I pity much more those who believe that it can disappear, that all religion should disappear."

20. *El Evangelista* 3 (December 20, 1879): 114–115.

21. *El Evangelista* 7 (May 31, 1884): 170.

22. *El Evangelista* 8 (May 30, 1885): 169.

23. *Annual Report of the Missionary Society of the Methodist Episcopal Church for the Year 1872* (New York: Printed for the Missionary Society, 1873), p. 10.

24. The process of organization under the direction of Thomas B. Wood was extended from June 1877 to June 1887.
25. *El Evangelista* 7 (December 7, 1884), p. 388.
26. "Statements of Accounts of the W.F.M.S. Work in Montevideo, Uruguay," August 1, 1887.
27. Cecilia Guelfi, circular, "Escuela Evangélica Gratuita," published in Montevideo, January 1879. At the end of the school year and on the occasion of final exams, *El Evangelista* reported: "Students who at the beginning of the year could not read have produced brilliant exams in reading, arithmetic, geography of the Republic, points of grammar, as well as a great understanding acquired through teaching with objects with regard to form, color, weight, sound, human bodies, plants, animals, minerals, etc. Vocal music and gymnastic exercises adopted at a very young age for the majority of students demonstrated that those very useful fields are not omitted from the complete program that the school conducts." *El Evangelista* 15 (December 20, 1879): 119.
28. Cecilia Guelfi de Bersiá, *Dos Vidas Fecundas* (Buenos Aires: La Aurora, 1940), p. 73. Also see *El Evangelista* 4 (December 25, 1880): 151. A short article is reproduced from *El Ferrocarril* in Montevideo in which the author congratulated "Miss Guelfi for the brilliant result that is crowning her efforts to elevate the education of her sex."
29. Wood, *Statements of Accounts of the W. F. M. S. Work in Montevideo, Uruguay*, August 1, 1887.
30. Guelfi, *Dos Vidas*, p. 108. The report appears to be dated November 1887.
31. *Actas de las Conferencias Anuales*, 1888. At the end of 1888, thirteen establishments continued operating, but with a noticeable loss of students, since the enrollment was 650 students and the teaching staff comprised twenty-seven teachers. See Guelfi, *Dos Vidas*, p. 107.
32. Simone Brandt-Bessire, *La correspondencia entre Daniel Armand Ugon y Tomás Bond Wood (1880-1890): un intento de estrategia misionera protestante conjunta entre Valdenses y Metodistas en las zonas rurales del Río de la Plata* (master's thesis, Instituto Superior Evangélico de Estudios Teológicos [ISEDET], Buenos Aires, 1997).
33. In Antonio Guelfi's last year, the schools suffered a significant reduction in enrollment, dropping from 951 to 661 students, a decrease of 290.
34. Edith Clarke de Ros-Jones, "Historia de Crandon (1879–1969)," mimeographed document, Montevideo, 1971, p. 12.
35. For the editor of *El Evangelista*, "School should be, in the eyes of the people, the court where one rewards and one punishes with the severe impartiality of justice; the pulpit of the truth; the sanctuary of faith; the stronghold raised against the discharges of ignorance; the temple of the light of the spirit; the holy ark of alliance, where souls float in order to free themselves of the general flood; the trench that defends; the holy and blessed mansion that nobody should desecrate." *El Evangelista* 2 (October 20, 1878): 61.
36. *El Evangelista* 2 (October 20, 1878): 37.
37. *El Evangelista* 3 (November 22, 1879): 81.

38. *El Evangelista* 9 (October 30, 1886): 347. It is important to note how, after January 1886, *El Evangelista* maintained a column in the newspaper where Consuelo Portea would be in charge of disseminating teachings that sought to shape the character of the children. See especially these 1886 editions: *El Evangelista* 9 (January 30): 35; (March 27): 99; (April 24): 130–131; (July 17): 227; (September 11): 290–291; (October 16): 330–331.

39. *El Evangelista* 9 (March 27): 99. The denominational press often printed maxims that declared the importance of recreation in the development of habits. For example, "There are no better amusements than those in which one recreates and the spirit is left well educated." *El Evangelista* 4 (February 5, 1881): 199.

40. *El Evangelista* 7 (May 31, 1884): 170–171.

41. With regard to the methods of teaching, *La Tribuna Popular*, in a short article referring to final exams in the Escuela Evangélica of the Aguada, commented, "The second group became known for the strength of its knowledge. It is evident that Miss Portea follows a good teaching method. The method she employs is the one that produces the best results: memorized lessons today do not allow the success that is required in the instruction." *El Evangelista* 7 (December 7, 1884): 388.

42. Guelfi, circular, "Escuela Evangelista Para Señoritas," published in Montevideo, January 1879. Thanks to the reports of annual exams published by the daily press, we have been able to reconstruct the program of study of the *Escuelas Evangélicas* of Montevideo for the period 1879–1886. In 1879, the *Escuela Evangélica Gratuita* No. 1 had a basic plan that stated: "Lessons about objects, writing, grammar, arithmetic, geography of the Republic, physiology and gymnastic exercises, morality and religion, sewing." Guelfi, *Dos Vidas*, p. 66. The currciulum also included "vocal music and gymnastic exercises." *El Evangelista* 3 (December 20, 1879). On the other hand, we know that in Trinidad and Durazno the program contained reading and the study of the Holy Scriptures, Latin, and English, as well as all of the primary and commercial subjects.

43. George Sabine, *Historia de la Teoría Política* (México City: Fondo de Cultura Economica, 1982), pp. 189–190.

44. For Thomas Aquinas, "Hence, we observe the same in all those who govern, so that the plan (*ratio*) of government is derived by secondary governors from the governor chief; thus the plan of what is to be done in a state flows from the king's command to his inferior administrators. . . . Since then the eternal law is the plan of government in the Chief Governor, all the plans of government in the inferior governors must be derived from the eternal law." *Saint Thomas Aquinas: The Summa Theologica*, tr. Laurence Shapcote, Second Part, Part I, "Treatises on Law," from Article 3, "Of the Eternal Law," vol. 18, *Great Books of the Western World* (Chicago: Encyclopaedia Britannica, 1996), p. 217.

45. In reference to the controversy with Catholicism in the educational field and the conception of political and social order, Jean Pierre Bastián says: "The affirmation of free will of the Christian subject was in itself a negation of Catholic corporativism, seeing that, while the first assumed the principle of free investigation on the part of the individual, the second was based on the idea that authority was as necessary to society as to man." Bastián, *Los Disidentes* (n.p.: Fondo de Cultura Económica, n.d.), p. 157.

46. *El Atalaya* 1 (November 16, 1901): 1.
47. A. Ardao has established three periods in its historical process. The first proceeds from its founding on September 5, 1868, until June 1872, the moment in which from its ranks surges the Club Racionalista as an autonomous expression but akin in its objectives. In June 1873 it acts again as a sole association given the disappearance of the Club Racionalista, and it remains as such until September 1877. Following this period, it unites with other minor assocations, forming what became called the Athenaeum of Uruguay. Ardao, *Racionalismo y liberalismo en el Uruguay* (Montevideo: Department of Publications of the University of Montevideo, 1962), p. 236. The author also indicates how, during this period, rationalism "under the philosophical protection of spiritualistic metaphysics of eclecticism," was becoming dominant, not only within the academic arena.
48. Minutes of the University Club, March 22, 1871.
49. Minutes of the University Club, March 24, 1871.
50. Minutes of the University Club, March 24, 1871.
51. *El Mensajero del Pueblo* 1 (May 7, 1871): 297.
52. *El Club Universitario* was the publication of the association. Founded on June 11, 1871, it had Manuel I. Méndez as its director and was last published in June 1873. To demonstrate the participation and principal role of J. F. Thomson, it should be noted that he acted as censor and editor of the newspaper 1872–1873.

    See C. M. de Pena, "The Religious Question," *El Club Universitario*, vol. 1, p. 2. The author put in evidence the dominant character of rationalism in the institution and the ideology of development when he affirmed: "In this way, the youth of today . . . gathers solicitous to assemble at the foot of the glorious insignia which wherever it has been displayed, has marvelously regenerated towns, has launched nations toward the realization of the great Rationalistic ideal, of the great Christian ideal: Liberty, Equality, Fraternity. The youth that gathers at the *Club Universitario* does not occupy itself with the religious question for vain pleasure, for pure literary pleasure; nor do we who today drive the regenerative banner of Rationalism make fire because of simple warlike spirit over the swaying bastions of Catholicism . . . . We come to defend the holy cause of the people, freedom of the spirit; to protest against the absurd and to combat it; to protest against all violence and to make it cease."
53. *El Club Universitario*, vol 1, pp. 46, 48. In the same news, the newspaper told of the triumph of the rationalist coreligionists over Thomson in the lectures of the club and of Thomson's attack from the pulpit of the Evangelical Temple.
54. Minutes of the University Club, lecture of July 30, 1873. Thomson contrasted as well the North American experience with France and Spain, both of which he predicted would not enjoy "the benefits of the Republic because in those nations the true religious spirit does not prevail." With regard to the historical experience of France, Thomson—and as did Protestantism in general—revealed his opposition to exacerbated rationalism. The French Revolution, in his understanding, deserved "a general and terrible abomination." See Minutes of the University Club, lecture of March 15, 1873. Thomson believed that there was no "salvation for the people without that blessed book with which the Puritans disembarked on the coasts of North America and that later contributed

to the permanent breaking of the bonds of the slave." The republics of the Plata, in his understanding, should adopt the religion of the "book," since this was the political instrument for excellence to reach "salvation," not only spiritual, of their "souls," but also the material "salvation" for freedom and progress.

55. Minutes of the University Club, lecture of February 11, 1876.
56. The "educative question" entered in discussion because of the appearance of the book, *De la Legislación Escolar*, by José P. Varela, who would be questioned by Carlos María Ramírez.
57. *El Evangelista* 7 (April 5, 1884): 112.
58. *El Estandarte Evangélico* 8 (April 18, 1890): 4. The editor told how Pastor Wood "revealed to us with a long pointer on several maps, which he had made to such an effect; the magnitude of the stars and the planets, as are seen through the telescope on their path through space, and with clarity . . . he indicated to us where the planet Saturn is found today, on its path of transference around the sun, forming an orbit, whose circle it spends approximately thirty years traversing."

See also *El Evangelista* 4 (January 8, 1881): 163–164.
59. *El Evangelista* 1 (December 15, 1877): 131. The references are to Louis Agassiz and Darwinism. See also "La Ciencia," *El Estandarte Evangélico* 8 (February 14, 1890): 1.
60. *El Estandarte Evangélico* 8 (February 14, 1890): 10.
61. See J. Míguez Bonino, "Wesley in Latin America: A Theological and Historical Reflection," in R. L. Maddox, ed., *Rethinking Wesley's Theology for Contemporary Methodism* (Nashville: Kingswood Books, 1998), pp. 169–182.
62. Here it is necessary to note the differentiation from certain areas of the Caribbean and Central America where the Methodist mission was directed from Great Britain, giving origin to Methodist churches with different characteristics.

7. Christian Mission in a Religiously Pluralistic Society

1. Robert Buckley Farlee, ed., *Honoring Our Neighbor's Faith* (Minneapolis: Augsburg Fortress, 1999). A close look at how these non-Christians are being received in several communities is provided in Diana L. Eck, *A New Religious America: How a "Christian Country" Has Now Become the World's Most Religiously Diverse Nation* (San Francisco: HarperSanFrancisco, 2001).
2. The Wesleyan quadrilateral is the concept developed by Albert C. Outler that John Wesley's theology comprised reason, Christian tradition, Scripture, and experience.
3. M. Thomas Thangaraj, *The Common Task: A Theology of Christian Mission* (Nashville: Abingdon, 1999), pp. 95–96, citing James A Scherer and Stephen B. Bevans, ed., *New Directions in Mission and Evangelism: Basic Documents 1972–1991* (New York: Orbis Books, 1992), p. 187.

8. The Future of Native American Ministry

1. Chief Seattle's words have been given in several different versions, so exact wording cannot be verified. One source that includes two versions is Eli Gifford and R. Michael Cook, *How Can One Sell the Air: Chief Seattle's Vision* (Summertown, Tenn.: Book Publishing, 1992). The version of Ted Perry on pp. 46–47 appoximates this quotation.

9. The Future of African Americans and Mission

1. Throughout this essay I will use "African American" and "black" interchangeably.
2. The reference is to West, *Race Matters* (New York: Vintage Books, 1994).
3. Wade C. Barclay, *Early American Methodism, 1769–1844*, vol. 1 of *History of Methodist Missions* (New York: Methodist Board of Missions, 1949), pp. xxxiv, 18, and 42, including note.
4. The term "edge cities" comes from Joel Garreau, *Edge City: Life on the New Frontier* (New York: Doubleday, 1991).

10. "Looking Forward Inwardly": The Future of Korean Mission

1. *Anatta*, "no self," as one of the so-called Fourfold Truths of Buddhist faith, articulates this point so well as to encourage us to learn from the Buddhist the art of negating oneself so we can be filled with God's descending Spirit, which is also the kernel of Christ's teaching. I have elsewhere claimed that the trouble with the Protestant "enthusiasm" to "Catch the Spirit" is that even when we think we caught the Spirit it may not be the Spirit of God but only a likeness of it created in our own image. The Buddhist teaching is that perhaps we should not attempt so much to "catch" the Spirit actively as to empty our hearts and cleanse our minds in quiet meditation "looking forward inwardly" so that the pouring Spirit of God might come and fill our spirits. I believe this sort of "inward waiting" is one of the most urgent tasks that most Protestants, if not all "religious" people, need to learn. As we shall see, however, this is not to insist on either one or the other but to strive diligently to keep the balance, which is believed to be the essence of spirituality. See Stephen S. Kim, "The Burning Heart: Passion for Holiness and Compassion for Humanity," in *The Burning Heart* (New York: General Board of Global Ministries, 1990), pp. 3–17.
2. This point has been shared by many participants in "Roots & Wings," the symposium referred to in the following. Particularly, see the greeting by Doochan Hahm, the chairperson of the Fortieth Anniversary Committee which organized the symposium, in the published symposium proceedings, *"Roots & Wings": An Invitational Symposium on the Future Ministry for the Korean-American Community*, ed. Kibong Kim (n.p.: Korean United Methodist Church of Greater Washington, 1994), p. iii.
3. "Task Force on Korean American Ministries: Report to General Conference 2000," p. 1.
4. "The Action Plan for Advancing Korean-American Ministries in the 2001–2004 Quadrennium," p. 10, lists six goals: (1) implement a comprehensive leadership

development program for clergymen, clergywomen, and lay leaders, with an emphasis on the United Methodist connection, partnership ministry, and crosscultural communication; (2) implement a vigorous leadership program for Korean-American clergywomen with an emphasis on leadership development, acceptance, and systematic integration in the life of the Korean-American ministry; (3) establish twenty new next-generation congregations and fifteen campus ministries; (4) strengthen the existing mission congregations and work toward establishing thirty new congregations; (5) recruit forty prospective next generation young men and women, with gender balance in mind, to attend United Methodist seminaries and encourage these seminary students to become ordained ministers in The UMC; and (6) create culturally relevant resource materials and a data bank to support Korean-American ministries and provide links to and within the connectional system.

5. I have articulated elsewhere this point of the importance of "informal" ministerial education in "One Hundred Years of Theological Education for the Korean-American United Methodist Churches" (in Korean) in Chan-Hie Kim, ed. *Mi-Joo Hanin Gamri Gyohoe Baek Nyun Sa* (*One Hundred Years of Korean Methodism in America* [working title]), to be published.

6. This point has been advanced by many historians of religions, including well-respected Korean historians whose work is included in Man-Yul Lee et al., *Hanguk Gidokgyo eui Yoksa* [*A History of the Korean Protestant Church*], 2 vols. (Seoul: The Institute of Korean Church History Studies, Christian Literary Press, 1989).

7. Love, "Contending Forces in the Global Arena," *Mission & Transformation in a Changing World: A Dialogue with Global Mission Colleagues* (New York: General Board of Global Ministries, United Methodist Church, 1998), pp. 15–24. The quote is from p. 23.

8. Literally, the mean (similar to the Aristotelian notion), *Chung-Yung* represents integrity of faith and life, theory and *praxis*, and even that of opposites. As a metaphysical principle, it is not unlike the Hegelian sense of thesis/antithesis in one way, but it is radically different from the dialectics in the sense that in the *Chung-Yung* view there never was duality to reconcile and synthesize. It is the radical opposite of dualism; in fact it rejects, in principle, onesidedness, divisiveness, and imbalance. It is the affirmation of the fundamental oneness or integrity of *anthropos* and cosmos. See Tu Wei-Ming, *Centrality and Commonality: An Essay on Confucian Religiousness*, revised and enlarged ed. (Albany, N.Y.: State University of New York Press, 1989).

9. On "thick description," see Clifford Geertz, *The Interpretation of Culture* (New York: Basic Books, 1973). For "contending forces," see Max Weber, *The Protestant Ethic and the Spirit of Capitalism*, tr. Talcott Parsons (New York: Charles Scribner's Sons, 1956 ed.). Also see Stephen S. Kim, "Methodist Missions to Korea," in William B. Lawrence, Dennis M. Campbell, and Russell E. Richey, eds., *People(s) Called Methodist*, vol. 2, *Forms and Reforms of Their Life* (Nashville: Abingdon Press, 1998), pp. 219–240.

10. "Glocal" refers to the interdependent nature of the real world between the global and the local. See Robert J. Schreiter, *The New Catholicity: Theology between the Global and the Local* (Maryknoll, N.Y.: Orbis Books, 1997).

11. Robert J. Harman, "Challenges of Mission in the Post Cold War Context," in *Mission & Transformation in a Changing World*, pp. 1–14.
12. I have expounded this point at length in "Methodist Missions to Korea."
13. My view is that the Roman Catholic Church in Korea has achieved much deeper reflective consciousness than the "hypersocialistic" Protestant church, which stresses its role as a social transformer. This is a subject that requires a major treatment.
14. The Amitabha Buddha is the "Buddha of Endless Light," one of the most important and popular buddhas of Mahayana Buddhism.
15. See my article, "Methodist Missions to Korea."
16. This is one of the top priorities for many reports on Korean-American ministries in the future, including the report of the General Conference Task Force on the Korean American Ministries to the 2000 General Conference.
17. Love, 19–20.
18. This is the so-called *Je-sa* controversy (or ancestor veneration controversy). I dealt with it in detail elsewhere: "Methodist Missions to Korea," pp. 229–33. Also see Young-Chan Ro, "Ancestor Worship: From the Perspective of Korean Tradition," in *Ancestor Worship and Christianity in Korea*, ed. Jung Young Lee (Lewiston, N.Y.: Mellen, 1988).
19. Jung Ha Kim, *"Roots and Wings,"* pp. 3–6.
20. John B. Cobb, Jr., *Beyond Dialogue: Toward a Mutual Transformation of Christianity and Buddhism* (Minneapolis: Fortress Press, 1982).
21. Unpublished paper she read at a conference held at Claremont in 1972, organized by John B. Cobb, Jr.
22. The six characteristics include uniqueness (everyone's *pal-ja* is different), inescapability (one cannot escape one's *pal-ja*), significance (it plays a significant role in one's major events or circumstances, such as the identity of one's parents, the identity of one's spouse, the time of one's marriage, how many times one will marry, the number of children, the time of one's death, one's standard of living, one's occupation, and any serious physical disability), emphasis on social relationships, conditionality (there may be conditions to avoid a misfortune), and interdependence (the events of a person's life are influenced not only by his or her own immediate family).
23. Hans Küng and Karl-Josef Kuschel, eds., *A Global Ethic: The Declaration of the Parliament of the World's Religions* (New York: Continuum, 1993).
24. See Tu Wei-Ming, *Centrality and Commonality*.
25. Sung-Bum Yun, *The Korean Theology: A Yellow Theology* (Seoul: Sun Myung Moon Wha Sa, 1972).
26. Unification of South Korea and North Korea has recently become the focal point of theological discussion in South Korea, and dialogue is occurring on many levels. The historic meeting of the two leaders (Dae-Jung Kim and Jung-Il Kim) in the fall of 2000 is being analyzed theologically as well as socially, economically, and politically. "Jubilee" ("Hee-Nyun"), a newsletter of the Committee on Korea Reunification and Reconciliation of the National Association of Korean-American United Methodist Churches, has been provid-

ing a forum for the exchange of ideas where the concepts of jubilee and reconciliation (Ephesians 2:14) are the themes around which much theological discussion is being conducted. One such dialogue happened in Chicago, December 7–9, 2000, with Dr. James Laney, former missionary to Korea and former U.S. ambassador to South Korea, as the keynote speaker. See the column by the Reverend Dr. Eun-Chul Cho, the editor of the newsletter. The committee has raised more than $375,000 in the past five years.

27. See Robert E. Buswell, Jr., *The Formation of Ch'an Ideology in China and Korea* (Princeton, N.J.: Princeton University Press, 1989).
28. Laurel Kendall, *Shamans, Housewives, and Other Restless Spirits: Women in Korean Ritual Life* (Honolulu: University of Hawaii Press, 1985).
29. Dong-Shik Ryu, *Moo-Gyo eui Yoksa wa Koo Jo* [*The History and Structure of Korean Shamanism*] (Seoul: Yonsei University Press, 1975, 1986).

11. A Latino Perspective

1. "Racial/Ethnic Population Trends Challenge United Methodists," United Methodist News Service, August 1998.
2. "The U.S. Hispanic Population Growing," *Archives* (October 12, 1999).
3. "Racial/Ethnic Population," United Methodist News Service.
4. "Who We Are, Where We Live," *Hispanic* (January–February 2000).
5. "Racial/Ethnic Population," United Methodist News Service.
6. Justo L. González, *Mañana: Christian Theology from a Hispanic Perspective* (Nashville: Abingdon Press, 1973).
7. Tradition has it that this term is a diminutive of the word *Mexicano*. This word was used as a derisive term to single out the mountain people who came to the market place in the cities. They had their own dialect and customs which were different from the city folk, who felt superior, and who started calling them "Mechicanos." Throughout the years the term was shortened to "Chicano." In recent years the new Latino of Mexican descent has taken the term and used it as a symbol of empowerment; this was called "Chicano power."
8. Statistics in this and the preceding paragraph come from *Hispanic*.
9. *Hispanic*.
10. Data supplied by the National Plan for Hispanic Ministries office, General Board of Global Ministries, New York.
11. José M. Fernández, "The History and Prospects of Hispanic Methodism in the Southern California–Arizona Conference of The United Methodist Church," Doctor of Religion diss., School of Theology at Claremont, 1973.
12. González, "Toward a Theology for a Hispanic Pastoral Praxis," *Occasional Papers*, no. 95, United Methodist General Board of Higher Education and Ministry, March 1999.
13. These and the preceding statistics come from "National Plan for Hispanic Ministry: The Report to General Conference 2000," *Daily Christian Advocate*, Advance Edition, pp. 831–836.
14. "National Plan," p. 831.

12. Women, Mission, and the Future

1. Cynthia B. Costello, Shari Miles, and Anne J. Stone, *The American Woman 1999-2000: A Century of Change—What's Next?* (New York: W.W. Norton, 1998), p. 33.

13. Youth and the Future of Mission

1. Although this precise figure is not reported in authoritative sources, it is estimated that "worldwide, 32% of the population was below the age of 15 in 1998, but that figure was 37% in LDCs [less-developed countries] outside China." *Britannica Book of the Year 1998* (Chicago: Encyclopaedia Britannica, 1998), p. 300.
2. Demographic data in this and the following paragraphs are taken from *Now Is the Time: The Millennial Generation Project, Seminar Notebook* (Nashville: General Board of Discipleship, The United Methodist Church, 1999).
3. *Now Is the Time.*
4. "Gen Xers" refers to "Generation X," also called "Baby Busters" and "twenty-somethings." The reference is to Americans born between 1965 and 1978. The term "Generation X" was coined by Douglas Coupland in his novel by that title.
5. From the Human Rights Watch web site, www.hrw.org.
6. U.S. Agency for International Development, *Children on the Brink*, quoted in *USA Today*, June 6, 2000.
7. See the web site, www.Rotary.org.
8. The 2004 General Conference adopted legislation creating a new Division on Ministries with Young People in the General Board of Discipleship. The new structure will absorb NYMO and the Youth Service Fund.

[Contributors]

Marvin B. Abrams is pastor of the Native American United Methodist Church of Southern California in Anaheim and is a clergy member of the California-Pacific Annual Conference. He has been an active participant in United Methodist programs and agencies related to Native American concerns.

N. Rubén Amestoy is the pastor of the Methodist Church in Alta Córdoba, Argentina, and is completing his doctoral degree in church history at Instituto Superior Evangélico de Estudios Teológicos (ISEDET), Buenos Aires.

Sudarshana Devadhar has served as a director of the General Commission on Christian Unity and Interreligious Concerns of The United Methodist Church. In 2004, he was elected bishop and assigned to the New Jersey Area.

James A. Dwyer is a member of the North Indiana Annual Conference and is a United Methodist missionary and pastor of the Peace Church, Munich, Germany, in the Germany Central Conference.

José M. Fernández is a retired member of the California-Pacific Annual Conference. He served as a pastor of La Plaza and La Trinidad churches in California and now resides in Douglas, Arizona.

John O. Gooch is a member of the Missouri East Annual Conference, has served as a staff member of the General Board of Discipleship, and is now a writer and consultant on youth ministries. He lives in Liberty, Missouri.

Peggy Halsey was formerly executive secretary for ministries with women, children, and families, Community and Institutional Ministries, General Board of Global Ministries, The United Methodist Church, New York, N.Y. She lives in Brooklyn, N.Y.

Robert A. Hunt is pastor of the English-Speaking United Methodist Church of Vienna, Austria, and is a United Methodist missionary. He formerly served as a missionary in Malaysia and is a member of the Southwest Texas Annual Conference.

Stephen S. Kim is E. Stanley Jones Associate Professor of Evangelism and Mission, Claremont School of Theology, Claremont, California.

Contributors

Néstor O. Míguez is part of the pastoral team of the First Methodist Church of Buenos Aires and teaches at the Instituto Superior Evangélico de Estudios Teológicos (ISEDET) as tenure professor of New Testament and member of the Oxford Institute for Methodist Studies.

Mercy Amba Oduyoye teaches at Trinity Theological College, Legon, Ghana, and has written and lectured widely on African church history and Christianity in Africa.

Anthony J. Shipley is pastor of Christ United Methodist Church in the Detroit Annual Conference and is the former associate general secretary for the National Program Division in the General Board of Global Ministries of The United Methodist Church.

Scott W. Sunquist is the W. Don McClure Associate Professor of World Mission and Evangelism at Pittsburgh Theological Seminary and was a lecturer in Asian church history at Trinity Theological College in Singapore 1987–1995. He is the editor of the *Dictionary of Asian Chrsitianity* (Grand Rapids, Mich.: Eerdmans, 2001).

Elizabeth S. Tapia is academic dean and professor of theology at Union Theological Seminary in Cavite, the Philippines. She is an ordained United Methodist pastor and has spoken at many church gatherings in her own country, the U.S., and Europe.

[Permissions]

AP/Wide World Photos: Photo of Army PFC Jessica Lynch, cover, p. 279.

Charles Cole: Photos of Buddhist temple and Praise Tabernacle, p. 154; Cities of Gold casino, p. 179.

General Board of Global Ministries, The United Methodist Church: John Goodwin photo of Nigeria student, cover, p. 17; Jim Stocker photo of young UMWS, p. 261.

Peter Williams for World Council of Churches: photo of Frederico Pagura, p. 146.

Phoenix Newspapers, Inc.: © Photo by Jack Kurtz of Border Patrol, cover, p. 224.

Ricardo Meredoni: photo of Windsor Village UMC, p. 186.

Richard Lord: photos of prenatal injection, Accra, Ghana, p. 7; Phnom Penh school, p. 33; Jakarta scholar and students, p. 55; Prague church, p. 99.

Robert Hunt: photo of women preparing for Muslim wedding, p. 51.

Scott Sunquist: photo of Miao boys in China, p. 29.

General Commission on Archives and History, The United Methodist Church: Thomas B. Wood, p. 126; John F. Thomson, p. 138.

United Methodist News Service: photos of Filipina evacuee, p. 69; Muslims and Christians, Philippines, p. 73; Smolensk students, p. 107; LA Muslims praying, p. 157; shawl dancer, cover, p. 170; Ben Hill UMC at Mutare, cover, p. 191; Honolulu sculpture, p. 206; Mongolia, p. 213; Chicano park, cover, p. 231; jet remains, Puerto Rico, p. 240; Iowa peace protestor, cover, p. 291.

[Index]

Action by Churches Together: 116; photo, 73.
Acts of the Apostles: 9, 164, 168.
Africa: 1–20; and Africans in Europe, 110, 111–114, 116, 117–118; and AIDS epidemic, 283; and bishops elected from, 194; and Christianity more alive there than in West, 72; and Global Justice Volunteers in, 287; and influence in Caribbean and South America, 122; and Methodist Church Ghana as outpost in Europe, 87; and Missioners of Hope in, 287. *See also* photos, cover, 7, 17.
African Americans: 183–202; and academies for African-American culture, 243–244; and concern for African diaspora, 199; and demographics in U.S., 258; as slaves returned to Africa, 2; and styles of mimicked in Africa, 9; and women in poverty, 253; as youth, 275. *See also* photos, cover, 186, 191, 261.
African Instituted Churches: 4, 6.
African Methodist Episcopal Church: 1, 88, 184.
African Methodist Episcopal Zion Church: 1, 88.
Africa University: 191, 265.
Agriculture: 116, 288.
Akrofi: 17.
Albania: 98, 116.
Albright, Jacob: 92.
All Africa Conference of Churches: 1.
American Bible Society: 128 *n13*.
American Church Board: 97.
Amitabha: 208.
Amity International: 29.
Amoah, Isaac: 113, 118.
Anatta: 204 *n1*.
Ancestral curse: 10.
Anglicans: in England, Ireland, and Scotland, 85; and mission to Nepal and Cambodia, 34–35; as parent to Methodism, 78; and Trinity Theological College, Singapore, 42; and Wesley as one, 83; mentioned, 81–82.

Antone, Hope: 74.
Apilado, Mariano: 66, 68.
Appalachian Service Project: 286.
Arechaga y Carvalho, Mr.: 139.
Argentina: 114, 122.
Armenia: 88, 115, 287.
Arminians: 125 *n5*.
Arredondo, M.: 138.
Asia: 21–75, 283. *See also* photos, cover, 29, 33, 51, 55, 69, 73, 213.
Asian Americans: 258, 271, 275. *See also* Korean Americans.
Assembly of God: 228.
Asuncion, Filomena: 68.
Atkinson, John: 113.
Atuel, Priscila R.: 70.
Austria: and central conference as including, 105; and Faith Conferences in, 103; and Francophone congregation, 111–112; and international ministry, 111; as place of German-speaking Methodism, 87; as place of least cause for optimism, 104; as related to Swiss church, 88; roots of Methodism in, 89.
Austria Provisional Annual Conference, 105 *n2*, 112.
Azariah, V. S.: 25.
Azarola, Enrique: 137, 139.
Azerbaijan: 88, 115–116.

Baby Boomers: 281.
Bahamas: 286.
Balkans: *See* names of countries.
Baltic states: 116. *See also* Estonia, Latvia, Lithuania.
Banerjea, Krishna Mohan: 25.
Baptists: and contrast with Arminians, 125 *n5*; and ethos in Germany, 106; as free church in Great Britain, 85; and Italy federation, 88; in Myanmar, 30; successful in Slovakia, 111.
Baraya, Namasta: 17.

[317]

Belgium: 87, 98.
Bell, Ray: 112.
Bermisa, Nila: 74.
Beslov, Zdravko: 95, 96.
Bhutan: 35.
Bishops' Initiative on Children and Poverty: 262.
Bishop W. T. Handy, Jr. Young Adult Missioners: 288.
Black Kettle (Native American): 178.
Blanco, Ramon Poza: 129–130.
Blasdell, Robert: 52.
Böhler, Peter: 87.
Bolivia: 122.
Bolleter, Heinrich: 100, 105 *n*2,111, 112.
Border Patrol: 222–225. *See also* Table 3, p. 249.
Bosnia-Herzegovina: 116.
Bowen, Mary E.: 134.
Brazil: 114, 122, 287.
British Methodists: and early efforts in Switzerland, 93; and founding of Methodism in Germany, 89; and Ghana still influenced by, 9; "going episcopal," 3; and international ministry in Germany, 113; and Italy church establishment, 88; and London Methodist Mission Society, 89; and support for Africa education, 5; and ties to Poland, 99; as widespread in British colonial areas of Africa, 1; mentioned, 79, 87, 92, 105, 106. *See also* "Resources Consulted," 119, Wesleyan Methodist Mission Society.
Buddhists: *Anatta* as a Fourfold Truth of, 204 *n*1; and devotion of admired by youth, 167; in early Indonesia, 46; and flunkyism of, 215; and "foolishness of cross," 157; and harmony as concern, 217; and influence on contemporary Koreans, 207; in Nashville, 276; number of in U.S., 154; as object of derision, 162; and preparation of self, 209; and Pure Land and Son forms, 217; and Shila period in Korea, 208; and weddings with Christians, 163. *See also* photo, 154.
Bulgaria: 94–97, 100.
Bulgaria Provisional Annual Conference: 105 *n*2.
Burma: *See* Myanmar.

Caldwell, Kirbyjon: 186, 201.
California-Nevada Annual Conference: 229.
California-Pacific Annual Conference: 172, 228–232, 236, 313.
Calvinism: 93, 102.

Cambodians: and Anglican and Methodist mission to, 34–35; in Europe, 112; and evangelism of Cambodia, 29; and mission of Singapore Methodist Church to, 34. *See also* photo, 33.
Canada: 3, 171, 275, 282.
Caribbean: and contrast between British and North American Methodism, 142 *n*62; and diaspora of, 199; and Methodist Church of, 87; and Methodists from in Florida, 229; and slaves brought from Africa, 222; and slaves returned to Africa, 2, 13; and youth project in, 286.
Castelar, Emilio: 129.
Catholic Relief Services: 116.
Central Conference of Central and Southern Europe: 95, 100, 105, 112.
Central Conference of Northern Europe: 100, 119.
Chaplains: 112–113.
Charismatics: in Africa, 4, 7; in Europe, 77, 118; in Latin America, 148–149.
Charter schools: 188–189.
Chávez, César: 245.
Chicano: 221.
Chief Seattle: 169.
Children: in Africa, 18; in African-American academies, 243–244; of African-American pastors, 201; at-risk work with by U.S. 2s, 288; and Azerbaijan work of UMCOR, 115–116; and Bishops' Initiative on, 262; and charter schools of African Americans, 189; and child labor, 282; and children killing, 239; and class isolation in U.S., 257; and Confucian filial piety, 210; and "dumbs up" theory, 193; and education of in nineteenth-century Uruguay, 127, 131, 133, 137; and hearing-impaired in Turkey, 116; and Hindu Sunday schools for, 162; in kibbutz, 243; killed in Boxer Rebellion, 21; of Korean-American immigrants, 203, 211; and Korean fatalism, 213–214; and medical work in Vietnam, 34; as members of people of God, 274; of Mexicans, 221; and México project of Interact, 289; and Muslim teaching of, 54; and Native American education of, 173–174, 176; Native American killed by Chivington, 178; and need for strong families, 280; as needy recipients of mission, 270; and network of women's groups in Philippines, 71; and number of among U.S. women, 251–252; and orphans, 265, 280; and responsibility of

young U.S. women for, 252; in Schools of Christian Mission, 263; as soldiers, 282; as Spanish-speakers, 225; starvation of in Wesley's England, 81; training teachers for in Philippines, 70; vulnerability of to HIV/AIDS, 253; mentioned, 33, 40, 172, 183, 192, 216. *See also* photos, 29, 33.

Chile: 122, 148, 241.

Chinese: associated with Christians in Malaysia, 53; and Boxer Rebellion, 21–22; and Hong Kong refugees, 41–42; and Kachin mission to China, 31; as Korean conqueror, 215; as language used by many in Southeast Asia, 42; and Malaysian missionary to China, 28–30; and mission initiatives in China and Hong Kong, 28–30, 35, 36, 41–42; and persecution of Christians, 35, 36; and Singapore ethnic Chinese serving in Africa, 43; and Singapore gang, 31; and Singapore Methodist Church mission to, 34; and Singapore Presbyterian church mission to Hong Kong, 27 *n11*; and Sung as missionary, 25. *See also* photo, 29.

Chivington, John A.: 178.

Christian Methodist Episcopal Church: 184.

Christian Missionary Society: 25.

Chung-Yung: 207, 216–218.

Church of Jesus Christ of Latter-day Saints: 285–286.

Church of the Nazarene: 88.

Claremont School of Theology: 172, 313.

Colonialism: in Africa, 2–3, 5, 11–12, 13, 15; in Asia, 22, 23; in Philippines, 66; as related to contextualization, 9; as related to globalization, 8; as related to racism, 16.

Commission on Christian Unity and Interreligious Concerns: 313.

Committee on Hispanic Ministries: 237.

Commonwealth of Independent States: 80, 105.

Communication: and *Christian Messenger and Examiner* in Africa, 17; and *Connection* newsletter in Europe, 110; and effect of global media, 260; and electronic media in age of millennials, 277–278; and electronic media as model of mission, 72; and *Evangelist* of MEC in Uruguay, 140–141, notes to chapter 6, passim; and *Literary Magazine* of University Club in Uruguay, 137; and "mission to six continents," 38; and *New World Outlook,* 264; and papers in Africa, 17–18; and radio and television as ways to reach Latinos, 241; and *Town's Messenger* of Uruguayan Catholics, 139. *See also* internet.

Communitarianism: 210, 235.

Community development: 270.

Community economic development: 186–188, 190.

Confucianists: and *Chung-Yung,* 216–218; as conservatives in China, 22; and filial piety of, 210; and flunkyism of, 215; and influence on contemporary Koreans, 207; and *Li,* 212; and Neo-Confucian ideals, 214; among non-Christians in U.S., 154; and Yi Dynasty in Korea, 208, 217; mentioned, 208.

Congregational development: 205.

Congregationalists: 85, 97, 106, 125 *n5.*

Connectionalism: and breakdown of, 264–265; of English-speaking congregation in Vienna, 111; as external aspect of Korean-American spirituality, 204; and leadership in Methodism tested by, 79; as place to encounter diversity, 257; and power of in multicultural conditions, 189; and relation to economic development, 190; and struggle of young German congregations to find way into, 106; works to prevent isolation, 96.

Contextualism: in Africa, 4–5, 9–10; and Latino theology, 232–233, 240; of liturgies, 10; and relation to inculturation, 8; and theology, 67.

Convention on Rights of the Child: 282.

Conversion: *See* evangelism.

Coronado, Francisco Vásquez de: 220.

Costa Rica: 147.

Costello, Cynthia: 253.

Côte d'Ivoire: 112.

Crutchfield, Stephanie: 70.

Cuba: 220, 221, 229.

Czech and Slovak republics: 98–100, 103, 105, 105 *n2.*

Daniels, Shermain: 261.

Davinson, Miss: 132.

Dayton, Donald W.: 125 *n5.*

Deaconesses: 267.

Deliverance Ministries: 4, 6, 8, 10. *See also* photo, 7.

Democratic Republic of the Congo: 112, 114.

Denmark: 101, 105 *n2,* 116.

Desert Southwest Annual Conference: 229.

Detroit Annual Conference: 184–185, 313.

Disabled: 116. *See also* photo, cover, 17.

Doctrinal standards (of Methodism): 79.
Domingo, Placido: 245.
Dong-Shik Ryu: 217.
Drees, Charles W.: 134.
Dunwell, Joseph Rhodes: 2.
Duremdes, Sharon Joy Ruiz: 65, 67, 69.
Durington, W. H.: 16.

East Timor: 48.
Ecology: as challenge to churches, 69; as concern of Filipinas, 71, 72, 74; as concern of youth, 279; as crisis in Philippines, 66; and missional priorities, 73; and Peace Corps, 288; and spirituality, 74; as task of women in mission, 68.
Ecuador: 122.
Ecumenicity: in Africa, 1, 14–16; ecumenicals and evangelicals as opposed, 158–159; in Latin America, 149–150; and missional shift to, 266; in Philippines, 66, 68, 69, 71, 72, 75; and World Methodist Council, 10; and World Missionary Conference, 51.
"Edge cities": 201.
Education: and adaptation to economics, 17; of Azerbaijan preschoolers, 115; and charter schools, 188–189; and colonialism in Asia, 22; and conversion a breaking away from worldliness, 129; and English Language College in Warsaw, 99–100; among indigenous Filipinos, 70; and lack of resources for in Africa, 6; of masses, 131; of Methodist Episcopal Church in nineteenth-century Latin America, 121–152; for mission, 263, 266; and missionary training centers, 74; and mission trips, 40; and need for attention in UMC, 189; for peace, 74; and Peace Corps, 288; in Russia, 108; and self-understanding of mission, 162–164; as success in Africa, 5; and Western form in Africa, 4; of women globally, 253. *See also* photos, 17, 33, 55.
Ekem, John: 113.
English Language College in Warsaw: 99–100.
Environment: *See* ecology.
Episcopal Church: *See* Anglicans.
Episcopal Relief and Development: 116.
Escalante, Jaime: 245.
Escande, Juan: 132.
Estonia: 101–102, 105. *See also* list, 105 *n2*.
Europe: 2, 11–16, 47–48, 77–119. *See also* names of countries.
Evangelical Association: 90, 92, 93.

Evangelical Methodist Church of Uruguay: 144, 147–148.
Evangelical United Brethren: 90, 92–93.
Evangelism: and abandonment of toward Muslims, 57; and Africans converting Africans, 6; and biblical view of conversion, 59; and contextualization in Africa, 8; and conversion as self-interest, 16; and English Language College in Poland as form of, 99; and evangelization as social change, 12; and "Kitchen Table" in Russia, 108; toward Latinos, 240; and Lausanne Congress on Evangelism, 158–159; among Muslims in Asia, 49–52; and proselytizing as undesirable, 71; and relation to social justice, 41; and "Silent Evangelism" of Mother Teresa, 167; as soul-saving in Africa, 3, 4; and southern diaspora Chinese concern for China, 29; and youth evangelizing youth, 293.
Expatriate congregations: 110.

Fabella, Virginia: 71.
Faith Conferences: 103.
"Familyism": 207–218.
Federal Republic of Germany: 105.
Feminism: *See* women.
Fiji: 27 *n11*.
Finland: 101. *See also* list, 105 *n2*.
First Corinthians: 157.
First Kings (Book of): 9.
First Peter, Letter of: 168.
Fitch, Douglass: 192.
Flake, Floyd: 184.
Fletcher, John William: 93.
Florida Annual Conference: 229.
France, Methodism in: with German-speaking conference, 104; as limited in Catholic country, 88; and number of congregations, 95; and united Protestant church, 87; and work among Hmongs, 112. *See also* list, 105 *n2*.
Franks, Dan: 112.
Free Evangelical churches: 117.
Freeman, Thomas Birch: 2, 5.
Free Methodist Church: 88, 171.
Füssle, Gottlob: 90.

Galatians, Letter to: 67.
Galvan, Elias: 245.
Garrett-Evangelical Theological Seminary: 185.

Index [321]

General Board of Discipleship: 112, 280.
General Board of Global Ministries (GBGM): absence of support from for English-Speaking Church in Vienna, 111; and Global Justice Volunteers, 287; and Martinez as president of, 245; and mission no longer purview of mission agencies, 260; and Native American Urban Initiative, 175; and Philippines project, 80; and web sites of, 119; World Division of, 180; mentioned, 203. *See also* National Division, United Methodist Committee on Relief, United Methodist Women.
General Board of Higher Education and Ministry: 112–113, 290.
General Conference Task Force on Korean American Ministries: 204–206.
"Gen Xers": 281.
Georgia (country): 88.
German Democratic Republic: 82, 96, 104–105.
Germany, Methodism in: and effort to identify needs, 106; and election of Methodist lay preacher to GDR parliament, 82; and founding of Methodist work in, 89; and immigrants in, 109; and issues between German and U.S. Methodists, 86; and Laity Abroad program, 112; and loss of membership in Methodist church, 104, 106; and National Socialism, 96; and settlements in eastern Europe, 101–102; and "Tent Mission Ministry," 109; and theological seminary, 96, 108; and Wesley's visit to Pietists in, 84; mentioned, 83.
Germany annual conferences: 105 *n2*.
Germany Central Conference: 104–105, 112. *See also* list, 105 *n2*.
Ghana: 1–19; and Asian missionaries working in, 27 *n11*; and Ghanaian ministry in Germany, 113; and Global Justice Volunteers, 287.
Ghandi, Mahatma: 160.
Gil, Juan: 140.
Gilbert, Nathaniel: 199.
Global Evangelization Movement: 26 *n7*.
Globalization: as bringing Christians in its wake to Asia, 54–55; and Christianity as absorption of European culture, 14; and communication, 11–13; as concern of Filipinas, 72, 74; and economic crisis in Philippines, 66; as enforcing colonial ethos, 8; and link between global market and religious priorities, 72; and Mining Act in Philippines, 69;

and threat to human dignity, 151; and United Methodist Women, 258.
Global Justice Volunteers: 287.
"Glocalism": 210–212.
God: *See* Jesus, Holy Spirit, Kingdom of God, mission of God, people of God, spirituality, Trinity.
Golden, Charles: 172.
González, Justo: and comment on missionaries of nineteenth century, 124; as Latino recognized for work in theology, 245; and new *praxis* for pastors, 243; and new theological paradigm for Latinos, 232–236, 240.
Goodfellow, William: 127, 128.
Gosa: 210.
Graft, William de: 2.
Great Commission: as discovery of ourselves, 45; and relation to other biblical texts, 45, 58, 65, 67, 156–157; as rescuing "the other," 5; and totality of for understanding mission, 155–156; and youth unmoved by sermon on, 278.
Guelfi, Antonio: 133–134.
Guelfi, Cecilia de Bersía: 132–133.
Gut (shamanistic ritual): 208, 210.
Gypsies: *See* Sinti and Roma.

Habitat for Humanity: 166, 286–287, 289.
Hae-Jong Kim: 204–205.
Handicapping conditions: 116. *See also* photo, cover, 17.
Handsome Lake (Native American): 175.
Handy, W. T., Jr.: 288.
Health care: in Armenia, 115; in Azerbaijan, 115; in Ghana and Nigeria, 4; and missional priorities, 73, 74; of Native Americans, 181; and Peace Corps, 288; in Philippines, 70; and PolioPlus program of Rotary International, 289; in Russia, 108; as traditional versus Western medical, 6; of women, 252, 253. *See also* HIV/AIDS, photo, 7.
Hearn, J. Woodrow: 219.
Hebrews (Letter to): 158.
Helvetia Confession: 79.
Henderson, Cornelius: 192.
Hernández, José: 245.
Hewett, Elizabeth: 134.
Hindus: and Bharatiya Janata Party of India, 36; as crusading and servant styles of Christians toward, 153–154; in early Indonesia, 46–47; and "foolishness of cross," 157; and hospitality of admired by youth, 167; invited

(Hindus, *continued*)
to join hands with Christians, 159–160; in Nashville, 276; and number of in U.S., 154; and practices derided, 162; starting Sunday schools, 162; and Sundar Singh as, 23–24; and weddings with Christians, 163.
Hispanics: *See* Latinos, Latin America.
HIV/AIDS: as augmenting need for health care in tropics, 6; as crisis in Africa, 283–284; and crisis in Philippines, 67; and Missioners of Hope working with victims of, 287; and orphanages required in wake of, 265; and U.S. 2 work with, 288; and women and children subject to, 253.
Hodge, Wilfred: 117.
Hollins, McCallister: 192.
Holmes, Zan: 201.
Holy Spirit: and critique of "Catch the Spirit," 204 *n1*; and dialogue requires openness to, 16; inspires innovation in mission, 166; and Jacoby recognition of irregular power of, 91; and mission directed by, 159; and power of required for mission, 59, 168; as related to mission of God, 160; as related to servanthood, 165; and spiritual disciplines, 204; as Sustainer in Scripture, 164. *See also* Great Commission, spirituality, Trinity.
Homelessness: 288.
Hong Kong: *See* Chinese.
Human rights: as byproduct of Christianity, 18; and child soldiers, 282; and Christians best served by, 60; in Italy in nineteenth century, 88; in the Philippines, 68; as problematic for Christians and Muslims in Asia, 53–54; in Uruguay in nineteenth century, 145; and violence against women and girls an issue of, 253.
Hungary: 89, 93, 101, 103.
Hungary Provisional Annual Conference: 105 *n2*.
Hyde, Minnie: 134.
Hyo: 211.

Ignatius of Antioch: 4.
Immigrants: 109, 222–225, 241.
Inculturation: 4, 6–9, 74.
India: associated with Christianity in Malaysia, 53; as country of Christian persecution, 35, 36; as mission base of Sundar Singh, 23–25; and Western support for initiatives of, 38.
India Missions Association: 26.

Indigenization: Bella Ramos as leader in Philippines, 70; in Europe, 105–106; as involvement of Christian women in Philippines, 71; in Korea, 39; in West Africa, 4, 16, 18.
Indonesians: and dialogue over meaning of Pancasila, 61; and evangelism of indigenous by student, 31–32; and independence, 52–53; and persecution of Chinese and Christians, 35; and spirituality, 73.
Instituto Superior Evangélico de Estudio Teológicos (ISEDET): 121 *n1*, 142, 313–314.
Interact: 289.
International Missionary Conferences: 51.
Internet: 259, 268, 270, 277. *See also* net addresses, 119.
Iraq: *See* photos, cover, 279, 291.
Ireland: and Anglican church in, 85; as resource, 119; and sojourners who became Methodists, 109; and United Methodist Church in, 87; and Wesley's ministry in, 83–84.
Islam: *See* Muslims.
Italy: 88.

Jacoby, Ludwig S.: 91.
Jains: 154.
Janelli, Dawnhee Yim: 212–214.
Japan: 215.
Je-sa: 211 *n18*.
Jehovah's Witnesses: 154.
Jesus: and abundant life, 65, 67, 187; and apologetic approach to Muslims, 49; and Asian woman studying words of with Senegalese, 43; and body of Christ, 235; and call to faith as coming from God, 59; and communications web offering redemption, 38; as crisis within Islam, 57; and dressing Christianity in Muslim garb, 56; and ecumenicity as witness to, 15–16; family of, 67; and grace offered to all, 118; and health, 5; Ignatius of Antioch quote, 4; and inculturation, 9; and Korean spirituality, 207; and Latino belief in salvation through, 228; and Lord's Prayer, 190, 235; and love of espoused by Mother Teresa, 167; and making disciples for, 154, 205; and message about as part of "golden age" of missions, 293; and ministry to whole person, 40–41; and mission as bringing abundant life, 65; and mission as liberation, 67; and mission as surrender for joy of loving God, 63; and mission as wit-

ness to, 9, 65; and Muslim questions about God, 61; as negating and fulfilling religion, 60; and normative models of mission, 57–59; as perceived by Native Americans, 170; and personal relation to, 281; and relation to *sharia*, 60; and religion of one of justice, 198; and religious pluralism in U.S., 153–154; and Scripture as basis for mission, 164; and second coming of, 236; and self-understanding of mission, 155–158; and Singapore youth's conversion, 32; and Spirit as preparing Muslims to hear, 62; and Sundar Singh conversion, 24; and teaching about in Vietnamese factory, 33; and theme of Myanmar mission, 30; unity in, 67. *See also* Great Commission, Kingdom of God, theology of mission.

Jews: conducting Bible study, 162; as fundamentalists, 285; invited to join hands with Christians, 159; and kibbutz in Israel, 243; and National Socialism, 96–97; in New Testament, 59–60, 157; among non-Christians in U.S., 154; and pluralism, 258.

John, Gospel of: and abundant life, 65, 67; and living faith and inculturation, 9; and relation to mission, 156–158, 160.

Justice: as aim of women's liberation, 71–72; as challenge for Filipino church, 67; church planting often excludes, 40; concern for lacking in Asia except for Philippines, 41; and economics, 71; and expectation of in conflict with theology of grace, 80; as expressive of evangelical affirmations, 146; and global justice as concern of youth, 292–293; as gospel message in midst of globalization, 151–152; and injustices toward Native Americans, 179; lack of and concern for in Boxer Rebellion, 21, 36; lack of in North Korea, 37; as part of sharing Christ, 65; as quality of follower of Jesus, 168; racial, 197–200; refugee treatment an issue of, 41–42; and relation to human rights, 53–54; as taking risks for individuals, 97; and Wesley's concern for social injustice, 81.

Kachins: 30–31. *See also* photo, 146.
Kaliningrad: 102.
Kapatiran Kaunlaran Foundation: 70.
Kaw Ma: 31–32.
Kazakhstan: 88.
Kenya: 283.
Kingdom of God: Asian Christians presenting as pilgrim in foreign land, 21; and challenge of mission among Southeast Asian Muslims, 45–46; as corporate, 198; giving up power an indicator of imminence of, 61; and gospel of Christ as refracting vision toward, 59; inclusiveness as part of Korean vision, 209; and Latinos as heirs of, 236; majority and minority having no place in, 199; realization of part of fundamental impulse of Christian mission, 57; true end of feminist struggle a society reflecting, 72; turning inward as related to looking forward to, 203; and worker-priests as committed to, 242.

Klaiber, Walter: 104, 105 *n*2, 112.
Korea Methodist Church: 87, 115.
Korean Americans: 113–114, 203–218.
Koreans: 39, 108.
Kosovo: 116.
Kurtz, Sebastian: 90.
Kwang-Shik Kim: 217.
Kwon Sang-Yeon: 211.

Lady Huntington: 1, 2.
Latin America: 121–152; and African diaspora in, 199; and AIDS epidemic, 283; and change from Catholicism in, 238; and Christianity more alive there than in Europe, North America, 72; its languages spoken in Europe, 114; struggles for justice contrasted with Asian missiology, 41.
Latin American Methodist Action Group: 237.
Latin American Provisional Annual Conference: 228–229, 232, 236.
Latinos: 219–249; and demographics in U.S., 258; and food program in Los Angeles, 174–175; and women as members of mission organizations, 271; and women in poverty, 253; as youth in U.S., 275. *See also* photos, cover, 146, 224, 231, 240.
Latitudinarianism: 215–216.
Latourette, K. S.: 125 *n*5.
Latvia: 101–102, 105, 286.
Lausanne Congress on Evangelism: 158–159.
Leadership development: 205, 233, 262.
Leviticus: 286.
Li (Confucianist propriety): 212.
Liberation Theology: 70–72, 147.
Liberia: 2, 287.
Link, J. C.: 90.
Lithuania: 101–102, 105, 106–107.
London Methodist Mission Society: 89.
Luke, Gospel of: 45, 58, 156, 161.

Index

Lutherans: and Augsburg Confession, 79; in Malaysia and Singapore, 42; and rationalism against which Methodism had to work, 102; successful in Slovakia, 111; in Sweden, 116.
Lynch, Jessica: 279.
Lyth, John: 89.

Macaspac, Paz: 70.
McCalmont, Cindy: 291.
McDonald, Duncan Black: 52.
Macedonia: *See* Yugoslav Republic of Macedonia.
Malaysians: and "civilizational dialogue" among religious communities, 61; and independence, 52–53; and Islamic history among, 46–50; and missionary to China, 28–30; and Muslim helping Christian during Ramadan, 45.
Maldonado, David: 245.
Mananzan, Mary John: 74.
Mandela, Nelson: 283.
Mann, Golo: 90.
Mark, Gospel of: 67.
Markay, David and Kristin: 107.
Martinez, Joel: 245.
Martyrdom: 35–37, 68, 91–92, 277.
Matthew, Gospel of: 167–168, 190, 278.
Meier, Jonathan: 291.
Meisel, Ulrich: 82.
Mendez, Juan Vera: 240.
Methodist Church Ghana: 2, 87, 117–118. *See also* Germany.
Methodist Church Nigeria: 2.
Methodist Church of the Caribbean and the Americas: 87, 117.
Methodist Church of Puerto Rico: 240.
Methodist Episcopal Church: and Bremen as European seat of, 92; in Bulgaria, 94; and establishment of mission in Uruguay, 127; and Guelfi a member of, 132; and Jacoby as missionary of, 91; in Latin America in nineteenth century, 121–152; and Methodist work in Switzerland, 92, 93; and North America constitution of, 79; and ordination of superintendents for, 81; Woman's Foreign Missionary Society of, 132, 133, 134.
Methodist Episcopal Church, South: 98, 99.
Methodist politics: 84.
Methodist sociology: 80–82.
Methodist theology: 78–80.
Metodistas Asociados Representando la Causa Hispano-Americanos (MARCHA): 237.
México: and drug traffic, 225; as exception to support of Liberation Theology, 147; and factories of with low wages, 197; and immigration to U.S., 221–224; and origin of term "Chicano," 221; and service project of Interact Club, 289; and symbiotic relation of border towns, 226; and U.S. influence in nineteenth century, 122; mentioned, 234, 241.
Mfantsipim Secondary School: 5.
Militarism: 37, 68–69.
Millennial generation: 275–285.
Millennium Fund: 115.
Miller, Craig: 280.
Milne, Andrés Murray: 127–128.
Minor, Rüdiger: 100, 105 n2.
Missiology: 41–42. *See also* theology of mission.
Missionaries: African American, 195–197; Asian, 23–25; as chaplains to traders, 11–12, 48; and culture of, 9; and difficulties with political system in West Africa, 12, 13; and Durington as indigenous African, 16; earliest in Ghana, 2; earliest in Nigeria, 2; as emigrating from Badagri, Nigeria, 15; and enlistment of young Filipinas as, 71; and European paired with Africans, 13–14; and Global Justice Volunteers, 287; and Hispanics as, 237, 238; initiators of education in Africa, 5; as instrumentalities of colonialism, 66; and king of Portugal as supporting, 15; and Missioners of Hope, 287; and Muslim-Christian encounters, 49–52; as needing interpreters, 14; and number from India, 26; and number of Western missionaries today, 25–27; as propagators of individual liberation, 17; as saving Africans from their own religions, 3, 8; and Schwenks in Philippines, 70; serving in Europe, 119; and short-term service, 255; and U.S. 2s, 288; and women as, 266, 267, 268; and young adult missionaries, 265, 270, 288. *See also* photos, 33, 126, 138.
Missionary Congress of Panamá: 143.
Missioners of Hope: 287.
Mission of God: based on Scripture, 164; and claims to power, 61; as related to women in mission, 271; as ushering in reign of God, 65.
Mission Society for United Methodists: 88.
Mission trips: 34, 40, 274.
Missouri East Annual Conference: 313.
Modayil, Sharon and Romesh: 113.
Models of mission: 57–59.
Mohammad: 50, 60. *See also* Muslims.
Mongolia: 215. *See also* photo, 213.

Moravian churches: 117.
Mother Teresa: 167.
Mountain TOP: 286.
Movimiento Estudiantil Cristiano: 149.
Mozambique: 114, 278, 284.
Mueller, Christoph Gottlob: 89–90.
Mueller, Reuben: 92.
Muslims: 45–63; in Africa, 3, 11, 12–13; and countries of persecuting Christians, 35, 37; and devotion of admired by youth, 167; as fundamentalists, 285; invited to join hands with Christians, 159–160; in Nashville, 276; and number in U.S., 154, 155; from Turkey and Central Asia, 78; and UMCOR work with in Turkey, 116. *See also* photos, 73, 157.
Myanmar: and Christians persecuted in, 35; and Methodist pastors studying in Singapore, 34; Presbyterian missionaries working in, 27 *n13;* and "300 for three years" evangelistic mission, 30–31; and Trinity Theological College work, 43.
Myanmar Institute of Theology: 30.

Nacpil, Liddy: 69.
National Association of Korean-American United Methodist Churches: 205.
National Committee on Korean American Ministries: 205.
National Council of Churches, Philippines: 69, 71.
National Division: 262, 314.
National Plan for Hispanic Ministry: 219, 237–238, 241, 244.
National United Methodist Native American Center (NUMNAC): 180.
National Youth Ministry Organization: 289, 290 *n8.*
Native American Comprehensive Plan: 181.
Native American International Caucus: 180, 181.
Native Americans: 169–182; as interns, 265; invited to join hands with Christians, 159; among non-Christians in U.S., 154; and urban initiative of, 175; and Wesley mission to, 84; and women in poverty, 253. *See also* photos, cover, 179, 224.
Neil, Stephen: 14.
Nepal: 34, 35, 38.
Netherlands: and Caribbean Methodists, 117; and colonial trade in Southeast Asia, 47–48; and Ghana ministries in Europe, 117–118.
Nevius, John L.: 39.
New age religionists: 154.

New World Outlook: 264.
Nigeria: and definition of success in mission, 15; and earliest missionaries as traders, 11; and evangelization in, 6; and founding of Methodism in, 1, 3; and language difficulties, 14; and Methodist Church Nigeria, 2; as Muslim country, 35; and traditional religion of, 10. *See also* photo, cover, 17.
Niza, Fray Marco de: 220.
Nordic and Baltic Area: 100, 107.
Northern Europe Central Conference: 105.
North Germany Annual Conference: 114.
North Indiana Annual Conference: 313.
Norway: 101, 105 *n2.*
Nova Scotia: 3.
Nusantera: 46.

O'Brien, Soledad: 245.
Ochoa, Ellen: 245.
Oklahoma Indian Missionary Conference: photo, 170.
Okure, Teresa: 8, 9.
Olmos, Edward James: 245.
Olsen, Oystein: 100, 105 *n2.*
Orthodox churches and tradition: affected by Methodist efforts on theological education, 101; and agreements with in Russia, 108; and countries predominantly Orthodox less open to Methodism, 88; and magisterial authority, 79; as male-dominated in Macedonia, 97; as mystical, 102; as religion of Serbs, 94.

Pacific Islanders: 27 *n11,* 275.
Pagura, Frederico: 146.
Pai, Manjeshwar Govinda: 157.
Pal-ja: 214–215.
Palos, José L.: 237, 244.
Pancasila: 61, 61 *n3.*
Parsis: 163.
Partnership in mission: 38.
Paternalism: 183.
Paul (Saint): 67, 157.
Paul, K. T.: 25 *n5.*
Peace Corps: 279, 288.
Pena, Carlos M. de: 138–139.
Peña, Frederico: 245.
Pentecostal Methodist Church of Chile: 148.
Pentecostals: 123, 148–149.
People of God: 273–275.
Peru: 122.
Philippines: 65–75; and Bible women in, 265; and Filipino missionaries in East Malaysia, 35; and Filipinos in Germany, 115.

Pliska, Linda: 113–114.
Pluralism: 74, 153–168, 258. *See also* photos 55, 73, 154, 157.
Poland: 88, 95, 98–100, 101.
Poland Annual Conference: 105 *n2*.
Pollero: 223–224.
Popes: Alexander VI, 15; John Paul II, 160, 242.
Portea, Consuelo: 135 *nn38, 41*.
Portugal: and Africa colonialism, 13, 14; and colonial trade in Southeast Asia, 47–48; and Methodist church in, 87, 89.
Poverty: as characteristic of Philippines, 66, 69; and children's emphasis on in UMC, 262; and children's escape from, 282; as context that speaks to Asian missionaries, 41; example of gospel related to moral changes in society, 125; and feminization of, 66; as Methodist concern in Uruguay, 145; and need for UMC to help Native Americans with, 181; problem of lack of control over one's life, 191–192; related to health, 6; of women, 253.
Presbyterians: and Asian serving in West Africa, 43; and churches in Great Britain, 85; and contrast with Arminians, 125 *n5*; and Korea mission, 39; and Liberation Theology, 147; and missionaries trained to speak African languages, 14; and missionary as executor of Singh's estate, 25; and missionary work in Korea, 27 *n13*, 34; and missionary work in Myanmar, 27 *n13*; and Singapore church sending missionaries, 27; and West Africa mission, 12; and Westminster Confession, 79.
Publications: *See* communications.

Quiocho, Ruth: 68, 74.

Racism: toward African Americans, 184, 192; and context for mission in Philippines, 67; of Europeans in Africa, 14, 15; faced by Native Americans in Southern California, 173; related to colonialism, 16; in United Methodist Church, 177; and women of color, 257–258.
Ramírez, Carlos María: 140.
Rascon, Alfred: 245.
Re-Imagining conference: 256.
Refugees: 41–42, 74. *See also* photo, 69.
Rhodes, Cheryl: 113.
Río Grande Annual Conference: 228–229, 236.
Rivera, Diego: 245.

Roman Catholics: Association of Major Religious Superiors, Philippines, 71; and colonization in North America, 124 *n4;* and deeper reflective consciousness in Korea, 208 *n13;* and difference with Methodists on political and social point of view, 136; and Fabella on aim of women's liberation, 71; and failure of Portuguese mission in West Africa, 14–15; and feminist vision of Bermisa, 74; and four kinds of dialogue, 166; and impetus for inculturation in Africa, 6–9; killed in Boxer Rebellion, 21; and Latinos as, 228, 238; and Liberation Theology participation in, 147; and magisterial authority, 79; and media attention, 260; as missionaries from India, 26; in the Philippines, 66; in Poland, 100; and Portuguese in Malaysia, 47–49; and protest against California missions, 178; as ultramontane, 102; and Uruguay Protestant-Catholic conflict, 130–131, 133, 137–141; and Wesley's letter to, 85; mentioned, 88, 125, 276.
Rotary International: 289.
Roye, Sandra: 170.
Russia: 100–102, 105, 107–108, 265; mentioned, 83, 215. *See also* photo, 107; list, 105 *n2*.
Rwanda: 284.

Samartha, Stanley: 165.
Sarasvati, Pandita Ramabai: 25.
Sarmiento, D. F.: 121.
Sarpong, Kwasi: 7–8.
Scandinavia: 100, 101, 116–117. *See also* list, 105 *n2*.
Schäfer, Franz: 110, 111.
Schmidt, George: 127 *n12*.
Schwenk, Richard and Caring: 70.
Self-emptying: 9–10, 63.
Sene-Gambia: 2.
Seneca Nation: 171, 172, 175, 176.
Senegal: 27 *n11*.
Serbia: 89, 93–94, 100.
Shamanism: 208–210, 215, 216.
Shanti, Margaret: 68.
Sharia: 13, 60–61.
Sherman Indian School: 175.
Sierra Leone: 1, 2, 5, 16.
Sikhs: 23, 154–155, 159–160, 276.
Sikkim: 35.
Singapore Center on Evangelism and Mission: 27.
Singapore Methodist Church: 32–34.
Singh, Sadhu Sundar: 23–25.

Sinti and Roma: 93, 95, 97.
Slavic Methodism: 100.
Slovakia: 89, 93, 111.
Social Gospel: 146.
Society for Saint Andrew: 286.
Society of Friends of Popular Education: 137.
Sommer, Carl Ernest: 96.
Song-bum Yun: 217.
Southeastern Jurisdiction Association for Native American Ministries (SEJANAM): 180.
Southern California Indian Center: 172–173.
South Germany Conference: 105 *n2*, 113, 114.
Southwest Texas Annual Conference: 313.
Spain: 87, 88–89.
Spirituality: Asian, 67, 210; and countertrend to traditional authority, 77; ecology-based, 74; feminist, 73, 236; in Ghana, 4, 7; indigenous, 74; Islamic, 54, 60; of Jesus, 198; of Korea, 39, 207, 208, 209, 212; of Korean Americans, 204; of mission, 62–63, 292; for missionary vocation, 57; as Native American, 172, 175–176, 178; and "revolutionary," 66, 68; and similiarity of Muslim and Christian approaches, 50; and social reform in Latin American Methodism, 124; in theological education, 72; of youth, 162, 280, 281.
Stewart, Carlyle Fielding: 185, 201.
Sticher, Hermann: 112.
Substance abuse: 225, 239.
Sufis: 47.
Sung, John: 25.
Svargaloka: 153.
Sweden: 101, 300.
Switzerland: and central conference as including, 105; and effort to identify needs, 106; and Füssle a convert, 90; and German-speaking Methodism, 87; and international ministries, 112; and number of congregations, 95; place of least cause for optimism in, 104; and roots of Methodism in, 93. *See also* list, 105 *n2*.
Syncretism: 62, 209.

Taoists: 154, 207, 208. 215.
Tasmania: 27 *n11*.
Tear Fund Netherlands: 116.
Thailand: 34.
Thangaraj, Thomas: 166.
Theology of mission: 40–42, 49–50, 59–62, 158–162.
Thomas Aquinas: 136 *n44*.
Thomson, John F.: and anti-Catholic controversy, 137; and move to Montevideo, 128; as spokesman for Protestantism in university debates in Montevideo, 139–140. *See also* photo, 138.
Tibet: 35.
Tinnevelly Missionary Society: 25 *n5*.
Tongsun Gido: 208.
Trajkovski, Boris: 82.
Trevino, Lee: 245.
Trinity, Holy: 45, 168. *See also* Jesus, Holy Spirit, Great Commission.
Trinity Theological College, Singapore: 28, 31, 42–43.
Turkey: 88, 95, 116.

U.S. 2s: 288.
Ugon, Daniel Armand: 142.
Ukraine: 98, 100, 101.
Ummah: 56.
Unión Latinoamericana de Juventudes Evangélicas (ULAJE): 149.
Union Theological Seminary, New York: 25 *n6*.
Union Theological Seminary, Philippines: 65, 70, 313.
United Brethren in Christ: 92.
United Evangelical Church: 68, 92.
United Evangelical Mission: 72.
United Methodist Campus Ministries: 290.
United Methodist Committee on Relief (UMCOR): 98, 115–116, 180. *See also* photo, 73.
United Methodist Women: 251–271; in Latino church in Los Angeles, 230; and president in Philippines, 70; and youth as members of, 290.
University Club: 137–141.
Uruguay: 121–152.

Vaca, Alvar Nuñez Cabeza de: 220.
Van, Edgar: 192.
Varela, Jacobo A.: 133.
Varela, José P.: 131–132.
Varner, Lee and Edith: 111.
Växby, Hans: 100.
Vietnamese: and evangelism of Vietnam, 29; and factory Bible study program to, 32–33; in Germany, 115; and Singapore Methodist Church mission to, 34.
Violence: and action against, 293; of children, 239; experienced by today's youth, 277; against women, 252–253, 262.
Virginia Annual Conference: 111.
Voglar, Harold: 57.

Voivodina: *See* Serbia.
Volunteers in mission: 255, 268, 286, 290.

Waldensian-Methodist Federation: 87, 88, 94.
Waldensian Evangelical Church of Uruguay: 134, 142.
Waldmann-Bohn, Sonja: 112.
Walls, Andrew: 1 *n1*, 2, 5.
Wesley, John: and first societies, of, 82, 86–87, 199; and "Model Deed" of, 79; as modernist, 84–85; and need for Latinos to hear his prophetic voice, 240; and personal commitment of, 86–87; and pragmatic efficiency, 78; and prevenient grace, 164; social and economic views of, 80–82; and structures for Methodist Church, 82–84; and world as parish, 6; mentioned, 91, 93, 109, 118.
Wesleyan Church: 88.
Wesleyan Methodist Mission Society: 2, 5, 14, 15.
Wesleyan quadrilateral: 79, 85, 155, 164.
Wesley College: 5.
Wesley Girls High School: 5.
Wesley Theological Seminary: 172.
West, Cornel: 191.
Western Jurisdiction Center for Native American Ministries (WJCNAM): 180.
Western New York Annual Conference: 172.
Williams, Cecil: 192.
Woman's Foreign Missionary Society: 132, 133, 134.
Women: Atuel as president of UMW in Philippines, 70; and Azerbaijan health care, 115; and Bible women in Philippines, 265; clergy, 268–270; and context at opening of twenty-first century, 251–253; and Korean-American leadership development, 205–206; in mission, 253–264; and Pakistan oppression of, 37; in Philippines, 65–75; and receptivity to in Latin America Methodism, 147; young women, 252, 263, 269–270. *See also* United Methodist Women.
Women's Division: *See* United Methodist Women.

Wood, Thomas B.: and comment on South America as opportunity for evangelism, 125; and establishment of educational network in Uruguay, 131–134; as founder of ISEDET, 142; as supporter of scientific-literary societies, 140–141. *See also* photo, 126.
Worker-priests: 242.
World Council of Churches: 1, 158.
World Division: 180.
World Methodist Council: 10.
World Missionary Conference of 1910: 51.
World wide web: *See* internet.
Wunderlich, Friedrich: 90–91.

Yoon Ji-Choong: 211.
Young Jin Cho: 204.
Youth: 273–293; and Africa youth fellowship, 18; decline of in Los Angeles congregation, 230; and demographics on African-American and Latino youth, 219; and Escalante as youth motivator, 245; and incidence of AIDS among black and Hispanic teen-age girls, 252; and interest in spirituality, 162; in Latin America, 149; as members of the UMW, 263; and "Mission of Peace" in northeastern U.S., 166–167; and Native American returning to tradition, 173–174, 177; and need to understand people of other faiths, 162; and parachurch groups in Europe active among, 88; in Philippines, 71, 72; and students at Trinity Theological College, Singapore, 28–30, 31–34, 43; as uncaring about connectionalism, 264; and young adult missioners, 265, 270, 288; mentioned, 160. *See also* photos, cover, 55, 73, 107, 261, 279, 291.
Youth Service Fund: 289–290, 290 *n8*.
Yugoslav-Macedonia Provisional Annual Conference: 97, 112.
Yugoslavia: 105, 112. *See also* Serbia.
Yugoslav Republic of Macedonia: 82, 97, 100, 105 *n2*.

Zimbabwe: 283, 284.

Please mail order with check payable to:
SERVICE CENTER
7820 READING ROAD CALLER NO 1800
CINCINNATI OH 45222-1800

Costs for shipping and handling for sale items:
$25 or less, add $4.65
$25.01–$60, add $5.75
$60.01–$100, add $7.00
Over $100, add 6.5%

For billed and credit card orders:
WEB ADDRESS: gbgm-umc.org/e-store
CALL TOLL FREE: 1-800-305-9857
FAX ORDERS: 1-513-761-3722
E-MAIL: scorders@gbgm-umc.org
If billing is requested, a $2.00 billing fee will be added.

| $ 14.95 PAPERBACK | STOCK #3645 |
| $ 21.95 HARDBACK | STOCK #2883 |